P9-CMP-521

FATEFUL VISIONS

FATEFUL VISIONS
Avoiding Nuclear Catastrophe

Edited by
Joseph S. Nye, Jr.
Graham T. Allison
Albert Carnesale

BALLINGER PUBLISHING COMPANY
Cambridge, Massachusetts
A Subsidiary of Harper & Row, Publishers, Inc.

International Standard Book Number: 0-88730-272-6

Library of Congress Catalog Card Number: 87-31836

Printed in the United States of America

Library of Congress Cataloging-in-Publication Data

Fateful visions.

   Includes index.
   1. Nuclear warfare. 2. Nuclear disarmament.
3. World politics—1985-1995. 4. International relations.
I. Nye, Joseph S. II. Allison, Graham T. III. Carnesale,
Albert.
U263.F39   1988   355'.0217   87-31836

ISBN 0-88730-272-6

Contents

Preface and Acknowledgments

Several years ago, our book *Hawks, Doves, and Owls: An Agenda for Avoiding Nuclear War* focused on a practical list of "do's and don'ts" to reduce the prospect of a major nuclear war between the United States and the Soviet Union over the coming decade. Yet we continued to ask each other: If all these options were taken, would that suffice? Was a security system based on nuclear deterrence not bound to break down over the long run? Indeed, that book concluded with a recommendation to reduce reliance on nuclear deterrence over the long term.

Our deeper dissatisfaction is shared by the larger public who wonder whether it will be possible to avoid nuclear catastrophe over the long term. More recently, both Ronald Reagan and Mikhail Gorbachev have proposed plans to reach such an objective. Their official plans are only two among many approaches. No one can foretell the future. But by careful analysis and comparison of the full range of publicly debated visions of a more desirable nuclear future, we can discover clues about the best directions to take. A vision of the future is essential. Such fateful visions deserve closer scrutiny than they have thus far received.

This book, like its predecessor, emerges from the multiyear Avoiding Nuclear War Project at the Center for Science and International Affairs at Harvard's John F. Kennedy School of Government. We are grateful to David Hamburg and the Carnegie Corporation for their support of the project. While the chapters are the responsibility of their authors, they were informed by many rounds of discussion in the Avoiding Nuclear War Study Group of the Center for Science and International Affairs. In addition to the authors, other members of the group included Bruce Allyn, Andrew Bennett, James G. Blight, Ashton B. Carter, Walter Clemens, Ivo Daalder, Tami Davis, Peter Feaver, Barry Fridling, Cristann Gibson, Thomas Graham, Fen Osler Hampson, Elisa Harris, Ronald Heifetz,

Tad Homer-Dixon, Jennifer Laurendeau, Mark H. Madsen, Ellen Meyer, Stephen Meyer, Philip Rogers, Douglas Seay, Kiron Skinner, Pamela Solo, and William Ury.

In addition, the idea of this book was shaped by two special Summer Conferences. We were joined in those efforts by Les Aspin, Robert Axelrod, Irven DeVore, Karl Deutsch, John Lewis Gaddis, Alexander George, Peter Goldmark, Morton Halperin, David Hamburg, J. Bryan Hehir, William Hyland, Mark Kramer, John Mack, Andrew Marshall, Ernest R. May, Walter McDougall, William H. McNeill, Robert S. NcNamara, Frederic A. Mosher, Jay Ogilvy, David Robinson, Henry S. Rowen, Thomas Schelling, Helmut Sonnenfeldt, Edward Warner, and Richard Zeckhauser.

In the spring of 1987, a conference was held at Harvard to review drafts of the chapters. We are grateful for the comments of Carl Builder, Walter Clemens, Randall Forsberg, David Hamburg, J. Bryan Hehir, Stanley Hoffman, Robert Keohane, Mark Kramer, John E. Mack, Stephen Meyer, Frederic A. Mosher, Jonathan Schell, Thomas Schelling, Gene Sharp, Louis B. Sohn, Richard Ullman, and George Weigel.

Finally, special thanks are due to James Blight, Robert P. Beschel, Jr., and David Welch for both their intellectual and their administrative skill in coordinating the project; to Melissa Baumann for her research and editorial assistance; and to Veronica McClure for the intelligence and patience with which she translated drafts into chapters.

Introduction

*Joseph S. Nye, Jr., Graham T. Allison,
and Albert Carnesale*

Imagine a modern-day Rip Van Winkle who falls asleep at the end of World War II, awakens in 1988, and asks how the great powers have assured their continued security since the war. Would our current situation seem plausible? U.S. and Soviet arsenals number over 50,000 nuclear weapons, most more powerful than the bomb dropped on Hiroshima; intercontinential ballistic missiles can deliver these destructive payloads in less than thirty minutes to any point on the globe; altogether we have built a potential for explosive power and radioactive contamination that may for the first time in history actually threaten the existence of life on earth—could we convince Rip that this world reflects a thoughtful vision of how to organize security?

Consider the questions he might raise. Since the United States and the USSR were allies when he fell asleep, how did they become hostile adversaries? Do the people of America really despise the Soviet citizenry (and vice versa) so much that they want to kill them by the tens or even hundreds of millions? Would the leaders of the two countries actually use these megatons of destruction to annihilate each other's societies? Are the people who created this system confident that it will not fail by accident or inadvertence? If it should, how would they justify what they had done? Undoubtedly Rip would ask more than once if he was really awake or was this "security system" merely a nightmare.

The current system seems plausible and acceptable primarily because of its familiarity. In fact, its major features were not deliberately designed, but emerged over time as a consequence of technology, competition, and piecemeal decisions. Under this system the great powers have enjoyed forty-two years without general war—a period twice as long as the time of peace following World War I. But if the system should fail tomorrow, a survivor (perhaps on some other planet) would undoubtedly conclude that its collapse was as certain as was the coming of World War I. Had Archduke Ferdinand not gone to Sarajevo in 1914, some other match would have lit the fuse. So, too, a nuclear holocaust would seem an inescapable consequence of the security system the great powers created in the decades after World War II.

Technologists can debate whether a major nuclear war could actually lead to the extinction of the human species. Predictions of a nuclear winter, in which clouds of dust and soot would destroy life on earth, have been exaggerated.[1] But a nuclear summer would be bad enough. Even if some people in remote parts of the globe were to escape destruction, a major nuclear war would end civilization as we now know it. Unfortunately, a conflict of such consequences, which we refer to as a catastrophic nuclear war, clearly is possible. All of the explosives used in World War II, in both the Atlantic and Pacific, could be encompassed in a single modern nuclear warhead—and there are more than 50,000 nuclear weapons in the world today.

The Risk of Catastrophe

Pessimists argue that nuclear catastrophe is inevitable. Since all human beings make mistakes, they observe, a system of security based on nuclear deterrence with vast numbers of weapons seems bound to break down at some point. Moreover, Murphy's Law—the proposition that whatever can go wrong will go wrong—seems to operate powerfully in large, complex organizations such as governments. Thus the pessimists have powerful intuitions on their side.

On the other hand, optimists argue that catastrophe is not inevitable. For example, if the prospects of a major nuclear war are 1 in 100, and if those odds can be reduced by 20 percent each year, then the chance that a major nuclear war will ever occur is about 5 percent.[2] But to reduce the risks of nuclear war by 20 percent a year for all future years is an extremely tall order. No one knows the true odds of a major nuclear war, but they probably lie somewhere between the fatalistic intuitions of the pessimists and the ambitious policy prescriptions of the optimists.

One central irony of nuclear weapons is that their very destructiveness has reduced the probability of both nuclear and conventional war among the major powers. Any political leader who contemplates war can see that the risk of nuclear destruction far outweighs any gains he might hope to achieve by war. Thus, nuclear weapons have engendered caution. The nuclear era has been an unprecedented period of peace between the major powers. The four centuries since the modern international state system began to evolve in Europe have been wracked by wars between the major powers. Some theorists have argued that such wars are inevitable because of competition for the dominant or hegemonic position in the interstate system. If so, the prospects for the future are indeed gloomy, for a Soviet–American war would then seem inescapable. Yet the United States and the Soviet Union have been the dominant powers in the international system for more than four decades and have managed to avoid any direct fighting. They have even evolved certain prudent practices to reduce the probabilities of war. For example, they regularly discuss arms control and regional issues, and have established special procedures for communication in times of crisis.

But even as nuclear weapons have reduced the probability of war between the major powers, they have increased potential destructiveness if war ever breaks out. Since the probability of war cannot be reduced to zero, the potential for catastrophe remains, particularly through accident, inadvertence, and nonrational factors.[3]

Conventional war can cause enormous destruction without resort to nuclear weapons. For example, World War II may have cost as many as 50 million lives. Some might argue that avoiding two or three conflicts of that scale over the course of a century justifies the risk of even a medium-scale nuclear war. But one can never be sure that a nuclear war would remain "medium." Because of their enormous destructive potential, the existence of large numbers of nuclear weapons means that the fate of the earth will always be at risk.

Beyond Deterrence?

Reliance on nuclear deterrence entails an ever-present possibility of catastrophe. Arnold Toynbee prophesied in 1948 that the nation-state and the split atom could not coexist on this planet.[4] One or the other had to go. The idea of abolishing nuclear weapons has been prominent in the peace movement since the beginning of the nuclear era. More recently it has moved from the fringes of political debate to a central position. For example, in March 1983, President Reagan raised the possibility of new advances in defensive technology to make nuclear weapons impotent and obsolete. In January 1986, Soviet leader Mikhail Gorbachev announced a two-phase plan to abolish all nuclear weapons by the end of the century. At the Reykjavik Summit in October 1986, Reagan and Gorbachev discussed the possibility of abolishing nuclear weapons over a similar time horizon.

The Reykjavik conversations were poorly prepared and confusing. According to the White House, "the President was reflecting his willingness to discuss the details, including timing, of a plan to eliminate all nuclear weapons, in conjunction with a plan to reduce conventional arms to insure conventional force balances." But some administration officials were skeptical. Assistant Secretary of Defense Richard N. Perle argued that "a nuclear free world is . . . empty propaganda." In his view, such arguments were "deployed by officials and politicians who fear that the public would not support them if they simply rejected outright Mr. Gorbachev's beguiling maneuver."[5] Regardless of differences of interpretation, the real significance of the Reykjavik discussions is that the issue of abolishing nuclear weapons had migrated from the fringes of the peace movement to the center of policy discussions.

Nuclear abolition is more complex than its first appears. The scrapping of weapons would not destroy nuclear knowledge. As Jonathan Schell and others who have written about nuclear abolition acknowledge, even burning all books and scientists would not eliminate the potential reinvention of nuclear weapons. They hope for "weaponless" nuclear deterrence, in which each nation is dissuaded from rearming by the fear that its rivals would do the same and return them all to the basic predicament they are trying to escape.[6] In effect, deterrence would depend not on the number of nuclear weapons in the arsenals but on the time it takes to turn knowledge into weapons (that is, numbers of days rather than numbers of weapons). Deterrence would rest on conventional force balances reinforced by the potential for reinventing nuclear weapons.

A more radical vision might go beyond deterrence. Such a world would require fundamental changes in international politics, such as creation of a world government so that states no longer need to rely on military force for their security. Or it might require major changes in social attitudes or in human nature so that it became unacceptable to use force to make gains or prevent losses in international affairs. Somewhat more modestly, such a vision might be realized in a world in which civilian-based resistance to any aggressive actions by other states would deny such aggressors any gains. But the threatened costliness of overcoming such civil resistance would still be a form of deterrence.

Practical people often dismiss weaponless deterrence or world federalism or civilian-based defense as utopian visions. But scoffers should ask themselves who would ever have envisioned the world we live in now. A series of incremental decisions has created a world in which the total obliteration of modern society is possible. What is more, those weapons can be delivered at intercontinental distances within thirty minutes. Advances in technology promise not only to shorten the time available for human decision but to spread the destructive capability to more nations and subnational groups.

The problem is not only the technology but the social system in which this destructive power is imbedded and the psychology and attitudes that accompany this new vulnerability. States nourish, polish, and elaborate their ability to do horrible damage to one another. In the United States and the Soviet Union, tens of thousands of people and a major share of national budgets are devoted to maintaining the system. It is hard to imagine that anyone would have invented this world as a deliberate act of policy. It would have been regarded as too fanciful, impractical, and dangerous. Yet we accept it simply because it is familiar. If the utopian visions of a safer world are judged against the design of the world we live in, they may not fare so badly.

Alternative Visions

Visions of a safer world, however impractical they may first appear, play an important role in raising our sights from the incremental decisions that have brought us to today's world. President Reagan's Strategic Defense Initiative, announced in 1983, has been criticized on a variety of practical, technical, and political grounds, but it has raised issues that deserve attention and has transformed the debate about the nuclear future. Similarly, abolitionist proposals, whether those of Mikhail Gorbachev or Jonathan Schell, have helped us to ask questions we had put aside under the pressure of day-to-day business.

Almost by definition, the probability of utopian solutions is currently low. We simply do not know. It is important, however, to avoid foreclosing such prospects and to investigate ways to keep possibilities open. Alternative visions of the future may keep us from being imprisoned by the tyranny of current events.

Expounding a vision of a safer world does not mean that such a world would really be safer. Visions that blind us to current reality can have disastrous consequencs, as can those that are poorly thought out or built on faulty assumptions. Not all visions of a safer world are accurate; some might have unintended consequences that would increase the risk of nuclear war or its potential destructiveness, or both.

The table below outlines ten visions of a world in which catastrophic nuclear war can be avoided. These are all worlds that seem to their proponents more desirable than our current situation. In other words, they avoid the simplistic "solution" of avoiding nuclear war by surrendering fundamental values. Thus, for example, a world dictatorship is not included in this list. While these are not the only desirable worlds that one could imagine, our list covers a broad spectrum of potential solutions, all of which have figured in the recent debate in the Western democracies about how to escape our nuclear predicament.

Some of these visions focus on changes in nuclear development, some on changes in the international system of states, and some on changes in domestic societies and politics. They fall into five major categories. Those in the first category involve radically reducing the vulnerability of populations and societies. The most dramatic vision here is the one we call "defense dominance," popularized by President Reagan with his Strategic Defense Initiative. An alternative view is the abolition of nuclear weapons. At the political level, this notion has been recently associated with Mikhail Gorbachev, while in the domestic American debate it was popularized in Jonathan Schell's book *The Abolition*. Closely related is the concept of hedged abolition, or reducing nuclear weapons

Publicly Debated "Desirable Worlds"

Radically Reduced Vulnerability of Populations and Societies
1. Abolition and Near Zero (Schell, McNamara)
2. Increased Accuracy (Wohlstetter)
3. Defense Dominance (Reagan)

Radically Reduced Reliance on Nuclear Weapons
4. Lengthen the Fuse (Halperin)
5. Non-provocative Defense and Civilian Resistance (Forsberg, Sharp)

Political Accommodation between the Superpowers
6. U.S.–Soviet Cooperation (Shulman)
7. Soviet Transformation (Kennan)

Radical Increase in the Relative Power of One of the Superpowers
8. Soviet Decline (Perle)

Transformation of the International System
9. Internationalism (Mitrany, Angell)
10. World Government (Clark and Sohn)

to near zero rather than zero. Robert McNamara, former secretary of defense, has popularized this view.[7] Albert Wohlstetter suggests a dramatically different approach, aiming at increased accuracy.[8] If we could hit only what we aimed at, we could drastically reduce the numbers and size of weapons and the collateral damage they would do. This would make deterrence more credible and thus reduce the probability of nuclear war as well as its destructiveness if such a war should occur. It would allow the discrimination between military and civilian targets required by theories of a just war.

A second set of proposals focuses on reducing reliance on nuclear weapons. One school urges "lengthening the fuse" leading from initial conflict to nuclear use. For example, Morton Halperin has argued that a policy of no first use, if taken seriously, would move nuclear weapons out of the front lines and regular forces and into reserve roles, making it difficult to use them early in any conflict.[9] A number of nuclear weapons would remain, but the prospect of their use would be greatly diminished. Another set of proposals stresses nonprovocative defense and civilian-based resistance. Randall Forsberg has suggested a world in which nations would agree not to intervene across borders and military forces would consist mostly of border guards.[10] Gene Sharp has suggested that an effectively organized civilian population could resist occupation and deny an aggressor the fruits of victory.[11] In some ways, such a world would generalize the type of defense used by countries such as Switzerland today.

A third cluster of visions focuses on political accommodation between the two superpowers.[12] In one view, the United States and the Soviet Union learn how to go beyond their current prudent practices and rudimentary regimes for cooperation in some security areas into a more fully developed framework of cooperation. Though nuclear weapons would remain, their threat would be greatly diminished by the reduction of the political hostility in which they are now embedded. Just as Britain and the United States each possess nuclear weapons without threatening the other, the United States and the Soviet Union could reduce the prospects of nuclear catastrophe by developing far-reaching cooperation. Another vision in this category rests on the prospect of change in the Soviet Union. Some believe that there must be a change in the nature of Soviet power and the foreign policy that follows from it before hostility can be reduced and cooperation enhanced. This concept was first suggested by George Kennan in a famous article published in 1947.[13]

Still another vision posits a radical change in the relative power of one of the superpowers. While it is possible that either nation's power might decline, the focus here is on a weakened Soviet Union. (Few Americans publicly advocate American decline.) Some would argue that a decline in Soviet power would remove tensions and hostilities that derive from and created the need for nuclear deterrence in the first place. Richard Perle and Richard Pipes are associated with this view.[14]

Finally, some visions of a safer world involve a broader transformation of the international system. One, which we call *internationalism*, presumes that if interdependence, communication, transnational ties, and international institutions are strengthened, nationalism will gradually weaken and a world will emerge in which sovereign states are less likely to engage in warfare.[15] Nations will be all in the same boat, or at least so closely tied together that the prospects of war will greatly diminish. Once again, though weapons may remain, the hostility in the relationship would be greatly reduced. The final vision we consider is world federation, in which states would give up a degree of their sovereignty, in particular their control over military forces and nuclear weapons, to a world government.[16] Rather than abolishing weapons, world federation would abolish some of the independence of the states, which nuclear deterrence is designed to protect.

Incomplete Visions

Some of these worlds are complementary, but others would be inconsistent with each other. Each focuses on certain parts of the problem and pays little or no attention to other parts. Almost all are "underspecified" in that they do not spell out all the conditions needed to make these worlds workable and desirable. They remind us of the proverbial blind men trying to understand the nature of an elephant through touch alone. One touches the trunk, another a leg, a third the tail, but none understands the whole elephant.

Theories of international politics suggest that five sets of assumptions must be spelled out to understand whether a world will be desirable or sustainable.[17] First, one would want to know something about the structure of international power. For example, how will power be distributed among major states? Will the current bipolarity between the United States and the Soviet Union continue? Will both countries decline so that there will be a multipolar balance of power? Or will there be an uneven decline that leaves the United States in a superior position? Will power be reorganized to form a single world government? The answers to these questions alter the context in which the various worlds will exist.

One also needs to make assumptions about the political processes that will characterize the international system. Processes are the means by which states relate to each other. What sort of relations will exist between the United States and the Soviet Union? Will they cooperate in developing rules and regimes for governing the relationship, or will there be no rules of the game? What about relations with other countries? Will there be rules that discourage the spread of nuclear weapons to new countries? To what extent will there be rules that discourage intervention across national borders? Will states control activities that cross borders, or will private groups and international institutions play large roles?

A third set of assumptions relates to the domestic politics of the major powers that possess nuclear weapons. Will the domestic politics be moderate or highly ideological? Will they lead to foreign policies that are expansionist or that focus on internal problems?

We also need to specify a fourth set of assumptions about nuclear weapons technologies. How many, how accurate, and what types of nuclear weapons will exist? How effectively will they penetrate defenses? What will be the relationship between nuclear offense and defense? Nonnuclear technologies, our fifth category, may also affect weaponry and other areas. For example, will high accuracy create nonnuclear strategic weapons to substitute for nuclear weapons? Will "smart" weapons give an advantage to defense over offense on the conventional battlefield? Will it be possible to maintain effective deterrence without nuclear weapons? What about new technologies of communications? Will they increase economic and social interdependence? Will that in turn transform the way states relate to each other?

Most of the publicly debated desirable worlds listed in our Table do not specify all of the assumptions necessary to determine the feasibility of their propositions. We would like to know how sensitive these hypothesized worlds are to the unspecified assumptions. Do variations in those assumptions overwhelm the desirable feature of a particular vision? Alternatively, what assumptions are needed to sustain the desirability of each vision? How would the world have to change to make these visions appear feasible?

Fleshing Out the Visions

Each chapter of this book begins by presenting the arguments made by the proponents of a particular alternative world and then turns to the missing information. What would have to be changed to make the world desirable and sustainable? Although it is difficult to change fundamental parameters immediately, over a longer period of time it becomes more plausible to imagine radical changes that would make the desirable worlds feasible.

This book looks at changes that might be possible over the next fifty years. Some changes could occur quickly; others may seem difficult even in half a century. The further out in time, the more difficult it is to assert the bounds of feasibility, either to rule in or to rule out particular changes. On one hand, fifty years seems an impossibly long time. For example, a book on the international balance of power written in the 1930s would not have considered nuclear weapons. Within another half century, drastic changes in biotechnology or climate may threaten the human species as much as our nuclear predicament does now. On the other hand, benign forces may become stronger. Even if fifty years is an impossibly long time, companies persist in forming pension schemes and this year's high school graduates assume a need to plan for the year 2038 — and we hope they are right.

This book is not an effort to project what the world will look like in fifty years or to describe it in any detail. Rather, we examine ten publicly debated desirable worlds and ask what fundamental changes in basic assumptions would be necessary for such worlds to be feasible and sustainable. This is a way of relaxing the constraints that reality places on our imagination in the current framework.

By relaxing such constraints and raising our sights beyond everyday policy concerns, we hope to gain perspective on the nature of our current predicament and to uncover a sense of direction for future policy. The public debate has focused too much on two visions, abolition and defense dominance. The most promising paths to the future may require a combination of desirable worlds. In any case, the effort to look closely at these fateful visions helps us to stretch our imagination beyond mere acceptance of the world as it is and raises important questions about alternative futures.

CHAPTER 1

Zero and Minimal Nuclear Weapons

James N. Miller, Jr.

We are here to make a choice between the quick and the dead.
That is our business.
—*Bernard Baruch, before the United Nations in 1946*

On June 14, 1946, less than a year after the bombings of Hiroshima and Nagasaki, Bernard Baruch presented the United States' plan for abolishing the atomic bomb. The plan called for the establishment of an International Atomic Development Authority vested with extensive powers for inspection and enforcement. Five days later, Andrei Gromyko offered a Soviet alternative: all nuclear weapons (then held only by the United States) would be destroyed, and their production and storage prohibited. Gromyko suggested no provisions for verification or enforcement; presumably such matters would be settled at a later date. No agreement was reached.[1]

On January 16, 1986, General Secretary Mikhail Gorbachev offered his plan for "ridding the earth of nuclear weapons...before the end of the century."[2] In response, President Ronald Reagan suggested that in a world without nuclear weapons, strategic defenses would be needed to provide insurance against cheating. In October 1986, these visions came head to head in Reykjavik, Iceland. Whether near-miracle or near-disaster, or simply a charade, the Reykjavik summit between Reagan and Gorbachev dramatically demonstrated the enthusiasm both leaders could muster for a world free of nuclear weapons.[3]

The logic of nuclear abolitionism is straightforward: nuclear weapons pose an unacceptable threat to the human race. In the more graphic phrasing of Jonathan Schell,

One day—and it is hard to believe that it will not be soon—we will make our choice. Either we will sink into the final coma and end it all or, as I trust and believe, we will awaken to the truth of our peril, a truth as great as life itself, and, like a person who has swallowed a lethal poison but shakes off his stupor at the last moment and vomits the poison up, we will break through the layers of our denials, put aside our fainthearted excuses, and rise up to cleanse the earth of nuclear weapons.[4]

Robert S. McNamara, secretary of defense under Presidents Kennedy and Johnson, has argued that while complete abolition will not be feasible for the foreseeable future, it is possible and desirable to move to minimal nuclear arsenals, comprising no more than a few hundred strategic nuclear warheads for each side. Behind this policy recommendation is the belief that since *any* nuclear use might escalate to a global holocaust, "nuclear warheads are not weapons—they have no military use whatsoever except to deter one's opponent from their use."[5]

This chapter examines proposals for the abolition and near-abolition of nuclear weapons. I consider first the abolition of all nuclear weapons everywhere, as proposed in the Baruch plan of 1946 and in the Gorbachev vision of 1986. Then I discuss proposals for near-abolition put forward by Robert McNamara and others: NATO and the Warsaw Pact would eliminate all tactical nuclear weapons, and the nuclear powers would each keep some tens or perhaps hundreds of strategic nuclear warheads.[6]

Abolition

Assume, for the sake of analysis, that all nations have agreed to abolish nuclear weapons. Perhaps some nations were bribed to accept these accords; others may have been coerced in some way. Two key questions remain. First, how will *verification* be undertaken to detect whether all nuclear weapons have been abolished and whether any new ones have been created? Second, what will be the response to violations—what will be done if it is discovered that a nation or other group is building or has hidden nuclear weapons?

Verification

There would be two main objectives in verifying compliance with an abolition agreement: discovering whether all nations had in fact divested themselves of their nuclear weapons, and promptly detecting the development of any new bombs. The former task would be much more difficult. Obviously, only nations (or other groups) that had nuclear weapons at the time of the abolition agreement could hide them. Unfortunately, however, it might not be clear just which nations were included in this category, and one country's nuclear weapons might be hidden on the territory of an ally.

Locating all of the world's nuclear weapons was a much simpler proposition at the time of the Baruch plan. In 1946 it was widely known that only the United States had nuclear weapons, and very few of them at that. Today, there are five acknowledged nuclear-weapons states: China, France, Great Britain, the Soviet Union, and the United States. Between them, these countries have over 50,000 nuclear weapons, most of which are held by the United States or the Soviet Union. There are also a number of threshold nuclear powers that may have or soon develop nuclear explosives, including Argentina, Brazil, India (which has carried out a nuclear test but claims not to have any bombs), Israel (which reportedly has a small stockpile of nuclear weapons), Pakistan, South Africa and Taiwan.[7] Most industrially developed countries, such as Canada, Italy, Japan, Sweden, Switzerland, and West Germany, currently have the capability but not the desire to develop nuclear weapons. As an abolition agreement neared completion, nuclear-capable countries would be tempted to hide weapons-grade plutonium or uranium, and/or ready-made bombs, if only out of fear that other nations would do the same. How would the abolition plan deal with this problem?

Mikhail Gorbachev suggested that "verification . . . would be carried out by both national technical means and through on-site inspection."[8] Nuclear warheads are too small, and too easily concealed, to allow complete verification of an abolition agreement by national technical means (primarily satellites and other sophisticated devices to intercept communications and literally see into other countries).[9] Inspections would therefore be an integral part of any agreement not based primarily on trust or on a willingness to accept the possibility of many hidden bombs.

Two considerations indicate that an acceptable basis for abolition would require unlimited inspections, with respect to both the number allowed and the area covered. First, nations giving up their nuclear arsenals would accept only a negligible chance that other countries had not done the same. Cheating with even one or two nuclear weapons could have military significance, or at least be so perceived. Second, sensitive military facilities would be a top priority for inspection. Indeed, the more sensitive a military or scientific facility, the greater the legitimate need for other nations to inspect it. The required inspections might entail "a level of intrusiveness that even [the United States] Constitution would not permit."[10] In any case, such extensive inspections would constitute a significant diminution of national sovereignty, which could take place only in a context of greatly reduced tensions between nations—not only between the United States and the Soviet Union, but between potential nuclear nations involved in regional conflicts (for example, Israel and the Arab states in the Middle East, India and Pakistan, and Argentina and Brazil). Allowing other nations to inspect one's most sensitive military installations without limit would otherwise be unthinkable. If tensions were reduced to this point, war would probably be perceived as extremely unlikely, so that inspections might serve primarily as a confidence-building measure.

Detecting whether nations were building new nuclear weapons, though less difficult than finding hidden bombs, would also be problematical. If weapons-grade uranium or plutonium could be stashed away before safeguards were in place, or covertly produced, then even international supervision of nuclear facilities could not ensure prompt detection of nuclear rearmament. Nations that did not have active nuclear weapons programs at the time of agreement would have a much more difficult task in trying to build nuclear weapons secretly.[11]

Under any arrangements for verification, there would be some risk that nations had stored away some nuclear bombs or would develop them. The next section considers how this risk would be managed.

Responding to Violations

The 1946 Baruch Plan called for "an international law with teeth in it" to undertake the "immediate, swift, and sure punishment" of violators.[12] To this end, the International Atomic Development Authority was to be given exclusive right to carry out research on atomic explosives; Baruch anticipated that it could use a small stockpile of atomic bombs to prevent or punish cheating.[13] Could such an authority be given exclusive access to the ultimate military power and remain anything short of a world government? The answer must be no. If a nuclear-capable nation were losing a conventional war, it would face powerful incentives to build nuclear weapons to stave off defeat. The international atomic authority would have to be able either to enter into a country during wartime to physically prevent nuclear rearmament, or to credibly threaten to disarm or punish a nation that built the bomb. Even Bernard Baruch, in presenting his more limited plan to the United Nations, indicated that a world government might be needed: "But before a country is ready to give up any winning weapons it must have more than words to reassure it. It must have a guarantee of safety, not only against the offenders in the atomic area but against the illegal uses of other weapons—bacteriological, biological, gas—why not?—against war itself."[14]

In his 1982 bestseller *The Fate of the Earth*, Jonathan Schell argued that abolishing nuclear weapons would require a revolution in international relations, that we could no longer "make do with a Newtonian politics in an Einsteinian world."[15] Two years later, in *The Abolition*, Schell changed his mind. While fundamental changes in world politics were still ultimately desirable, he now argued that nuclear weapons could be abolished without abolishing the nation-state system. This could be done by establishing a state of "weaponless deterrence," in which each side would be deterred from rebuilding nuclear weapons by the knowledge that the other side would respond in kind.[16]

Even if nuclear weapons were abolished, Schell recognized, nuclear *knowledge* would still exist. Thus a successful abolition agreement could provide only a temporary reprieve from the threat of nuclear extinction, until nations could rearm and start a nuclear war. But perhaps this reprieve could be extended indefinitely. As long as it were abundantly clear that any stockpiling or building of nuclear weapons would lead to a renewed arms race, nations would be deterred from doing so. Or, if nuclear weapons were used, retaliation would follow once the assaulted nation rebuilt its arsenal. No advantage could be gained by cheating. "The task for strategy in a nuclear-weapon-free world," wrote Schell, "would be to design a capacity for nuclear rearmament which could not be destroyed in a first strike by a nation that took the lead in rearmament by abrogating the abolition agreement, secretly or openly."[17]

How would nations' capability for rearmament be assured? A country might have many nuclear weapons plants to reduce the chances that an opponent could destroy all of them. This would be extremely expensive, and would complicate verification enormously, as each plant would have to be inspected. Nuclear facilities might be hidden, but then there could be no verification that nuclear weapons were not being created. Schell suggested that the proliferation of nuclear capabilities (as opposed to the weapons themselves) to many countries would increase the stability of weaponless deterrence, as nations could join together to fight any country that violated the abolition agreement. Such an increase in nuclear capabilities, however, would make it much more difficult to verify that nations were in fact abiding by the abolition agreement. And since many more nations would be able to spoil the arrangement by rearming, the result would almost certainly be a decrease, rather than an increase, in stability.

Schell, like President Reagan, has argued that strategic defenses could provide an insurance policy against cheating in a nuclear-weapon-free world. (Schell, however, differs with the president by insisting that strategic defenses must be put in place only *after* nuclear weapons have been abolished. Otherwise nations would respond to defenses by increasing their nuclear arsenals.[18]) Indeed, defenses might protect both a nation's citizens and its capability to rearm, supporting an abolition agreement by decreasing the advantage that would go to a nation that violated it. However, if strategic defenses were themselves vulnerable to attack, they would be of no help. If one side had a superior defense, that side would be in a much better position to manipulate the risk of war (and nuclear rearmament) to political or military advantage. Finally, even perfect strategic defenses would not defend against all threats. "It would not be essential to possess nuclear weapons in order to destroy nuclear facilities," Thomas Schelling has observed. "High explosives, commandos, or saboteurs could be effective."[19]

In the event of a war, peacetime verification procedures would probably not provide adequate assurance that no nuclear weapons were being built. Therefore, once a conventional war began, or was believed likely, a nuclear rearmament race would almost certainly ensue. Destroying an adversary's capability to build nuclear weapons would be the top military priority, perhaps a matter of national survival. Since the first nation to finish rearming might use a small number of nuclear weapons to military advantage, or for political blackmail, it would be important not only that rearmament capabilities be secure, but that the time required for rearmament be approximately equal among nations. Otherwise, the runner-up in the rearmament race, when it had finally procured some nuclear bombs, might have already lost the military engagement or succumbed to blackmail.

It seems unlikely that the American public would strongly support an agreement for zero nuclear weapons—witness citizens' fears during the "bomber gap" and the "missile gap." Moreover, there is strong public support for nuclear deterrence. For example, almost three-quarters of those questioned in a 1985 Harris Survey believed that the threat of instant nuclear retaliation had helped to keep the peace between the United States and the Soviet Union.[20] If any nation were suspected of cheating on an abolition agreement, there would be overwhelming domestic pressures to abrogate the agreement.

For public opinion to help sustain an abolition agreement, there may have to be a shocking event—a series of disasters at nuclear plants, a nuclear war between two smaller powers (e.g., India and Pakistan), or a nuclear war involving the superpowers. Otherwise it is difficult to imagine, in the foreseeable future, the wholesale transference of allegiance from individual nations to an international authority, or to humankind at large. The most likely path to an agreement to abolish nuclear weapons may be a nuclear war.

Abolishing nuclear weapons would require more than the agreement of the five established nuclear weapons states; the cooperation of all nuclear-capable nations would be needed. If a single nation refused to abide by an abolition agreement, other nations would have three choices. First, they could accept the nation's nonparticipation and allow it to be the world's only nuclear power. This seems highly unlikely. Second, the other states could try to bribe or coerce the hold-out to accept the provisions of the agreement. The chances seem remote of persuading a nation's leaders to give up on what would be considered the most critical component of national power and security. Attempting to coerce a nation to give up its atomic arsenal raises the prospect of starting a nuclear war to abolish nuclear weapons. Finally, all nations could give up on the abolition accord because of the failure of one state to participate. This would seem by far the most likely, and perhaps the only plausible, alternative.

As long as nations remain sovereign, then, abolishing nuclear weapons will be possible only when *all* nuclear-capable nations are willing to agree to and abide by an abolition agreement. Without fundamental changes in both the domestic politics of nuclear-capable states and a vast reduction in national sovereignty, however, unlimited inspections would be impossible, and there could be no assurance that countries (or subnational factions) were not violating an abolition accord. Without virtually perfect verification, the agreement would be likely to unravel, as nations hid or built nuclear weapons out of fear that others were doing the same.

Ironically, the same fear that would push nations to cheat—that others may be cheating—would also inhibit them from taking advantage of any violations.[21] For if one nation could hide or secretly build nuclear weapons, could not others as well? And if one country attacked another that had stockpiled bombs, it would face the prospect of prompt retaliation in kind. If a nuclear attack were threatened rather than undertaken, then other countries could begin to rearm openly, while not ruling out the possibility that they might have hidden bombs themselves, to deter the offending nation from immediate attack.

An equal ability to hide nuclear weapons, then, would be critical to the stability of a world where nuclear weapons were supposed to have been abolished. Nations, however, do not have an equal ability to hide nuclear bombs, and there is no reason to believe that such an equality could be established. More open societies, such as the United States, would be at a disadvantage to closed societies like the Soviet Union in hiding nuclear weapons.[22] Perhaps more importantly, political tensions would be acute in a world where nations were suspected of cheating on the most important international agreement ever made. Under such circumstances, domestic pressures for rearming could be overwhelming.

In principle, equal abilities to hide nuclear weapons, like secure abilities to rearm, would be needed to ensure a stable post-abolition world. Why not incorporate the stability given by the possibility of equal numbers of hidden nuclear weapons explicitly into the agreement, and allow each country to keep a small number of nuclear warheads for "deterrence only"? This would avoid the problems of establishing an equal ability to hide nuclear weapons: by reducing the military value of cheating with a few weapons, it would reduce the incentives to do so. In any case, getting to a world with zero nuclear weapons would almost certainly require passing through a world with very few. I turn next to proposals for minimal numbers of nuclear weapons.

Near-Zero Nuclear Weapons

Secretary of Defense McNamara has argued that it will not be possible to eliminate nuclear weapons in the foreseeable future, since there would be no way to verify such an agreement. However, McNamara continues, it would be possible and desirable to move to a world with very few nuclear warheads, which would be used only as a deterrent to nuclear use by others.[23] Similarly, President Jimmy Carter has put forward as the "penultimate solution" short of abolition an arrangement with "each side retaining small, exactly balanced, relatively invulnerable forces, confined either to submarines located in havens or to missiles in silos, which would be impossible to destroy except by the expenditure of the attacker's entire arsenal."[24]

Like abolitionists, advocates of near-abollition recognize the need for an acceptable balance in conventional forces. (McNamara, for example, calls for a moderate conventional build-up by NATO, presumably unmatched by the Warsaw Pact.) Assuming for the moment that this criterion is met, four questions remain. First, just what would be the balance of nuclear forces, not only for the United States and the Soviet Union, but for other present and potential nuclear powers as well? (Could an arrangement be found that was acceptable to all?) Second, could strategic stability be ensured with very few nuclear warheads on each side? Third, how would compliance with the agreement be verified? Finally, how would the transition be made from today's world with tens of thousands of nuclear weapons to a world with perhaps only tens? While these questions cannot be definitively answered, the following discussion considers some of the arguments that have been made and the issues they raise.

The Nuclear Balance for Near-Abolition

What sort of arrangement might be reached for near-abolition? In a purely bipolar world, parity would be easy to define, if not to achieve: each side would have the same number, and kind, of nuclear warheads. (The problem would be more complicated if the two sides differed in the capability of their strategic or civil defenses, or their willingness to absorb a nuclear blow.) With more than two nuclear-weapons states, however, an equal number of warheads for each would mean that a coalition of several could have a great advantage over the others. For example, if China, France, Great Britain, the Soviet Union, and the United States each had 50 nuclear warheads, each country would face a potential coalition of 200 nuclear bombs to its 50. A multipolar world, then, would make an agreement to move to near-zero nuclear weapons difficult to achieve, and probably unstable. Any change in alliances could completely alter the distribution of nuclear power. The possibility of still more nations acquiring nuclear weapons compounds the problem.[25]

How low the superpowers might be willing to go, then, would depend in part on the nature of other countries' nuclear forces. It seems extremely unlikely that the Soviet Union would agree to become one of several equal nuclear powers, given the largely correct Russian perception that "every nuclear weapon in the world is either in the Soviet Union or aimed at the Soviet Union."[26] Indeed, pre-eminence in nuclear weapons is a potent symbol of superpower status for both the Soviet Union and the United States. The most plausible schemes for near-abolition would probably preserve a rough parity between the superpowers, and inequality between the superpowers and other countries.

Although it does not seem likely, other nuclear powers might abolish their arsenals if the two superpowers would cut back to very few nuclear weapons. The procurement of good, but not perfect, strategic defenses by the superpowers would reduce the value of small deterrent forces; China, France, and Great Britain might go to zero nuclear weapons rather than increase their forces enough to overcome a very good Soviet defense. In this sense, good strategic defenses by the superpowers would increase bipolarity and could thus improve the chances of reaching an agreement for near-abolition.[27] However, since strategic defenses would also reduce the value of a small deterrent force for the superpowers, they might be less willing to reduce their own strategic arsenals. Similarly, China, France, and Great Britain might instead increase their nuclear forces to overcome Soviet defenses, or shift to other means of delivery (e.g., cruise missiles). Finally, some nuclear weapons are not aimed at either the United States or the USSR, and so superpower defenses would not eliminate the value of small nuclear forces.

One arrangement for near-abolition might have the Soviet Union and the Western nuclear-weapons states (France, Great Britain, and the United States) move to equal numbers of warheads, while China kept a much smaller nuclear force. For example, the NATO alliance and the Soviet Union might each retain a total of 500 nuclear warheads, while China would keep only 100. The Soviet Union would then face a potential coalition of 600 nuclear weapons, not overwhelmingly more than its own 500. On the Western side, either the United States would have to allow itself to be somewhat inferior to the Soviet Union in nuclear warheads, or Great Britain and France would have to eliminate their arsenals completely. An alternate solution, which would carry its own problems, would provide the United States with the authority to launch all 500 Western nuclear weapons, with Great Britain and France each having independent authority to launch 100 of the warheads.[28] Thus, parity would be maintained between the United States and the Soviet Union, while Britain and France would each have an independent capability equal to that of China.

Verification and Compliance

To meet political concerns, the verification of an agreement for near-abolition would have to be extremely thorough. From a military perspective, the requirements for verification depend on the size and the vulnerability of each side's allowed nuclear forces. The lower the number of allowed nuclear warheads, the greater the value of building or hiding any number of additional warheads, and hence the greater the need for thorough verification. For example, suppose one side could hide, or quickly build, 100 warheads; if it thereby created an advantage of 110 to 10, that is far more significant than an advantage of 1,100 to 1,000 warheads.

Any arrangement of forces for near-abolition must squarely face the tradeoff between ease of verification and the vulnerability of forces. Perhaps easiest to verify would be an agreement that each side could have the same number of fixed, land-based intercontinental missiles—but even then, national technical means alone might not be adequate to verify that no countries had extra missiles and the capability to reload launchers. At the other extreme, each side might be allowed to deploy a certain number of warheads on any systems it chose. Such an arrangement could be virtually impossible to verify even with extensive inspections.

Allowing each side to "hedge" with a few nuclear weapons would reduce the dangers of a breakout from the agreement, but would make verification more difficult. Under an agreement to abolish nuclear weapons, even one warhead would constitute a violation. If some small number of warheads were allowed, it would be more difficult to verify compliance with the agreement. Inspections would be required to ensure that nuclear warheads were not installed on such dual-capable delivery systems as cruise missiles, fighter planes and bombers, and even artillery. Since inspecting delivery vehicles could not rule out the possibility of stockpiles of nuclear warheads elsewhere, extensive inspections of nuclear weapons labs would also be necessary. Since weapons-grade plutonium and uranium could also come from nominally civilian nuclear facilities, international control of nuclear energy would have to be extended to cover all sensitive facilities (enrichment and reprocessing plants).

Verification would be much easier if nuclear-weapons states were simply not allowed to manufacture nuclear warheads. Either nuclear powers would have to make do with some fraction of the weapons they had at the time of the near-abolition agreement (thus combining very deep cuts with a freeze on the procurement of new warheads), or an international nuclear weapons plant might be established on neutral territory. In the latter case, any building of nuclear weapons, or the discovery of a warhead that had not come from the international plant, would constitute a clear violation.[29]

How many nuclear weapons could a country hide? How many nuclear weapons could be built before being discovered? These questions are difficult, perhaps impossible, to answer with any precision. Yet they are critical. If, for example, countries could hide or develop arsenals of 100 nuclear weapons before being detected, then a force to hedge against violations would have to be large enough so that 100 nuclear weapons would not upset the military balance. Moreover, it would seem prudent to allow some margin for error in any estimate of other nations' nuclear potential.

The Stability of Nuclear Deterrence at Low Numbers

According to advocates of minimal nuclear arsenals, the ultimate goal of military policy and arms control should be "a state of deterrence at the lowest [nuclear force] levels consistent with stability."[30] The standard notion of "stability" is that, under any foreseeable circumstances, each side will have "much more than the minimum required strike-back capability."[31] Thus, under stable deterrence, no likely changes in technology, military doctrine, or the political relationship (e.g., a severe crisis) would make a first strike seem appealing. This definition, however, leaves open the question of what would constitute an adequate strike-back capability. As noted by Bernard Brodie, a pioneering strategist of the nuclear age, "It is one thing to say that we have more than enough weapons for deterrence, but who is to say—and convince others—how far that number can reasonably drop before deterrence is in fact diminished?"[32]

There are four very different schools of thought on the requirements for stable nuclear deterrence (in roughly increasing order of the demands placed on nuclear arsenals): equal destruction, assured destruction, victory denial, and leadership punishment.[33] These schools are to a certain extent ideal types, and each has at least some merit under certain circumstances.

The *equal destruction* view of deterrence holds that as long as each side expects to receive about the same level of damage in a second strike as it could deliver in a first strike, it should be deterred from attacking. Parity in destructive power is sufficient for deterrence, and "in a world of approximate parity, the lower the mutual threat is, the better."[34] The ideal outcome, of course, would be a situation where destructive capabilities were virtually nonexistent.

Proponents of nuclear deterrence through equal low levels of destructive capacity are skeptical about the long-term stability of nuclear deterrence; eventually, they believe, it is likely to fail. Thus strategic arsenals should be cut, and both strategic and civil defense measures should be undertaken to increase our chances of survival. As one member of this school wrote, "If deterrence of an all-out war is unreliable, and if all-out war, however devastating, is likely to happen at least every hundred years or so, the death of our nation is assured within the foreseeable future unless we protect our ability to survive and recover."[35] A state of near-abolition that was both "hedged" with a few nuclear weapons and "insured" with strategic and civil defense might be the ideal arrangement, in the view of advocates of deterrence through an equal destruction capability.

The *assured destruction* view has been well described by Paul Warnke, an assistant secretary in McNamara's Department of Defense:

What really counts for deterrent purposes is . . . the adversary's understanding of the absolute magnitude of the devastation that would be inflicted on him if he initiates nuclear war. From our standpoint, deterrence means that the number of Russians sure to die must be unacceptable, whether greater or lesser than the number of Americans sure to die.[36]

This view, that an ability to destroy a significant portion of the adversary's society in a second strike is both a necessary and a sufficient condition for nuclear deterrence, is called finite (or minimum) deterrence. Since assured destruction is taken as the sine qua non of nuclear deterrence, an agreement to reduce warheads to too low a number could leave each side holding just a few huge nuclear bombs. Indeed, as the strategist Herman Kahn noted, the ultimate finite deterrent would be a single nuclear weapon, a "doomsday machine" that would automatically be triggered to destroy the world in the event of a nuclear attack on the United States.[37] Advocates of finite deterrence would point out that the needed deterrent effect comes from the capability for assured destruction, not the plan to carry it out automatically in case of war. In the event of a Soviet attack, the United States' response might be limited, or indeed might never come at all.

How many nuclear weapons would be required for deterrence through an assured destruction capability? Certainly, advocates of finite deterrence agree with George F. Kennan that "the present Soviet and American arsenals . . . are simply fantastically redundant to the purpose in question."[38] McNamara suggests that the United States and the Soviet Union would each need fewer than 500 strategic warheads.[39] Admiral Noel Gayler, a former director of the National Security Agency, would set the balance at an even lower level: 100 nuclear weapons on each side should be "plenty to remove any value of clandestine development and deter use."[40]

An assumption that nuclear warheads can have no military value might lead a nation to aim all its nuclear weapons at cities (as opposed to military targets), to be used only if the other side attacked cities. If an adversary used nuclear weapons against military targets, however, what would be the response? If the only alternatives were no nuclear response and an attack against cities, the former might well be preferable. While the Soviet Union might be deterred by even a small chance that the United States would strike Soviet cities, the question remains as to what to do if deterrence failed. (One answer, of course, is the present U.S. and NATO strategy of flexible response, which is meant to give the United States "the capability to react to a Soviet counterforce attack without going immediately to a counter-city attack."[41])

The *victory denial* school would use nuclear weapons on the battle-field as a last resort to stave off military defeat. Such use may have a greater chance of remaining limited than would a first use of nuclear weapons against cities (whether the attack was "intentional" or occurred because cities were located near military targets). Since a strategy of victory denial could, in principle, mean a use of nuclear weapons that was proportional to the provocation and largely limited to combatants, it holds at least some hope of being consistent with a just war tradition. (How much hope depends on one's view of limiting a nuclear war.) While recognizing that nuclear weapons are different from conventional weapons, proponents of victory denial argue that nuclear first use could at least be potentially justified if weapons were directed against a limited set of targets. Escalation, of course, would still be a risk. Joseph Nye argues, for example, that:

Targeting nuclear weapons to destroy advancing Soviet armies (and the bridges, railheads, and narrow points through which they must pass and the supply depots they must rely upon)...could deny the Soviet Union the gains from aggression while exposing it to additional dangers. Innocent people would be killed in such an attack, but far fewer than in a massive counter-city strategy.[42]

It is not clear how many nuclear weapons would be required to deny the Soviet Union victory on the battlefield. The answer depends largely on the balance of conventional forces and the specific balance and type of nuclear forces. Numerical requirements for nuclear weapons may be increased in order to hold a reserve force of nuclear weapons to deter the other side from attacking cities.

The *leadership punishment* school argues that neither assured societal destruction nor the denial of a military victory is necessarily enough to deter the Soviet Union from using nuclear weapons. The United States must be able to severely punish the Soviet leadership itself, by targeting numerous Communist Party leadership posts. In the view of Colin Gray, "The threat to the rule of the Communist Party of the Soviet Union should be thought of as the United States's [sic] 'Sunday punch,' intended to deter the Soviet Union from striking at U.S. cities."[43] Some argue that the United States must also be able to impede the Soviet Union's ability to recover after a nuclear war, by destroying vital economic assets or targeting specific ethnic groups in order to maximize the difficulties Russian leaders would face in reconstituting Soviet society after a nuclear war.[44] Not surprisingly, advocates of leadership punishment would argue vigorously against any move to very low numbers of nuclear weapons.

These four schools—equal destruction, assured destruction, victory denial, and leadership punishment—have very different ideas of what it takes to deter the Soviet Union from attacking the United States or its allies with nuclear weapons. Indeed, the answers range from almost nothing (for equal destruction, as long as it is symmetric) to practically everything (for leadership punishment). Only the equal destruction school would support a move to levels of destructive capability insufficient to destroy a significant portion of society. It is ultimately impossible to know exactly what retaliatory threat would deter the Soviet Union, or any other country, from initiating a nuclear attack. (It is worth noting, however, that the Soviet Union, unlike the United States and NATO, has *declared* that it would not be the first to use nuclear weapons.) The question of what deters nuclear attack may be relevant only in times of deep crisis or during a major conventional war, situations with which we have fortunately had little experience.

Zero or Near-Zero Nuclear Weapons and the Risk of War

The standard wisdom holds that eliminating or greatly reducing nuclear weapons, other things being equal, would increase the likelihood of conventional war. This is a powerful argument, for it would be difficult to argue that the risk of escalation to all-out nuclear war provides *no* deterrent against conventional hostilities. Those who favor moving to zero or minimal nuclear arsenals hope, first, that an escalation from conventional to nuclear war would then be less likely; and, second, that any nuclear war that did occur would be less destructive.

It is a moot point whether the abolition of nuclear weapons would make the world safe for conventional war: nuclear weapons could be rebuilt, and so *nuclear* war would still be possible. The relevant question is whether abolition or near-abolition would reduce the perceived risks of initiating a conventional conflict and so make it more likely; the answer depends on judgments concerning the likely behavior of future national leaders. I believe a major conventional war would be more likely under abolition or near-abolition. Other things being equal, the presence of large numbers of nuclear weapons—and NATO's stated intent to use them to avoid defeat in a conventional conflict—must have a greater deterrent effect than would much smaller numbers of nuclear weapons meant for nuclear deterrence only, or the threat to rebuild nuclear weapons. However, the greater the danger posed by a breakdown of abolition or near-abolition (as long as it is symmetric), the more "weaponless deterrence" or "minimum deterrence" would extend to deter conventional war as well.

A *nuclear* war would probably also be more likely under abolition or near-abolition, but its potential destructiveness would be much less than in the current world of over 50,000 nuclear weapons. Although nuclear weapons could be rebuilt, it is difficult to imagine that they could quickly return to present levels after a war broke out. On the other hand, numbers of warheads do not necessarily reflect destructive power. A few huge bombs, quickly made, might be dropped on major cities, killing many millions of people. Still, a return to current destructive potential would seem unlikely.

The more important question is whether the *expected* destruction from nuclear war would be greater or less under abolition or near-abolition; the answer depends on one's assessment of relative probabilities of the incentives future leaders may have to use nuclear weapons. My judgment is conditional. *If* there were extensive cooperation to set up a disarmament regime that could reliably detect the hiding or rebuilding of nuclear weapons, then the expected destruction would be less under abolition or near-abolition than in a world of assured destruction. As discussed earlier, however, satisfying this condition would require wholesale reductions in national sovereignty. Except under appropriate political conditions, vast reductions in nuclear forces could make both conventional and nuclear war more likely. As one analyst observed:

Trading nuclear war for conventional war would be a tempting bargain except for escalation. If we allow the risks of conventional conflicts to increase by making nuclear conflict less credible, then through the backdoor of escalation, the net effect may be perverse: it may ultimately increase the risks of nuclear conflict.[45]

A critical question is whether the "crystal ball effect" of nuclear weapons would remain: whether future leaders will have internalized the message that a nuclear war could never be won and must never be fought.[46] Greatly reducing the numbers of nuclear weapons could make any remaining weapons seem more usable, since the chances for catastrophe would be lessened. If nuclear war were less likely at very low numbers, it would not be because of the reductions per se, but because leaders' attitudes or military strategy had changed. Vast reductions in nuclear arsenals could, however, be an important political symbol of a change in strategy away from nuclear war fighting, or of a great improvement in U.S.–Soviet relations.

Advocates of abolition and near-abolition have suggested a number of ways to make up for the lost deterrent effect of nuclear weapons. Robert McNamara calls for a moderate conventional build-up by the West, while Mikhail Gorbachev's plan for abolition stresses the need for a negotiated reduction of conventional forces.[47] Jonathan Schell suggests that conventional arms control and "defensive defenses" would support an abolition agreement.[48]

Would a negotiated reduction in conventional forces increase the stability of a world with very few nuclear weapons? Other things being equal, a reduction in conventional arms would increase, rather than decrease, the military value of a small number of nuclear weapons. The hope behind proposals for reductions in conventional arms to accompany very deep cuts in nuclear weapons is that other things would *not* be equal. Deep reductions in conventional and nuclear forces might reduce the fears of attack on both sides, particularly if reductions in conventional forces left an arrangement of "defensive defenses."[49]

It is worth briefly considering the effect of greatly reducing nuclear weapons on the chances for "inadvertent" nuclear war brought about by the accidental or unauthorized launch of nuclear weapons or the catalytic use of nuclear weapons by a third party.[50] It would seem that the chance of accidental or unauthorized use would decline with the number of nuclear weapons. But drastically reducing the numbers of weapons may also reduce a nation's confidence that it can withstand a first strike against its nuclear weapons without being disarmed. If a country attempted to increase its second-strike capability by loosening control over nuclear weapons or by moving to a strategy of "launch on warning," it might thereby increase the probability of an accidental or unauthorized launch of nuclear weapons.[51] The net effect of vast reductions of nuclear arsenals on the likelihood of accidental or unauthorized use would depend on the controls that were placed on remaining nuclear weapons, and the strategy for their use. A reasonable objective would be the capability of ensuring no immediate second use.[52] This would require making command and control, and the nuclear forces themselves, able to withstand a first strike with high confidence. If the small nuclear forces were given simplified missions, this task would be easier to accomplish, and the chances for accidental or unauthorized launch could be reduced.

As for catalytic third-party use, the effects of near-abolition are uncertain. The United States and the Soviet Union have agreed, along with other signatories to the Non-Proliferation Treaty, "to pursue negotiations in good faith in effective measures relating to cessation of the nuclear arms race at an early date and to nuclear disarmament."[53] Fulfilling their treaty obligations by greatly reducing nuclear arsenals could put the superpowers in a better position to argue for increasing controls over nuclear proliferation to other countries. It may become increasingly difficult for the United States and the Soviet Union to argue that they need enormous arsenals of nuclear weapons for their security, but that even small arsenals are detrimental to the security of other countries. On the other hand, a vast reduction in America's nuclear arsenal could encourage U.S. allies to follow France and Great Britain and develop their own nuclear weapons. The net effect of vast reductions in nuclear arsenals on proliferation and the likelihood of third parties using nuclear weapons would depend very much on the perceived balance of nonnuclear forces in Europe, the Middle East, the Korean peninsula, and other areas of potential conflict.

Other Weapons of Mass Destruction

In his 1986 abolition proposal, Gorbachev also called for the complete elimination of chemical weapons and "a ban on nonnuclear arms based on new physical principles that, in terms of their destructive capability, approach nuclear or other means of mass destruction."[54] Indeed, what would be the point of abolishing nuclear weapons only to replace them with other weapons of mass destruction? Extensive controls on the research and development of new means of mass destruction would be important in a world where the United States and the Soviet Union had few or no nuclear weapons. Such controls may be as important for controlling each side's fears about the other as for controlling the weapons themselves.

The Transition to Very Low Numbers

A rapid transition to a world with very few or no nuclear weapons does not seem likely. Indeed, there are advantages to a more gradual process of disarmament. It would allow confidence to be built over time. Dividing the process of disarmament into small steps might make cooperation more likely by reducing the military advantage that could be gained by breaking the agreement.[55] (See the discussion of U.S.–Soviet cooperation in Chapter 6.) Procedures for verification and enforcement could be phased in over time, responding to changes in technology and taking advantage of any improvements in political relations. In addition, there would be more time for the development of conventional weapons that could substitute for nuclear weapons in military roles. Finally, other negotiations that would support a near-abolition agreement, such as a balancing of conventional forces and a prohibition on other means of mass destruction, could take a long time to complete.

A leisurely pace of nuclear disarmament, however, would also carry risks. Nuclear weapons technology might progress to an unstable balance at which incentives to go first in a crisis are great; verification could be made more difficult by a continuing move to "dual-capable" systems, such as cruise missiles, that can carry both conventional and nuclear warheads; the proliferation of nuclear weapons to other countries might accelerate; and the political relationship between the superpowers might deteriorate rather than improve.

Conclusions

Abolishing nuclear weapons without abolishing war would require the full cooperation of all nuclear nations. If a single nuclear-capable country refused to participate, the abolition agreement would break down. Even with comprehensive verification and the participation of all nations, establishing a stable relationship of "weaponless deterrence" would be extremely difficult. It is not clear how nations could establish equal abilities to rearm and to hide nuclear weapons; yet without equal abilities, a world where nuclear weapons had been proscribed but where conflicts could lead to war would be unstable. The involvement of any nuclear nation in a war or serious crisis would probably prompt rearmament by all.

Improvements in verification technology seem unlikely to substantially increase the chances that any cheating on an abolition agreement would be promptly discovered; comprehensive inspections would be a vital part of any agreement to reduce the numbers of nuclear weapons to the hundreds or lower. The virtually unlimited inspections that would accompany the abolition of nuclear weapons would require a significant reduction in the secrecy of military activities, possible only if the U.S.– Soviet relationship were radically transformed. (For a discussion of such a transformation in superpower relations, see Chapter 7.) The alternative to unlimited inspections for abolition is a public willingness to accept hidden nuclear weapons—an unlikely prospect given the United States' history of anxiety about the "bomber gap," the "missile gap," and the "window of vulnerability." The more limited, but probably still extensive, inspection regime that would accompany a move to some hundreds of nuclear warheads seems much more plausible. But while allowing each side to have a limited nuclear arsenal would reduce the incentives for cheating, the political tensions associated with verification and compliance would presumably persist, both inside the United States and between the superpowers. Managing these tensions would be critical, and perhaps difficult.

There are several important differences between a world with a few hundred nuclear weapons and one with none at all. First, since the expected benefits from cheating should be less if each side has some nuclear weapons, the incentives to cheat should also be smaller. On the other hand, the chances of being caught cheating would probably be less under near-abolition, since under abolition the discovery of one nuclear warhead or the initiation of production would constitute a clear violation.

Second, an abolition agreement would be supported by strategic defenses that could protect rearmament capabilities—and people—thereby reducing incentives to break the agreement. Whether strategic defenses would help in a move to near-abolition depends on the assumptions made about the requirements of deterrence: only if approximately equal destruction is deemed adequate would population defenses be desirable. Under a strategy of minimum deterrence (as suggested by most proponents of minimal nuclear arsenals), population defenses would not help and could hurt, while defenses of retaliatory forces could help— if they were invulnerable and not subject to upgrading to population defense.

Finally, the appropriate balance of conventional forces may be quite different under abolition and near-abolition. For abolition, it might be best to maintain conventional forces at a fairly high level, to minimize the effect of cheating with a few nuclear weapons; conventional weapons could substitute for nuclear weapons to a certain extent (at least to deter rearming). The desired balance of conventional forces under minimum nuclear arsenals, like the balance of strategic defenses, would depend on the nuclear strategy used. If, for example, the deterrence strategy were victory denial, then a conventional balance sensitive to the use of a small number of nuclear weapons might be desirable; under a strategy of minimum deterrence, the conventional balance should be robust to limited nuclear use.

If the present technological trend toward increasingly accurate and destructive conventional weapons continues, the chances for vast reductions in nuclear weapons may improve. Further developments in emerging-technology conventional weapons could be a mixed blessing, however, if they blur the firebreak between conventional and nuclear weapons.[56] Technological improvements in conventional weaponry may, over the long term, reduce incentives to procure nuclear warheads for war fighting, though it is not now clear how far a process of "conventional substitution" or a movement to "defensive defenses" may go. (For a discussion of these questions, see Chapters 4 and 5.) Conventional explosives are unlikely to displace nuclear weapons completely as a threat to cities.[57] Even the massively destructive firebombings of World War II—in Dresden, Hamburg, and Tokyo—pale in comparison with the destruction that could be wrought by a few thermonuclear bombs.

Political rather than technological factors will probably determine the prospects for vast reductions in nuclear weapons. If more policy makers come to believe that nuclear weapons could serve no military purpose, this conviction—whether or not it is in any sense "correct"—may reduce the perceived need for nuclear weapons more than would any foreseeable technological changes. (Of course, each side must also believe that the other side shares this conviction.)

With vastly reduced superpower nuclear arsenals, there may be increased incentives for nuclear proliferation, particularly among American allies who see the U.S. nuclear umbrella being pulled back to the American coast, or folded up entirely. An agreement between the superpowers for minimal nuclear arsenals that did not take account of U.S. allies' security needs could be disastrous for both the United States and the Soviet Union. (A significant concern underlying the Soviet Union's interest in signing the Non-Proliferation Agreement was the possibility that West Germany would acquire nuclear weapons.)

Several factors create pressures for having fairly substantial numbers of nuclear weapons (i.e., in the hundreds rather than the tens). First, one cannot know how much nuclear power is required. That will depend on particular circumstances, and may change with the leadership of the Soviet Union and other countries. There is a natural tendency toward conservatism, toward the view that "what *surely* deters the Soviets is the chance of all hell breaking loose once war begins."[58] Second, it is difficult to know how many nuclear weapons the other side might have hidden, or might quickly build. Hence, it is reasonable to possess at least enough nuclear weapons to ensure national security against any foreseeable level of cheating by others. Finally, other nations besides the United States and the Soviet Union now possess nuclear weapons, and this is likely to remain true in the future. Unless the superpowers are willing to become one of several equal nuclear powers, they will be reluctant to reduce nuclear weapons to levels close to those of other nations.

All in all, I believe an attempt at abolition in the near term would probably increase the expected damage from both conventional and nuclear war. With extensive international cooperation to provide a politically acceptable and strategically stable balance of nuclear weapons, establish verification procedures, and produce a robust conventional balance — long-term goals that will be extremely difficult to achieve — minimal nuclear arsenals would (in my judgment) be likely to reduce the risks of nuclear war.

It is impossible to predict the form of an arms control agreement for vast reductions in nuclear arsenals that would be acceptable to all present and potential nuclear powers, sometime in the indefinite future. However, most of the goals that would reduce nations' incentives to acquire and maintain nuclear weapons — limiting the proliferation of nuclear weapons technology and materials; establishing a more stable balance of conventional forces; increasing controls over other weapons of mass destruction; reducing international tensions and building mutual confidence between the superpowers; and developing a greater capacity for the nonviolent resolution of regional disputes — are worth pursuing whatever the number of nuclear weapons in the world.

Smart Weapons and Ordinary People: Implications of Increasingly Accurate Long-Range Missiles

Albert Carnesale

The men, women, and children who fight and die in armed conflicts over the next several decades will differ little from those who fought and died in previous wars. The offensive and defensive means by which they conduct their battles are likely to have changed far more.

Some small fraction of the changes in hardware will be revolutionary in character, introducing entirely new kinds of military systems, having impacts similar to those accompanying the earlier introduction of machine guns, tanks, aircraft, radar, aircraft carriers, reconnaissance satellites, ballistic missiles, and, most importantly, nuclear weapons. One such revolutionary change may be the widespread deployment of effective defenses against ballistic missiles. The feasibility and desirability of this vision of the future are subjects of intense debate, as discussed in Chapter 4.

Evolutionary changes are easier to anticipate. In particular it seems clear that offensive weapons, particularly ballistic missiles and cruise missiles, will be able to deliver nuclear and nonnuclear payloads with markedly improved accuracy to targets at long ranges, up to and including intercontinental distances.[1]

The availability of smart weapons has little bearing on combatants' ability to destroy cities or other large "soft" targets. Even today, it is hard to miss a city. When intercontinental ballistic missiles were introduced in the early 1960s, their accuracy was on the order of a couple of miles; now it is closer to a tenth of a mile; soon it will be reduced by another order of magnitude. Missing the center of a metropolis by two city blocks would have little effect on the damage caused by the arriving nuclear explosive. The same cannot be said of small, hard (i.e., blast-resistant) military targets, such as missile silos and command-and-control bunkers. The vulnerability of such targets depends very much on the distance between the target and the point of explosion, as well as on the amount of explosive energy released. Indeed, against small, hard targets, greater accuracy contributes more to the likelihood of successful attack than does higher yield. For example, a twofold improvement in accuracy is as effective as an eightfold increase in yield, and a tenfold accuracy improvement would permit a thousandfold decrease in yield with the same destructive effect. With markedly improved accuracy, reduced-yield explosives, perhaps even conventional explosives in some cases, may be sufficient to destroy many military targets now vulnerable only to high-yield nuclear weapons.

To the extent that increased accuracy is accompanied by reduced explosive yield, either nuclear or conventional, the principal effect would be to lower the collateral damage resulting from attacks on small targets. Of course, improved accuracy need not necessarily be accompanied by reduced yield. Military planners might continue to use high-yield weapons with the more accurate delivery systems, either to increase the likelihood of target destruction or to avoid developing, testing, producing, and deploying a newly designed nuclear or conventional warhead. In this case, accuracy improvement would have little or no effect on collateral damage. Proponents of accuracy improvement, however, invariably envisage simultaneous yield reduction. Indeed, their arguments rely heavily on advantageous reductions in collateral damage.

It is claimed that the deployment of high-precision long-range delivery systems carrying conventional warheads or nuclear warheads of markedly reduced yield would enhance deterrence of conventional aggression against our allies or other areas of vital interest; more nearly satisfy the "just war" criteria calling for proportionality and discrimination in deterrence threats and in responses to failures of deterrence; and reduce the chances that a failure of deterrence might cause a nuclear winter threatening the survival of the human species. Still more benefits would accrue to systems precise enough to permit replacement of nuclear warheads by conventional ones. Supplementing our nuclear arsenal with nonnuclear strategic weapons would improve the U.S.–Soviet balance of conventional forces and provide militarily effective unmanned means for limited attacks; it would also shift to the adversary the burden of escalation to nuclear war.

These claims appear modest in comparison with those made for the other visions of the future explored in this volume. Advocates of precise delivery systems have not portrayed them as a basis for a world in which we would no longer rely on nuclear deterrence for our security (although some of the claims come uncomfortably close). A world of low-yield nuclear and nonnuclear smart strategic weapons is far more likely to be realized than more visionary scenarios. Almost all observers would agree that this evolutionary technological change is likely to occur and that it will be militarily important. The claims of its advocates deserve careful consideration.

Weighing the Claims

Enhanced Deterrence

Liberals and conservatives, religious leaders and atheists, idealists and pragmatists, experts and laymen—all abhor the notion of relying on threats of nuclear retaliation to deter aggression against ourselves, our allies, or areas of vital interest to us. Some would remedy the situation by reducing reliance on retaliatory threats, followed by near or total abolition of the nuclear weapons themselves. Others would cure the same disease by improving the weapons in ways that make them more usable and, therefore, the threat of their use more credible.

These prescriptions represent polarized approaches to the dilemmas of usability and credibility. Paradoxically, as the Harvard Nuclear Study Group observed, "Nuclear weapons can prevent aggression only if there is a possibility that they will be used, but we do not want to make them so usable that anyone is tempted to use one." At the same time, threats of nuclear use are inherently somewhat suspect:

The threat of retaliation which best deters aggression is a credible threat, one which the potential attacker believes the defender actually intends to execute if he is attacked. The credibility of nuclear threats is often in doubt, however, for this simple reason: a nation that retaliated might be attacked again and suffer even more.[2]

There are no obvious resolutions of these dilemmas; indeed, the West (and, one suspects, the East as well) has been struggling with them since the dawn of the nuclear age. It is hardly surprising that some observers push for moving to one extreme while others pull in the opposite direction.

Albert Wohlstetter is an articulate advocate of moving toward greater usability, with particular emphasis on accuracy improvement and concomitant yield reduction. In his words:

The Western establishment only recently has begun to face up to the possibility that the Soviets may use conventional force decisively. It continues to evade the military, political and moral problems of responding in contingencies where the Soviets might use *nuclear* force decisively and still leave both sides a large stake in avoiding suicide and universal ruin.... The West has limited options and needs more and better ones in order to deter the plausible attacks.[3]

We should be prepared to use discriminating offense strategies, tactics and precise weapons with reduced yields and deliberately confined effects...to select targets of a sort, number and location that will accomplish an important military purpose and yet contain the destruction.[4]

All other things being equal, the "more and better" retaliatory options provided by more precise weapons with reduced yields would clearly enhance deterrence. But so would the addition of virtually any military capability to our current arsenal. The questions of interest relate to the adversary's response to the added capability and to the net effect on the likelihood and consequences of nuclear war.

The real value of smart weapons would not lie in enhancing deterrence of attacks against the U.S. homeland. More than ten thousand U.S. nuclear weapons are already within range of the USSR. If this force is insufficiently daunting, the addition of some conventional or low-yield nuclear strategic weapons to our arsenal is unlikely to make much difference. If any threat is credible, it is that we would respond in kind to an attack on the United States.

Extended deterrence is more problematic. While we have the *ability* to punish the Soviet Union for any aggression it might commit against our allies or other areas of clear importance to us, the *credibility* of a threat to do so is doubtful. When two nations are engaged in a conflict that does not involve attacks on their national territories, initiation of such an attack would drastically alter the nature of that conflict, and this qualitative change far outweighs the technical characteristics of the weapons employed. Reduction of potential collateral damage is unlikely to reduce significantly the barriers to attacking the adversary's homeland, especially when the adversary is a nuclear superpower. The choice of weapons is not insignificant, but it is overshadowed by the far more difficult decision of whether to violate the adversary's homeland sanctuary.

What might be the Soviet reaction to a U.S. attack on the Soviet homeland with conventional or low-yield nuclear weapons? Would it be markedly different from the response to a U.S. attack employing high-yield weapons? Most important, is there any reason to believe that the Soviets *would* retaliate against a homeland attack by high-yield weapons but *would not* retaliate against a homeland attack by low-yield weapons? Most likely, the specific characteristics of the weapons used to violate their motherland would have little bearing on their decision whether to retaliate. Then what purpose would the U.S. smart weapons have served? If the Soviet arsenal also included smart low-yield weapons, the collateral damage done by a retaliatory attack on the United States could be held to a minimum. Otherwise the exchange might result in comparable damage to the military targets on both sides and far greater damage to the civilian sector of the United States than of the USSR.

Improving the West's capabilities to fight a conventional war in Europe, the Persian Gulf region, or other areas perceived as important potential objects of Soviet aggression would help deter such action. In this regard, precision-guided nonnuclear weapons can play a role. Short-range systems, such as antitank missiles for battlefield use, have been in our arsenal for some time. Intermediate-range systems, such as terminally guided cruise missiles launched from land, sea, or air, would be used to stop the reinforcement of Warsaw Pact troops by attacking airfields, rail and road networks, communications facilities, and second-echelon forces well beyond the front lines. Long-range smart nonnuclear weapons could cover targets such as these wherever the line of battle might be. By helping to offset Soviet local advantages in conventional forces, these smart weapons enhance extended deterrence.

As long as extended deterrence rests ultimately on the willingness of the United States to escalate a regional conflict to an attack on the homeland of a nuclear-armed Soviet Union, it will be in trouble. The acquisition of smarter longer-range systems for use in conventional conflict outside the superpower homelands would help to deter Soviet aggression just as would other improvements in the West's general-purpose forces. The threat of using such weapons against targets within the Soviet Union, however, is unlikely to be sufficiently credible to add much to extended deterrence.

Proportionality and Discrimination

In a 1983 pastoral letter, the American National Conference of Catholic Bishops reminded us of the moral principles underlying the doctrine of "just war."[5] The bishops elucidate both the conditions that would allow the resort to force (the *jus ad bellum* criteria) and the conditions under which a just war must be conducted (the *jus in bello* criteria). Of particular

relevance to the issues raised by smart strategic weapons are the principles of proportionality and discrimination.

> In terms of the *jus ad bellum* criteria, proportionality means that the damage
> to be inflicted and the costs incurred by war must be proportionate to the good
> expected by taking up arms. . . . This principle of proportionality applies through-
> out the conduct of the war as well as to the decision to begin warfare.[6]

In the *jus in bello* context, the rule of proportionality and discrimination
requires that "response to the aggression must not exceed the nature of
the aggression" and "prohibits directly intended attacks on non-com-
batants and non-military targets."[7] The bishops recognize the difficulty
and importance of questions related to the definitions of *intentional, non-
combatant,* and *military.* Nevertheless, they maintain that the two principles of proportionality and discrimination "in all their complexity, must
be applied to the range of weapons—conventional, nuclear, biological,
and chemical—with which nations are armed today."[8]

Albert Wohlstetter offers high-precision low-yield strategic weapons
as a partial solution to the bishops' moral quandary. In an essay focused
largely on the bishops' letter, he writes:

> My own research and that of others has for many years pointed to the need
> for a much higher priority on improving our ability to hit what we aim at and
> only what we aim at. . . . The danger of Soviet aggression is more likely to be
> lessened by a Western ability to threaten the military means of domination than
> by a Western ability to threaten bystanders.[9]

"Increased precision," Wohlstetter goes on to say, "would improve our
ability to avoid the unintended bombing of innocents with nuclear or
conventional warheads."[10] Thus, in his view, smart weapons that cause
low collateral damage will not only enhance deterrence, they will also
address the bishops' condemnation of "retaliatory action which would
indiscriminately and disproportionately take many wholly innocent lives,
lives of people who are in no way responsible for reckless actions of their
government."[11]

Of course current nuclear arsenals permit a substantial degree of discrimination in launching attacks. For example, with existing weapons the
United States could attack important Soviet military forces and installations in remote, sparsely populated areas (e.g., along the trans-Siberian
railway or on the Chinese border), with little collateral damage. There is
no doubt that low-yield warheads would kill fewer bystanders than high-
yield ones, and that fewer dead would be better than more. The relevant
arguments against smart strategic weapons, especially nuclear-armed

ones, reflect two basic concerns: first, a greater capacity to fight wars might increase the likelihood that they will be fought; second, the more nuclear weapons come to resemble conventional weapons, the lower will be the barrier to nuclear use. Noting these concerns, the bishops "oppose... strategic planning which seeks a nuclear war-fighting capability that goes beyond the limited function of deterrence [and] proposals which have the effect of lowering the nuclear threshold and blurring the difference between nuclear and conventional weapons."[12] Finally, there remains the question of what might happen after the low-collateral-damage weapons were used. Would the war remain limited? If not, the smart weapons would merely have smoothed the ascent of the escalation ladder to large-scale nuclear use, and perhaps even to global catastrophe. This issue too is addressed by the bishops, who are "highly skeptical about the real meaning of 'limited.'.... In our view the first imperative is to prevent any use of nuclear weapons and we hope that leaders will resist the notion that nuclear conflict can be limited, contained or won in any traditional sense."[13] Thus, while Wohlstetter joins the bishops in urging adherence to the principles of proportionality and discrimination, he differs as to how that might be achieved. In particular, he sees smart strategic weapons as a partial solution, whereas the bishops see them as part of the problem.

The Burden of Escalation

The turn of the century will see... the emergence of capabilities for intercontinental strategic conflict without nuclear weapons.... It is not too early to begin thinking about the implications of technological developments which will once again make it possible to attack important military targets deep inside the homelands of the super-powers with non-nuclear weapons.... a revolution is on the way.[14]

With these words, Carl H. Builder concludes his comprehensive and notably objective analysis, "The Prospects and Implications of Non-nuclear Means for Strategic Conflict." He identifies four trends favoring the development of nonnuclear strategic weapons: (1) the growing reluctance to use nuclear weapons; (2) the accelerating pace of modern conflict, which reduces the value of attacking urban and industrial areas and increases the importance of destroying military forces; (3) the increasing concentration and fragility of modern military forces, which makes them more vulnerable to attack; and (4) the availability of new technological means for "precise, discriminatory attacks at global ranges."[15] Builder has no doubt as to which of these trends provides the strongest driving force:

> The most important incentive for the development of non-nuclear strategic weapons springs from the presumption... of a growing *reluctance* to use nuclear weapons. If that presumption is incorrect, then not only are non-nuclear weapons easily countered by a nuclear response, but the principal incentive for their development also disappears. On the other hand, if the presumption is correct, then the incentive for their development will exist and a nuclear response to their use will be an awesome and uncomfortable step.[16]

However high the barrier to use of nuclear weapons, it is likely to shrink considerably in the minds of those whose national vulnerability has been abused. A nation on whose territory the adversary has detonated weapons (whether conventional or nuclear) is presumably less reluctant to use nuclear weapons than is one whose homeland sanctuary has not yet been violated. While the use of nonnuclear strategic weapons clearly is less provocative than the use of their nuclear counterparts, an attempt to shift the burden of nuclear escalation by attacking the adversary's homeland with conventional explosives may make it all the more likely that the burden will be taken up.

Implications

The introduction of highly accurate intercontinental weapons will certainly not be the only important change in the global political-military situation in the decades ahead. While we cannot predict with confidence what those other changes might be, it is useful to raise some of the possibilities and to explore their implications for a world with precise long-range weapons.

Nonnuclear Strategic Weapons

Who will possess the precise intercontinental weapons of the future? All too often analysts fall prey to the "fallacy of the last move" by considering a world that differs from the present one only in that some beneficial change is made in the forces of the West. Is it reasonable to imagine that only the United States will have these new long-range systems, or will the Soviets, perhaps lagging by several years, acquire them as well? Will the addition of nonnuclear strategic weapons to the arsenals of both superpowers serve U.S. interests? Would not their use by the Soviets against a small number of selected targets, especially port facilities, in

Western Europe or other potential theaters of conflict, or even in the United States, hamper our reinforcement capabilities even more than our use against comparable Soviet targets would hamper theirs? If these weapons shift the burden of escalation to nuclear war, to which side would it be shifted? And will other nations besides the current super-powers gain access to these inherently more usable weapons? How would their proliferation affect the likelihood of conventional war and, ulti-mately, of escalation to nuclear war?

The effectiveness of the new weapons also is open to question, since neither the weapons themselves nor the countermeasures that will be employed against them have yet been designed. Carl Builder describes the countermeasures problem to be faced by nonnuclear systems:

Non-nuclear weapons, unlike their nuclear counterparts, will depend upon pre-cision delivery and terminal homing to ensure that their much more modest de-structive power is brought fully to bear on the target. Such precision delivery will necessarily rely upon sensors which are subject to familiar countermeasures, including jamming, decoying and masking. . . . If non-nuclear weapons require precise placement at some critical point or aspect of a target, then only that point or aspect needs . . . additional protection to defeat the attack. If communications are required between elements of the weapon system—to enable remote designa-tion of individual targets for example—then those, too, are subject to jamming or signal exploitation.[17]

Believing that "the familiar game of measure and countermeasure" will continue to be played, Builder concludes that, "while non-nuclear stra-tegic weapons seem destined to be more vulnerable to countermeasures than their nuclear predecessors, it is not apparent that they will always be significantly or unacceptably so."[18] True, but "always" is a very long time. For the foreseeable future, nonnuclear systems are likely to be sig-nificantly more vulnerable to countermeasures.

Nuclear Weapons

What changes in nuclear arsenals might be expected as a result of the introduction of highly accurate long-range delivery systems?

As precision of delivery continues to improve, lower-yield nuclear weapons will be able to perform some of the military functions currently assigned to higher-yield ones, and one would expect the new systems to replace the old as part of the continuing process of force modernization. Greater precision also will provide opportunities for employing high-yield weapons to destroy some targets (such as superhardened silos for intercontinental ballistic missiles and deep underground bunkers) that had previously been relatively invulnerable to attack. The current generation of delivery systems is entirely adequate to destroy large soft targets, particularly urban/industrial areas.

Not even the staunchest advocates of nonnuclear strategic weapons predict the extinction of nuclear systems. Wohlstetter sees them as having "a large political importance...in reducing the pressures to resort to nuclear weapons."[19] "They give us choices."[20] Builder addresses the matter directly:

[The] advent of non-nuclear capabilities would offer no prospects for elimination of nuclear weapons, nor even their replacement in the ultimate threat to destroy cities. Thus, the consequences of full-scale nuclear war, at least in contemplation of societal destruction, are not likely to change because of emerging capabilities for non-nuclear strategic conflict.[21]

Moreover, Builder expresses concern that the emergence of effective non-nuclear systems might stimulate "increasing public pressure for substantial reductions in the super-power arsenals of strategic nuclear weapons." He cautions against yielding to such pressure on these grounds: (1) "the effort to supplant most strategic arms by non-nuclear replacements... is almost certain to involve higher costs"; (2) "nuclear arms have become premier symbols of national power"; and (3) "the transition to a world of significantly reduced nuclear arsenals for the super-powers...could be a very unstable process."[22]

It has been suggested that the danger of societal destruction might be eliminated by removing from nuclear arsenals the high-yield weapons and retaining only the low-yield weapons. Prospects for such action appear bleak. First, as indicated previously, high-yield nuclear weapons may be the only means available for destroying superhard targets of substantial military significance. Second, the ability to extinguish the adversary's society is seen by many as the "ultimate deterrent" not only to attacks on our homeland, but also to some lesser acts of aggression that might escalate uncontrollably. This capability becomes all the more essential as more nations acquire nuclear arsenals. Third, enormous damage can be done to a society with a sufficient (and not unreasonably large) number of low-yield nuclear weapons. High-yield weapons just make the task easier. Fourth, verifying that an adversary's nuclear arsenal contained no high-yield weapons would be an enormous, perhaps impossible, challenge.

If the nuclear threat to civilization is to be removed, it will not be through the accuracy improvements that enable the weapons of one nation to hit a bull's-eye in the homeland of another. And even if nuclear weapons were to disappear irreversibly, civilization would remain vulnerable to human actions. We can draw on other means of mass destruction, such as chemical and biological weapons and weather modification. If nuclear weapons—to date, the devices of choice—became unavailable, is it likely that great powers, and those aspiring to be great powers, would abjure the other options as well?

Political Dimensions

What of the political characteristics of the world in which increasingly accurate strategic weapons will exist? For example, how will the implications of those weapons depend on the structure of the international system, the nature of the political relationships among the key elements of that system, and the domestic politics within nations? These aspects of a world with smart weapons have yet to be addressed by the analysts.

It is difficult to imagine how the advent of smart strategic weapons would depend on whether the structure of international power were multipolar or bipolar, or whether there existed strong international organizations or security regimes. Yet somehow we suspect that these factors would be strongly influential. Domestic politics are also likely to be important. How many societies will be willing to devote a greater portion of their national treasure to supplant nuclear strategic weapons with conventional ones; that is, intentionally to get "less bang for the buck"? Even if some were willing to do so, the rationality and morality that foster adherence to the principles of proportionality and discrimination are not uniformly present in all societies, nor at all times in any given society. In nations whose domestic politics are highly ideological and volatile, the rationality and morality on which the vision of a safer world of smart weapons depends are likely to be in short supply, and shorter still in times of war.

Conclusion

However opaque the future may be, we can confidently predict continuing improvements in the accuracy of long-range delivery vehicles and in the destructive efficiency of the weapons they deliver. With these new smart systems, the explosive energy required to destroy most kinds of military targets, particularly small hard ones, will decline, thereby permitting reductions in the yields of the nuclear warheads intended for attack against such targets and, in some instances, the substitution of nonnuclear for nuclear weapons. An attack against a given set of targets by these less powerful weapons would, of course, cause less collateral damage than would an attack by the same number of high-yield nuclear weapons.

Because of the lower collateral damage, using or threatening to use smart weapons would seem more rational and more moral (or less irrational and less immoral) than using or threatening to use their high-yield nuclear predecessors. This raises an all-too-familiar paradox: on the one hand, more usable weapons provide the basis for more credible threats and therefore should be more effective as deterrents to war; on the other hand, other things being equal, more usable weapons are more likely to be used. The controversial issues associated with smart strategic weapons are reflections of this paradox.

In the course of modernizing its strategic forces, the United States has for years been replacing some higher-yield nuclear warheads with lower-yield ones. Continuation of this trend will have little effect on the likelihood or ultimate consequences of nuclear war. The acquisition of effective nonnuclear strategic weapons, however, would represent a qualitative change in America's arsenal. By helping to redress the imbalance of conventional forces between East and West, these weapons could strengthen deterrence of Soviet aggression in regions far from the U.S. homeland. This enhancement of extended deterrence would flow from the potential for militarily effective use of smart intercontinental-range conventionally armed weapons against Soviet and Warsaw Pact land, sea, and air forces outside Soviet territory. (If the Soviets also had nonnuclear strategic weapons, it is not at all clear that the net effect on the balance of conventional forces would benefit the United States, or that extended deterrence would be enhanced rather than undermined.)

Threats to use smart conventional weapons against targets in the Soviet homeland would contribute little to extended deterrence. Such threats would hardly be realistic, since their implementation almost certainly would stimulate a Soviet nuclear response against targets in the American homeland. The Achilles' heel of extended deterrence lies in the credibility of the U.S. threat ultimately to escalate a regional conflict to strategic war between the superpowers. Smart weapons will not solve that problem.

The opportunities smart weapons provide for proportionate and discriminate use are mixed blessings. First, there is the obvious confrontation with the usability paradox. Second, the acquisition of a strategic arsenal covering the full range of explosive energy, from conventional warheads to very-low-yield "mini-nukes" and on up through multimegaton monsters, is bound to blur the distinction between conventional and nuclear weapons—a distinction that has been considered to be of fundamental importance. Third, the notion that low-collateral-damage weapons can be used advantageously assumes there will be no escalation to use of far more destructive weapons. Few earthlings would want the survival of civilization on their planet to depend on self-restraint by the nuclear superpowers in the wake of a homeland-to-homeland nuclear duel.

The fear of Armageddon would be alleviated if the nuclear powers would "lop off the top" of their arsenals—that is, eliminate all high-yield nuclear weapons. Unfortunately, however, certain perceived military and political needs (such as the destruction of superhard silos and bunkers and the possession of a city-busting "ultimate deterrent") are best met by high-yield weapons. Thus, nuclear low-yield and nonnuclear smart weapons are far more likely to supplement than to replace traditional strategic arsenals.

The addition of smart weapons to the enormous array of destructive devices already in the hands of ordinary people offers little prospect for meaningfully reducing the risk of catastrophic nuclear war.

CHAPTER 3

Defense Dominance

Charles L. Glaser

A prudent restraint from aggressive violence that is based on acknowledgment that the world is too small to support a nuclear
war is a healthier basis for peace than unilateral efforts to build
defenses. I like the notion that East and West have exchanged hostages on a massive scale and that as long as they are unprotected,
civilization depends on the avoidance of military aggression that
could escalate to nuclear war.

—Thomas C. Schelling

The possibility of an enormously destructive nuclear war has generated
interest in strategic defenses that would protect the United States. Proponents argue that defenses are desirable because they would reduce the
costs of a nuclear war. Perfect defenses would make the United States
invulnerable even to a deliberate full-scale Soviet nuclear attack. Near-
perfect defenses, while allowing the Soviet Union to inflict enormous
damage, would greatly reduce the costs of an all-out war and increase
the prospects for rapid U.S. recovery. In addition, defenses could reduce
the costs of other types of attacks. They might stop an accidental Soviet
attack from damaging the United States, thus reducing the probability
that such an accident would trigger escalation to all-out war. Moreover,
defenses that were highly effective against the Soviet force would probably be even more effective against other states with nuclear weapons.

A variety of other rationales have also been advanced: Deploying
strategic defenses might reduce the fear created by the possibility of nuclear war, make U.S. security less dependent on Soviet decisions, reduce tensions and add stability to superpower relations, and provide the

An earlier version of this chapter appeared in the Fall 1984 issue of *International Security*.

foundation for a more moral national security policy. Such motivations were invoked by President Reagan when he initiated the current debate over strategic defenses. He called for a shift from a world in which both superpowers have assured destruction capabilities—that is, from a world of mutual assured destruction (MAD) capabilities—to a world of highly effective defenses.[1]

I've become more and more deeply convinced that the human spirit must be capable of rising above dealings with other nations and human beings by threatening their existence. Feeling this way, I believe we must thoroughly examine every opportunity for reducing tensions and for introducing greater stability into the strategic calculus of both sides.... Let me share with you a vision of the future which offers hope. It is that we embark on a program to counter the awesome Soviet missile threat with measures that are defensive.[2]

This speech launched the Strategic Defense Initiative (SDI) and set in motion a fundamental re-evaluation of U.S. nuclear policy.[3]

Lt. Gen. James Abrahamson, director of the SDI Office, presents a similar view of why effective defenses are desirable:

The policy of mutual assured destruction has worked reasonably well, if you say we haven't destroyed ourselves yet. And then you look at the trends in the world, in terms of how easy it is to build missiles now, and you say "Do we want to rely on this kind of concept for our children forever?" It's really a search for a strategy of what some people call mutual assured survival. I can't understand why it is that so many people find that that's so distasteful.[4]

Opposition to defending the United States is based largely on the judgment that near-perfect defense against a massive Soviet ballistic missile attack is infeasible. (By *near-perfect defenses* I mean systems that can deny one's adversary an assured destruction capability.)[5] Authoritative studies show there is virtually no hope that the "star wars" concepts now under research will provide near-perfect defense in the foreseeable future.[6]

A variety of factors combine to dim the prospects for near-perfect defense. First, enormous technical progress is required. Large advances in various individual devices—for example, lasers or other spaced-based weapons—will be needed before a highly effective ballistic missile defense can be deployed. Once developed, moreover, these devices must be combined into an efficient system capable of surviving attack. Second, because the Soviet offense is very large compared with the number of U.S. cities, U.S. defenses would have to be extremely effective. Given today's forces, a 99 percent effective defense would be expected to allow approximately 100 Soviet nuclear weapons to reach the United States, leaving the largest U.S. cities vulnerable. Third, if the United States develops defenses that are highly effective against today's offenses, the Soviet Union could deploy a variety of countermeasures and/or increase the size of its force. To remain near-perfect, the U.S. defense would have to offset all such Soviet efforts.

The question of whether perfect or near-perfect defenses are actually desirable has been left largely unexamined.[7] The implicit assumption is that if effective ballistic missile defense (BMD) could be developed and deployed, then the United States should pursue the BMD route and the associated change in nuclear strategy.[8] Even analysts who strongly oppose SDI on technical grounds tend to believe that highly effective defenses, if feasible, would be desirable. In the view of the Union of Concerned Scientists, for example, "If it were possible to put in place overnight a fully effective, invulnerable defense against nuclear weapons, there could hardly be serious objections to doing so."[9]

Nevertheless, the desirability of highly effective defenses is the central question. If near-perfect defenses would create a world far safer than MAD, then even a slight chance of eventually deploying them might justify pursuing extensive research and possibly taking some risks in current policy. But if MAD is preferable to a world of near-perfect defenses, then, even if near-perfect defenses are feasible, the United States should pursue policies to preserve MAD.

This chapter analyzes the desirability of perfect and near-perfect defenses. To examine the issues that lie beyond the technical feasibility of BMD, I hypothesize a world in which the superpowers have deployed perfect or near-perfect defenses. My analysis does not depend on the type of strategic defenses deployed. The issue is how effective the superpowers' defenses are against each other's offenses. I focus on the situation in which both superpowers have highly effective defenses and ask whether such a world might be preferable to our current one, in which both countries maintain redundant assured destruction capabilities?[10]

I leave aside the hypothetical case in which only the United States achieves near-perfect defenses. For one thing, it is unlikely that the United States could maintain a technological advantage that would permit this outcome. Furthermore, symmetric deployment is an especially interesting case to consider because of the intuitive appeal of reducing U.S. vulnerability without threatening Soviet security. Proponents of SDI see this as a strong selling point of defense dominance, arguing that MAD is morally unacceptable because in this world the United States threatens enormous destruction. They also argue that defenses will reduce superpower tensions. Such beliefs are evident in the remarks of President Reagan and General Abrahamson quoted above. Similarly, former Secretary of Defense Caspar Weinberger argues that "President Reagan's SDI vision seeks to move *all* mankind away from our unsettling state of total vulnerability."[11] Clearly, these claims do not apply to a world in which only the United States has effective defenses.

Any final conclusion about near-perfect defenses, however, must consider the case in which only the United States has such effective defenses. Further, we would need to consider the transitions to these worlds. For example, if the transitions are very dangerous, then even if the end state would be desirable, the United States might still decide in favor of preserving MAD. In addition, a complete analysis would include the case in which only the Soviet Union has near-perfect defenses.

This chapter does not address the question of less-than-near-perfect defenses.[12] These systems raise fundamentally different issues since the superpowers remain in MAD. Less-than-near-perfect defenses may have some value, but they cannot reduce the costs of an all-out superpower war. However, since some argue that deploying less effective BMD systems is a step toward highly effective systems, beliefs about the desirability of near-perfect defense are important in the debate over less-than-near-perfect defenses.

A world in which defenses win the competition against offenses, thereby eliminating the superpowers' assured destruction capabilities, is often described as one of *defense dominance*.[13] I will refer to the world in which both superpowers deploy highly effective defenses as BAD (Both Are Defended).[14] In other words, this chapter asks: Could BAD be preferable to MAD?

Perfect Defense

What are the strategic implications of perfect defenses? There is a widespread presumption that perfect defenses are desirable if feasible, and this is the goal toward which many advocates of strategic defense, including President Reagan, wish to move. Yet a world of perfect defenses has two major shortcomings that might make it less safe than our current nuclear situation.[15]

First, there could be no guarantee that perfect defenses would remain perfect. The technical challenge of developing and deploying a defense that would make the United States invulnerable to nuclear attack is enormous. The difficulty of maintaining such a perfect defense indefinitely is likely to be far greater than developing it in the first place. Consequently, so-called perfect defenses should not be seen as a permanent technological solution to the dangers posed by nuclear weapons. It is far more likely that a world of perfect defenses would decay into a world of imperfect defenses, returning the superpowers to MAD.[16]

The likelihood of decay would create a number of related dangers. A world in which strategic defenses made both superpowers invulnerable to nuclear attack would be extremely sensitive to even small improvements in the ability of one country's offense to penetrate the adversary's defense. For example, the ability to penetrate the adversary's defense with ten warheads would provide the potential for enormous destruction when compared with no destruction. Moreover, faced with large offenses, both superpowers would fear even more substantial degradations of their defense—decreases of a few percent in the effectiveness of one's defense could allow many hundreds of warheads to penetrate. The country that first acquired even a small capability to penetrate the adversary's defense might attain an important coercive advantage: nuclear attack could be threatened with impunity since effective retaliation would be impossible, given the adversary's inability to penetrate one's own defense.[17] Recognizing that the adversary is likely to acquire a similar capability—that is, that one's defense will not remain impenetrable—could create pressure to reap the benefits of the strategic advantage quickly. This time pressure would be especially strong if one's advantage could be used to prevent the adversary from acquiring the capability to penetrate one's defense.

By contrast, when both superpowers possess redundant assured destruction capabilities, which is the case today in MAD, the addition of tens, hundreds, or even thousands of warheads would not significantly change either country's capabilities. As a result, the probability of gaining a strategic advantage is extremely low, especially when each superpower is aware of and reacts to changes in the other's nuclear force.

In a world of impenetrable defenses, the dangers that result from this sensitivity to small offensive improvements would be increased by the strong incentives the superpowers would have to defeat each other's defense. Each country could be expected to make the acquisition of a strategic advantage a priority. Moreover, because there could be no guarantee that one's defenses would not be degraded, even a country that did not want to acquire an advantage would feel compelled to acquire additional strategic capabilities. Such a country would want to improve its defense to offset anticipated improvements in the adversary's offense.

In addition, there would probably be a strong instinct to improve one's offense as a hedge against being unable to offset the adversary's enhanced offense with improvements in one's defense. Unfortunately, one's adversary could not be certain that these strategic programs were intended only to preserve an equal capability. Consequently, even if both countries would prefer to remain in a world of perfect defense, an interactive competition that threatened to reduce the effectiveness of the defenses would probably ensue. (BAD would also be sensitive to relatively small changes in vulnerability when the defenses were near-perfect. This lack of "robustness" to changes is examined in greater detail below.)

The second problem with BAD is that superpower conventional wars would probably be more likely than in MAD. Today's nuclear forces greatly increase the potential costs of any direct U.S.–Soviet military confrontation. Thus nuclear weapons help deter conventional war by increasing its risks. Impenetrable defenses would eliminate this contribution. Virtually all analysts believe that the superpowers' current strategic arsenals help deter conventional war, though they may disagree about which features are most critical for that function.[18]

Perfect defenses might be in the United States' security interest despite the increased probability of conventional war. Still, there is an important tradeoff to consider. As World Wars I and II demonstrated, global conventional wars can be extremely destructive. The net effect of increasing the probability of major conventional war, while eliminating the possibility of more destructive, but extremely unlikely, nuclear war, might not be positive. The evaluation of this tradeoff would involve many factors, including the probability of nuclear and conventional wars with and without perfect defenses, the size and costs of these wars, and the availability of options for reducing the probability and costs of conventional war. Here I can only call attention to this tradeoff, not resolve it.

Imperfect Defense and the Probability of War

Understanding security in a world of perfect defense is relatively easy because with impenetrable defenses there is no possibility of a strategic nuclear war.[19] The problem is more complicated in a world in which near-perfect defenses have been deployed. Since the United States would be vulnerable to Soviet strategic nuclear attack, we need to evaluate the U.S. ability to reduce the probability of such an attack.

The following analysis considers cases in which both superpowers have near-perfect defenses; that is, each can deny the other an assured destruction capability. Implicit in this formulation is a relationship between one country's offense and the adversary's defense. When defenses are imperfect there will always be, at least in theory, an offense sufficiently large to provide an assured destruction capability. Therefore, for one country's imperfect defense to deny the adversary an assured destruction capability, either the size of the adversary's offense must be limited or the defense must be able to expand and improve to offset increases in the size of the offense. This analysis does not examine the feasibility of achieving these conditions. It assumes the establishment of a world in which neither the United States nor the Soviet Union has assured destruction capabilities.

The probability that the United States will avoid war with the Soviet Union depends on three features of the nuclear situation:

1. *The U.S. ability to deter premeditated Soviet nuclear attack.* Deterring this type of attack requires that the Soviet Union believe that the net effect of starting a nuclear war would be negative—that is, that it would be worse off after the war than before it. Surprise attacks, including the infamous "bolt from the blue," fall into this category. So do limited nuclear attacks employed as a means of coercive bargaining and certain counterforce attacks employed for damage limitation.[20]

2. *The crisis stability of the nuclear forces.* In a crisis, one or both superpowers might fear a nuclear attack by the other. If striking first is believed to be preferable to being struck first, and if a country believes that the probability that the adversary will strike first is sufficiently high, then launching a first strike would be preferable to taking a chance on being struck first. This type of first strike is commonly termed a *pre-emptive attack.* Unlike a premeditated attack, the country launching a pre-emptive attack would expect to be less well off after the war than before it. The crisis stability of the nuclear forces is a measure of how severe a crisis must be (or how high one's estimate that the adversary will strike first must be) before striking first becomes one's best option.[21]

3. *The robustness of U.S. forces.* The adequacy of U.S. forces depends not only on their ability to reduce the probability of pre-emptive and premeditated attacks, but also on how sensitive this ability is to potential changes in Soviet forces. The more easily the Soviet Union could build forces that would either make a premeditated attack attractive or significantly increase the incentives for pre-emptive attack, the greater the probability of a nuclear war. The robustness

of the U.S. nuclear force is a measure of the difficulty the Soviet Union would encounter in trying to reduce U.S. security.

These three measures are frequently used to assess the adequacy of U.S. nuclear forces. Past analyses have asked what capabilities are required to minimize the probability of war. Essentially all answers include the need for an assured destruction capability. Here we will explore how the elimination of assured destruction capabilities by mutual deployment of defenses would affect the probability of nuclear war.

Premeditated Attacks: Is Assured Destruction Necessary for Deterrence?

If Soviet defenses eliminated the U.S. assured destruction capability, the United States would lack what is now generally accepted to be the most basic requirement for deterring Soviet nuclear attacks. But closer examination of cases in which both superpowers deploy defenses shows that the United States could maintain the capability to deter premeditated Soviet attacks without possessing an assured destruction capability.

The United States now formulates its force requirements recognizing that it could be annihilated by the Soviet Union. Specifically, the standard argument holds that the United States can best deter Soviet annihilation by credibly threatening retaliatory annihilation.[22] But deterring this attack would become unnecessary if, by deploying defenses, the United States eliminated the Soviet Union's annihilation capability. Thus the United States could still have an adequate deterrent when the superpowers eliminated each other's annihilation capabilities by deploying defenses.

What capability would the United States need to deter attacks against its homeland when defenses had denied the Soviet Union an annihilation capability? Deterrence requires that, even after a Soviet attack, the United States be able to inflict costs greater than the benefits the Soviet Union would achieve by attacking. Thus, to determine the U.S. retaliatory requirement we must estimate the value the Soviet leaders would place on attacking the United States.

Analysts are rarely explicit about why they believe the Soviet Union would ever launch an all-out attack on U.S. cities. We can reasonably question whether the Soviet Union would ever do so. Still, since such an attack is not impossible, the United States should plan to deter it. This requires estimating the value the Soviet Union might place on attacking

U.S. cities. One possibility is that the Soviet Union would attack U.S. cities to weaken the nation, reducing U.S. ability to oppose Soviet pursuit of expansionist foreign policy objectives. This rationale may underlie analysts' current concern about countervalue attacks; presumably they fear that the Soviet Union might annihilate the United States to become the dominant world power.

To deter this type of attack, the United States would need forces capable of weakening the Soviet Union as much as the Soviet countervalue attack could weaken the United States. The United States could satisfy this requirement with a countervalue capability roughly equivalent to that of the Soviet Union. In fact, this is a very conservative requirement. U.S. retaliation would do far more than deny the Soviet Union an increase in relative world power; in addition, it would inflict direct costs by destroying targets the Soviets value.

Because the Soviet Union could attack first U.S. forces and then U.S. cities, the U.S. forces should provide a countervalue capability essentially equal to the Soviets' both before and after a Soviet counterforce attack. I will call this an *equal countervalue capability*. On the basis of similar considerations, Freeman Dyson has argued for this requirement, terming the concept "live-and-let-live."[23]

Alternatively, the Soviet Union might use its nuclear capability to coerce the United States. The potential benefits of such a course are more obvious than those of actually attacking U.S. cities. To avoid being coerced, the United States must be confident of its ability to deter Soviet attacks. A large disparity in U.S. and Soviet countervalue capabilities could undermine the United States' credibility, thereby reducing its confidence in its deterrent. Consequently the United States would have to maintain an equal countervalue capability in order to deny the Soviet Union the coercive use of its nuclear forces.[24]

The implications of the equal countervalue requirement are significantly different from those of the assured destruction requirement. The equal countervalue requirement explicitly couples U.S. and Soviet capabilities to inflict countervalue damage. According to the equal countervalue requirement, if the United States can reduce the Soviet Union's ability to inflict countervalue damage, then the United States can afford to have its retaliatory capability reduced by the Soviet Union. Moreover, improvements in Soviet defenses that reduce the damage the United States could inflict on the Soviet Union could be compensated for by improvements in U.S. defenses. Both the United States and the Soviet Union can satisfy the equal countervalue requirement at all levels of vulnerability to attack. In contrast, the assured destruction requirement demands that the United States have a retaliatory force capable of inflicting a specific level of countervalue damage independent of the Soviet ability to inflict damage. It demands that improvements in Soviet defenses be offset either by an increase in the size of the U.S. offense or by an increase in the ability of the offense to penetrate the Soviet defense.

Crisis Stability: What Would Be the Effect of Defenses?

There is a common belief that defenses capable of eliminating an adversary's assured destruction capability would decrease crisis stability: a country that can protect itself (that is, a country that can deny its adversary a second-strike annihilation capability) is more likely to strike pre-emptively in a crisis.[25] Under what conditions is this proposition correct?

Crisis stability depends on the decision maker's incentives to strike pre-emptively in a crisis. The decision to pre-empt would depend on a comparison of the costs of being struck first with those of being struck second.[26] If the adversary has an assured destruction capability, then there would be little, if any, incentive for a rational decision maker to pre-empt. A pre-emptive attack could not deny the adversary an annihilating retaliatory capability, so a decision maker who anticipates a countervalue attack would see little difference between the costs of being struck first and second.[27] In MAD, the vulnerability of the adversary's forces does not create significant pre-emptive incentives. The adversary's force is sufficiently large that the surviving fraction would still be able to inflict the damage required for annihilation.

If one's defense eliminates the adversary's assured destruction capability and if the adversary's retaliatory capability is partially vulnerable, then pre-emption might reduce the damage from an all-out countervalue attack. As a result, a decision maker who anticipates a countervalue first strike would have an incentive to pre-empt. Since without defenses there would be virtually no incentive to pre-empt (because the adversary could maintain its assured destruction capability), deploying defenses that eliminate assured destruction capabilities would decrease crisis stability.

However, we reach a different conclusion if the adversary's retaliatory capability is invulnerable to a first strike. In this case, the adversary's retaliatory strike would be as costly as if it had struck first—that is, the costs to one's own country of suffering an all-out countervalue first strike and second strike would be essentially equal. So, because the adversary's forces are invulnerable, there is no incentive to pre-empt.

Deploying defenses that can survive attack would reduce societal vulnerability but would not create pre-emptive incentives.[28]

We should not overestimate the practical significance of this observation. An invulnerable retaliatory capability requires not only that the forces be invulnerable, but also that attacks against the command and control system would not reduce the size of the possible retaliatory attack. These conditions might not be achievable. Moreover, space-based defense is likely to be highly vulnerable, which could increase pre-emptive incentives. Consequently, while in theory defenses that eliminate assured destruction capabilities need not decrease crisis stability, in practice they probably would.

The fundamental insight we can draw from this discussion is that survivable defenses do not by themselves create incentives for pre-emption. In this case, the source of pre-emptive incentives would be offensive force vulnerabilities. Therefore, the effect of defenses on crisis stability should not be evaluated without considering the vulnerabilities of the offensive force to a counterforce attack. By reducing the adversary's retaliatory capabilities, one's defenses can increase the significance of the adversary's offensive vulnerabilities.

To preserve crisis stability, the United States could pursue programs to reduce the vulnerability of its offenses. Area defenses, although not designed specifically for this mission, could increase force survivability, as could many other approaches, including the deployment of point defenses.[29] If effective area defense were feasible, then defenses could also make forces and command and control highly survivable. Deploying effective survivable defenses might then reduce crisis stability only slightly.

Robustness: The Primary Inadequacy of Defensive Situations

We do not live in a static world and cannot simply evaluate U.S. security as though both superpowers' forces could be held constant. Instead we must also examine the effect of changes in Soviet forces on U.S. security and the probability of these changes. More specifically, we must evaluate not only the U.S. ability to deter premeditated Soviet attack and to create crisis stability, but also the probability of changes in Soviet forces that would undermine these capabilities.

The robustness of U.S. forces is a measure of the difficulty the Soviet Union would encounter in trying to reduce U.S. security.[30] All else being equal, the more easily U.S. security could be jeopardized by changes in Soviet forces, the less desirable the situation. A world that would be highly desirable if the two countries' forces could be held fixed, but that lacks robustness, might not be preferable to one that is less desirable when the forces are imagined fixed, but that is more robust.

I have already discussed the lack of robustness of a world in which both superpowers have deployed perfect defenses. This section extends that analysis to mutual deployment of near-perfect defenses. The conclusion remains the same: BAD would be much less robust than MAD.

The following discussion compares the difficulty the Soviet Union would have undermining the U.S. ability to deter premeditated Soviet attacks in BAD and MAD. It assumes that the requirement for deterrence of premeditated attacks (that is, the equal countervalue requirement) is initially satisfied.

The robustness of U.S. nuclear forces to changes in Soviet forces depends on two related factors. First is the magnitude of the change in potential countervalue damage required for the Soviet Union to be less deterred from launching a premeditated attack. For example, how large an increase in Soviet countervalue capability is required to provide a significant advantage? The second is the technical difficulty the Soviet Union would have achieving this increase. For example, assuming the Soviet Union must increase its countervalue capability by fifty warheads, how difficult would this be to accomplish? The combination of these two factors determines the overall difficulty of acquiring a strategic advantage. Both factors tend to make BAD less robust than MAD.

My discussion of perfect defenses focused on the first factor, the magnitude of the change, and argued that even small countervalue changes could have strategic significance. Situations in which near-perfect defenses had been deployed would suffer from the same sensitivity, although less severely. Imagine three cases: (1) both superpowers have impenetrable defenses; (2) each can penetrate the other's defense with ten warheads; and (3) today's world, in which both superpowers have assured destruction capabilities. Now imagine an improvement in Soviet forces that enabled fifty additional warheads to penetrate. The addition to Soviet capabilities would be most significant in the case of impenetrable defenses. Fifty penetrating warheads would provide the Soviet Union with a large advantage in the ability to inflict damage. Its still impenetrable defense would enable the Soviet Union to attack the United States without fearing retaliation and to threaten attack with high credibility. If the superpowers started with ten penetrating warheads, the addition of fifty penetrating warheads to the Soviet capability would be less dangerous for the United States, although still worrisome. The change would significantly increase the Soviet countervalue capability, quite possibly providing an advantage in coercive capability. However, the U.S. ability to retaliate would reduce the coercive value of the Soviet advantage. In MAD, however, the addition of fifty warheads to the Soviet arsenal is insignificant—even thousands of new warheads would not significantly increase the Soviet ability to damage the United States.

In general, the less vulnerable the United States is to Soviet attack, the more sensitive its security is to improvements in Soviet capabilities.[31] This conclusion can be restated specifically in terms of defenses: the smaller the number of warheads that could penetrate U.S. defenses, the more sensitive its security would be to improvements in the Soviet ability to penetrate its defenses. As a result, BAD tends to be less robust than MAD.

The technical difficulty of gaining a strategic advantage depends on the size of the requisite change. Since a much larger change would be needed in MAD than in a world of near-perfect defenses, the Soviet Union would probably have a much harder time gaining an advantage today than it would in BAD.

Other considerations reinforce this conclusion. Low vulnerability requires defenses that are nearly perfect. By enlarging its offense and adding countermeasures, the Soviet Union can force the United States to deploy increasingly effective defenses simply to maintain a given level of vulnerability. Increasing the effectiveness of defenses tends to increase their cost at the margin, making it more difficult to offset changes in the adversary's offenses.[32] Thus even if near-perfect defenses are ever deployed, the prospects for maintaining low vulnerability seem small. In contrast, the U.S. assured destruction capability is relatively easy to maintain. It is not necessary that a large percentage of the U.S. offense survive Soviet attack and penetrate Soviet defenses. Instead, the offense needs only 100, or possibly a few hundred, surviving penetrating weapons. So the Soviet Union is likely to face a much greater technical challenge in trying to defeat the U.S. assured destruction capability than in trying to defeat near-perfect U.S. defenses.

Further, in MAD, diversifying one's offense increases the challenge facing the adversary's defense. For example, to deny the United States the ability to inflict high levels of damage, Soviet defenses must be highly effective against both ballistic missiles and strategic bombers. Just the opposite is true in BAD: the ability to penetrate with a single type of delivery system can eliminate low vulnerability. To preserve its low vulnerability in BAD, the United States would need to continue to defeat improvements in all types of Soviet delivery vehicles. This is obviously harder than continuing to defeat any single system. Thus, for what could be termed structural reasons, BAD could not be made as resistant to change as MAD.[33]

A lack of robustness would not be so dangerous if the United States and the Soviet Union lacked incentives to try to alter the nuclear balance. A political environment in which the superpowers did not try to gain a strategic advantage would reduce the need to make BAD resistant to change. But in fact the superpowers would feel tremendous pressure to try to defeat the adversary's defenses. Even if BAD were made highly robust, neither superpower could have high confidence in this robustness: a country could not be sure that its adversary could not develop offenses that would undermine its defenses. Neither superpower could overlook this uncertainty because its security would be sensitive to small changes and because the adversary's incentive to pursue a strategic advantage would be obvious. So, while proponents of strategic defenses promise a more stable and less frightening world, in fact BAD would be much more competitive than MAD, and the United States would be unable to satisfy its security requirements with high confidence.

The pressures generated by this strategic environment would make it quite difficult for the superpowers to reach arms control agreements that might increase the robustness of BAD.[34] When security is sensitive to small variations in forces, cooperation will seem especially risky. And given our limited success in negotiating strategic arms control treaties when both countries have redundant assured destruction capabilities, we have little reason to be optimistic.

Having raised the possibility of arms control, I should distinguish between two cases in which strategic defenses help reduce the superpowers' vulnerability to attack. The first is that of defense dominance. Cooperation is not necessary to reduce the superpowers' vulnerability since each country's defense can win the race against the other's offense. This relationship between offense and defense is most important in a world in which the superpowers engage in military competition. If they were not competing, then the ability of the defense to dominate the offense would not be tested and might not be important. In the second case, defense dominance does not prevail, but defenses might help the superpowers to reduce their vulnerability if combined with limits on their offenses. Here the key to reduced vulnerability is cooperation, not defense; this case shares more with disarmament than with defense dominance.

This distinction is important since, contrary to proponents' claims, deploying defenses in the foreseeable future is unlikely to encourage extensive cooperation. The more likely result is that defenses will make it far more difficult to reduce offenses. Each country's defenses reduce the ability of the adversary's offenses to perform their missions—thus increasing the marginal value of additional warheads.[35] On the other hand, once the superpowers are already committed to reducing their vulnerability through cooperation, defenses might help reduce the risks of cooperating.[36] But these necessary conditions for ambitious arms control agreements do not exist in today's world.

Overall, then, the probability of nuclear war would be greater in BAD than in MAD. In static conditions, the United States might be able to deter premeditated attacks and to maintain crisis stability as well in BAD as in MAD. However, the world would not be static, and the superpowers would compete for strategic advantage. Because BAD would be far less robust than MAD, this competitive armament would be more likely to create the conditions and opportunities for a nuclear war.

Could Defense Create a Preferable Nuclear World?

A comparison of alternative worlds requires a measure that combines the two U.S. security objectives: to minimize the probability of war and to minimize the costs if war occurs. Examining either dimension alone is insufficient to understand the net effect of a shift from MAD to BAD. For example, a policy that would reduce the damage of a nuclear attack, but would also increase the probability of the attack, might not improve U.S. security. The correct measure of security is the expected cost of a war, defined as its probability multiplied by its costs.

It is crucial to keep these two aspects of U.S. security in mind when analyzing defenses. Much of the debate over BMD tends to ignore the need for simultaneous evaluation. Proponents emphasize that defenses might reduce damage. Opponents argue that deploying BMD would increase the probability of nuclear war by undermining deterrence and decreasing crisis stability. Neither of these arguments is sufficient for drawing a conclusion about area defenses: each looks at only one aspect of U.S. security. Previous sections examined the probability. Here we compare the costs of war in BAD and MAD and consider the tradeoffs required to conclude which world is preferable.

If U.S. security depended only on the probability of nuclear war, then, since the probability of war would be higher in BAD, mutual deployment of highly effective defenses would decrease U.S. security. However, because defenses would decrease the damage of certain wars, they would have some positive effects as well as negative ones. In general, their net effect is therefore indeterminate.

To see this point in greater detail, consider the possible paths to nuclear war. First, assume that the superpowers' forces are held constant, that the superpowers have deployed near-perfect defenses, and that the equal countervalue requirement is satisfied. The Soviet Union might launch a premeditated attack even when the requirements for deterrence are satisfied; this is true today, when both superpowers have assured destruction capabilities, and it would be true in BAD. The damage in an all-out countervalue war would be lower in BAD. Since the probability of premeditated nuclear war might not be greater in this world of near-perfect defenses, the expected costs along this path to nuclear war could be lower than in MAD.

The damage from a pre-emptive war could be lower in BAD than in MAD.[37] The probability of pre-emptive war, and therefore the expected costs of a pre-emptive attack, would depend on relative crisis stability. If BAD were less stable in crises than MAD, then the probability of pre-emptive attack would be higher. In this case, BAD would have a higher probablity of pre-emptive attack and lower costs if the pre-emptive attack occurred. Therefore, it is unclear whether the expected costs from pre-emptive war would be greater in BAD or MAD. If, on the other hand, BAD were as stable in a crisis as MAD (which is possible if the retaliatory capabilities and defenses are invulnerable), then the expected cost along the pre-emptive path would probably be lower than in MAD.

Now suppose the superpowers' forces are not held constant. Both the United States and the Soviet Union might deploy forces that increase their adversary's vulnerability or decrease their own. Here the damage in BAD might not be lower than in MAD. Superpower competition might restore one or both countries' assured destruction capabilities. The potential damage would not be determined by the status quo forces. If a country could build its way out of BAD (i.e., regain its assured destruction capability), then its adversary might suffer costs as high as in MAD. The expected costs of nuclear wars resulting from changes in the status quo could be greater in BAD than in MAD. Although the adversaries begin in a world of near-perfect defenses, the damage of war is not constrained by the status quo forces and might not be lower than in MAD; moreover, because of the lack of robustness in BAD, the probability of nuclear war along this path is higher.

In addition to the paths examined above, defenses might also reduce the costs of an accidental Soviet attack or an attack launched by another state with nuclear weapons. Assuming that defenses do not somehow increase the probability of these attacks, they would reduce the expected costs along these paths.

All in all, although defenses could reduce the damage done by certain types of wars, this positive effect would tend to be offset by the increased probability of wars resulting from BAD's lack of robustness and possibly from its lower crisis stability. Consequently, the net result of both superpowers' deploying near-perfect defenses might be to decrease U.S. security.

This conclusion runs counter to the commonly held belief that BAD, and so-called defense dominance, would be clearly preferable to MAD. Even after making the best case for mutual highly effective defenses (that is, ignoring technical and economic feasibility, the effect on the probability of superpower conventional wars, and a number of other issues discussed briefly at the end of this chapter), MAD might be preferable to a world in which the superpowers' defenses drastically reduced their vulnerability to nuclear attack.[38]

The policy implications of this conclusion are obvious, and profound. Whether the United States could be more secure in a world of highly effective defenses should no longer be viewed primarily as a technological issue. The United States should examine more completely the strategic and political issues associated with defense against nuclear attack before making a decision to pursue such a fundamental change in nuclear strategy.

Additional Problems with Strategic Defense

Several additional factors further weaken the case for pursuing highly effective defense.

Uncertainty

The effectiveness of U.S. defenses would be uncertain, and small uncertainties would be highly significant. In addition to the uncertainties inherent in the operations of complex systems, the effectiveness of defenses would be uncertain because of the severe limits on possible testing. The defense could not be tested against a full-scale attack or against Soviet offenses. And while effectiveness against deployed Soviet offenses could be estimated, there would always be reasonable questions about Soviet penetration aids that could be quickly added to their offensive force.

Small uncertainties would be significant because, given the large offensive forces that are currently deployed, a small difference in the percentage of penetrating weapons would translate into a large difference in destructive potential. The uncertainties involved with a perfect defense would probably be large enough to leave the United States unsure whether it was vulnerable to an annihilating attack by the Soviet Union. While the strategic implications of this uncertainty are ambiguous—in some cases it might enhance deterrence—uncertainty about necessary capabilities would frighten political leaders and exacerbate superpower tensions.

Uncertainty would affect U.S. policy in a number of ways. First, the nation would never feel adequately defended. (Nor would the Soviet Union.) Even without uncertainties, some would always argue that the United States needed additional defense to protect itself against Soviet attacks and as a hedge against Soviet offensive breakthroughs. These arguments would be more telling than those made about the inadequacy of today's offenses since defensive capability would become redundant only after the defenses were perfect. The existence of uncertainties would probably lead to unrelenting requests for additional defenses, yet fulfilling these requests would yield little satisfaction and add little to the public's sense of security. Because uncertainties would persist, even fantastic advances in strategic defense would not reduce domestic fear of nuclear war.

Second, uncertainty would fuel fears that the Soviet Union had a superior defensive capability. Prudent military analysis could require that uncertainties be assessed in favor of Soviet defense and against U.S. defense. As a result, even if the United States and Soviet Union had comparable defensive capabilities, the United States could not be confident that it was maintaining capabilities adequate to deter the Soviet Union. This conclusion would contribute to the demands for improving U.S. defenses. This uncertainty might not increase the probability of war. If both countries employed these conservative assumptions, uncertainty might reduce the danger of low robustness. On the other hand, if political leaders believed that the uncertainties created strategic inferiority, they might feel pressure to run greater risks to protect their basic interests. This could increase the probability of war.

Allies

Any comprehensive analysis of BAD must consider the reaction of U.S. allies and the implications for their security.[39] If strategic defense were believed to increase the probability of conventional war, then we should expect tremendous resistance from our European allies. Many expect a conventional war in Europe to be so costly that it is almost as unacceptable as a nuclear war. A second concern focuses on the vulnerability of allies to nuclear attack. U.S. allies are unlikely to support a policy that drastically reduces U.S. vulnerability while leaving them highly vulnerable. A third concern would be the effect of defenses on the independent deterrent capabilities of the French and the British. A highly effective but imperfect Soviet defense would leave the United States with a modest retaliatory capability, but would probably eliminate the value of these independent European deterrents.

Suitcase Bombs and Future Nonnuclear Technologies

The ability to defend effectively against ballistic missiles, cruise missiles, and bombers could greatly increase the importance of clandestinely delivered nuclear weapons. Nuclear bombs could be placed on Soviet ships and commercial airplanes or could be carried into the United States by Soviet agents. These alternative types of delivery are possible today, but are far less important because the Soviet Union has such a large arsenal.

These alternative forms of delivery would not necessarily render defense useless. The Soviet ability to deliver weapons clandestinely in a crisis might be severely limited; hiding weapons before a crisis would be risky unless early detection was known to be impossible; and the damage from clandestine attacks might be less extensive than is currently possible without defenses. Still, the observation that defense against the delivery systems that are most important today would not eliminate vulnerability to nuclear attack raises basic issues about strategic defense. What threats must the United States be able to defend against? How would a "partial defense" (that is, a defense against standard delivery systems) affect the political and military uses of nuclear weapons?

In addition, we need to consider future nonnuclear means of mass destruction. These might be biological or chemical weapons far more destructive than the existing varieties. Moreover, entirely new types of destructive capabilities might be invented. Would future strategic defenses that work against nuclear capabilities also be highly effective against these still unknown threats? If not, then the United States might be just as vulnerable as it is today.

Multipolarity

In the future many nations may have large nuclear arsenals capable of surviving attack. Would the United States be more secure in a multipolar world of countries with perfect or near-perfect defenses or in a multipolar world of countries with redundant assured destruction capabilities?

To begin, we need to reconsider our definitions of perfect and near-perfect defenses. A defense that is perfect against one country's offense might provide essentially no protection when attacked by two or more large nuclear powers. Nevertheless, I will continue to term this a perfect defense. Similarly, an imperfect defense that is capable of eliminating one adversary's assured destruction capability will be considered near-perfect.

Highly effective defenses run into problems in a multipolar world that would not exist in a bipolar world. First, the requirements for deterring a premeditated attack cannot be satisfied by all countries. In BAD, both countries can have equal countervalue capabilities, and a position of purity is sufficient to allow the United States to maintain the capabilities required for deterrence. In a multipolar world this would no longer be possible. If each country has an equal countervalue capability against each of its adversaries, then it lacks such a capability against an alliance of adversaries.[40] This problem could be avoided in a multipolar world of countries with assured destruction capabilities. Each country could maintain the capability to annihilate all its adversaries.

The possibility of each superpower maintaining forces sufficient to deter all of its adversaries, even against the most threatening alliance, makes strategic nuclear multipolarity quite different from prenuclear multipolarity. Kenneth Waltz argues that the danger in multipolar worlds stems from uncertainty:

With three or more powers flexibility of alliances keeps relations of friendship and enmity fluid and makes everyone's estimate of the present and future relation of forces uncertain.... Russia and America depend militarily mainly on themselves. They balance each other by "internal" instead of "external" means, relying on their own capabilities rather than on the capabilities of allies. Internal balancing is more reliable and precise than external balancing. States are less likely to misjudge the strength and reliability of opposing coalitions. Rather than making states properly cautious and forwarding the chances of peace, uncertainty and miscalculation cause wars.[41]

The dangers of multipolarity might not arise in a world of many states with highly redundant assured destruction capabilities. However, these dangers would exist in a multipolar world of near-perfect defenses.

This last point leads us directly to the second danger of a multipolar world with near-perfect defenses: the robustness of U.S. forces would be even more tenuous than in a bipolar world. More countries would be able to defeat U.S. defenses, making low vulnerability more difficult to maintain then in a bipolar world. Further, U.S. security would depend heavily on alliances. If it could not maintain its share of allies, the United States would fall into strategic inferiority. Unless alliances were quite inflexible, which is unlikely in a world of true multipolarity, the United States would have little confidence in the future adequacy of its forces.

Once again, a multipolar world of assured destruction capabilities would not encounter these problems – U.S. forces could be quite robust. A highly redundant force could be made relatively insensitive to changes in adversaries' forces and the United States would not need to depend on superpower allies.

Any final conclusions about these multipolar worlds must consider that war occurring in the defensive world might be less costly than war in the assured destruction world. Still, the difficulties of maintaining adequate capabilities, and the intense competition that is sure to result, count against the multipolar world of highly effective defenses.

Conclusion

Strategic defense and the prospect of being invulnerable to nuclear attack have undeniable appeal. But even perfect strategic defense cannot return us to a prenuclear world. BAD has not been studied as carefully or extensively as MAD. There are, however, reasons to believe that BAD would be more complex and more difficult to manage than MAD.

The best of worlds in which both superpowers have perfect or near-perfect defenses would not be as good as today's world of redundant assured destruction capabilities. In all but the case of perfect defense, the United States would still depend on deterrence for its security; the lack of robustness in BAD would make it sensitive to small changes in forces and would create strong incentives to pursue threatening improvements in offenses; the acquisition of these forces would increase the probability of nuclear war; the probability of large conventional wars between the superpowers and their allies might well increase; and the threat posed by clandestinely delivered nuclear weapons would be much more significant than today.

Any serious policy for deploying defenses must address the dangers that would result from the difficulty of maintaining low vulnerability. Even if defenses greatly reduced U.S. vulnerability, this capability could not be made highly robust. The lack of robustness would be particularly dangerous because BAD would be a highly competitive world in which superpower cooperation was extremely difficult. President Reagan and other proponents of BMD have suggested that effective defenses would eliminate the need for offenses.[42] This outcome is extremely unlikely. Deploying defenses would probably lead to an intense offensive and defensive nuclear weapons competition and to tense, strained superpower relations. Arms control agreements to limit or reduce offensive nuclear forces would be difficult, if not impossible, to negotiate. Thus the prospects for improving security by shifting to a world of effective defenses seem especially gloomy.

No evidence indicates that the U.S. interest in highly effective defense is based on a complete analysis of a world of near-perfect defense. Unfortunately, a world in which both superpowers deployed effective defense would be far less attractive than its proponents suggest. Even on the most optimistic asumptions, BAD would probably be less secure than MAD; with more realistic assumptions, we find that deploying BMD would reduce U.S. security. Until a convincing argument is presented for this fundamental change in nuclear weapons policy, the United States should give priority to living safely in a world of mutual societal vulnerability, pursuing with renewed determination a prudent policy of offensive weapons acquisition and strategic arms control.

CHAPTER 4

Lengthening the Fuse:
No First Use and Disengagement

Daniel J. Arbess and Andrew M. Moravcsik

U.S. foreign policy turns ultimately on the deterrent power of the American nuclear umbrella—the rock on which the renaissance of the West since 1945 was built and the foundation for its security.
—*Eugene V. Rostow*

The U.S. declaratory doctrine of deliberate escalation is a Grand Illusion or a Great Lie, a pretension that we would allow America to be destroyed in an attempt to save Europe.
—*Richard K. Betts*

Few Americans realize that under specific circumstances it is official American policy to initiate nuclear war.[1] Since the creation of the NATO alliance in 1949, the defense of Europe has been backed by an explicit American threat to use nuclear weapons first. If Western conventional defenses in Europe threaten to crumble, the strategy of "flexible response," officially adopted by NATO in 1967, reserves the option to respond with nuclear weapons. A similar policy underlies the defense of East Asia and the Middle East. On several dozen occasions, the United States government has secretly contemplated or openly threatened the use of nuclear weapons in support of diplomatic goals.[2]

Most American strategists favor this policy, but few do so because they believe that the use of these weapons would bolster the battlefield position of Western defenders.[3] Instead, they believe that the prospect of sudden catastrophic losses, perhaps even the total annihilation of its homeland, will deter a superpower from even contemplating conventional aggression. Nuclear weapons, they contend, not only alter the calculus of costs and benefits facing an aggressor; they render such a calculation irrelevant. Because the sheer horror of their use changes the way nations think about war, nuclear weapons are, as one strategist describes them, "the ultimate deterrent."[4]

But the policy of first use contains an internal contradiction. As long as it succeeds in keeping the peace, first use appears perfectly rational. But once a conventional war breaks out, a defense based on nuclear retaliation is a potentially catastrophic liability. When facing an opponent with a secure nuclear retaliatory capability, first use would likely be suicidal. American strategists no longer contemplate immediate nuclear attacks on the Soviet homeland, as they did in the 1950s; instead, they speak of flexible response and nuclear options. But General Bernard Rogers, formerly supreme allied commander in Europe, has estimated that if the Soviets attack, NATO will have only a few days to deliberate before turning to nuclear weapons.[5] In short, if deterrence breaks down, the policy of first use will be exposed either as a bluff or as a doomsday machine.

In recent years, the consensus in favor of a deterrent based on first use has been attacked by a growing number of statesmen and strategists. They question even the modest reliance on nuclear weapons required by flexible response and call on the United States to take steps to make them more difficult to use early in a conflict. Although such proposals have been advanced since the 1950s, they have multiplied since the publication in 1982 of a celebrated article in *Foreign Affairs* by McGeorge Bundy, George Kennan, Robert McNamara, and Gerard Smith. These four distinguished statesmen argue that "the one definable firebreak against the worldwide disaster of general nuclear war is the one which stands between other kinds of conflict and any use whatsoever of nuclear weapons. To keep that firebreak wide and strong is in the deepest interest of mankind."[6] In their view, defense against aggression should rely more heavily on conventional forces or on the "existential" uncertainty created by the mere presence of nuclear weapons, rather than strategies for actually using nuclear weapons first.

In effect, measures for making nuclear weapons less readily usable "lengthen the nuclear fuse." There is a range of proposals for lengthening the fuse. At one end of the spectrum are slight modifications in existing procedures and deployments that increase control over nuclear weapons and strengthen conventional forces; in the middle are proposals that remove nuclear weapons from the front, place bureaucratic obstacles in the way of their use, and plan for conventional war; and at the far end of the spectrum, the United States would sever some of the defense commitments that might put the American homeland at risk, with corresponding reductions in both conventional and military forces. All of these measures can be overridden in wartime. Thus, none reduces the risk of first use by either side to zero. But by placing obstacles in the way of first use, each proposal attempts to precommit Western nations, led by the United States, to a more prudent nuclear policy.

While some of these proposals may appear dramatic, their implementation would largely be a matter of aligning military doctrine and deployments with a long-term trend among political leaders against seriously considering the first use of nuclear weapons.[7] Former secretaries of defense and state have testified that they recommended as a principle against any plan for nuclear first use.[8] The Soviet Union has already adopted a declaratory policy of no first use. While the requirements of flexible response prevent the United States from making a similar pronouncement, it is clear that some members of the U.S. government have already informally adopted a de facto policy of no first use. There appears to be emerging, between the superpowers, a norm against first use.[9] In recent years, overt incidents of nuclear diplomacy, as well as high-level consideration of the deliberate use of these weapons, have declined markedly.[10]

In the first two sections of this chapter, we present the criticisms of first use and the various proposals to lengthen the fuse. In the third section, we examine various scenarios by which war could break out. In the final two sections, we attempt to specify the conditions under which the various proposals to lengthen the fuse would reduce the likelihood of nuclear war.

Criticism of First Use

Objections to first use fall into three categories. In the eyes of its critics, a defense based on first use is indiscriminate, uncontrollable, and destabilizing. The first criticism is that nuclear weapons cannot be used discriminatingly; the collateral damage is certain to outweigh any reasonable aim. Critics argue that since nuclear first use is such a destructive and irrational step, conventional forces provide a more credible deterrent. This is particularly true in the Third World, where the stakes are relatively low. Most strategists reject the notion that first use favors an undermanned or outgunned defender.[11] Indeed, if nuclear weapons are disconnected from the overall military infrastructure, U.S. conventional forces abroad could probably be used more effectively and with less risk.[12] Former Secretary of State Robert McNamara succinctly sums up the first criticism: "Nuclear weapons serve no military purpose whatsoever. They are totally useless—except only to deter one's opponent from using them."[13]

At the same time—and this is the critics' second objection—nuclear weapons render warfare uncontrollable. Nuclear first use is a dangerous bluff. If deterrence fails and a conventional war breaks out, extensive plans for first use may become a self-fulfilling prophecy. In part, the danger stems from the tendency of decision makers to resort to standard operating procedures in a crisis; even if they perceive the situation correctly and maintain control over operations, they may feel that they have no choice but to cross the nuclear firebreak. An even greater danger, according to many critics of flexible response, is that control over the situation will be lost. The integration of thousands of nuclear weapons into conventional defense strategies increases the likelihood of nuclear war breaking out inadvertently through accidents, unauthorized use, miscalculations, and pre-emption.[14]

Advocates of a longer fuse believe the danger of uncontrolled escalation is real. There is an inherent tension, for example, between NATO's political and operational requirements. Nuclear weapons are stored in a limited number of depots throughout Europe and are thus vulnerable to a Soviet pre-emptive strike. To reduce the risk of such a strike, NATO leaders may feel compelled to authorize dispersal of battlefield nuclear weapons while deliberations about their use continue. Yet once nuclear weapons are dispersed, political control would become more difficult to ensure. Unless command and control remains utterly reliable, authority might be delegated to field commanders, increasing the likelihood of unauthorized or accidental use and giving the Soviets incentive to interdict those operations.

"The Western alliance is thus posed with a dilemma," according to a group of ten prominent statesmen and strategists, writing jointly in the *Atlantic Monthly*.

If NATO, during a political crisis in Europe, felt that a conflict in Europe was imminent, it might move to scatter its vulnerable nuclear assets in order to protect them. Soviet leaders, on the other hand, might very well interpret such an action as preparation for a NATO nuclear attack. NATO's alternative would be to allow these weapons to remain concentrated and vulnerable to a preemptive Warsaw Pact strike—nuclear or conventional. In either case Soviet leaders would be under pressure to deploy the weapons quickly—and NATO field commanders would be under pressure to use them quickly.[15]

Uncontrolled first use could also be an unintentional by-product of the current tight integration of nuclear and conventional forces. Nuclear alerts, naval movements, and other deployments of integrated forces might trigger a dangerous process of "action and reaction, [creating] an operational momentum towards first use."[16] Conventional operations might, for example, provoke first use by threatening strategic nuclear systems on land or at sea.[17]

Even if Western soldiers and statesmen initiate nuclear war in a deliberate and controlled manner, critics contend that they will inevitably lose control. Once the superpowers cross the firebreak, escalation to an all-out strategic nuclear exchange may well be inevitable. For a nuclear war to remain limited, the two sides would have to agree on specific limits on weapons and targets. As one group of critics observes: "This unprecedented feat of diplomacy would have to be achieved in a state of crisis and uncertainty unknown to history, with each side holding in reserve a nuclear arsenal that could carry the conflict to virtually any level of destruction. . . . It would be reckless to assume that escalation far beyond the battlefield could be averted. . . ."[18]

A third objection links the short fuse to destabilizing military doctrines and economic policies. In order for the strategy of extended nuclear deterrence to be credible, critics assert, the United States must adopt a counterforce posture at the strategic level. In other words, American strategic missiles must be deployed in such a way as to threaten Soviet missiles in their silos. According to critics, this posture undermines both crisis stability and arms control. Earl Ravenal argues that such a posture demands that the United States maintain a first-strike capability: "A damage-limiting attack against hard targets is a demanding requirement, in numbers and characteristics of weapons. And, to have its intended effect, it must be preemptive."[19] The consequences, according to Ravenal, are grave: "It is its adherence to alliance commitments that skews the United States strategy toward counterforce targeting and warps American doctrines of response toward first use of nuclear weapons, prejudicing crisis stability and increasing the chance of escalation to nuclear war."[20] The trend toward counterforce, some argue, has pushed American policy away from the objectives of arms control, and particularly away from the norms against counterforce and damage limitation established by the Anti-Ballistic Missile and Strategic Arms Limitation Treaty of 1972.

Some supporters of disengagement argue that the United States is economically as well as militarily overextended. The high cost of American military spending in support of current alliance arrangements, Sherle Schwenninger and Jerry Sanders contend, locks the United States into a worsening economic position vis-à-vis its main competitors.[21] According to David Calleo, the United States has resorted to a series of destabilizing international economic policies—trade deficits, sudden devaluations, inflation, and now the accumulation of debt—in order to finance an overextended foreign policy. In the long run, Calleo predicts, superpower war will be less likely and the international system more stable if we deliberately withdraw from commitments now, rather than abandoning them later amidst international economic turmoil brought about by the United States' inability to continue in its role as a hegemonic power.[22] Melvyn Krauss predicts that U.S. withdrawal from Europe would reduce the incentive of Europeans to free ride. Once this incentive is removed, increased European defense spending would compensate for American reductions, thereby creating a stronger and more balanced Western defense.[23]

Lengthening the Fuse: No Early Use, No First Use, Disengagement

To evaluate specific proposals, it is necessary to distinguish between lengthening the fuse as a *principle* and as a *policy*.[24] Declarations alone do not reduce the probability of first use unless they redirect strategic planners "to prepare realistically for conventional defense without contemplating early use of nuclear weapons."[25] In their 1982 article, Bundy and his colleagues recommended that the United States issue a declaration of no first use and consider methods of strengthening conventional defense in Europe, but they declined to recommend specific changes in military deployments, tactics, or decision-making procedures. Nor did they draw any implications for areas outside Europe.[26] Since then, many more detailed proposals have been advanced. Broadly speaking, these schemes fall into the three categories introduced above: no early use, no first use, and disengagement.

No Early Use

Advocates of no early use support measures to raise the threshold at which nuclear weapons are used and to maintain command and control on the battlefield. Among these measures are stronger conventional forces or a conventional arms control agreement, decreased vulnerability of existing nuclear weapons, deployment of weapons farther from the front, and tighter and more centralized control over the authorization of first use.

In varied forms, no early use has gained wide support even among those who continue to accept flexible response as the basis of Western defense.[27] Four distinguished German critics of the Bundy group's manifesto advocate both a build-up of nonnuclear forces and an arms control treaty establishing conventional parity in Europe.[28] General Rogers has called for a conventional build-up requiring annual increases of 4 percent (in real terms) in NATO defense budgets, including the enhancement of capabilities for using conventionally armed missiles to disrupt and interdict forces far behind Warsaw Pact lines.[29] Samuel Huntington has proposed the creation of a "conventional retaliation" option in Europe, in which allied forces would launch a retaliatory counteroffensive into East Germany and Czechoslovakia, cutting Warsaw Pact supply lines, undermining the support of Soviet satellites, and improving NATO's position in negotiations to terminate the war.[30]

All of these proposals implicitly concede that Western defense relies too heavily on nuclear first use. Yet each is conservative in spirit, for each is entirely consistent with the general outlines of flexible response.[31] None rests on reassessment of the Soviet threat, renegotiation of political agreements between allies, or rearrangement of bureaucracies within national governments. Above all, none requires a definitive renunciation of nuclear first use.

No First Use

A second, far more ambitious form of lengthening the fuse is a policy of no first use. The *Atlantic Monthly* group advocates "military plans, training programs, defense budgets and arms negotiations" based on the assumption that the United States "will not initiate the use of nuclear weapons."[32] As first steps in this direction, they propose an immediate policy of no early use in Europe, cessation of weapons modernization programs predicated on first use, elimination of dual-capable systems, the creation of separate command and control procedures for nuclear weapons, a policy of no early second use, eventual no first use outside Europe, firm rejection of strategic first use and counterforce targeting, and abandoning the Strategic Defense Initiative.[33] Johan Holst has enumerated a number of additional measures that may be necessary to transform no first use from principle into policy: withdrawal of nuclear artillery and air defense munitions from Europe, and controls on the introduction of high-technology conventional weapons that could raise the velocity of warfare beyond the current capacity to control it.[34]

In a recent book, Morton Halperin elaborates a policy of no first use based on the premise that nuclear weapons cannot be used rationally in a military conflict.[35] Accordingly, control over all nuclear weapons should be placed in the hands of an "entirely separate structure...totally divorced from the command structure for conducting conventional combat operations." A small force of invulnerable nuclear weapons, numbering several hundred at most, should replace present NATO nuclear forces. These weapons should be used exclusively for "demonstration" shots, never for tactical purposes. In the Third World, including the Korean peninsula and the Persian Gulf, Halperin recommends a policy of unconditional no first use and the eventual withdrawal of all American nuclear forces, whether naval or based on land.

Halperin argues that strategic nuclear weapons should be configured to prevent early first or second use, thereby reducing the chance of accidental or ill-considered firings. First-strike weapons should be eliminated from the arsenal, perhaps by deploying a large percentage of the force in the form of slower, less powerful cruise missiles. The ability of weapons and the centers that command and control them to survive attack should be strengthened, while we move toward an eventual bilateral limitation on the number of warheads. The redeployments should be implemented by a presidential directive "indicating that strategic nuclear forces will not under any circumstances fire first."

Disengagement

Some believe that no early use and no first use do not go far enough. According to Earl Ravenal, "Americans are faced with an increasingly demarcated choice: the salvation of Europe, or their own solvency and safety."[36] Ravenel argues that the United States should disengage from the defense of Europe and other allies as part of a broad alternative conception of foreign policy. "Globally," he writes, "we would draw back to a line that has two mutually reenforcing characteristics: credibility and feasibility; a line we *must* hold, as part of the definition of our sovereignty, and that we *can* hold, as a defense perimeter and a strategic force concept that can be maintained with advantage and within constraints over the long haul."[37] Advocates of disengagement disagree over which security interests are truly vital, but most foresee a partial or total withdrawal from Europe, with the forces either deployed elsewhere or demobilized.

Assessing Proposals for Reform

The debate over lengthening the fuse is fundamentally a debate over where to strike the balance between assuring that Soviet aggression is adequately deterred and avoiding crisis instability or loss of control. Advocates of a longer fuse contend that by making nuclear weapons more difficult to use, or by giving civilian leaders more, direct control over the decision, we can reduce the probability of inadvertent, accidental, pre-emptive, or ill-considered first use without significantly increasing the chances of a deliberate Soviet attack. By diminishing U.S. reliance on nuclear weapons, lengthening the fuse may also reduce demands for the damage-limitation capability associated with first use and counter-force weapons, thereby opening up new opportunities for arms control.

Those who praise the nuclear option as "the rock on which the renaissance of the West" is built question the claim that a longer fuse will promote stability and controllability of crises.[38] Drawing an analogy to the failure of the Munich Agreement to deter Hitler, they fear that nuclear war will arise as a result of a failure to deter the Soviets. A longer fuse, they believe, increases the chance of conventional war. Since a major conventional war is the most likely road to nuclear holocaust, they argue, widening the firebreak increases the chance of nuclear war. As Josef Joffe writes: "With nuclear weapons withdrawn, and the risk of immediate escalation set aside, a conventional lunge, stopping well short of the new nuclear perimeter in the West, will look visibly less irrational than under current circumstances . . . if nuclear weapons are the queens of deterrence, their removal from the board will liberate the conventional pawns from the restraints of the game."[39] Some supporters of first use go so far as to concede the desirability *in theory* of greater reliance on conventional forces, but note that Western nations are unwilling to commit the resources necessary to achieve decisive conventional superiority over the Soviet Union, while Third World allies lack the means to do so. Thus, the threat of first use remains the most cost-effective and politically expedient form of defense.

Paths to War

How are we to choose between these positions? Ideally, strategists would calculate the probability of nuclear war under the various possible scenarios. But it is impossible to assign reliable quantitative values to the variables needed to assess the probability and costs of war given a certain strategic doctrine or force posture.[40] We simply do not know enough about the resiliency of conventional defenses, the probability of escalation, and the future intentions and perceptions of the potential antagonists. More importantly, such a calculation must take into account the political context in which first use is considered. Accordingly, in this chapter our assessment of proposals for lengthening the fuse is largely *qualitative,* relying primarily not on calculations of military might, but on a comparison between three political scenarios by which nuclear war might break out. In order to determine how war is most likely to break out, we examine three scenarios: a Soviet bolt from the blue in Europe, spill-over from Eastern European uprisings, or a catalytic conflict in the Third World.[41]

A Bolt from the Blue.   Although the foundation scenario for NATO strategy is a Soviet lunge in Central Europe, this is a relatively unlikely path to war. Yalta and Helsinki have, to a certain extent, legitimized the Soviet role in Eastern Europe, and the USSR has difficulty sustaining even its current commitments. On balance, the Soviet Union profits economically, politically, and militarily from the status quo in Europe. Compared to a sudden attack, the Soviet Union could gain a great deal in the way of trade and technology transfers at less cost by opting for continued détente in Europe. And even if Soviet leaders harbor overtly aggressive intentions, traditional geopolitical logic dictates that they eschew the heavily armed Central European front and expand someplace where the risks and costs of conventional advance are lower. Accordingly, Jonathan Dean concludes that "the main contingency for which the NATO alliance was established – to deter or repel deliberate Soviet attack aimed at the conquest of Western Europe – has become increasingly remote, so remote that it has become negligible."[42]

Eastern European Uprisings.   A second scenario, more likely than the first to provoke nuclear war, begins with anti-Soviet uprisings in Eastern Europe, which might provoke the Soviet Union to take desperate measures to avoid losing control over its satellites. But since the conventional superiority of the Warsaw Pact in Europe depends largely on Eastern European troops, the Soviet Union would be unlikely to initiate hostilities unless it faced direct Western provocation in the form of covert intervention or political interference. On the other hand, if the USSR found a real or perceived justification for such fears, and if the crisis were long and violent, even a clear noninterventionist stance, as was taken in Czechoslovakia in 1968, might be inadequate to assure the Kremlin.[43]

Third World Conflicts.   The most likely path to nuclear war between the superpowers has its roots in the Third World, where political conditions are unstable, where both sides' interests are ambiguously defined, and where the resulting risks of misunderstanding or misjudgment are most acute. Most crises involving the threat of first use have taken place in the Third World. Nuclear war might break out in situations where the West is hopelessly outnumbered, as in some views of Soviet intervention in Iran; through escalation involving forward-based weapons at sea; or through accidental, unauthorized, or pre-emptive use when both sides' integrated forces are alerted.[44] Conventional conflict in the Third World may also spill over into the European theater. If the Soviets assume that the probability of war is high, pre-emptive strikes against Western nuclear assets in Europe may become a strategic priority. Michael MccGwire concludes that the nuclear threshold is less likely to be crossed as the result of an outright Soviet urge to aggression than as a by-product of "the momentous decision that world war was unavoidable."[45]

A Balanced Deterrent

Several lessons can be drawn from this brief analysis. First, crisis stability and controllability, particularly once a conventional crisis is under way, are at least as important as a strong peacetime deterrent. In most of the scenarios by which nuclear war might plausibly break out, misunderstandings, misperceptions, fears of pre-emption, failure to control forces in the field, or simply lack of an alternative play a prominent role. Second, there is in many cases a tradeoff between crisis stability and control on the one hand and deterrence on the other. Doctrines and postures designed to enhance deterrence can undermine crisis stability and control during wartime, or create a situation in which either side may decide to use nuclear weapons first.

It would be unwise to rest Western defense planning solely on the doves' best-case scenario, in which the Soviets are assumed to be over-deterred even without nuclear weapons. The weakness of the hawks' argument, on the other hand, is not (as is often maintained) that it is a worst-case assessment, but that it fails to acknowledge that there are *several* worst-case assessments. By focusing on only one scenario—potential Soviet aggression—hawks promote doctrines and capabilities that make other scenarios more likely. It is an oversimplification to regard first use and the nuclear guarantee as the most likely cause of war or as the primary factor that prevents war. A balance must instead be struck between the objectives of deterrence stability, crisis stability, and controllability. Postures that overemphasize one objective to the detriment of the others may be dangerous. In order to reduce the chance of nuclear war, the United States and NATO should pursue a strategy of *balanced deterrence:* a posture designed to reduce the overall likelihood of nuclear war by all paths.[46]

Our analysis suggests that the best way to achieve this goal is to adopt measures blocking nonrational paths to war. NATO's current short fuse provides an imbalanced deterrent. While the United States and NATO continue to focus strategic decisions on the danger of sudden attack in Europe, whether a pre-emptive strike during crisis or a premeditated bolt from the blue, the Soviet's primary concern is with the "Sarajevo factor," the fear that an uncontrollable chain of events could lead to world war. Current strategy implicitly concedes the importance of this fear: since the threat of nuclear retaliation is in many ways incredible, its effectiveness must rely heavily on an element of uncertainty—on the possibility that nuclear weapons might be used accidentally, inadvertently, or hastily in a conventional conflict. But in wartime, this uncertainty might lead to catastrophe.

Managing the Tradeoff

Proponents of a longer fuse argue that NATO's present strategy increases the likelihood of general war while attempting to deter the lesser threats of Soviet aggression and blackmail. But would lengthening the fuse tip the scale in the other direction, leaving the Soviet Union inadequately deterred? Would gains in crisis stability and controllability outweigh the potential losses in deterrence?

Most proponents of a longer fuse are sensitive to the deterrence side of the equation, emphasizing the need for it to be coupled with measures to strengthen conventional defense or negotiate conventional arms control. Underlying this view is a basic consensus that under current circumstances NATO's conventional capabilities would be inadequate to resist a sudden concerted Soviet advance (although given adequate time to mobilize, Western conventional defenses in Europe and East Asia are adequate).

Just how far the fuse could safely be lengthened without conventional compensation depends on how the Soviets respond to marginal changes in nuclear deployments. Here there will be critical differences of opinion. Those who feel that Soviet behavior is shaped predominantly by the fear of American missiles will support minimal no early use proposals, but argue strenuously for more reliable conventional defenses to compensate for any move away from first use. Others believe that the

Soviets are highly constrained by the benefits of the status quo, the political and economic costs of aggression, the existence of small French and British nuclear forces, and what McGeorge Bundy has termed "existential" deterrence (the fear and uncertainty induced by the mere existence of nuclear weapons, independent of the precise mode of deployment).[47] They will be prepared to lengthen the fuse with less compensation.

The latter view is the more plausible. The credibility of a nuclear defense does not rest primarily on the particular mode of deployment. There is little reason to believe that it makes much difference to the Soviets whether nuclear weapons used against them are launched by Americans or Europeans, early or late in the conflict, or from cruise missiles or battlefield launchers. Moreover, if our analysis is correct, and the danger of nonrational use outweighs the danger of deliberate use, *some* lengthening of the fuse would reduce the overall probability of nuclear war, *even without any conventional compensation.*

Each of the three proposals considered here—no early use, no first use, and disengagement—can claim *under certain conditions* to reduce the probability of nuclear war by moving toward a more balanced deterrent. Let us first consider the military conditions under which each proposal would be desirable. Then we will turn to long-term political conditions.

No Early Use. Under almost any conceivable circumstances, adoption of measures to assure that weapons and command and control systems would survive the early stages of an attack—the minimal no early use proposal—would reduce the probability of nuclear war. Steps to ensure that decisions about nuclear weapons would be made in a deliberate and prudent manner would block nonrational paths to nuclear war without diminishing the overall deterrent—thereby satisfying both hawks and doves. Reasoned opposition to these measures could come from but one group: those who believe that the threat of Soviet attack is so immediate that it outweighs all the evident risks of nonrational use, and that the Soviets are restrained from such an attack only by their fear that Western missiles might go off inadvertently. In our view, this is an implausible ground for opposing no early use.

Proposals to increase the ability of weapons to survive conventional and nuclear attack would be one particularly important aspect of this minimal no early use position. Current NATO plans also foresee an improvement in theater command and control.[48] The problem of unauthorized use might be addressed through further changes in command systems, for example by developing more reliable Permissive Action Linkages

(PALs)—locks on nuclear weapons that require centralized authorization to open. Ground and air-based weapons now require PALs, but many have yet to be upgraded to 1980s standards. Such controls might be extended to naval weapons, many of which can currently be fired without encountering a PAL lock. A new generation of PALs, working by secure radio links, might allow civilian officials even greater control. Withdrawing nuclear weapons farther from the front lines would reduce the risk of early use, controlled or inadvertent. Ideally, the bulk of theater nuclear defense should consist of mobile missiles stationed far behind the front lines.[49]

No First Use. If we accept the assumption that the present first use policy is dangerously imbalanced, some movement toward reduced reliance on nuclear weapons and their replacement with nonprovocative conventional forces is clearly desirable. Many Western officials agree that NATO relies too heavily on nuclear weapons and that the prospects of pre-emptive or inadvertent war are real. Responding to these concerns, current NATO plans foresee reductions in the number of battlefield nuclear weapons from 5,895 in 1985 to 4,082 in 1992.[50]

Exactly how far the trend toward no first use should go depends, as we have seen in the preceding section, on the deterrent value ascribed to conventional forces, the extent to which the mere existence of nuclear weapons provides an existential deterrent to aggression, and assessments of the Soviet threat. In the absence of mutually negotiated reductions, however, it is safe to assume that some minimal nuclear force is required to deter Soviet use of theater weapons in Europe. This requirement places a lower bound on reductions in arsenals.

Paradoxically, proposals for no first use (and no early use) that involve a large build-up of conventional forces tend to be more risky than those that do not. Some such proposals, such as those for deep strikes and conventional retaliation, might move us even further away from a balanced deterrent. To be sure, conventional retaliation offers advantages. It might deflect some of the wartime damage away from the Federal Republic of Germany, lead to gains of territory that could be used to bring the Soviets to the negotiating table, and increase the cost of war to the Eastern Europeans, thereby diminishing their support for the Soviet cause.[51] But the advantages of conventional retaliation may well be outweighed by its liabilities. Insofar as it poses an offensive threat, a strong conventional force undermines the crisis stability side of the equation.

Retaliation may inadvertently threaten Soviet strategic assets, thereby opening up new paths to nuclear war, while encouraging pre-emptive thinking in NATO.[52] Even though NATO perceives itself as the defender, it will be under pressure to shoot first if the steadfastness of its forward defense depends on the early destruction of enemy rear assets. Moreover, a counteroffensive capability might pose a more realistic threat of conventional intervention in Eastern Europe. The resulting Soviet fears of invasion could be extremely destabilizing, particularly in the case of an Eastern European uprising.

Nonprovocative defense or conventional arms control would permit us to lengthen the fuse without these disadvantages. Such a defense also promises to be less costly than conventional alternatives.[52] A clearly nonprovocative defense posture could give NATO a more nearly sufficient capacity for defense, while minimizing crisis instability. Because NATO would not possess the structural capacity for strikes deep within Eastern Europe, the Soviet incentive to strike westward would be reduced, as would the likelihood of rapid escalation or spillover from a crisis in Eastern Europe or the Third World. The most desirable way to create a nonprovocative conventional defense would be to include it within the framework of ongoing conventional arms control negotiations, such as the successor to the Mutual Balanced Force Reduction talks. An arms control package combining reductions in shorter range nuclear weapons with negotiated limitations on conventional forces could raise the nuclear threshold while redressing perceived imbalances in the conventional constellation of forces. Even quite conservative analysts support this alternative, although doubts remain about its feasibility.[54]

To a greater extent than no early use, the desirability of no first use depends on assessments of the overall East–West military balance, as well as the current state of military technology. Massive increases in Soviet or regional power vis-à-vis the West or developments in weapons technology radically favoring conventional attackers might upset the conventional balance and require a different balance of policies—one more concerned with deterring deliberate aggression.[55] With these exceptions, however, proposals for no early use and no first use maintain their desirability across a wide range of situations. Whatever assumptions are made about the structure of the international system—for example, an increase in the number of major actors and the relative decline of the superpowers—a longer fuse remains desirable. Indeed, a long fuse would be most advantageous in a world where nuclear weapons have proliferated.

Similarly, a longer fuse is consistent with many assumptions about the state of military technology. One immediate technological threat, however, should be noted. The recent trend toward the miniaturization of nuclear weapons, if projected into the future, threatens to narrow the firebreak between conventional and nuclear war. New technologies tend to breed new strategies and bureaucratic support. Once introduced, miniaturized weapons may prove difficult to remove.

Disengagement. Disengagement risks significantly weakening the credibility of Western defenses. Thus, advocates of disengagement must rely on a number of highly uncertain assumptions about the underlying military reality. The first of these assumptions is that the Soviet threat of attack is negligible; the second is that allies will compensate for American withdrawal by increasing their own defense efforts; and the third is that American strategic deterrent forces, along with European ground troops, are enough to deter aggression. None of these is utterly implausible, but they introduce a higher level of uncertainty into the analysis than the more conservative no early use and no first use proposals.

Disengagement, for example, runs a higher risk than more moderate proposals of upsetting the military balance. American withdrawal would be aimed at reducing the risk of nuclear war to the United States, but it does not necessarily reduce the chance of nuclear war in Europe or elsewhere. It is unclear how realistic such a policy of isolation is, given the global reach of modern conventional weapons. The security of Europe and Japan—and, through them, Korea and the Middle East—would remain vital interests. Should war break out in any of these areas, an isolationist America would probably be dragged into the conflict under less advantageous circumstances than it would have faced had it remained engaged.

Lengthening the Fuse: The Long Run

The preceding analysis suggests that by lengthening the fuse, American defense policy can move closer to a balanced deterrent and thereby reduce the chance of nuclear war, at least in the short term. But how stable would these proposals be in the long term? Here we consider four long-term factors that constrain policies of lengthening the fuse: domestic politics here and abroad, political relations between the United States and its allies, international economic stability, and the political climate between the superpowers.

Domestic Politics

On both sides of the Atlantic, there is solid public support for the principles behind policies of lengthening the fuse. Since the 1950s, public opinion in both Europe and America has consistently rejected the first use of nuclear weapons.[56] As Halperin argues: "No one who could be elected president...needs to be told that the American people would accept a policy that involved reduced reliance on nuclear weapons.... Most Americans believe that their government has been working all along for [their] elimination...."[57] Strong public support for arms control should also extend to support for a longer fuse, if the two proposals are linked rhetorically. Reductions in U.S. reliance on nuclear weapons and increases in civilian control, however, may encounter opposition in some branches of the American military.[58]

In comparison with the bold declarations favored by early advocates of no first use, many concrete measures to lengthen the fuse—reforms in command and control procedures, changes in the deployment of conventional forces, moderate reductions or redeployments of nuclear weapons, and altered strategies for their use—have the advantage of being highly technical and outside public scrutiny, and therefore potentially less controversial. Only a few of the specific policies considered in this chapter would be sure to encounter significant opposition abroad. European publics reject increased spending, for example, although they support stronger conventional defense as a concept. Observers of European politics seem to agree that there is little political support for the 4 percent annual increases in military spending needed to fund General Rogers's proposed conventional build-up.[59] A number of less expensive nonprovocative defense options involve fortifying the intra-German border, which in turn would symbolically underscore the division of Germany, prompting stiff German opposition.[60] The United States must take care when altering the terms of its nuclear commitment not to create the perception, either in the East or the West, that its broader commitment to its allies has eroded. Thus, although both European and American public opinion may favor a longer fuse, little would be gained by broad public declarations.

Alliance Relations

Allied governments constitute the most serious constraint on the effectiveness of policies to lengthen the fuse. Although there is strong elite support for conventional arms control, the current policy of flexible response reflects a delicate compromise between the desire of European elites for a firm nuclear guarantee and American fears of escalation. But the prospect that its revision could create deep disharmony within the alliance is often exaggerated. Open disagreements and a lack of coordination between allies are common within NATO and other American security alliances and do not constitute a case against reform. European politicians, for reasons that have more to do with electoral politics than military strategy, routinely oppose changes in the status quo.

Two other threats must be considered as well. First, some contend that without the current U.S. commitment, Europe will be vulnerable to Soviet intimidation. The resulting "Finlandization" of Europe would in the long run weaken the West, encourage further Soviet aggression, and increase the chance of nuclear war—under circumstances highly unfavorable to the West.[61] Fortunately, this commonly heard scenario is probably not very realistic, at least in Europe. The Soviets have attempted to coerce Western European states in the past, but without success. With its superior economic strength and continuing political vitality, Western Europe is unlikely to permit itself to be Finlandized. It is far more likely that in the event of a U.S. withdrawal from Europe, French and German policy would approximate that of Sweden, a hardy neutral that spends a greater percentage of its resources on defense than do most NATO nations. As Jonathan Dean argues, "The concerns of U.S. leaders about the steadfastness of others in the face of Soviet pressures often reflect a supercilious assessment of the superior toughness of Americans and the lesser fiber of foreigners, as well as some exaggeration of Soviet capabilities."[62] The Finlandization scenario, however, may be somewhat more appropriate to the Third World.

The response of our allies poses a second, more plausible threat of war.[63] Rather than capitulating, the allies may well overcompensate for a decreased American commitment with forward deployments of their own nuclear (or chemical and biological) weapons. With greater numbers of front-line states deploying weapons, the chance of catastrophe might increase. The existence of a reliable American nuclear guarantee has helped to restrain a number of U.S. allies, including Korea, Taiwan, and perhaps even Japan and West Germany, from joining the nuclear club. This consideration weighs particularly heavily against proposals for disengagement, but even smaller steps toward lengthening the fuse may trigger an allied reaction. When the United States and the Soviet Union recently began serious negotiations to limit theater nuclear weapons, for example, the French almost immediately pushed forward with a five-year plan to develop new chemical weapons.[64] Pakistani and Korean attempts to acquire nuclear technology in the late 1970s were also widely interpreted as a reflection of doubts about the American commitment to its defense.[65] The nuclearization of such U.S. allies might also be perceived by the Soviet Union or China as a direct threat, thereby triggering a downward spiral in political relations and increasing the danger of war. The constraints imposed by alliance relations suggest that the transition to a world with a longer fuse will have to be managed carefully. The transatlantic and transpacific security bargains are complex, based on a delicate balance of risks, and any attempt to alter the bargain must take into account the response of allies.

International Economic Stability

Those who doubt that the United States can sustain its alliance commitments over the long run without courting international economic disaster deserve more serious attention than they get. The recent accumulation of domestic and international debt by the United States is an epochal event, one that calls into question the enormous cost to the United States of its postwar military deployments. High investments in defense may sap the dynamism of the American economy. In coming years, some U.S. conventional forces will likely be shifted from Europe to the Third World. If an East–West conflict is likely to start in the Third World, as we have argued, this may in fact be optimal for both the United States and its allies. Moreover, there is little doubt that U.S. defense spending will be cut substantially in the next decade. Some moderate withdrawals are inevitable.

Nevertheless, it remains unclear whether, as critics contend, U.S. military spending must lead to international economic instability. Nor is it obvious that disengagement is the only solution. We simply do not know enough about the linkages between defense spending and economic growth to judge. Recent studies demonstrate persuasively that (at least until the Reagan military build-up) the major NATO nations have shouldered roughly equivalent burdens within NATO.[66] Moreover, the balance of payments effects of U.S. participation are offset by payments from host countries. Any effort by the United States to adjust the burden may simply weigh down other nations, with no net improvement in the world economy. Given the lack of conclusive evidence and the obvious disadvantages of disengagement, it seems most prudent to wait and see, rather than adopt an extreme policy in expectation of the worst.

Superpower Relations

The success of proposals for lengthening the fuse depends most directly on the state of political relations between the superpowers. Since the primary mission of U.S. nuclear weapons (and most of the world's standing conventional forces) is to deter big-power conventional war, long-term prospects for more ambitious measures reducing reliance on nuclear weapons are directly linked to the stability of the conventional peace between the superpowers. In Europe, where superpower confrontation has been most intense, the trend is favorable. As Jonathan Dean observes, the European confrontation has reached a watershed. Over the next twenty years, there is a possibility of "gradual decline or attrition of the confrontation under the combined impact of arms control, political measures and budgetary shortages."[67]

More radical proposals for lengthening the fuse—including steps toward a partial withdrawal of U.S. troops from foreign commitments—should be seen as a possible benefit of more cordial relations and greater cooperation between the superpowers. The prospect of Soviet military action against Western Europe is likely to arise, as we have seen, only as a result of the escalation of some lesser conflict in Eastern Europe or the Third World, and even then, only if the Soviets are convinced that world war has become inevitable. The key to reducing long-term reliance on nuclear weapons both in Europe and elsewhere may thus lie in limiting political and military confrontation in the Third World. Here the prospects are less favorable. Although superpower intervention in the Third World seems to be becoming more expensive and less effective, there has not yet been any enduring decline in the actual use of force.[68] If conventional intervention becomes less attractive over the long run, the need for nuclear deterrence should diminish accordingly. Then more radical reductions in the role and size of nuclear arsenals may become possible.

Conclusion

Hawks, concerned that nuclear war might result from deliberate Soviet aggression invited by Western weakness, resist proposals to lengthen the fuse unless they are coupled with much stronger conventional forces. Doves, concerned that nuclear war is most likely to come about inadvertently, pre-emptively, or simply for lack of an alternative, call for a longer fuse even without compensation. Proposals to lengthen the fuse offer ways of striking a balance between these two concerns. Precisely where the balance should be struck, however, depends on the military and political ramifications of the proposal and on the political and psychological assumptions made about Soviet intentions. Table 1 summarizes the conditions under which the three proposals discussed in the chapter are desirable.

As we move from no early use to disengagement, the desirability of the proposals rests on increasingly uncertain assumptions. No early use proposals promise to reduce the likelihood of nonrational paths to war without significantly degrading the deterrent against deliberate attack. No first use aims to fashion a more balanced deterrent. To the extent that our current posture overemphasizes the threat of a deliberate all-out attack, while neglecting the threats of pre-emptive and inadvertent nuclear use, the substitution of conventional forces for nuclear forces is in principle desirable—*even* if the reductions in nuclear weapons are not offset by increases in conventional forces. Conventional forces must be deployed in a manner unambiguously nonprovocative. Because of the threat of proliferation and the cost of conventionalization, a conventional arms control agreement offers the optimal precondition (although not a necessary one) for the introduction of a longer fuse. Because their effects are felt indirectly, it is easy to overlook bureaucratic reforms, such as those proposed by Halperin. But doctrinal statements and bureaucratic procedures that reinforce separate procedures and controls for nuclear weapons would be indispensable parts of any policy of lengthening the fuse.

Disengagement is the most radical of the proposals considered here, and the least predictable. It compounds the problems raised by more moderate proposals and is nearly certain to lead to major political and diplomatic upheavals. Proponents of disengagement assume that the Soviet Union is overdeterred, that existential deterrence is strong, and that an American withdrawal from these areas will lead to increased allied defense efforts, a more equitable distribution of burdens, and thus a more stable deterrent. But other, less desirable political alternatives are also possible, including nuclear proliferation and the erosion of political will and military strength in the West. Although the threat of Finlandization has been wildly exaggerated, American disengagement might lead to higher overall levels of military spending in the West, nuclear proliferation, and, nevertheless, weaker defense. Advocates of disengagement are correct to point out that budget constraints will prevent the United States

Table 1. Lengthening the Fuse: Conditions of Desirability

Proposal	Specific Measures	Military Conditions	Political Conditions
No Early Use	More survivability, tighter PAL control, clearer command structure, rearward deployment, stronger nonprovocative conventional forces.	*Desirable* Increases crisis stability without eroding deterrent significantly. Forces must be nonprovocative.	*Desirable* Little public or elite reaction; low cost.
No First Use	Reduce nuclear forces; bolster nonprovocative defense or negotiate conventional arms control. Separate conventional and nuclear commands.	Reductions *desirable* up to a point, even without adding conventional forces; *desirable* thereafter, at some rate of substitution, down to a minimum needed to deter enemy first use.	*Conditionally desirable* if Soviet threat moderate, cost affordable and allied reaction moderate.
Disengagement	Withdrawal from nuclear and conventional commitments of extended deterrence.	*Conditionally desirable* only if there is some compensation for U.S. withdrawal.	*Desirable only under highly uncertain conditions*: Soviet threat very low; allies increase spending without proliferation; existential deterrence strong.

from maintaining its current commitments to NATO, but it is doubtful that complete withdrawal is the preferred response.

There is long-term political support among Western publics for many no early use and no first use proposals, and perhaps for a limited disengagement of American forces. Increasingly, there is elite support as well. Proposals to lengthen the fuse offer a realistic way of building on the progress of the past four decades and ensuring the continued avoidance of nuclear war.

CHAPTER 5

Nonprovocative and Civilian-Based Defenses

Stephen J. Flanagan

> Thus it came about that the conquerors grew afraid of the con-
> quered and their nerves wore thin and they shot at shadows in
> the night.
>
> —*John Steinbeck*, The Moon is Down

A number of Western analysts have argued that a major source of international insecurity is fear of aggression based on worst-case assessments
of other states' military capabilities. Robert Jervis and George Quester
have attempted to demonstrate how offensive strategies and force postures make war more likely by promoting a Hobbesian competition for
limited security.[1] Among states with antagonistic relationships, military
preparations, particularly those with the potential for ready application
to offensive operations, are themselves part of the security problem. This
assessment has been reflected in Western defense policy debates as well.
The West German Social Democratic party's August 1986 policy statement, "Peace and Security," characterizes the problem this way:

Security concepts continue to be dominated by fear and the threat and counter-
threat of force. . . . As long as armaments programmes and strategic planning are
based on the worst-case assumption, no security problems will be solved, rather
new ones will be created. The general feeling of being under threat, which is both
a cause and a consequence of the arms race, can only be overcome through negotiated, inter-bloc security.[2]

These theorists and practitioners see the situation in Central Europe
as a concrete and extremely dangerous illustration of this problem. There

NATO and the Warsaw Pact confront each other with what are seen as excessively large, heavily armored, and highly mobile forces that are ideally suited for offensive warfare. The military doctrines and training activities of both sides have offensive aspects that exacerbate fears of hostile action. States on both sides of the East–West divide have adopted strategies and force postures that assume that the likelihood of military aggression by the other bloc in a crisis is quite high. Thus, some analysts argue, a shift to military capabilities and doctrines that left states structurally incapable of conducting offensive military actions, or even the replacement of traditional military forces with plans for civilian-based resistance to any use of force, would stabilize European security. They contend that such a shift in national defense postures would be reassuring to domestic populations and neighboring states but credible enough to deter aggression and guarantee a country's survival if deterrence failed.

A few analysts, including Randall Forsberg, have applied this concept to the causes of insecurity on a global scale. Forsberg has proposed a "new approach to arms control," which seeks to limit all nations' military forces to nonprovocative territorial defense, by way of negotiations over a fifty-year period.[3]

Finally, several European analysts and the American scholar Gene Sharp have advocated replacement of traditional military forces with integrated strategies of nonmilitary civilian-based resistance to any aggression.[4] Sharp applies the history of passive and active resistance to aggression to the contemporary security dilemma of neutral states in Europe. He characterizes that dilemma as a choice between accepting an inevitably uncertain nuclear guarantee from another power and developing a nuclear or robust conventional deterrent of their own. If deterrence failed, Sharp contends, the destructive power of both nuclear and modern conventional weapons would result in devastation that would vitiate any notion of victory. Thus he advances an alternative concept of deterrence based on a society's clear expression of its determination never to accept external domination of its political life. A state could accomplish this by preparing its populace and institutions to resist and subvert civil and military instruments of state control, if deterrence fails.[5] Where possible, the defending country would also attempt to create international problems for the aggressor state. In essence, Sharp advocates a system in which the conquerors would grow afraid of the conquered, as Steinbeck suggested in The Moon is Down, his novel about the resistance to the Nazi occupation of Norway.

As an alternative to the current structure of bipolar nuclear deterrence, a system in which states shifted to purely defensive military postures has received considerable attention among the leftist "alternative defense" community in Western Europe. It remains to be seen whether any country we will be able to develop military capabilities that absolutely cannot be used aggressively or at least ones that are both deterring and nonthreatening to antagonistic states.

This chapter outlines the principal characteristics and arguments supporting three alternative security regimes: nonprovocative defense; nonintervention and defensive defenses; and civilian-based resistance. It then considers changes in the international system that would be needed for realization of these visions. All these proposals share a central premise: that the security of individual states and regional and global stability could be enhanced if no country had any significant capability to conduct extraterritorial military operations. This notion that offensive military capabilities are as much a cause as a manifestation of hostility among states surfaced during the 1930s and in much more sophisticated analyses of the last decade as an explanation of the origins of World War I.[6] It warrants further scrutiny.

Nonprovocative Defense

Context

Concern about the instability caused by the offensive military capabilities of modern armed forces has long been widely felt in West Germany and among the left elsewhere in Western Europe. In the early 1950s, former Wehrmacht General Staff Officer Bogislav von Bonin proposed that the new Federal Republic of Germany develop a nonprovocative defense system quickly and at a modest cost by erecting a network fifty kilometers deep of camouflaged field fortifications manned by small cadres all along the inner-German border. Von Bonin's interest in a purely defensive German front line reflected a desire to avoid provoking a build-up of Soviet invasion forces in East Germany.[7] His ideas, however, were quickly eclipsed by the Adenauer government's decision to develop heavy armored forces. Nonetheless, as Helmut Schmidt, hardly an advocate of alternative defense concepts, wrote in 1962, "The optimum goal of German defense policy and strategy would...be the creation of an armaments structure clearly unsuited for the offensive role yet adequate beyond the shadow of a doubt to defend German territory."[8] Contemporary advocates of nonprovocative defense believe that this goal has been obscured. Indeed, they find the heavily armored, highly mobile forces of NATO and the Warsaw Pact a major source of instability and tension in Europe because of their offensive capability. Members of the East–West Pugwash Study Group on Conventional Forces in Europe contend that crisis stability is threatened by the following characteristics of the military forces on both sides of the European divide: "increased emphasis on time-critical weapon systems; increased numbers of targets for pre-emptive strike; increased numbers of weapon systems that appear to be capable of crippling defences and which thus raise the pressure for pre-emptive attack."[9] In place of the current military structures, these theorists would field much smaller military forces structurally incapable of offensive operations.

Another rationale for eliminating all offensive military potential is found in the Social Democratic party's proposal for an East–West partnership in the search for common security (*Sicherheitspartnerschaft*). As the party's 1986 policy paper suggested, "The alliance must make allowance for the political and military concerns of our eastern neighbours. It must, therefore, clearly articulate the defensive character of its strategy by placing the emphasis on border-area defence."[10] For those who hold this view, East and West face a common threat: the risk of war through miscalculation. The current politico-military situation seems inadequate for stability and lasting peace. Both alliances should support the transition to this new security partnership. Arms control agreements removing the threat of attack would be the most important instruments for developing this partnership. Ultimately, a new world political order should be based on agreed procedures for the peaceful settlement of disputes, and war should be proscribed as a means of achieving political objectives.

The member governments of the Warsaw Pact have advanced a similar assessment of the causes of instability in their 1986 Budapest Appeal and May 1987 Berlin proposals for arms control in Europe.[11] The Eastern governments have called for 25 percent reductions in force levels in Central Europe to be accompanied by "reciprocal withdrawal of the most dangerous offensive types of weapons" and adoption of "strictly defensive" military doctrines by both sides. NATO governments are clearly troubled by the offensive plans and capabilities of the Warsaw Pact, but are quick to point out that the Alliance has always had a defensive strategy. The problem here is that both alliances have forces that *could* be used for offensive operations, and neither believes the other has purely defensive intentions. Nor do the two have a common understanding of the scope and character of defensive operations.

Defense Military Concepts and Europe

The alternative defense debate in Europe comprises two general schools of thought, characterized as the radical and moderate approaches. The former, which tends to be unilateralist an implementation, stresses the importance of reshaping the role of the European states in NATO, developing a nonnuclear Europe, and changing the social structure. The moderate version, reflected in the thinking of the Social Democratic party, seeks to strengthen the European pillar of the Alliance and envisions using bilateral arms control to achieve phased denuclearization of all of Europe and to increase the ratio of reserve forces to standing armies.[12]

Egbert Boeker and Lutz Unterseher have offered a clear definition of nonprovocative defense:

The build-up, training, logistics and doctrine of the armed forces are such that they are seen in their totality to be unsuitable for offence, but unambiguously sufficient for a credible conventional defence. Nuclear weapons fulfill at most a retaliatory role.[13]

Most nonprovocative proposals are based on concepts of territorial or area defense, in which defenders seek to exploit the natural terrain and, in some instances, urban sprawl to wear down an aggressor. They also share an assumption that defenders have decisive advantages over attackers. This assessment, based on technology and history, is not a revolutionary notion. Carl von Clausewitz argued that defense is intrinsically "the stronger form of war," and that the "advantage of the ground" rests with the defenders, who inhabit the territory and know its contours.[14] As will be seen, however, nonprovocative defense concepts depart from Clausewitz in application.

Another common assumption of these concepts is that the most significant recent breakthroughs in military technology will augment the defender's natural advantage in future conflicts. While mobility and armor have only marginally improved an attacker's ability to advance, there have been quantum leaps in both reconnaissance capabilities, which will reduce the attacker's advantage of surprise, and the lethality of individual conventional weapons systems, which allow for a more effective dispersed defense.[15]

Western proponents of this posture advocate exploiting some of the same technologies—new surveillance systems, precision-guided munitions (PGMs), remotely piloted vehicles, and air defenses—that NATO commanders find attractive, but the nonprovocative defenders propose to use them in a much more reactive fashion. Capabilities for deep forward strikes are seen as a threat to the Warsaw Pact that would undermine crisis stability.

A few other common characteristics of these nonprovocative defense concepts should be noted. By deploying small, dispersed forces in less populated areas and forgoing military defense of urban centers, these proposals seek to increase crisis stability by providing few targets worth pre-empting before a war starts. Similarly, because airfields and other support facilities provide tempting targets for hostile aircraft and missile attack, these concepts avoid or limit the role of air forces.[16] Moreover, advocates emphasize that nonprovocative defense would further increase stability by developing a new kind of military balance not to be measured in traditional "bean count" fashion, but "in terms of relative chances of successfully denying an aggressor his victory, without calling destruction on the civilian population."[17] Little attention has been paid to naval forces by these theorists, although some do mention the desirability of shifting to weapons systems designed for purely coastal defense, and assume that freedom of navigation will be maintained by the United States.

Four general types of nonprovocative defense concepts have emerged in recent years: area defense (*Raumverteidigung*); wide area covering defense (*raumdeckende Verteidigung*); the fire barrier (*Grenznahe Feuersperre*); and integrated and interactive forward defense. All seek to deter aggression by denial. If deterrence failed, defenders would attempt to ensnare any aggressor in a web of small engagements, avoiding any decisive battle, thereby precluding a clear victory.

Horst Afheldt, one of the earliest proponents of this general approach, supports a concept of area defense that would replace NATO's large heavily armored units with static light infantry, organized in 10,000 formations of twenty to thirty men each. These small units, armed with antitank guided weapons, would each defend ten to fifteen square kilometers of territory with which they were very familiar.[18] In the forward area these units would be composed of active duty forces who would guard against surprise attack. Rear areas would be covered by local reserve units.

All these "techno-commando" units would be both difficult for the attacker to locate and unsuited for offensive operations. Conversely, any efforts by an aggressor to concentrate forces would be disrupted by precise fire from short-range artillery and rockets based in dispersed patterns deep in rear areas. Afheldt has argued that these units, armed with their ATGWs and knowledge of the terrain and supported by short-range rocket and artillery batteries, all linked together by an integrated communication system, could be effective in diminishing the size and momentum of a Warsaw Pact offensive close to the inner-German border.

A number of similar concepts have gained some political support in Europe. Former Bundeswehr Major-General Jochen Loser has proposed a "wide-area territorial defence" in which a frontier defense zone would be established 80 to 100 kilometers deep, with barriers and blocking units channeling attacking tank forces toward concentrations of fire.[19] Loser advocates deployment of a network of light infantry "shield" brigades in the forward zones currently occupied by allied forces to wear down an attacker in a series of small engagements. These shield units would cooperate with traditional Allied and German units in the transition period. Once the transarmament process was completed, however, light units would make up the bulk of the shield (for covering defenses) and sword (for repulsing attacks) forces. Loser's scheme would require a doubling of the number of brigades in the Bundeswehr by expanding the reserves. He would maintain the bulk of these units in the second echelon for counterattack against breakthroughs. Loser's concept makes extensive use of air and missile defenses, and does not rule out the ultimate use of nuclear weapons.

Norbet Hannig and Albrecht von Muller have advanced similar ideas for multilayered, nonprovocative forms of forward defense.[20] In both concepts, the first layer would be a "fire-belt" four to five kilometers wide along the inner-European divide. No NATO troops would be deployed in this *cordon sanitaire*, which would be inundated with remotely delivered fire. The next layer would be composed of small units of light infantry armed with PGMs to deal with breakthroughs. Successive layers would be defended in von Muller's plan by heavily armored but dispersed units backed up by a network of local, semimobile, territorial defense units, whereas Hannig proposes to deal with breakthroughs by redirecting 180° the missiles that constitute his fire barrier.

The West German Study Group on Alternative Security Policy (SAS) has advanced a nonprovocative defense proposal called "interactive forward defense" that integrates elements of several concepts described above. The SAS proposal has three components: a static containment force composed of decentralized light infantry units employing reactive tactics; a rapid commitment force composed of mechanized infantry, armor, and cavalry forces with limited mobility; and a rear protection force to cope with penetrations and airborne assaults. The first two components would be made up of active-duty NATO units, with the latter filled out by reserve forces. As SAS chief theorist Lutz Unterseher explains, the static warfare units would maintain area control and deplete an adversary's momentum by harassing advancing units and channeling them into areas where they would be vulnerable to attack by the mechanized forces.[21]

The military thinking and some of the political goals of these German strategists are echoed in a number of other European proposals, such as those of the British Just Defence organization and the Alternative Defence Commission.[22] In advocating a denuclearized posture of "defensive deterrence" decoupled from U.S. strategic forces, the latter group concedes that the political imperatives of forward defense require NATO to retain or even expand its large standing armies, but argues that more systematic preparations for territorial defense should also be explored as an alternative.[23]

Not all nonprovocative defense proposals have come from Europe. In the United States, Richard Smoke has argued for a gradual transition in NATO, over fifteen years or more, toward a strategy that relies primarily on conventional forces "unambiguously capable only of defense" and backed up by secure, second-strike nuclear forces for deterrence of any nuclear use by an opponent. Smoke expects a continuing erosion of political support for NATO's current nuclear first-use policy. As he puts it, "democratic societies that feel relatively secure cannot forever base their strategy on what amounts to a threat of global suicide."[24] Nonetheless, Smoke's strategy owes much of its credibility to the "residual nuclear deterrence" or existential deterrence that would underpin it. Whether it would be more stable than the current situation is addressed below.

A Global Nonintervention, Defensive Defense Regime

Randall Forsberg has applied some of the principles underlying nonprovocative defense concepts to explain the causes of national insecurity on a global scale. She has proposed development of "a regime in which the big powers and other northern industrial states entered into multilateral agreements not to intervene directly, with their own military forces in the Third World."[25] The near-term goals of this plan are to promote self-determination in the Third World, to facilitate resolution of regional security problems by disentangling them from the East–West competition, and to reduce the risk of superpower competition that could lead to nuclear war. Forsberg does not specify how nations might be motivated to pursue this conversion, but concedes that such arrangements could only be initiated in a climate of greater East–West trust and harmony than prevails today. Over the long term, Forsberg believes, this regime would foster the development of democratic institutions and a stable peace among the big powers. This new world order would be conducive to restructuring all nations' military forces, either by negotiations or as a consequence of independent national decisions based on reduced threats to nonprovocative territorial defense roles. The nations of the world could then reduce their aggregate defense expenditures from $950 to $100 billion annually by converting their large standing armies to border guards. Ultimately the restructuring could lead to a just, stable peace that might allow for negotiated abolition of all nuclear weapons.

For Forsberg the principal security problem is separating the potential intervening nations, defined as those "big powers" and "other northern industrialized nations" mainly concerned with the East–West or Sino–Soviet conflict, from countries in the Third World, which are largely focused on local or regional questions. Forsberg notes that these seven northern countries (the United States, USSR, China, Japan, Great Britain, West Germany, and France) comprise the bulk of the "modern military system" and have the greatest resource base for future military power. Only the superpowers are likely to intervene in the Third World on a large scale, she notes. Nonetheless, an agreement by the seven big countries, perhaps in concert with the other industrialized nations, to convert their military forces to border guards would revolutionize the world military system and reduce the chances and risks of global conflict.[26] Forsberg contends that this transformation of the military system would have a trickle-down effect limiting conflict potential in the Third World by virtually eliminating most military R&D and arms transfers.

Forsberg envisions several possible "transition paths" to this new world, involving different arrangements of six basic changes in the big powers' standing armed forces:

1. Elimination of (mostly U.S. and Soviet) nuclear war-fighting systems and the renunciation of first use of nuclear weapons.
2. Ultimate elimination of the minimum nuclear deterrent forces that would remain after the war-fighting systems were abolished.
3. Conversion of the large standing armies in the northern tier to small forces equipped with short-range weaponry, which would provide for a strong territorial defense but pose no real threat of aggression.

4. Withdrawal and dismantling of Soviet troops stationed in Eastern Europe and a "Finlandization" of that region.
5. Elimination by the industrial nations of long-range air forces and ocean-going warships.
6. Renunciation by the big powers of any future large-scale, unilateral conventional military intervention in the Third World.[27]

She freely admits that these changes would not be possible without dramatic shifts in international political relations.

The principal question for Forsberg is not whether, but *when* and *in what order* these changes should take place. She suggests that the first step toward this new world should be a package including the abolition of nuclear forces for extended deterrence (change 1) and development of nonprovocative conventional defenses in Europe (change 3). Similarly, she notes that development of nonprovocative conventional defenses in Europe would not have the desired effect, making the USSR feel more secure about withdrawal from Eastern Europe, unless the NATO countries abolished their long-range air forces and ocean-going navies. Thus changes 4 and 5 would be closely linked to the implementation of changes 1 and 3. Forsberg considers ways to cut into this "seamless web" of military interests and concludes that change 6, ending direct, large-scale military intervention in the Third World, offers the best starting point without increasing the risk of war. The big powers do not consider their vital interests as deeply involved in the Third World as in Europe, she argues. Thus a Third World nonintervention regime would help instill and reinforce inhibitions against the use of force as an instrument of power and a legitimate means of resolving conflicts. Forsberg concludes that this new regime cannot be enforced. Rather, it can only function as a product of perceived self-interest.

Civilian-Based Defense

Context

In his review of the security dilemmas of small neutral states, Gene Sharp rejects deterrence by either nuclear or large-scale conventional forces as unstable and incapable of providing a genuine defense. As Sharp puts it, "the capacity to defend in order to deter has been replaced by the capacity to destroy massively without the ability to defend."[28] Development of a nuclear force by any of the small European states would require breaking with international efforts to curb proliferation and accepting a nuclear commitment with all the uncertainties so often reflected in West European angst concerning extended deterrence. Sharp argues that the reach of modern conventional weaponry vitiates the traditional notion of defense at the frontier and that the destructive power of these systems means that a protracted nonnuclear war would result in devastation of one's own territory. Thus, Sharp concludes, war and traditional preparations for war have lost much of their rationale as instruments of national policy for these states.

For Sharp, the greatest weakness of NATO's present deterrent strategy is that it can fail with catastrophic consequences. Neither a policy of no first use of nuclear weapons nor a purely conventional defense overcomes this basic flaw. As Sharp sees it, traditional military means cannot both deter and defend populations. He argues that any viable defense system should provide remedial means for protecting a society after deterrence has failed. His system of civilian-based defense is intended to provide for the security of small states in the current global situation with the tacit recognition that it has wider applications in a changed world order.

Three decades earlier, an Englishman, Sir Stephen King Hall, reached similar conclusions about the need for an alternative to nuclear deterrence. King Hall proposed that the European NATO allies switch to a defense policy based on "political and moral force" and prepare their populations for nonviolent resistance to occupation. He advocated maintaining conventional forces sufficient to provide token resistance to a Soviet invasion during the transition to a civilian-based defense, at which time the limited remaining military forces would be used for internal security functions.[29]

Definition and Operational Characteristics

The term *civilian-based defense* (CBD) is used to describe a broad array of nonviolent political, social, economic, and psychological instruments of power. There are three general methods of civilian-based defense: nonviolent protest and persuasion; social, economic, and political noncooperation and boycotts; and nonviolent intervention. Widespread training of the population in the various tactics of civilian-based defense forms the basis for a reactive strategy that seeks to frustrate efforts of any government or hostile group to achieve political or economic aims by the use of force.[30]

Civilian-based defense might influence an opponent through conversion, nonviolent coercion, or persuasion. In the first case, the defenders attempt to convince the invading force that their cause is unjust and that they should defect or cease and desist. Nonviolent coercion is a more familiar method, essentially an effort to deny an aggressor the fruits of its action by noncooperation. Persuasion is an effort by an international forum to orchestrate political and other pressures that cause an opponent to change its policy.

Civilian-based resistance is largely the province of the peace research community in Europe and to a lesser extent in the United States. In several neutral European countries, CBD forms a small part of operational defense plans. Several other Western governments have studied the utility of CBD or are now doing so.

Advocates of civilian-based defense focus on spirals of conflict rather than the stability of deterrence. CBD seeks to cut off the potential for conflict by providing a nonprovocative means of ensuring security. Relying on extended nuclear or conventional deterrence or developing large military forces of their own, Sharp argues, would make the small European countries potential targets. However, a state with an extensive CBD plan might still be perceived as a threat by a neighboring government with uncertain domestic support. Sharp notes that the Soviets might find adoption of CBD in Western Europe threatening to their internal control because of the possible emulation of these nonviolent methods in Eastern Europe or parts of the USSR.

There are three general ways in which CBD might be applied: as an adjunct to a strategy that used nuclear weapons, traditional conventional forces, or nonprovocative defenses; as a substitute for conventional and nuclear defense in special circumstances such as a coup d'état or defeat of military forces; or as a permanent and complete alternative defense policy. Here we consider the role CBD could play in a world where the role of nuclear and/or conventional military deterrence is greatly reduced or eliminated, the circumstances under which CBD might become the strategy of various countries, and ways to accomplish the transition to this world.

Widespread adoption of CBD is virtually unthinkable unless nuclear weapons had been entirely abolished; even then it is not clear how CBD would deter nuclear rearmament. CBD would appear to undermine the credibility of any nuclear escalation strategy backed by a minimal deterrent force. If a nuclear state had extensive CBD plans, it would imply that nuclear weapons might not be used to preclude the loss of national territory. Given that dramatic political changes would be needed for the elimination of all nuclear weapons, it might well be possible, in that context, to achieve multilateral agreement on a CBD regime as the new ultimate guarantor of each state's security. Clearly, this would be a world with an unprecedented degree of cooperation among states, and probably a greatly diminished level of perceived military threats. In this world, one can imagine CBD serving as either a substitute for conventional military defenses or as an ultimate deterrent after the collapse of a traditional or nonprovocative conventional military defense.

The process of shifting completely to CBD, or transarmament, also appears much less complicated in this nuclear abolitionist context. Most schemes for transarmament envision a very long-term snowballing process initiated by the example of several small countries, which would convince the rest of the world of the viability of CBD as they moved from partial to total reliance on this strategy for their defense.[31] CBD could be imposed by mutual agreement of the denuclearized states or by some form of world government or other international mechanism established to enforce the nuclear disarmament process.

Assessments and Unanswered Questions

Nonprovocative Defense: A Preliminary Assessment

The proposals for nonprovocative defense described in this chapter have dubious deterrent effect in themselves, because they falsely assume that the problems faced by the attacker and defender are thoroughly different. Most of these concepts leave the defender with limited capability for offensive counterattack for repulsing or evicting invading forces. A more effective deterrent would blend some elements of punishment *and* denial. A state that relies on the pure form of deterrence by denial, inherent in the nonprovocative defense concepts, runs the risk of tempting a potential aggressor to wear down its defenses. A related operational shortcoming is that these concepts advocate largely reactive measures to be undertaken after an attack has begun, making them highly vulnerable to surprise attack.

Most of the current European concepts, particularly Afheldt's, focus too narrowly on the threat of heavily armored assaults. The NATO countries and most industrialized states confront multidimensional security threats, including combined air and ground force operations. According to a study by the Dutch Ministry of Defence, these antitank-oriented defense postures could be severely degraded by infantry attacks supported with artillery fire.[32] Such defenses could also stimulate and be overtaken by a technical arms race in anti-tank guided weapons (ATGW) countermeasures and new forms of armor. These ATGW units may also be subject to piecemeal destruction by heavy mechanized forces. Finally, all of these concepts are premised on the realization of some immature conventional weapons technologies and on the unverifiable assumption that these emerging technologies are shifting combat advantage to the defense.

Systems analysis studies in Germany have suggested that at least some of these alternative defense options are more cost-effective than aspects of the Bundeswehr's existing Active Defense plans. Several analysts involved in these studies have argued that these traditional and alternative defense concepts should be considered in a more integrative rather than a mutually exclusive fashion. One study concluded that "incorporation of properly designed reactive defense into NATO's existing force structure could indeed contribute to a significant improvement of NATO's forward defenses," even without the availability of emerging technologies.[33]

The advocates of defensive defense have shown how their ideas would operate in the countryside, but have generally neglected to indicate how these concepts would be applied in urban settings. Instead, most have simply stated that they would avoid, as much as possible, conducting defensive operations in cities. This would be a particularly difficult feat in a country with West Germany's development density. This lacuna may be partly explained by political sensibilities in West Germany, where discussion of urban warfare is hardly popular. Theorists who have broached the urban problem, such as Wilhelm Nolte, have suggested that civilian resistance in the cities would be the most appropriate adjunct to their territorial defense concepts.[34] However, given the nature of the Central European landscape and most modern industrialized states, urban welfare is likely to be a significant aspect of future conflicts. Thus one of the principal dividends touted by advocates of nonprovocative defense is avoiding the massive societal destruction likely to accompany modern conventional warfare.

All these theorists agree that war would be much less likely to erupt by miscalculation if the West adopted a defensive defense posture unilaterally. Moreover, they argue, if this deterrent did fail, it would be much easier to terminate a war with less capable forces on one or both sides than currently exist. In a similar vein, it is argued that the East's incentives to pre-empt NATO militarily would virtually disappear if the West had no offensive capability. Conversely, they contend, NATO's current offensive nuclear doctrine and any offensive conventional military plans provide a convenient rationale for the sustained Soviet buildup. Finally, most advocates of this posture feel that it could, in the long run, facilitate the evolution of a new politico-military situation in Europe, and may be essential to ending the division of the continent.

Thus most European supporters of nonprovocative defense concepts assume the security problem for NATO and the Warsaw Pact is to adapt the military means of the two sides to their defensive political goals. Without addressing the dubious notion that the Soviet Union has purely defensive goals in its military planning vis-à-vis Western Europe, this assumption illustrates another problem in applying these notions on a global scale. Could nonprovocative defense concepts deter a state with clearly hostile political objectives? For example, would a nonprovocative Iraqi defense posture have deterred Iranian attacks over the past seven years? Similarly, in reference to Randall Forsberg's model, the absence of superpower involvement in the Persian Gulf would hardly have precluded the Iran–Iraq war or other Third World conflicts rooted in unique cultural, historical, and economic antagonisms.

The moderate proponents of nonprovocative defenses advocate multilateral negotiations to achieve the desired force structures. The more radical advocates would pursue these changes unilaterally, while offering unspecified "incentives" to the East to emulate this shift in its own military posture. It is hard to envision why the East would wish to reduce its military edge in Europe after the West made such a dramatic unilateral shift. Similarly, it is difficult to envision circumstances other than mutual decline or development of some form of world government under which the United States and the USSR, with their global interests, would agree to adopt a defense posture incapable of projecting power. It is likely that nonprovocative defenses would have to be adopted unilaterally by various small states. Such shifts actually seem more likely when a balance of power continues to provide global or regional stability.

The Defensive Defense World

The applicability of nonprovocative and civilian-based defense strategies has been discussed thus far largely in the context of the present East–West confrontation in Europe. Their application in various future worlds, including those discussed in this volume, remains to be examined.

As the preceding discussion shows, it is difficult to establish precisely what distinguishes defensive from offensive weapons systems and strategies; these difficulties are compounded when one considers the question in global perspective. The defensive nature of any military forces rests in their application and in the perception of their likely application. Even if two large states negotiated defensive force postures and strategies vis-à-vis one another, these same capabilities might still look very threatening and provocative to a smaller third state not party to the accord.

Similarly, even if one could define a purely defensive military force, with no capability to project itself into another country, those forces might still be used for purposes of aggression. There would be no stopping the Soviet Union from loading several divisions of border guards into Aeroflot aircraft and attempting to impose its will on a less powerful third country that had also agreed to field only border guards.

Other critical questions need to be addressed, such as the militarization of society in a defensive defense world. The shift from large standing and/or professional armies to large groups of citizen-soldiers may not be attractive to authoritarian societies with marginal political legitimacy. The Soviet Union would hardly find appealing the prospect of decentralized reserve forces forming the backbone of its defenses, nor would many countries in the Third World. These reserves would represent a potential threat to governmental control and hence to domestic and possibly regional stability.

The proposition that large offensive military capabilities are in themselves a trigger of war needs more detailed analysis. It is not at all clear that a regime of defensive defenses will be more stable than our current predicament. After all, much of world military history concerns conflicts between forces that were essentially border guards.

Civilian-Based Defense

It is difficult to envision any circumstances in the next fifty years, short of nuclear abolition and universal subscription to certain norms of international behavior, whereby nonviolent civilian resistance could be the sole basis of any state's security strategy. In worlds such as our own, CBD can supplement with a limited effect nonnuclear defense postures of neutral states, particularly as a safeguard against the collapse of military resistance to external aggression. However, even in this context, history shows that it is difficult to sustain such efforts for very long or with much success in the absence of external military support. To realize a national defense strategy based solely on civilian-based resistance, a modern state would also require a degree of domestic political cooperation unprecedented in history. This level of organizing could also lead to societal factionalization, more disruptive subnational conflicts, or, if imposed in a highly centralized, coercive way, to an authoritarian social order. Negotiating this strategy into a world ordering principle might even be beyond the reach of a supranational government. Like nonprovocative defense, CBD suffers from a credibility problem due to its inability to punish an aggressor. It relies exclusively on a state's convincing an adversary that its population is willing to suffer extreme repression to deny achievement of certain political objectives. The effectiveness of this deterrent would ultimately turn on the value of the objective at issue to both the attacking and defending state. If the objective had equal value to both states, a stable political situation might result. However, an aggressor state might be motivated to attack if it sensed the defender's willingness to suffer for a principle was low.

Advocates of CBD also need to specify how their system would deal with efforts by hostile states to exert influence short of invasion. How could CBD address violations of a state's territorial integrity by another country seeking easy access to a third state? Sharp dismisses the importance of safeguarding territory, but erosion of territorial control could undermine the credibility of even a CBD deterrent posture.

Finally, neither CBD strategies nor nonprovocative defenses solve the problem of catastrophic failure, which their advocates see as the central problem with nuclear and traditional conventional deterrence. Failure of any of the three alternatives reviewed in this chapter could also result in total societal destruction. In addition, all three postures examined here offer less convincing deterrents to aggression than do nuclear weapons or large conventional forces.

CHAPTER 6

From Confrontation to Cooperation: Transforming the U.S.–Soviet Relationship

Sean M. Lynn-Jones and Stephen R. Rock

We must go behind the missiles to the Cold War itself.
—*E. P. Thompson*

Confrontation is not an innate defect in our relations; it is an anomaly. It is not inevitable that it should be maintained. We consider an improvement in Soviet–American relations not only necessary, but also possible.
—*Mikhail Gorbachev*

The two superpowers have nothing to gain by eternal conflict.
—*Henry Kissinger*

In 1985 the *Christian Science Monitor* held a contest. In response to its request for essays on how peace might come to the world by the year 2010, over 1,300 entries poured in. The essays presented many different scenarios for the evolution of a peaceful world, but the one theme sounded most often was the need to improve U.S.–Soviet relations.[1]

The idea of removing the threat of nuclear catastrophe through a fundamental transformation of superpower relations—from confrontation to cooperation—makes sense to many people. It is surprising, therefore, that this notion has been ignored in much of the contemporary debate on reducing the risk of nuclear war. Many recent proposals instead emphasize the need to control the nuclear arsenals of the United States and the Soviet Union. George Kennan, Robert McNamara, Jonathan Schell, Richard Ullman, and others have called for major reductions in superpower stockpiles or even the complete elimination of nuclear weapons.[2]

These proposals, as well as President Reagan's vision of perfect defenses against nuclear attack, reflect the conviction that the size and composition of nuclear arsenals are the primary factors influencing the likelihood and destructiveness of nuclear war.[3]

Despite widespread concern about the risks of a major nuclear war between the United States and the Soviet Union, relatively little serious attention has been paid to how improved U.S.-Soviet relations might, in themselves, reduce the danger of war between the superpowers. Improved relations are often seen as a prerequisite for reducing nuclear arsenals or as a likely result of negotiated arms limitation agreements. But the widespread preoccupation with numbers of weapons has obscured the essential truth that political relations between the two countries may have a powerful effect on the likelihood of nuclear war regardless of the size and composition of superpower nuclear arsenals. Great Britain, France, and China possess (or will soon possess) the capability to inflict substantial damage on the United States in a nuclear exchange, but few worry about that prospect, because the United States has good political relations with each of these countries.[4]

This chapter will explicate the arguments for a far-reaching political accommodation between the United States and the Soviet Union. We will attempt to spell out what a world of U.S.-Soviet cooperation might look like. We will examine some scenarios of how U.S.-Soviet relations might be fundamentally transformed over the next fifty years. Finally, we will analyze the costs and benefits associated with such a world, to see how desirable it would really be.

What Would a World of U.S.-Soviet Cooperation Look Like?

A fundamental transformation of U.S.-Soviet relations would radically change the basis for international security and the role of nuclear weapons. In the present U.S.-Soviet relationship, war is avoided at least partly through the fear of mutual destruction. Deterrence is regarded as an important means of maintaining the peace, and the composition and levels of U.S. and Soviet nuclear forces receive close attention. As Lawrence Freedman points out, "the political framework has been taken too much for granted and strategic studies have become infatuated with the microscopic analysis of military technology and the acquisition of equipment by the forces of both sides."[5] In a world in which the U.S.-Soviet political antagonism is assumed to be permanent, debates about the risk of nuclear war revolve around questions of force levels, missile accuracy and vulnerability, the possibility of strategic defenses, and the reliability of command and control systems. If U.S.–Soviet relations were placed on a friendly footing, however, these factors would be much less relevant. As in the case of Britain and the United States, the possession of nuclear weapons by both sides, and the nature of the strategic balance, would be of far less concern.

Nuclear deterrence as a means of preventing war has been much criticized on both ethical and practical grounds. Many critics of deterrence argue that a transformation of the U.S.–Soviet political relationship is the best way to achieve a substantial reduction in the risk of nuclear disaster. One such analyst, Michael MccGwire, claims that "the danger of war stems from the adversarial nature of the Soviet–American relationship, not from their nuclear arsenals." He suggests that "deterrence dogma" has diverted attention from "the central importance of the Soviet–American political relationship as the potential source of global war."[6]

The notion of avoiding nuclear war by improving U.S.–Soviet relations is intuitively logical and very appealing as a solution to the problems of nuclear deterrence. Yet few of its proponents have offered detailed visions of what a world of U.S.–Soviet cooperation might look like. MccGwire, for example, exhorts us "to tackle the root of our immediate problem, namely East–West relations in general and Soviet–American relations in particular," but he provides no specific suggestions about what sort of relationship is necessary or how it might be attained.[7] As William Hyland has noted, "we have rarely thought out the concrete terms of a settlement with the Soviet Union."[8]

Walt Rostow and George Liska are among the few analysts who have offered outlines of a world in which the United States and the Soviet Union have fundamentally transformed their adversarial relationship.[9] It is important to stress that such a transformation would go well beyond détente. Détente is a framework for reducing tension and managing rivalry between two basically antagonistic countries.[10] In a world of U.S.–Soviet accommodation, however, the political differences that divide the superpowers would no longer be a potential source of war. The superpowers would have either resolved such differences or found more important common interests to override them. Moscow and Washington would have a relationship of the type Karl Deutsch calls a "security community," in which countries "will not fight each other physically, but will settle their disputes in some other way."[11] Détente might be the start of a process that would eventually lead to such a relationship, but it would not be the endpoint.

In a world of U.S.–Soviet cooperation, the major issues that now divide the two countries would presumably have been solved. The issues most frequently identified as central to the current antagonism are nuclear weapons, the control of Europe, and conflicts in the Third World.[12] The precise nature of the superpower dispute in these areas is often remarkably vague.[13] Nor is it always clear whether these differences are primarily a cause or a consequence of U.S.–Soviet hostility. In any event, it is difficult to imagine a world of U.S.–Soviet accommodation in which these issues remained unresolved.

Nuclear Weapons

If political factors are the root causes of U.S.–Soviet rivalry, nuclear weapons will have little independent influence on superpower relations or the risk of war. But the existence of huge nuclear arsenals aimed at one another can hardly be conducive to improved U.S.–Soviet relations. Thus any real transformation would probably be accompanied by serious attempts at arms control or disarmament. Such agreements would not only symbolize and solidify the new relationship, but could also decrease the probability or destructiveness of an accidental conflict.

A variety of efforts in this direction can be envisioned. Cooperation between the United States and Soviet Union could include major reductions in nuclear forces that would leave both countries with a secure second-strike capability.[14] Potentially destabilizing technologies could be prohibited or regulated by mutual agreement. Strategic defenses, for example, might be prohibited *or* deployed subject to U.S.–Soviet understandings that would render them stabilizing.[15] Nuclear arsenals would still exist, but the process of competitively arming would come to a halt. In the absence of a technological or quantitative arms race, suspicions that one country was seeking nuclear superiority would be laid to rest. With an improvement in political relations, more intrusive verification would become possible. Measures to reduce the risk of accidental war, such as the Hot Line and U.S.–Soviet crisis centers, would also be continued and expanded. Increasing interchanges between U.S. and Soviet military staffs could provide reassurance about the nonthreatening nature of doctrines and force structures.[16] The two superpowers would intensify their efforts to implement the Nuclear Nonproliferation Treaty and might also seek agreements with other nuclear powers on force ceilings.[17]

Reconciliation in Europe

Europe has been the central theater for U.S.-Soviet rivalry since 1945. Accommodation between Washington and Moscow would almost certainly include political and military agreements that would transform the confrontation between NATO and the Warsaw Pact. Walt Rostow envisions negotiated reductions in the military forces of both alliances and an increase in national political freedom in Eastern Europe.[18] George Liska foresees the United States accepting a greater Soviet diplomatic role in Western Europe in return for the loosening of Soviet control over Warsaw Pact members. The resulting arrangement might be one in which Eastern Europe was "Finlandized" while Western Europe was "Hollandized."[19] Many Europeans on both sides of the Iron Curtain have called for similar changes that would gradually overcome the division of Europe into rival blocs. The elements of such proposals generally include reductions in the U.S. and Soviet military presence in Europe; removal of nuclear weapons from Europe; greater autonomy from the United States for Western Europe; and increased political freedom and autonomy from the Soviet Union in Eastern Europe.[20] Whatever their precise details, visions of a stable end to U.S.-Soviet rivalry in Europe usually are based on a reduced superpower military presence in that continent and the acceptance of greater European autonomy.[21]

Rivalry in the Third World

Although the stakes have been lower than in Europe, U.S.-Soviet rivalry in the Third World has posed many obstacles to improved superpower relations. Many critics of the détente of the 1970s claim that Soviet "adventurism" in the Third World undermined U.S. attempts to build a more cooperative relationship. Others point out that Moscow and Washington were incapable of devising mutually acceptable "rules of the game" to govern their involvement in regional conflicts.[22] Indeed, many people believe that the most likely scenario for the outbreak of nuclear war involves a superpower confrontation over the Middle East or the Persian Gulf. The stability of any far-reaching improvement in U.S.-Soviet relations would thus depend on achieving a modus vivendi in the Third World.

Two basic approaches to ending U.S.-Soviet rivalry in the Third World appear theoretically possible. The first is the establishment of a superpower condominium in which the United States and the Soviet

Union would exercise joint control over regional conflicts.[23] As Alton Frye has suggested, "the superpowers would bargain directly—not only on bilateral issues but also on arrangements to be imposed on other states whose disputes threaten to ignite wider war."[24] Similarly, George Liska has argued that a "far-reaching concert" amounting to a "quasi-condominial partnership" is needed to prevent regional conflicts from threatening world peace.[25] A condominial approach to such conflicts might include mutual guarantees of the security of Third World states or even joint peace-keeping forces. Moscow and Washington would act in concert instead of competing for power and influence.

The second approach calls for superpower disengagement from areas of competition. Randall Forsberg contends that U.S. and Soviet intervention in the Third World is the most dangerous use of force in the contemporary world. Instead of arguing for joint action to control Third World conflicts, she advocates an end to all U.S. and Soviet interventions: "The interventionary function of armed force must be replaced by a more democratic international system in which the extraordinary size and wealth of some nations no longer give them the right or the duty to act as global policemen."[26] Such proposals rest on the simple logic that U.S.-Soviet war will become less likely if the number of points of conflict can be limited. They also assume that regional conflicts are not always indigenous but are sometimes stimulated by U.S. and Soviet intervention.[27]

Any U.S.-Soviet regime to manage regional conflicts would probably include elements of both condominium and disengagement, depending on the level of superpower cooperation that was possible and the interests at stake for each in a given region. Both superpowers might, for example, be able to withdraw from much or all of Africa. In the Middle East, however, joint security guarantees and mediation might be necessary to avoid conflicts with a dangerous potential for escalation. Over time, disengagement might become more prevalent as power devolved to countries of the region. George Liska envisions U.S.-Soviet condominium as a means of managing the transition to greater stability in the Third World. He argues that "the perils [of such a transition] suggest the benefits of de-emphasizing U.S.-Soviet contention in the Third World in favor of jointly overseeing the long, unavoidably crisis-ridden process of forming viable national and regional orders there."[28]

Maintaining U.S.-Soviet Cooperation

U.S.-Soviet accommodation almost certainly would include a number of processes or institutions intended to ensure that superpower relations did not revert to hostility. As President John F. Kennedy said in his June 1963 American University speech, "Peace is a process—a way of solving problems." U.S.-Soviet cooperation might include regular summits and other contacts and consultations on nuclear forces and regional issues. Over time, these talks might be integrated into multilateral institutions. As U.S.-Soviet cooperation increased, such consultations might include economic issues. If the Soviet Union abandoned its autarkic tendencies, it might ultimately join the economic summits held by the major Western industrial powers, as well as institutions such as the Organization for Economic Cooperation and Development and the General Agreement on Trade and Tariffs. Cooperation could also be pursued in a variety of other areas, including scientific research, environmental protection, space exploration, and promotion of economic development in the Third World.

Pathways to U.S.-Soviet Accommodation

Many people find a fundamental transformation of U.S.-Soviet relations utterly implausible. When asked if it might be time to start thinking about how to end the Cold War, a senior State Department official reportedly replied, "Oh, it hadn't occurred to us that the Cold War might end."[29] This judgment can be found across the political spectrum. From the conservative end, Robert W. Tucker argues that "the structural and ideological determinants of the Soviet-American conflict are such that even a quite successful détente can be expected to affect only the margins of the relationship."[30] Liberals such as Robert McNamara and Hans Bethe agree that "profound differences and severe competition will surely continue to mark U.S.-Soviet relations."[31]

There is no shortage of explanations for U.S.-Soviet rivalry. Many scholars claim that the bipolar structure of the international system guarantees that the two superpowers will remain hostile.[32] Others argue that its commitment to Marxist ideology ensures that the Soviet regime will regard the United States as an adversary and will attempt to spread communism throughout the world. Marxists counter that the United States—the world's leading capitalist power—is inherently aggressive and imperialist. Even if only one of these ideological arguments is true, U.S.-Soviet cooperation would appear to be a remote possibility. Some observers do not emphasize ideology, but point to a long tradition of Russian xenophobia, paranoia, and expansionism.[33] Finally, many analysts claim that misperceptions, misunderstandings, and mutual suspicion generate U.S.-Soviet hostility even where there are no real clashes of interest. Taken together, these arguments suggest that the U.S.-Soviet competition is an over-determined phenomenon.

U.S.-Soviet rivalry has become such an enduring feature of world politics that it is often taken for granted. But this does not mean it will persist forever. Relations between the two countries have varied in the past. In the last fifty years, the United States and Soviet Union have entered into a wartime alliance and an era of détente in addition to periods of acute enmity. We should remember, moreover, that today's friendly relations between France and Germany or the United States and Japan would have been virtually unimaginable fifty years ago. As Marshall Shulman argues, "Predictions about anything so complex as the adversary relationship between the Soviet Union and the United States are probably best written in ink that is guaranteed to fade almost immediately."[33] At the very least, it is important to suspend doubt about the feasibility of U.S.-Soviet cooperation in order to think more clearly about how we might get from here to there. Even the most dubious skeptic may admit that certain developments, however improbable, could make U.S.-Soviet accommodation possible.

Structural Changes in the International System

Historically, great powers have frequently improved their relations in response to a threat from a third country. Before World War I, Britain and France, as well as France and Russia, patched up their quarrels when Germany acquired the potential to dominate Europe. During World War II, U.S.-Soviet cooperation reached its apogee when the two countries allied to fight Hitler. France and Germany went to war three times in seventy years, but since 1945 their common fear of Soviet domination has helped them to become friends and allies. In the future, the rise of a powerful rival to both the United States and the Soviet Union might prompt a sweeping reconciliation.

At present, however, no such rival looms on the horizon. In the next fifty years, only China seems poised to make a bid for superpower status, but daunting economic challenges will limit its global role for decades. A reunified Germany might be a potentially formidable rival, but neither the United States nor the Soviet Union is likely to permit German reunification. Japan has become the world's second-ranking economic power, but has shown no inclination to revive its aspirations for military power or to develop nuclear weapons.

Even if a third superpower emerged, the United States and the Soviet Union would not necessarily join forces against it. Depending on the configuration of power and the perceptions of threats, the third country might ally with the Soviet Union against the United States (or vice versa). The Soviet Union, after all, initially sought accommodation with Nazi Germany through the 1939 Molotov–Ribbentrop pact and aligned with the Western allies only after Hitler invaded it in 1941. In the absence of firm alliances, an unstable pattern of triangular rivalry might emerge, posing even greater dangers than the existing stable pattern of intense, but predictable, bipolar competition.

U.S.–Soviet cooperation might also be stimulated by structural changes that posed new but independent threats to each superpower. China for example, might become more threatening to the Soviet Union, but not to the United States, while the United States might confront increasing difficulties with Mexico and other Latin American countries. U.S.–Soviet differences might then seem less important than these regional concerns, prompting U.S.–Soviet reconciliation.

Shared concern about the gradual loss of global influence might also bring about U.S.–Soviet accommodation. George Liska argues that superpower cooperation is "the sole alternative to decline relative to third parties, regardless of how distant this prospect currently seems."[34] Moscow and Washington might cooperate to maintain their duopoly on world power rather than compete while other countries gained in relative power.

This scenario is more plausible than the emergence of a third superpower. If present trends continue to diffuse power away from the United States and the Soviet Union, it may even be likely. Nevertheless, Moscow and Washington would need tremendous foresight and consistency of purpose to cooperate to avoid the erosion of bipolarity. The two superpowers would share an interest in maintaining their relative power, but in a situation of mutual decline either might be tempted to seek short-term advantages at the expense of the other instead of long-term gains through cooperation. A perception of uneven decline could tempt one country to exploit its apparent superiority, creating fears in the other that might lead it to contemplate preventive war.[35]

Domestic Changes in the United States or the Soviet Union

Many observers have argued that domestic changes in the Soviet Union could enhance the prospects for U.S.–Soviet cooperation.[36] President Ronald Reagan has said that "significant democratic steps" are needed "for a fundamental improvement in relations between East and West."[37] If the Soviet Union became more democratic, less committed to Marxist-

Leninist ideology, and more interested in promoting economic welfare at home, it might be less hostile to the United States.

Although the Soviet regime has survived for seventy years, evolutionary or revolutionary changes could conceivably lead to the emergence of a liberal-democratic Russia during the next fifty years. The USSR already has shown considerable capacity for change: Gorbachev's regime is very different from Stalin's. Even President Reagan, who once saw the Soviet Union as an "evil empire," now sees "movement toward more openness, possibly even progress toward respect for human rights and economic reform."[38] Nevertheless, a fundamental change in the Soviet system of government is highly unlikely. Despite Gorbachev's widely heralded attempts at economic and political reform, the apparatus of Communist party rule remains in place. The current changes may be tactical attempts to enable the Soviet system to compete more effectively with the United States, not fundamental changes in the political system or its ideology. Moreover, the United States probably can have no more than marginal influence on the nature of the Soviet system. The USSR has steadfastly resisted attempts to impose changes from outside, as President Carter's human rights campaign amply demonstrated.

Whether a democratic Soviet Union—or a socialist United States—would lead to U.S.-Soviet cooperation depends on the extent to which ideology determines superpower relations. Since the early days of the Cold War, the ideological aspect of the U.S.-Soviet rivalry has become muted, but the competition continues nonetheless. If a bipolar international system always produces rivalry between its two leading members, domestic changes will have at best a limited effect.[39] Michael Doyle's exhaustive study of democracies and war suggests, however, that democratic countries virtually never go to war with one another.[40] Although there is no historical precedent for the existence of two democratic countries as the leading powers in a bipolar system, Doyle's conclusions lend plausibility to the hypothesis that a democratic Soviet Union would cooperate with the United States. Even if internal change did not lead to a reorientation of Soviet foreign policy, it would still remove some obstacles to U.S.-Soviet cooperation by quieting U.S. critics who argue against maintaining friendly good relations with a government that violates human rights.

Changes within the United States could also contribute to U.S.-Soviet cooperation. Without accepting Marxist arguments that the capitalist economy and military-industrial complex in the United States are the sole factors driving U.S.-Soviet rivalry, one can agree that U.S. domestic politics have exacerbated superpower tensions. Opportunities to improve

U.S.–Soviet relations may have been overlooked because of internal political factors. The visceral fear of communism that was expressed in the McCarthyism of the 1950s has probably prevented the United States from making more efforts to cooperate with the Soviet Union. Moreover, the inconsistent and erratic course of U.S. foreign policy has confused and frustrated the Soviets and complicated efforts to cooperate. As George Kennan has argued, "the motivations for American policy toward the Soviet Union from the start have been primarily subjective, not objective, in origin. They have represented for the most part not reactions to the nature of a certain external phenomenon (the Soviet regime) but rather the reflections of emotional and political impulses making themselves felt on the internal American scene."[41] Merely overcoming these domestic barriers to consistency and coherence in U.S. policy toward the Soviet Union would not transform U.S.–Soviet relations. However, it is hard to imagine that the relationship can be significantly improved without a more stable U.S. policy toward Moscow.

Technological and Economic Change

Many analysts have argued that the need to maintain economic growth rates and competitiveness will motivate the United States and the Soviet Union to ameliorate their rivalry. Friendlier relations would allow the two superpowers to invest greater resources in their economies. Walt Rostow has recently claimed that advanced technologies and rising educational levels in the developing countries "are accelerating the diffusion of power away from both Washington and Moscow and posing domestic challenges that render the ideological aspects of the cold war increasingly anachronistic."[42] He suggests that new technologies in the fields of microelectronics, genetic engineering, industrial materials, lasers, communications, and robots will be absorbed by the many developing countries—including India and Mexico—that have trained a large new cohort of scientists and engineers. The challenge of Third World competition in these areas will require new domestic and international economic arrangements for the industrialized countries. The Soviet Union will have difficulty maintaining its power in this new international economy and will cooperate with the United States and other industrialized countries.[43] Others with similar visions of the future refer to the emergence of "the new age of geoeconomics."[44]

Rostow's scenario assumes that the Soviet Union will decide that it must take part in the development of new technologies and that it must cooperate with the United States. However rational such a course might be, it is by no means certain that Soviet leaders will follow it. Liberal theories of international relations traditionally have held that the quest for economic welfare will lead states to avoid military conflicts.[45] In practice, however, many countries have been more wedded to maintaining military power than liberal theorists would have predicted. On the eve of World War I, Norman Angell wrote in *The Great Illusion* that the economies of Europe were so interconnected that war would be impossible because it would have catastrophic economic effects.[46] He was right about the economic catastrophe, but wrong about the impossibility of war. History suggests that statesmen do not always make choices using the same standard of rationality as liberal theorists. Even if Rostow is correct about the likely evolution of the world economy, the Soviet Union might respond to such changes with a temporary foreign policy retrenchment, domestic reforms to increase productivity and innovation, and a more aggressive campaign to steal or buy Western technology. Indeed, Gorbachev's current policies could be interpreted as fitting into this pattern. Nevertheless, Rostow's vision reinforces the sense that the diffusion of power away from the superpowers will continue and perhaps even accelerate. The technological and economic changes he identifies may help to convince Washington and Moscow that their relative power will decline even more rapidly in the absence of U.S.–Soviet cooperation.

Greatly Heightened Fear of Nuclear War

Many advocates of U.S.–Soviet cooperation claim that the risk of nuclear war is so great that the United States and Soviet Union should recognize that they have no choice but to improve relations. The two superpowers obviously share an interest in avoiding mutual annihilation. The evidence, however, indicates that this common interest alone is not sufficient to transform the U.S.–Soviet relationship. Fears of nuclear catastrophe have in the past motivated the superpowers to lessen tensions. The trauma of the Cuban missile crisis led to the Limited Test Ban Treaty and other cooperative efforts. But fears of nuclear war have not yet been sufficient to produce a fundamental transformation of U.S.–Soviet relations. Indeed, each relaxation of tensions has been followed by a period of renewed confrontation and heightened competition. The apparent stability of the current strategic balance (compared with the situation in the late 1950s or early 1960s) may further limit the motivation provided by fear of nuclear war.

An acute crisis or even a limited nuclear war might leave U.S. and Soviet leaders more concerned about the dangers of nuclear war. Herman

Kahn once claimed that in the aftermath of a limited nuclear exchange the U.S. president and Soviet general secretary would immediately talk on the telephone and agree to implement the Clark–Sohn plan for world government.[47] Even if U.S. and Soviet leaders did not go that far, they still might agree to reconcile their differences for the sake of avoiding another nuclear conflict. However, few would advocate risking even a small nuclear war as a means of improving superpower relations.

Nonnuclear catastrophes might also generate incentives for U.S.–Soviet cooperation. For example, the two superpowers might join forces to combat a climatic disaster, epidemic disease, or environmental crisis. In the next fifty years such a crisis is indeed possible, though hardly predictable. Early 1970s predictions of an ecological disaster that would bring about U.S.–Soviet cooperation appear to have been greatly exaggerated. Even the threat of a major catastrophe might not be sufficient to produce a reconciliation. The superpowers would probably have unequal stakes in many climatic or ecological crises. A small increase in global temperatures, for example, might threaten to turn U.S. wheatfields into a dust bowl while increasing the fertility of Soviet farmlands.

Changes in the Process of U.S.–Soviet Interaction

If the United States and the Soviet Union already have at least latent interests in cooperation, U.S.–Soviet accommodation could come about through a gradual change in the process of interaction between the two countries. Those who favor this approach believe that geopolitical and ideological obstacles to U.S.–Soviet cooperation may be less important than mutual misperceptions, misdefined interests, and other damaging psychological effects of the "malignant social process" of Soviet–American interactions.[48] In their view, relations could be dramatically improved through constructive processes of cooperation that would halt, and then reverse, the spiral of hostility that has plagued superpower relations since the beginning of the Cold War.[49]

Strategies of De-escalation. Several specific strategies of de-escalation have been proposed that might establish and perpetuate more cooperative superpower relations. One particularly prominent and enduring strategy is Charles Osgood's Graduated Reciprocation in Tension-reduction (GRIT), described most fully in his 1962 work, *An Alternative to War or Surrender.*[50] GRIT requires that the United States undertake a series of unilateral tension-reducing initiatives. These would inspire the Soviet Union to reciprocate, beginning a process of cooperation and counter-cooperation. Osgood insisted that the initiatives be graduated in risk, according to the degree of reciprocation obtained from the USSR.[51]

Closely related to GRIT is the strategy of gradualism, proposed by Amitai Etzioni in his 1962 volume, *The Hard Way to Peace*.[52] Gradualism was to operate in three stages. First, the United States would take some unilateral, symbolic steps to reduce international tensions. Next it would make substantive concessions, expecting the Soviet Union to reciprocate. Finally, the United States would suggest bilateral negotiations that would result in simultaneous and matched concessions. At this last step in the process, significant arms reductions would occur and important political questions would be resolved. Like Osgood, Etzioni insisted that his strategy entailed little if any risk to the United States because it involved a series of graduated steps and could be stopped at any point.

The "tit-for-tat" approach, given strong support by Robert Axelrod in his *The Evolution of Cooperation*, resembles GRIT and gradualism, but calls for the party that initiates the cooperative process to reciprocate at every turn the behavior of the other side.[53] The response to cooperation is cooperation, while the response to defection is defection. The strategy is predicated on the notion that the second party will soon recognize that its defection means mutual defection, whereas its cooperation means mutual cooperation. Once this is seen, the only rational strategy is to cooperate.

Perhaps the latest entrants into the de-escalation game are the international regime theorists.[54] Regimes, which consist of norms, rules, and procedures, may evolve in many areas, but in the case of the United States and Soviet Union have been confined largely to security affairs. The Nuclear Nonproliferation Treaty is the prime example of a U.S.–Soviet security regime. The two superpowers have cooperated over almost twenty years to prevent the spread of nuclear weapons.[55] A less successful, but still important, security regime is the U.S.–Soviet SALT/START strategic arms control process and its accompanying institutions.[56] Scholars have become increasingly interested in the ways in which regimes promote the redefinition of individual interests and the evolution of common ones. It appears that regimes facilitate the learning of cooperation, and theorists have begun to investigate not only how this occurs, but whether the learning of cooperation in one issue area—for example, crisis management—might spill over into other aspects of relations.[57]

Areas of Cooperation. The gradual de-escalation of the U.S.–Soviet rivalry could be pursued in a wide variety of areas.[58] Some authors have argued that expanded U.S.-Soviet trade and joint efforts to deal with common problems of health, the environment, and world hunger "would encourage a psychological pattern and attitude of cooperation."[59] Even Edward Teller, for example, proposes U.S.-Soviet projects in the "development of ocean-food resources, and work on weather prediction and modification," arguing that "joint work forges the human links that lead to understanding."[60] Daniel Deudney claims that "a two-part agenda—involving deep-space pioneering on the one hand and global habitability studies and information security on the other—could, over time, help transform the U.S.-Soviet relationship."[61] High-level contacts between U.S. and Soviet government officials may be a particularly promising way of developing common interests and perspectives in the long run. Indeed, many advocates of U.S.-Soviet cooperation press for greatly expanded contacts of all types and at all levels—between political leaders, scientists, businessmen, athletes, writers, artists, and ordinary citizens. Consistent with this theme, the International Group of the Aspen Institute has called for a pattern of "sustained engagement," involving heightened interaction and cooperation in the political relationship, the security relationship, the economic relationship, and other spheres, including science, the humanities, education, medicine, and technology.[62]

The Dynamics of De-escalation. Although advocates of change in the process of U.S.-Soviet interaction sometimes differ in their assessments of how far superpower cooperation might be expected to evolve, virtually all view it as having a spiral dynamic. In other words, cooperation breeds cooperation—for several reasons. First, cooperative ventures—such as contacts, trade, and functional interaction—may provide both sides with more and better information about one another's capabilities and intentions. Such information may enable them to forego worst-case analyses and to engage in further cooperative efforts that would otherwise have seemed too risky.[63] Second, cooperation may help each side appreciate the legitimacy of the other's interests.[64] This "realistic empathy" may enhance both sides' willingness to compromise.[65] Third, cooperation may cause the states to redefine their own interests. This might occur because of the internalization of a norm of cooperation, which would increase the benefits of one's own cooperation and the costs of defection.[66] Alternatively the experience of cooperation might modify perceptions of the other side. One will be more willing to risk a cooperative strategy if the other seems likely to reciprocate. Fourth, because cooperation reduces tensions, it facilitates the settling of disputes. As Morton Deutsch points out, "excessive tension reduces the intellectual resources available for discovering new ways of coping with a problem or new ideas for resolving a conflict."[67] Finally, cooperation promotes a trusting, friendly atmosphere in which sensitivity to similarities and common interests is increased, while the salience of differences is minimized.

Assessing De-escalation. Unfortunately, evidence for the success or failure of de-escalation comes mainly from computer simulations or psychology experiments that use individual human beings as subjects, not from the diplomatic record of states in the international system.[68] One study of GRIT and gradualism concluded that the strategy had been employed only once in the last twenty-five years, in the so-called Kennedy Experiment.[69] Proposed by President John F. Kennedy in June 1963, the initiative succeeded in producing matched reductions in defense budgets by the United States and Soviet Union until mid-1965, when Kennedy's successor, Lyndon B. Johnson, asked Congress for supplemental appropriations to fight the war in Vietnam.[70] Some additional examples of de-escalation have been noted. Steven Spiegel argues that the United States and the People's Republic of China have followed a "calibrated détente strategy" in recent years.[71] Deborah Larson suggests that a GRIT strategy led to the 1955 Austrian State Treaty and accompanying "spirit of Geneva."[72] Relations between Egypt and Israel since the historic meeting of Begin and Sadat may reflect a similar dynamic.[73] But a long list is difficult to compile, and it is harder still to argue that anything like a fundamental transformation of relations has occurred via this route alone.

The current superpower hostility is not merely the consequence of misperceptions, misdefined interests, or other problems largely psychological in origin. Even if all such barriers could be removed, other obstacles would still persist.[74] The more realistic proponents of de-escalation as a path to peace recognize this difficulty. Herbert Kelman admits that "international conflicts typically evolve out of real conflicts of interest and ideological differences that cannot be attributed simply to misperception and distrust" and that "overcoming these barriers does not in itself resolve a conflict."[75]

There is no historical precedent for a fundamental transformation of the relationship of two great powers through a gradual evolution in their process of interaction. Previous cases of great power reconciliation suggest the need for a common enemy or cultural and political similarities.[76] Still, improving the process of interaction between the United States and the Soviet Union might remove some of the obstacles to cooperation.

Indeed, one can argue that unless the psychological barriers produced by dysfunctional processes of interaction are removed, favorable changes in the structure of the international system or in the domestic politics of the two countries will not lead to better relations. For example, the United States was slow to awaken to the possibility of rapprochement with China because the two countries were not interacting constructively. More than a decade after the Sino–Soviet split, most Americans still viewed China as part of an international communist monolith and therefore incapable of any meaningful accommodation. Finally, of all the factors affecting superpower relations, the process of U.S.–Soviet interaction may be the one most easily manipulated. The two countries will find it difficult, if not impossible, to control the international distribution of power over the long term. Neither will be able to exercise much influence over the domestic politics of the other. But a change in the process of superpower interaction could be initiated quickly and then expanded by conscious policy decisions on the part of the two governments.

Multiple Pathways

Just as the U.S.–Soviet antagonism appears to have multiple causes, a fundamental transformation of U.S.–Soviet relations seems most likely to occur as the result of mutually reinforcing changes along several dimensions—in the structure of the international system, in the domestic politics of the superpowers, in the processes of interaction between them, perhaps even in the fear of war. The transformation of relations between France and Germany in the years following World War II illustrates this point. The reconciliation of these once-bitter enemies was encouraged by their relative decline and the emergence of the Soviet threat, by the virtual eradication of Nazism in Germany and the establishment of a stable democratic government there, and by the horrors of the conflict just ended. It was also facilitated by the establishment of new patterns of Franco-German interaction, particularly within the European Community. These patterns, over time, appear to have brought about a measure of trust and the perception of common interest unprecedented in the history of these two countries.

Evaluating a World of U.S.–Soviet Cooperation

To many, it will seem axiomatic that political accommodation between the superpowers would produce a more desirable world—a world in which the risk of nuclear catastrophe would be reduced dramatically. Nevertheless, there are some conditions under which U.S.–Soviet cooperation might not significantly lower the risk of war. Moreover, in a world in which U.S.–Soviet cooperation plays a significant and positive role, other values may have to be sacrificed for the sake of political accommodation.

The Risk of War

Paradoxically, while U.S.–Soviet cooperation would be more likely in a world that was not bipolar, this same erosion of bipolarity would render an accommodation less likely to reduce the danger of nuclear catastrophe. As we have noted, the emergence of a third superpower could create powerful incentives for U.S.–Soviet cooperation. However, the rivalry between such a power, on the one hand, and the United States and the Soviet Union, on the other, would pose a significant threat to world peace. Historically, Hitler's Germany has been the only rival powerful enough to bring about a U.S.–Soviet alliance. The emergence of a similar threat—from a nation that would probably possess nuclear weapons—would be a high price to pay for U.S.–Soviet cooperation. Moreover, in a multipolar world, U.S.–Soviet cooperation might actually engender third-country hostility. If a U.S.–Soviet condominium developed, other powerful nations might see their ambitions being thwarted and become belligerent, further raising the risk of war.[77]

A mutual decline in the relative power of the United States and Soviet Union that promoted U.S.–Soviet cooperation would also render that cooperation less relevant to the problem of avoiding war. In such a world, the U.S.–Soviet rivalry would no longer be the major axis of conflict. Other political rivalries at both the nuclear and conventional levels might pose more significant threats to peace. Moreover, the relative weakness of the United States and Soviet Union would leave them unable to manage or control these rivalries in a condominial fashion.[78]

Other American Interests

Far-reaching U.S.–Soviet cooperation might require the United States to renounce some of its traditional hopes for the liberation of Eastern Europe or for improvements in human rights in the Soviet Union. Whether one accepts this argument depends on one's interpretation of Soviet motivations. If it is true, as some have suggested, that the Soviets continue to dominate Eastern Europe largely out of fear, as a precaution against an aggressive and hostile West, cooperation and a transformed relationship might be the one thing that would actually induce the Soviets to loosen their control.[79] Similarly, if, as some have claimed, putting pressure on the Soviets to observe human rights is counterproductive, and the Soviet system becomes more repressive when the country is faced with external threats, cooperation with the Soviet States might actually promote liberalization within the Soviet Union.[80] As advocates of cooperation see it, the United States has made very little progress in pursuing these goals through confrontation in the last few decades; a cooperative strategy may therefore be well worth a try.[81]

Transition Problems: Deterrence Failure, Alliance Cohesion, Reversal

A fundamental transformation of the U.S.–Soviet relationship is most likely to occur gradually. As Walt Rostow has noted, "exit from the cold war should be viewed as a process—probably protracted—of getting from here to there."[82] The transition from confrontation to cooperation might create additional problems and dangers.

The first potential difficulty is deterrence failure. In a world of U.S.–Soviet accommodation, deterrence failure would not be a major problem because deterrence would no longer be the primary means of avoiding superpower conflict. During the transition from the present U.S.–Soviet relationship to a more cooperative one, however, either country might act aggressively if it interpreted the other's willingness to cooperate as evidence of weakness or irresolution. Critics of the U.S.–Soviet détente of the 1970s often claim that American attempts to cooperate with the Soviet Union only encouraged Soviet "adventurism" that led to crises in the Middle East, Angola, the Horn of Africa, and the invasion of Afghanistan.[83] The argument is plausible, but not necessarily correct. For example, Moscow's expansionist policy of this period could be attributed as easily to Soviet readings of the post-Vietnam anti-interventionist mood in the United States as to the belief that the pursuit of détente implied a lack of American resolve. A gradual build-up of cooperation, with reciprocity required for continuation, would make the strategy less risky than might be suspected. Moreover, given the present danger of a nuclear conflagration, some risk may be well worth running.

In any case, greater risk could be partly offset through crisis management procedures. Such manifestations of U.S.–Soviet cooperation, including the Hot Line and possible future U.S.–Soviet military communications links, would presumably reduce misunderstandings in crises instead of allowing them to spiral out of control. Even if an initial miscalculation led to a crisis, such procedures might keep it from escalating. Indeed, the 1973 Middle East Crisis, sometimes cited as evidence of the dangers of détente, may be interpreted as a success. Richard Stevenson argues that "the most important feature of the crisis was that the superpowers co-operated effectively in its resolution."[84] It may therefore be crucial to couple improvements in the atmosphere of interaction with concrete measures to reduce the risk of nuclear war. Finally, increased contacts between Soviets and Americans at various levels and on various issues might reduce the possibility of mutual misperceptions and therefore the probability of dangerous miscalculations.

The second problem that might be associated with the period of transformation is the weakening of alliance cohesion. The sort of settlement many envision for Europe would necessarily loosen alliance bonds in both NATO and the Warsaw Pact. U.S.–Soviet cooperation might also alienate America's allies if it required that certain rules be imposed on them against their wills. For example, joint action by Washington and Moscow in nonproliferation might involve the enforcement of an unpopular ban on the export of nuclear technologies. Or a reduction in the perceived threat from the Soviet Union—a consequence of collaboration—might make European countries and Japan less willing to accommodate the United States on economic or other issues in the interest of alliance solidarity. Experience during the era of détente suggests that some such effects would occur. But a loosening of alliance bonds would not necessarily harm the U.S. security position as much as cooperation with the Soviet Union would improve it. If the Soviet Union were less threatening, there would be less need for a cohesive coalition to oppose it. In any event, once a world of U.S.–Soviet cooperation was firmly established, alliance cohesion would no longer be a salient concern.

The third difficulty that might be associated with the transition period is the problem of premature reversal. If cooperation began and then faltered, the resulting disillusionment and attempts to assess blame might leave U.S.–Soviet relations worse off than before. Thus, for instance, unfulfilled expectations following U.S.–Soviet cooperation in World War II may have intensified the Cold War, and disappointment and mutual recriminations following the détente of the 1970s may have heightened the animosity of the present decade. One may argue, however, that the risk of worsening U.S.–Soviet relations is insignificant compared with the potential for improving them. Moreover, as a historian of recent U.S.–Soviet diplomacy has pointed out, failed détentes of the postwar era have not left U.S.–Soviet relations worse off than before. Indeed, though all these experiments eventually deteriorated, each resulted in a net improvement in superpower relations and an enhanced capacity for further collaboration.[85]

Conclusions

The principal problem with visions of U.S.–Soviet cooperation is feasibility. It takes a vivid imagination to envision a future in which Washington and Moscow overcome the many obstacles to a fundamental transformation of their relationship. Nevertheless, it is possible that common interests will emerge in the next fifty years. The superpowers already share a common interest in avoiding nuclear war, and they may recognize that each has a stake in the continued existence of the other as a great power. A common fear of rapid mutual decline and international instability could motivate U.S.–Soviet cooperation to manage the transition to a more multipolar world. Attempts to improve the process of superpower interaction, such as the development of security regimes, could help create a cognitive environment that would facilitate cooperation even if they did not in themselves transform the U.S.–Soviet relationship.

U.S.–Soviet cooperation is likely to become less promising as a means of avoiding nuclear catastrophe if the world becomes less bipolar. If nuclear proliferation, superpower decline, and the rise of regional powers combine to reduce U.S. and Soviet power, U.S.–Soviet relations will have less impact on the risk of nuclear war. A superpower condominium will become impossible. However, joint efforts to manage the move toward a stable future beyond bipolarity might reduce the dangers inherent in such a transition.

The most important lesson to be learned from speculating about the future of U.S.–Soviet relations is that the Cold War will not last forever. Every historical epoch eventually comes to an end. Virtually all contemporary strategic analysis proceeds from the assumption that U.S.–Soviet political accommodation is out of the question. Thinking about a world in which U.S.–Soviet relations are transformed fundamentally at least prompts us to reconsider this assumption and to plan for alternative futures.

CHAPTER 7

The Long-Term Moderation of Soviet Foreign Policy

Robert P. Beschel, Jr.

The USSR wants normal relations with the United States. There is simply no other sensible path from the standpoint of the interests of both of our nations and of mankind as a whole.
—*Leonid Brezhnev, 1981*

The Soviet Union is our antagonist and will be for the indefinite future.
—*Arthur Hartman, former American ambassador to Moscow, 1987*

Could a change in Soviet foreign policy transform U.S.–Soviet relations so that we would no longer fear a major nuclear war between these two states? This possibility is one of the more likely alternative worlds considered in this book. It would not require a fundamental technological breakthrough, a transformation of the international system away from the nation-state, or a change in the nature of state interaction. Indeed, if some analysts are correct, Mikhail Gorbachev may currently be pursuing such a reorientation in his drive to bring "new thinking" (*novoye myshleniye*) into Soviet foreign policy.[1]

This alternative, which emphasizes Soviet rather than American change, has been most Americans' preferred method of escaping from both nuclear and prenuclear security dilemmas.[2] Unlike many of the other alternatives, a significant moderation in Soviet policy seems highly unlikely to have negative repercussions for the United States.[3] This sentiment would not be universal; fears of a joint U.S.–Soviet condominium were prevalent in Europe during détente and would probably be revived. In addition, certain nations (such as Cuba, Egypt, and India) would find their special status, and their economic and security assistance, threatened by a reduction in superpower tensions. Even in the

United States, critics on the right would argue that such a change could be quite dangerous, by lulling the American public into a false sense of security that the Soviets would then exploit. Others, on the left, would maintain that U.S.–Soviet enmity is much more influenced by the structural requirements of modern capitalism, or the need of the military-industrial complex to manufacture an enemy, than by the nature of Soviet foreign policy. And yet an overwhelming majority of Americans would see a moderation in Soviet foreign policy as an unmitigated blessing.

Unfortunately, sharp disagreements persist even among Americans who would like to see the Soviet Union change. Some of these disputes center on the nature of a moderate Soviet foreign policy. Some have emphasized that the Soviets must modify their beliefs and renounce their objective of world revolution or their tactics of using any means in pursuit of this end. Others have emphasized the need for a change in Soviet behavior in the international arena. Still others have attacked the "evil" nature of the Soviet domestic regime. Walter Lippmann once remarked that we could define "moderation" as the point at which Soviet children are born singing "God Bless America."[4]

Other disagreements have centered on how this world of Soviet moderation might come about. This debate reflects fundamental differences within the American academic and policy community as to the sources of Soviet foreign policy and the roots of Soviet–American enmity. Some American scholars maintain that there can be no fundamental improvement in U.S.–Soviet relations without a transformation of the Soviet domestic system. Others believe that Soviet foreign policy is driven by external factors (such as the distribution of power within the international system) and can "mellow" without significant domestic changes. Still others maintain that Soviet foreign policy is currently moderate and defensive, and that an improvement in superpower relations will require a change in U.S. policy.

Greater analytic clarity can focus these debates, but is unlikely to resolve them. Since 1917 American attempts to understand the Soviet Union have been marked by disagreement as to what constitutes a mellow Soviet foreign policy and how it might be obtained. Since no "objective" definition is possible, Soviet mellowing must be addressed within the context of a particular author's views on the topic.

This chapter will examine the views of four leading students of international affairs on how Soviet–American enmity might be reduced. Two of these scholars, Richard Pipes and George Kennan, have envisioned a transformation of the Soviet Union itself as an essential step toward the eventual improvement of U.S.–Soviet relations. Walter Lippmann and Marshall Shulman, on the other hand, maintain that U.S.–Soviet relations can be improved without fundamental changes in the Soviet domestic regime.

Taken together, these authors represent the major poles of the American debate over the last forty years concerning the roots of Soviet foreign policy and the nature of the Soviet threat. Kennan's "X" article inspired the policy of containment, while Walter Lippmann offered the foremost critique of this doctrine when it was first enunciated.[5] Richard Pipes and Marshall Shulman are eloquent representatives of the "hard versus soft" debates in contemporary American Soviet policy. Both are distinguished academics with extensive policy experience – Shulman during the Carter administration and Pipes during the early years of the Reagan administration.

The Arguments

In his famous 1947 article, "The Sources of Soviet Conduct," George Kennan identified two principal influences on Soviet foreign policy:

The political personality of Soviet power as we know it today is the product of ideology and circumstances: ideology inherited by the present Soviet leaders from the movement in which they had their political origin, and circumstances of the power which they now have exercised for nearly three decades in Russia.[6]

Kennan did not believe there was a one-to-one correspondence between the principles of Marxism-Leninism and specific Soviet actions. Instead, he argued that ideology contributed to an "innate antagonism between capitalism and Socialism," which ensured that Moscow would never believe it had any sincere community of aims with capitalist powers. The United States should not be misled by tactical maneuvers, for the underlying characteristics of Soviet foreign policy "are basic to the internal nature of Soviet power, and will be with us, whether in the foreground or the background, until the internal nature of Soviet power is changed."[7]

By resisting the expansion of Soviet influence, Kennan believed the United States could bring about a change in the character of Soviet power. Three steps were necessary to accomplish this objective.[8] The first was the re-establishment of a functioning balance of power, ensuring that Western Europe and Japan would remain outside the Soviet orbit. The second step was the encouragement of the cracks and fissures that Kennan believed would inevitably develop in the international communist movement. This would blunt the Soviet Union's ability to use this movement for its own purposes. Finally, the United States needed to slowly guide and direct the "shape" of Soviet power. Kennan's most famous injunction (an admonition that he later lamented was formulated quite poorly) was that the United States needed to be willing to contain Soviet pressure "by the adroit and vigilant applicant of counterforce at a series of constantly shifting geographical and political points."[9]

Kennan believed that Soviet power bore within it the seeds of its own decay, and that this decay was already well advanced. Internally, revolutionary ardor was likely to give way to calculations of self-interest and a drifting away from Moscow, particularly within the satellite nations and foreign communist parties. Externally, reality would eventually grind down the messianic pretensions of Marxism-Leninism. "No mystical, Messianic movement," Kennan wrote, "can face frustration indefinitely without eventually adjusting itself in one way or another to the logic of state affairs."[10]

Kennan's original "X" article did not examine what a mellowing of Soviet power would look like. In another *Foreign Affairs* article in 1951, he warned against expecting the emergence of a liberal-democratic Russia along American lines. Instead, one should look for a Russia that:

...would be tolerant, communicative and forthright in its relations with other states and peoples. It would not take the ideological position that its own purposes cannot finally prosper unless all systems of government not under its control are subverted and eventually destroyed. It would dispense with this paranoiac suspiciousness we know so well...It would consent to recognize that this outside world is not really preoccupied with diabolical plots to invade Russia and inflict injuries on the Russian people.[11]

While Kennan's analysis was receiving a widespread and sympathetic hearing in Washington, Walter Lippmann strongly criticized it in a series of *New York Herald Tribune* articles published in the late summer of 1947.[12] Lippmann agreed that the United States needed to face up to the realities of Soviet power and squarely address them. However, he strongly disagreed with both Kennan's analysis of the roots of Soviet foreign policy and Kennan's prescriptions for American policy.

In particular Lippmann took issue with Kennan's argument that containment required the use of "unalterable counterforce" at every point where the Soviets showed signs of encroaching. Lippmann viewed this formulation as a "strategic monstrosity" that would allow the Soviet Union to set the agenda. It would require continual and complicated intervention by the United States to maintain an anti-Soviet coalition; it would require vastly increased defense expenditures; and it would require that we "stake our own security and the peace of the world upon satellites, puppets, clients, agents about whom we can know very little."[13]

Lippmann also criticized Kennan's assumption that ideology and the circumstances under which power was seized and retained were the key determinants of Soviet foreign policy. Instead, he saw Soviet policy as far more Russian than Marxist-Leninist in character. The postwar settlement in Europe was dominated by traditional czarist ambitions, realized in the wake of the Red Army's victorious advance into the center of Europe, and not by the ideology of Karl Marx.[14]

Lippmann was quite skeptical of Kennan's contention that Soviet power contained the seeds of its own decay and would collapse if confronted by the United States. Such hopes were the product of "wishful thinking," and not the proper grounds for the American people to "stake their entire security as a nation upon."[15] Maintaining instead that "the heart of our problem is the presence of the Red Army in Europe," Lippmann advocated a negotiated solution that would eliminate the Soviet and American military presence on European soil and re-establish a traditional balance of power through the reunification and neutralization of Germany.[16] While Lippmann did not believe that such actions would eliminate Soviet and American antagonism altogether, he felt they could "decisively" reduce the threat that the Soviet Union posed to the West.

The basic arguments between Kennan and Lippmann persist today. Richard Pipes believes there was a great deal of utility in the doctrine of containment as originally enunciated by Kennan.[17] Indeed, his analysis and policy prescriptions parallel many of Kennan's original beliefs. Both Kennan and Pipes maintain that Soviet hostility toward the West is the product of internal conditions within the Soviet regime.[18] Both believe that Soviet power bears within it the "seeds of its own decay"; and that this is well advanced.[19] Both emphasize the need for vigorous American resistance to Soviet gains, which will eventually force domestic changes within the Soviet Union. And both believe these changes will bring a more pacific Soviet policy toward the West.

The two scholars differ as to how such a change will come about. Kennan sees the change as resulting from a reorientation in Soviet perceptions, brought about by the failure of Marxism-Leninism to realize its messianic vision and the contradictions inherent within Soviet power.

This failure, in turn, will provoke a more "realistic" assessment of the international situation and presumably an abandonment of the innate hostility between communism and capitalism.

Pipes is skeptical that the *nomenklatura* (the Soviet ruling elite) would voluntarily reorient itself toward pursuing a more pacific foreign policy. The factors that contribute to Soviet enmity—and particularly, the close link between external expansion and the domestic legitimacy of the Soviet state—are too strong to be overcome under normal circumstances.[20] Pipes believes that Soviet antipathy toward the West will not change fundamentally unless the Soviet elite is confronted with a severe crisis in the Soviet political and economic system.[21]

Such a crisis will force the *nomenklatura* to undertake various political and economic reforms that will weaken its grip on the nation. The result will be greater public participation in government, a shift of attention inward, and a more pacific Soviet foreign policy. Pipes maintains that democratization would "act as a brake on the regime's hitherto unbridled appetite for conquests because, much as they may be flattered by the might of Russia, its citizens have other concerns, closer to home."[22]

According to Pipes, a coordinated Allied policy of economic denial would have a profound effect in promoting the ultimate moderation of the Soviet regime.[23] Should the West pursue such a policy successfully, the *nomenklatura* would soon face an economic crisis that would force it into economic and political reform.

Marshall Shulman is strongly critical of Pipes's position.[24] In particular he questions the contention that Soviet expansionist behavior is rooted in the nature of the Soviet system and can be modified only through fundamental domestic change.[25] Shulman maintains that this position overemphasizes the influence of Marxist-Leninist ideology and underemphasizes the "notable pragmatic nation-state responses that have characterized Soviet foreign policy in response to the external environment."[26] Although the Soviets continue to employ ideology rhetorically, Shulman believes they have clearly yielded to more pragmatic operational guidelines. The Soviet Union is more like a traditional great power pressing for a role commensurate with its status than a revolutionary nation bent on refashioning the status quo in its own image.[27]

Shulman also takes issue with Pipes's contention that a revolutionary situation exists within the Soviet Union. Downplaying the gravity of Soviet internal dissent, he argues that severe U.S. pressure is likely to make the Soviets even more truculent and militaristic.[28]

Shulman proposes a strategy in which the United States is "firm" without being bellicose. He believes the clashes of interest that underlie East–West problems are unlikely to disappear in the near future.[29] However, even without a fundamental transformation in U.S.–Soviet relations, evolutionary changes could occur that will allow these two nations to exist at a much reduced level of enmity. Shulman's hopes depend on both changes in the international system and greater "rationality" in the conduct of U.S.–Soviet relations.

On the first score, Shulman sees the world emerging from the strict bipolarity of the Cold War into greater complexity and diversity. The restoration of Europe and Japan, the rise of North–South issues, and the increasing independence of movements of national liberation from Moscow have all reduced the importance of the U.S.–Soviet rivalry.[30] Americans need to understand the local dynamics of political upheavals and realize that the Soviet Union is only a complicating factor—not the source—of regional instability.[31]

These changes in the external environment are (or should be) paralleled by a more sophisticated understanding of the roots of Soviet and American enmity. Shulman maintains that U.S.–Soviet relations have frequently demonstrated an interactive or spiraling effect, in which "oversimplified and emotionally colored stereotypes of the other" created a "cycle of reactions that took on a life of their own, disproportionate to and only partly related to the real conflict of interest involved."[32] He views the arms race as a particularly dangerous manifestation of this cycle, and his writings are full of injunctions to bring it under prudent control.[33] As a long-term strategy, the United States should seek to reduce these exaggerated misperceptions by encouraging more enlightened views on the part of Soviet leaders. Americans should incorporate incentives as well as constraints into their dealings with the Soviet Union and seek Soviet help in managing the superpower rivalry in a prudent and restrained fashion.[34]

In summary, Kennan and Pipes see the Soviet threat as primarily political in nature. Military factors are important and should not be ignored. But the fundamental problem posed by the Soviets is that—because of ideology and political culture or the requirements of domestic legitimacy—the Russian elite does not perceive that there can be any long-term community of interests between the Soviet Union and the West. Any redirection of Soviet policy must entail a mitigation of this innate hostility.

Lippmann and Shulman are far less worried about any fundamental Soviet enmity toward capitalist powers. They view the military element of Soviet power as the essential problem. For Lippmann, it was the position of the Red Army in Central Europe and the threat it posed to vital Western interests. For Shulman, it is the arms race and the dangers of nuclear war. Moderation in this context means a willingness to join with the United States in reducing these threats.

These four authors also differ as to how moderation will be achieved. Kennan and Pipes view the Soviet system as containing the seeds of its own decay. For Kennan, the fatal flaw is an inadequate world view coupled with a general tendency for empires to fall apart; for Pipes, it is a failing economic system. Both Lippmann and Shulman disagree with these contentions, and maintain that changes in the international system—combined with skillful diplomacy—will reduce the Soviet threat to a manageable level.

Analysis and Implications

Of the arguments considered in this chapter, Walter Lippmann's recommendations are least applicable to international realities in the late twentieth century. His criticisms of Kennan were brilliant and in many respects quite prescient. His arguments for the neutralization of Germany (which he believed would eliminate the presence of Soviet troops in Central Europe and the need for a vigorous counteractive American response) have resurfaced under various guises over the last forty years.[35] But Lippman's argument has been eclipsed by the changes in military technology. With the development of ballistic missiles, the Soviet Union can threaten Western population centers without invading them. Removing the Red Army from its forward position would make the job of seizing and holding territory more difficult, but it would not free the West from the coercive leverage of the Soviet Union.[36]

If superpower disengagement from Europe took place, some alternative security arrangement would be necessary. There is no shortage of innovative proposals, yet most of them contain serious flaws.[37] For all its problems, the European status quo has been remarkably successful at keeping the peace; most students of international affairs would agree that Europe is currently one of the most stable regions in the world.[38] Although some may lament the level of militarization on the continent and others may be frustrated by the lack of freedom in Eastern Europe, the burden of proof rests with those who argue for radical departures from the current system of alliances. It is not clear that such changes would decrease the risks of war without increasing the risk to fundamental Western values.

Even a satisfactory resolution of the question of Europe would probably not lead to a fundamental moderation in Soviet foreign policy or U.S.–Soviet enmity. The superpower rivalry has become global in character, and other regions—such as East Asia and the Middle East—are now important, by virtue of their location or natural resources, to the global distribution of power. A superpower confrontation is much more likely to break out in these regions, where the stakes are high and the interests much less well defined, than in Europe, where clear spheres of influence exist.

At the core of Marshall Shulman's argument is the belief that changes in the nature of the international system will (or should) combine with internal perceptual shifts, both Soviet and American, to bring about a more prudent management of the superpower rivalry. As discussed below, there is evidence that Soviet perceptions are being reoriented along the lines he describes; his other contentions, however, are less persuasive.

Shulman is rather vague in spelling out just how a breakdown of the postwar bipolar system will reduce Soviet and American tensions. He appears to assume that the restoration of Europe and Japan will combine with increases in the salience of North–South issues to make Soviet–American differences "seem less important."[39] Other scholars have maintained that multipolarity would lead to more flexible alignments, further decreasing the risks of U.S.–Soviet confrontation.[40]

These arguments represent just one side in a very complex and unresolved debate. Within the literature on international affairs, disagreement continues as to whether a multipolar or a bipolar world is more stable. This debate hinges on differing assessments of factors such as flexibility and uncertainty.[41] Though Shulman may ultimately be correct that a multipolar system is more stable, this conclusion is by no means obvious, and he fails to address the numerous potential complications that would accompany such a world.

In addition, it is not clear that bipolarity is eroding. The United States and the Soviet Union now account for a smaller share of world production, and there is greater diversity and complexity in their alliance relationships. Some scholars have argued that these changes are relatively superficial, however; by most indexes of power, the superpowers are still clearly the dominant players in contemporary international relations.[42] Important empirical and conceptual problems relating to the measurement of power make it impossible to resolve these disputes in a systematic fashion.[43]

Thus Shulman's argument that broad transnational forces are working to transform U.S.–Soviet relations quickly becomes mired in tedious and inconclusive debates. And yet, stripped of its vague references to changing international realities and placed within the context of traditional power politics, his argument contains an important element of truth. Balance-of-power theory predicts that the emergence of another superpower could cause the Soviet Union to seek close ties with the United States to secure a counterweight against this third party.[44] This has been true historically: the presence of common enemies—Britain and France in the nineteenth century, Germany and Japan in the twentieth—has always provided powerful incentives for both Imperial Russia and the Soviet Union to cooperate with the United States.

Although the rise of a threatening third power would probably improve U.S.–Soviet relations, this would not necessarily diminish the risks of catastrophic nuclear war. A nuclear exchange between the United States and the Soviet Union would probably become less likely. However, the dangers of conflict between this third party and either the United States or the USSR could actually increase the aggregate probability of nuclear war.

Could Soviet moderation be obtained without changes in the nature of the international system? Shulman's views suggest that such a reorientation is possible given appropriate Western policies. From his perspective, Soviet foreign policy is quite flexible when it encounters obstacles. If pushed too hard, the Soviets are likely to become truculent and militaristic. But given the proper combination of carrots and sticks, the Russians can be coaxed to behave in a fashion that is not antithetical to Western interests.[45]

Other scholars are less convinced. Richard Pipes, for example, maintains that attempts to "teach" or "educate" the Soviets are bound to be futile.[46] Henry Kissinger has argued that Russia's history of repeated invasions has reinforced an inherent Soviet xenophobia that is impervious to Western attempts to assuage it.[47] Kennan's "X" article emphasized that ideology perpetuates the Soviet belief that there can be no long-term harmony of interests between the Soviet Union and the capitalist West (although Kennan also believed that the Soviet view of the outside world would slowly become less hostile and paranoid).

As events of the late 1970s demonstrated, Shulman was too quick to assume that the Soviets valued moderation and restraint over the enhancement of their power and prestige. Instead of cooperating with the United States to create a world that was "more responsive to the desire of people everywhere for economic well-being, social justice, political self-determination and basic human rights," the Soviets sought to exploit American retrenchment after Vietnam for the sake of concrete foreign policy gains and the enhancement of their revolutionary credentials.[48] Perhaps Shulman's conclusions were merely premature; the jury is still out as to whether Gorbachev's changes represent a fundamental reorientation in Soviet foreign policy or merely the pursuit of old objectives with new tactics (as the general secretary himself professes).[49]

If Shulman is too ready to assume a substantial Soviet willingness to cooperate with the West, Pipes errs in insisting that such cooperation cannot take place unless the Soviet Union is transformed and its economic and political processes are made more democratic. This assumption is rooted in Pipes's belief that the *nomenklatura* requires a foreign class enemy to justify its own existence.[50] Other scholars have also argued that as long as the successors of Lenin and Stalin remain in power (and perhaps even afterward), the Soviet elite will attempt to legitimize its rule by positing an external threat, ensuring continued hostility between the Soviet Union and the United States.[51]

Legitimacy is a complex phenomenon, and this argument is woefully underspecified. First, there is the question of whose support is necessary for the *nomenklatura* to survive. The Soviet regime makes differing demands on different social groups, and the requirements for legitimacy are likely to vary accordingly. It is enough for peasant farmers in Siberia to acquiesce passively to the dictates of the regime while being indifferent to its ultimate fate; such an attitude would be a far more serious matter in a cadre of senior Red Army officers.

Seweryn Bialer has argued that elite legitimacy (as opposed to popular legitimacy) is of greatest importance in communist systems.[52] During the post-Stalin era, he maintains, the Soviet elite has been quite supportive of the regime. Disagreements have usually occurred within the context of a general acceptance of the Party's right to rule; there have been none of the severe cleavages that have periodically marked the dissolution of communist power in satellite regimes.

A given regime can draw on various resources to establish its legitimacy. Legitimacy is enhanced by ideology, but it also has roots in historical experience, political culture, regime performance, and simple tradition. In the Soviet case, the requirements for mass legitimacy appear to be linked more closely to domestic concerns—the provision of goods and services and the prospects for social mobility within the Soviet Union itself—than to the existence of a capitalist West or to Soviet successes and failures on distant continents.[53]

Finally, ideological legitimacy is not immutable, but can be finessed. Marxism-Leninism is frequently ambiguous in its treatment of specific problems, and its name can be invoked to support a broad range of policy options.[54] Under the proper circumstances, even the most fundamental ideological principle can be explained away.[55]

These considerations suggest that a foreign class enemy is not absolutely necessary to provide domestic legitimacy to the Soviet regime. Certainly the fear of capitalist encirclement has been used in the past to justify repressive measures and great sacrifices, and the inclusion of more and more nations in the "progressive camp" has strengthened the Soviet claim that the "correlation of forces" is shifting in their favor. Yet the ultimate survival of the regime will probably have more to do with the availability of bread in Kiev, or the presence of indigenous party leadership in Kazakhstan, than with the existence of an external capitalist threat.

Pipes does not discuss in detail the relationship that he assumes exists between domestic reform and moderation in Soviet foreign policy. He indicates broadly that the requirements for increasing economic decentralization will result in greater domestic political liberalization, which in turn will bring about a more pacific Soviet foreign policy. Clearly major changes in the Soviet economy will be required if it is not to fall behind Western advances in technology and production techniques. Various serious structural problems make the Soviet economy ill adapted to develop and use advanced technology in the workplace.[56] Yet it is not clear that the changes needed to correct these problems will automatically lead to improved Soviet relations with the West.

For one thing, the Communist party is unlikely to be presented with a strictly dichotomous choice between maintaining its monopoly over information and modernizing the economy. It can opt for partial or intermediate solutions that would retard the spread of advanced technology, but allow the party to retain some measure of control over information.[57] A more fundamental problem with Pipes's argument is the lack of a clear connection between Soviet domestic liberalization and moderation in Soviet foreign policy. Charles Gati has argued that the adoption of a softer line abroad has frequently coincided with a domestic crackdown on various forms of dissent.[58] Dimitri Simes suggests that a Soviet leader's credibility might suffer if change at home were coupled with a perceived softness abroad.[59]

Pipes offers little hard evidence to back up his assertion that a more democratic Soviet Union would exercise greater restraint in international affairs. Indeed, there is some evidence that democratization might even increase Soviet assertiveness abroad. The limited public opinion data available indicate that Soviet citizens are generally supportive of Soviet aspirations toward great-power status and proud of the gains their country has made in recent years. (These views are especially prominent among younger Soviet citizens.)[60] This evidence may not be enough to overthrow the traditional Kantian assumption that democracies are more peaceful than autocratic forms of government.[61] Yet we simply do not know enough to assert without reservation, as Pipes does, that a more democratic Soviet Union will also be more pacific in its foreign policy.

These qualifications do not decisively refute Pipes's contention that the need for economic reform in the Soviet Union may result in a transformation of Soviet foreign policy. Indeed, Pipes recently claimed that events in Gorbachev's Russia were bearing out his hypothesis.[62] But the changes currently taking place in the Soviet political and economic system are not necessarily the product of the processes that Pipes describes. One would like to see better evidence of the causal connections Pipes assumes—and particularly of his allegation that greater public participation will result in a less adventurist Soviet foreign policy.

Kennan believed that the realities of international politics would combine with an inner crumbling of Marxist-Leninist ideology to produce a more sober and less paranoid perception of the external world. On both counts, his judgments appear to have been vindicated by history.

The erosion of Marxism-Leninism as an important force in Soviet foreign policy can be seen along several dimensions. Soviet dominance of the international communist movement, for example, is clearly much diminished since the Stalin era, when foreign communist leaders would be summoned to Moscow and "disappear" while their parties continued to follow Moscow's directives resolutely (often at significant cost to themselves). Many factors have contributed to this gradual dissolution of Soviet supremacy.[63] By the early 1980s, Soviet domestic and foreign policy was being openly criticized by other communist parties—criticism that provoked a stinging response from Moscow.

Gorbachev's recent statement that relations among communist parties must "rule out any monopoly on truth" and any notion of a "center" within the socialist world represents a departure from previous Soviet attempts to rebuke and isolate parties that had gone too far in their criticism of the USSR.[64] It also represents a formal acknowledgment of the dissolution of Soviet hegemony over the world communist movement.

This dissolution was envisioned by Kennan, who predicted in the 1940s that "Russian Communism may some day be destroyed by its own children in the form of the rebellious Communist parties of other countries."[65]

In other areas the ideological fervor of Soviet foreign policy has declined unsteadily. During the latter half of the 1970s, the Soviet leadership attempted to restore some of its lapsed revolutionary credibility by supporting movements of national liberation in the Third World. Although such ventures were costly in terms of relations with the West, they enhanced the standing of the Soviet Union among Third World radicals and countered criticism that it had abandoned its legacy as a revolutionary power.[66] These activities also gave the Soviets some concrete foreign policy successes that suggested the correlation of forces was continuing to shift in Moscow's favor.

It now appears that Soviet policy is being reoriented. Instead of ringing declarations on the shifting correlation of forces, Gorbachev acknowledged at the 27th Party Congress that the process of change in the Third World "has encountered considerable difficulties." Gone are blanket offers of military and economic support; the Party program that came out of that conference stated only that the Soviet Communist party has "profound sympathy" for the aspirations of peoples who have experienced colonial servitude.[67]

The extent of these changes should not be overemphasized. Military assistance to countries such as Nicaragua, Angola, and Afghanistan has increased under Gorbachev. The Soviets are consolidating their position in the nations where they already have a significant investment, and they are being "moderate" only in hesitating to take on new commitments. Yet this retrenchment marks a further decline in the perceived Soviet need for solidarity with movements of national liberation and for an ever-growing socialist camp. The tradeoff between solidifying relations with the West and retaining the revolutionary legitimacy of the Soviet state is clearly being resolved in favor of the former objective.

Finally, Soviet perceptions of international affairs have become much more varied and sophisticated since Kennan's "X" article appeared in *Foreign Affairs*. At that time Stalin insisted that the world was divided into two camps and that war between capitalism and socialism was inevitable. History was viewed as unfolding in a linear direction from capitalism to communism; American foreign policy was held to be directly controlled by a few Wall Street monopolists, and the capitalist system was thought to be on the verge of collapse.

All of these perceptions have been considerably modified and refined since 1947. Under Khrushchev, the "two camps" theory was abandoned, along with the Stalinist concept of a single, linear progression toward socialism. Khrushchev also argued that nuclear weapons necessitated a reformulation of the Soviet doctrine that war between capitalism and socialism was inevitable. A peaceful transition to socialism was now possible.

The years since Khrushchev have seen further modifications. Soviet views of the American foreign policy process have become much more sophisticated, giving far more attention to public opinion and the interplay of the president, Congress, and the bureaucracy.[68] The ultimate collapse of capitalism is no longer predicted; Gorbachev recently remarked that "the present stage of the general crisis does not lead to any absolute stagnation of capitalism and does not rule out possible growth of its economy and the mastery of new scientific and technical trends."[69] A few Soviet writers have even hinted that the Cold War arose out of misperceptions on *both* sides.[70] Some Soviet economists have argued that Third World countries with "capitalist-oriented" economies will tend to grow more rapidly because well-rounded development seems to be dependent on foreign investment and integration into the capitalist world market.[71]

These shifts in perception represent concessions to reality of the type that Kennan predicted. All of these developments—Soviet loss of hegemony over the international communist movement, the declining need to buttress Soviet revolutionary legitimacy, and the modifications in Soviet perceptions of international affairs—suggest that, despite of the flaws noted by Lippmann, Kennan's "X" article accurately assessed the likely evolution of Soviet foreign policy in the postwar era. Two important questions remain, however: is this evolution irreversible, and how far will it go?

The answer to the first question is a rather complex and qualified yes. There has been a steady erosion in Soviet ideology and its influence, both direct and indirect, on Soviet foreign policy. The more Marxism-Leninism interacts with reality, the more it is necessary to modify and adapt its premises in light of experience, and the more qualified and tenuous its conclusions become. In this sense, Gorbachev's changes are the outgrowth of an evolution in Soviet thought that transcends Gorbachev himself and his political fortunes.

Along this long-term trend, there may be cycles of ideological resurgence that could significantly retard the move toward moderation. These cycles might arise from two sources: domestic pressures culminating in a conservative reaction, or major crises in the West undermining the credibility of American political and economic institutions.

Certain powerful domestic interests within the Soviet Union would suffer from a reorientation of Soviet foreign policy toward closer relations with the United States. The most obvious is the Red Army. In the eyes of the Soviet military, a less threatening international environment would decrease the need for large defense expenditures, weaken Soviet morale, destroy vigilance, and reduce the importance of Defense vis-á-vis other ministries in the Soviet bureaucratic hierarchy.[72] There is ample historical evidence that the Ministry of Defense has always been reluctant to support a relaxation of tensions with the West; it was apparently a particularly forceful critic of détente in the early 1970s.[73]

For similar reasons, the state security organs would not welcome closer relations with the West. In their study of various interest groups within Soviet politics, Skilling and Griffiths found the KGB to be the most reactionary element of Soviet society.[74] As head of the KGB, Yuri Andropov went to elaborate lengths to emphasize the need for vigilance to counteract the imperialist threat. He asserted that a "real danger" would confront the forces of peace and progress as long as imperialism existed.[75]

Industries that specialize in defense production would also tend to resist the redirection of resources away from their sector, and thus to be skeptical of any Soviet accommodation with the United States that threatened their privileged status. These industries occupy a commanding position in the Soviet economy.[76] They have close ties with the armed forces and probably share much of the military's personal and organizational antipathy toward improved relations with the West.[77]

Finally, certain elements within the Communist party have sought to ensure that Soviet foreign policy shows "the right degree of ideological strength."[78] Under the leadership of Boris Ponomarev, for example, the International Division of the Party's Central Committee staunchly advocated a militant line in foreign policy. Pomonarev was recently retired under Gorbachev, and his job was given to the long-time Soviet ambassador to the United States, Anatoly Dobrynin—perhaps indicating an attempt to reorient this dimension of Soviet foreign policy toward closer relations with the West.

Although these groups could be expected to oppose improved relations with the United States, virtually all Western observers believe that they are controlled by the Politburo."[79] The police, who functioned as an autonomous unit under Stalin, have been demoted and their arbitrary authority has been curtailed. The Soviet military-industrial complex may exert some influence during a succession in leadership, but it generally appears content to support the regime as long as its basic needs and interests are satisfied.[80] Even if one subscribes to a pluralist model of decision making within the Soviet Union, a general secretary who has secured himself in office commands enough resources to circumvent any potential political opposition. He may not be able to go as far and as fast as he would like in reorienting Soviet foreign policy, but the countervailing tendencies are not strong enough to stop him.[81]

Perhaps more dangerous than any opposition group is an attitude that pervades Soviet society—an underlying hostility to the outside world and a desire to keep Russia "pure" from foreign influence.[82] This sentiment, which recalls the Slavophile movements of the nineteenth century, is tolerated in official circles. If close ties with the West brought an influx of capitalist decadence, and particularly if they led to political agitation similar to the unrest recently experienced in China, pressure would probably mount across institutional lines to insulate Russia from the West. Such pressure would be difficult for any but the most powerful general secretary to ignore.

There is a second way in which Soviet moderation could be reversed. In the past, certain events (which proved to be transitory) have prompted the Soviet leadership to assume that the correlation of forces was shifting in their favor. The rapid Soviet economic growth in the 1950s, combined with growing ties to the Third World, provided the substance behind Khrushchev's boasts that the Soviet Union would bury the West and achieve full communism within twenty years. In the 1970s, the achievement of strategic parity with the United States, coupled with American retrenchment after the Vietnam war, convinced Brezhnev that the forces favoring socialism were indeed on the rise. These perceptions in turn were largely responsible for the rise in Soviet activism at the end of the decade.

The Soviet leadership currently perceives itself to be in a period of retrenchment and consolidation. However, should *glasnost* (openness) and *perestroika* (restructuring) appear to be bearing fruit, or should the West enter a period of profound social and economic crisis similar to the 1930s (or, to a lesser extent, the 1960s and early 1970s), Soviet perceptions of the benefits of their ideology and social system vis-á-vis the West might well change. Their confidence in the inevitability of socialist triumph might be sufficiently bolstered that they would again embark on an activist course in foreign policy.

Finally, there is the question of how far the Soviets will go in making specific changes in their foreign policy. Seweryn Bialer writes that there

are certain immutable, absolute Soviet priorities: the security of the Soviet homeland and the preservation of communist rule within both the
USSR and the Soviet empire in Eastern Europe.[83] Next comes a group
of priorities that carry variable weight. Among these, Bialer lists the enhancement of Soviet international influence (including the establishment
of ties with nations friendly to the Soviet Union and the isolation of
states hostile to it) and economic priorities (the desire to promote the in-
flow of technology from industrialized capitalist countries, secure agri-
cultural imports, and obtain credits). The goal of supporting revolution
abroad ranks low on this list of priorities.

Soviet second- and third-tier objectives are being reshuffled. Economic
goals have become increasingly important, while solidarity with various
revolutionary movements has slipped even further down the list of priorities. Soviet moderation—whatever form it ultimately takes—will not
jeopardize the fundamental concerns of the Soviet leadership: the security of the Soviet state or the primacy of communist rule in the Soviet
Union and Eastern Europe.[84] The forms of domination may change over
time, but the substance of control will not be compromised willingly.

Conclusions

Virtually all U.S. observers concur that a moderation of Soviet foreign
policy is inherently desirable. There is less agreement about what this
world will look like, and how we will get there.

For Lippmann and Shulman, moderation means a Soviet willingness
to engage in negotiations to reduce the military threat to both societies.
Shulman maintains that it also means joining the United States in a type
of restrained competition, in which neither side seeks to gain a unilateral
advantage over the other.

Neither of these proposals can be ruled out a priori, yet both are either underspecified or neglect serious complications. Lippmann rightly
criticizes Kennan for only vaguely specifying how a "mellowing" in Soviet policy will occur, and yet his own solution is dated, neglects serious
complications, and fails to reduce the Soviet threat decisively. Shulman
sketches a somewhat better world, but grounds his argument in the neb-
ulous and unverifiable contention that certain changes in the international system will reduce the salience of the superpower relationship.
He also tends to overemphasize the incentives for the Soviet Union to
cooperate with the United States and to underestimate the degree of

Soviet antipathy (whether ideological or not) toward the West. Although events may ultimately follow the course he predicts, those developments may not be due to the causal factors on which he focuses.

Pipes foresees no moderation in Soviet foreign policy until domestic change forces the Soviet regime to renounce its hostility toward the West. His assumption that the Soviets require an external enemy to legitimize their domestic authority is almost certainly overstated. And, as Shulman and Charles Gati argue, greater American pressure will not necessarily result in a more liberal Soviet regime, and liberalization within the Soviet Union will not necessarily lead to a more moderate Soviet foreign policy. Pipes's argument would be enhanced if he examined its causal connections more carefully.

Ironically, Kennan's argument, the oldest of the positions considered in this chapter, is probably the most accurate. Kennan foresaw the dissolution of Marxism-Leninism as a potent ideological force in international affairs; he also foresaw the decline in ideologically motivated behavior and the modification of Soviet perceptions under the influence of international realities.

If Kennan is correct, the reorientation of Soviet policy will be a less dangerous transition than if it depends on the rise of a third power that threatens the Soviet Union enough to compel it to seek good relations with the United States for balance-of-power reasons.[85]

How far the changes predicted by Kennan will go, and whether they can be reversed, remains an open question. Russian political culture is unlikely to shed its long-standing xenophobia in a few decades, let alone a few years. But maximum security for the Soviet Union may not continue to mean maximum insecurity for many other states. Gorbachev's recent pronouncement that no state can have security at the expense of others seems to reflect an important new awareness of how Soviet (as well as American) actions can affect the arms race and the stability of the contemporary international system.[86] One hopes that such statements are not merely a tactical ploy to buy time to transform the Soviet domestic system before embarking on more expansionist foreign policy, but instead mark an evolution in Soviet thought concerning international affairs. It is still too early to tell.

The question of Soviet moderation is not a one-sided issue. A transformation in Soviet policy toward the United States will depend at least in part on American actions. Should the United States fail to respond appropriately, then Soviet moderation could lose out to more hard-line alternatives. An extremely conciliatory U.S. policy is not necessarily required, but a certain amount of moderation will be needed to encourage the Soviets to continue.

A moderate American Soviet policy must be supported by the American public at large. It is here that some of the most pervasive difficulties in improving Soviet–American relations will be encountered. Although Americans all want to see moderation in Soviet foreign policy, they remain deeply divided over what *moderation* means. Since there are bound to be limits beyond which the Soviets will not go—Soviet children are not going to be born singing "God Bless America"—Americans must learn to live with a Soviet Union whose moderation is likely to be ambiguous and fall short of many of our expectations.

These ambiguities in interpreting the nature of Soviet foreign policy will be reflected in American policy debates for a long time to come. One hopes that these disagreements will not prevent the United States from pursuing policies that will facilitate the processes of Soviet moderation. Despite their flaws, Kennan's original recommendations—which combine a firmness in resisting Soviet expansion with a subtle encouragement of Soviet moderation—have been successful and should not be discarded lightly. Perhaps his most important injunction is that America "need only to measure up to its own best traditions and prove itself worthy of preservation as a great nation."[87] Kennan astutely realized that, in the long run, it is the success of the American political and economic system that will create the greatest impetus for Soviet moderation.

CHAPTER 8

Prospects and Consequences of Soviet Decline

Kurt M. Campbell

It is my view that the most important and indeed most neglected question in contemporary international relations scholarship is: what will the West do when and if the Soviets decline? How we answer that question will perhaps determine whether there will be war or peace in our time.
> —*Raymond Aron to Hedley Bull at their last meeting,*
> *International Institute for Strategic Studies,*
> *London, November 1982*

In 1987, after his first visit to the Soviet Union in a decade, former Secretary of State Henry Kissinger spoke to a distinguished gathering in New York about the ambitious agenda of Soviet leader Mikhail Gorbachev. After reviewing the results of high-level meetings and intimate discussions in Moscow, Kissinger concluded with some thoughts about what Gorbachev's fledgling attempts at reform might mean for the United States. "The United States essentially faces two stark futures relating to Gorbachev's bold program for domestic revival," he explained. "The first future to be feared would be if Gorbachev succeeds and the Soviets emerge stronger than before; the second future to be regarded with some apprehension envisions Gorbachev's failure and a nuclear armed, domestically failed Soviet state." To this, another member of the delegation that traveled to the USSR responded, "while I share your concern for a future world where the Soviets have blasted ahead, I do not share your fears about a future in which the Soviets have buckled. I believe a world with the Soviets in decline is infinitely preferable and indeed safer than the world we live in today."[1]

A Soviet decline from superpower status has been the inspiration and ultimate objective for an eclectic collection of American politicians, strategists, and commentators. Indeed, the belief that the USSR is undergoing an inevitable and irreversible decline has profoundly influenced U.S. policy toward the Soviet Union during the Reagan presidency. While forecasters have long disagreed about the ultimate prognosis for the Soviet system, it is often simply taken for granted that a Soviet slippage would enhance American security and reduce the risks of a cataclysmic nuclear conflagration. There has been considerable controversy about the measurement of Soviet decline, but not about its potential consequences.

This chapter explores some of the conditions associated with a potential future decline of the USSR. In evaluating the feasibility and stability of a world order in which Soviet power is dramatically reduced, I shall review the work of those who advocate pushing the Soviets "onto the trash heap of history"[2] as well as the literature on the performance of Soviet society, particularly its purported sources of weakness. The Soviets' perceptions of the current state of their system are also discussed, along with their likely response to a Soviet slide and the structural changes it might induce in the present world system. A central question is whether the fall of the USSR would increase or reduce the risks of nuclear war. Finally, I offer some recommendations about how the United States should manage, or simply cope with, a transition to a world in which the Soviets have lost superpower status.

Visions of Decline

The words of American proponents of Soviet decline have served as a battle cry for those seeking a more assertive foreign policy towards the USSR. Irving Kristol has said,

We are not going to achieve any stability in this world or reach any level of satisfaction, or attainment, in American foreign policy until the Soviet Union has been pushed into an ideological reformation—that is to say, until the Soviet Union ceases being a political regime with an established religion called Marxist-Leninism imposed on the Soviet people. To achieve such a reformation and a lapse in Soviet power is a worthy goal of American foreign policy in the twilight years of the twentieth century and beyond.

Elliot Abrams observed that "there are clear signs of stress and fracture in the very foundations of Soviet power. American policy should be formulated to take account of these chinks." Likewise, Richard Perle has spoken of a need for a "sustained and concerted U.S. policy designed to check Soviet power abroad and challenge it at home."[3]

In perhaps the most important article about Soviet decline, "Living with a Sick Bear," Henry S. Rowen argues that because of continued economic stagnation, the USSR is in the midst of a profound societal malaise. After cataloguing the many ills and irregularities plaguing the nation, Rowen concludes that "even allowing for perceived differences in interest among Western nations, arguably the collective interest of the West lies in letting the Soviet system decay." Rowen believes that the United States must do nothing to assist the Soviets to retool and redirect their economic system, "because even small increments of outside support might enable that system to continue in ways that are dangerous to our health. But it should be some comfort that even the foolish, coerced, and venal capitalists probably won't be able to save that system."[4]

Given the enthusiasm for a withering away of Soviet power, there has been surprisingly little systematic thinking about a future world order in which the USSR has been relegated to a sub-superpower status. Advocates of policies intended to press the Soviets into decline have had little to say about the structure and stability of such a world, beyond expressing a general belief that in some ways it would resemble the brief period of American hegemony immediately after World War II. (Proponents of decline tend to focus more on American strategies to achieve concessions in the Soviet Union's military posture, Third World enterprises, or its human rights record.) Furthermore, while there is general agreement about the benefits the United States would reap from a Soviet decline and about the tactics needed to challenge the Soviets, this policy school comprises quite divergent views on what is ultimately desired for the Soviet Union.

For instance, pragmatists would like to see an inward-looking, domestically preoccupied Soviet elite that has been deterred or discouraged from international adventurism.[5] Some ideological reformers openly support the overthrow of the ruling Soviet party *apparat* and the dismantling of the Marxist system in favor of a democracy (presumably along the lines of the parliamentary system of the *Duma* and the brief tenure of President Kerensky in 1916).[6] Still others are concerned that the introduction of capitalism into Russia would make the country an even more powerful and potent adversary and these observers would only be satisfied once Russia is relegated to the status of a third-class power.[7] However, while their ultimate motivations are remarkably varied, this diverse group of scholars and political pundits has formed a common front in support of U.S. policies designed to test the Soviets severely.

Today the most important arenas for waging a metaphorical war of attrition with the USSR are thought to be in nuclear weaponry and in the Third World. For instance, an important factor influencing President Reagan's decisions to press ahead with an early deployment of a missile defense system and to abandon the SALT II treaty limits is said to have been a belief that the USSR can no longer keep up with the United States in the strategic competition. Reagan's thinking was purportedly influenced by a CIA review of the Soviet economy headed by Henry Rowen, which concluded that Moscow could not increase its current level of defense spending because of the terrible problems of the economic system.[8] Echoing these same sentiments, Kenneth Adelman wrote not long ago that "the Soviets already have their accelerator near or on the floor" and cannot significantly increase their strategic weapons production.[9]

Likewise, the challenge of the Reagan Doctrine in the far corners of the Soviet Union's Third World empire is also seen as a way to speed the Soviet decline. Irving Kristol has applauded the American crusade to sponsor anticommunist insurgents and argued that "small defeats" in Angola, Nicaragua, or Afghanistan could "shake the Soviet regime" and undermine its legitimacy at home.[10] Similarly, Richard Pipes has reasoned that Soviet power rests on "the notion of invincibility" and that if Russian proxies suffered a humiliating defeat abroad, there would be "immediate domestic consequences."[11]

In addition to a desire to gain the upper hand in the strategic competition and inflict a loss of credibility on the Soviets in the Third World, there has been wide support for an assortment of other policy initiatives intended to weaken the USSR. For instance, proponents of Soviet decline firmly endorsed the Reagan administration's decision to boycott the Soviet natural gas pipeline to Western Europe as well as attempts to shore up high-technology leaks flowing eastward.[12] The former was intended primarily to deny the USSR badly needed hard currency while the latter sought to impede public and clandestine attempts by the USSR to gain access to Western technology. There has also been a general opposition to any public forums between Westerners and official Soviets which might be seen to confer legitimacy on the ruling regime or benefit Soviet propaganda.[13]

In many ways, American conservatives' current zeal for Soviet decline mirrors the traditional Marxist prophecies about the inevitable collapse of capitalism. Ever since the successful conclusion of the Bolshevik revolution, Soviet leaders and propagandists have predicted the ultimate demise or transformation of the international capitalist system.[14] Indeed, General Secretary Mikhail Gorbachev devoted nearly the first third of his speech to the 27th Party Congress in March 1986 to the contemporary crisis of capitalism in the West.[15] The USSR has consistently maintained, despite all evidence to the contrary, that the United States will eventually experience a wrenching collapse of capitalism that will ultimately lead to a socialist system of government and organization of the means of production.

In recent years, Americans have fastened on the idea of Soviet decline, appropriating Marxian language to make their predictions. This curious reversal of roles has led commentators to speak of a "shift in the global correlation of forces" away from communism and of the "internal contradictions of the Soviet system" when arguing about the inevitability of Soviet decline.[16] President Reagan himself cited the obligation to counter "Soviet imperialism" in the Third World during his enunciation of the Reagan Doctrine at the United Nations.[17]

The superpowers' penchant for envisioning each other's withering away is remarkably imaginative, given the stability and continuity of both Soviet Russia and capitalist America over the last fifty years. Indeed, it is little more than a decade since Henry Kissinger observed that the United States would have to assume a less important role in the international system, in part because of the rise of Soviet power.[18] Clearly the current belief in Soviet decline is related to a desire to return to the brief postwar period of unquestioned American superiority and security from external threats. (At least one analyst, however, questions the assumption that the brief American monopoly of nuclear power amounted to a "nuclear golden age."[19]) Predictions of Soviet doom have the same appeal as the president's Strategic Defense Initiative (SDI): both visions reflect a fundamental desire to remove the Soviet threat, either by erecting a technological shield over the United States or by bringing about the ultimate crumbling of our rival superpower.

The Possible Sources of Soviet Decline

The recent attention to Soviet vulnerabilities is based on more than simple nostalgia for the past. Over the last several years forecasting has emerged as an increasingly important area of Sovietology. Western tools and techniques for measuring Soviet performance have improved dramatically since the advent of satellite reconnaissance, and a growing academic and specialist literature is devoted to assessing the failings and fallability of the Soviet system. Some of this work is highly speculative and uninformed, but a significant portion has spurred useful debates and discussion, opened new areas of inquiry, and generally advanced Western understanding of the USSR. Despite the increase in capabilities and interest, however, there remains no general consensus among Soviet specialists about the long-term prognosis for the Soviet Union.[20] A brief review of Western writings on the subject will help frame a discussion of the potential causes and consequences of Soviet decline.

Perhaps the most important work on Soviet decline has appeared in the field of economics. Since the dramatic downturn in Soviet economic performance in the late 1960s, there has been considerable speculation about a possible future collapse of the Soviet economic system.[21] Traditional smokestack industries have faltered, and the Soviet Union has not yet joined the information revolution underway in the capitalist world. Indeed, the rigid planning system that set the foundation for the USSR's rapid industrialization in the 1930s has proven itself ill suited to meeting the challenge of high-technology enterprises in the 1980s.[22] If Soviet backwardness in information processing and microcircuitry persists, the USSR may ultimately face severe challenges from the West on the technology front.[23]

Soviet nationality problems have also received considerable attention from Western scholars. A number of important studies consider the potential for revolt among non-Russian groups in the USSR, notably in Central Asia.[24] Among the possible indications of a nationality problem are the fact that Slavs and other white Soviets constitute a decreasing percentage of the total Soviet population; the disparity in standards of living between the western areas of the USSR and the Moslem republics in the south; and the relative lack of non-Russian representation in the Soviet government.[25] The 1987 uprisings in Kazakhstan have been interpreted as proof of a widespread ethnic opposition to Soviet rule.

Other commentators have focused on the vagaries of the Soviet political process as a potential source of domestic instability, noting the difficulties associated with political succession and leadership transition.[26] A related problem is the perceived difficulty of maintaining the tenuous balance of bureaucratic power within the government.[27] In one frequently considered scenario, the Communist party loses power to the Soviet military, the KGB, or both during a protracted succession crisis or foreign policy debacle.

Yet another branch of the literature examines the potential for a failure of Soviet agriculture or a serious shortage of various natural resources. With disappointing wheat harvests since the 1960s and increasingly large purchases of Western grain since the mid-1970s, the Soviet Union has become increasingly reliant on foreign food supplies.[28] A hard currency shortfall, brought on by reduced Soviet earnings from petroleum, gold, and diamond sales, might make it difficult to finance the expensive purchases of Western grain. Western scholars have long debated the possibility of a Soviet energy or natural resource crisis. There are widely conflicting reports about the security or vulnerability of the Soviet supply of various primary products, including petroleum, vanadium, platinum, gold, and chromium.[29]

Finally, some Western scholars have held that Soviet rule at home could be undermined by defeats or setbacks abroad. There was unceasing speculation in the early 1970s that the bloody border disputes over the Amur River would set off a major war between the Soviet Union and the People's Republic of China.[30] Ever since Soviet troops intervened to crush the Hungarian uprising in 1956, it has been predicted that widespread dissent in Eastern Europe would one day shake the foundations of Soviet power.[31] Most recently, the promulgation of the Reagan Doctrine to challenge the USSR in the Third World has been viewed as a means to roll back Soviet power on the peripheries and undermine the Soviet notion of the "irreversibility" of communist rule.[32] "By demonstrating that Communist revolutions are reversible," writes Robert W. Tucker, the Reagan Doctrine is expected to "explode a crucial myth. Once that happens, this view holds, the ground under the Kremlin will shake as it has not shaken in a very long time."[33]

To those Western writings about potential Soviet decline have recently been added some dire predictions and warnings—scathing critiques delivered *not* in the West but from inside the USSR. General Secretary Gorbachev and a few like-minded technocrats and economists around him have called for sweeping changes in the management of Soviet industries, the conduct of party affairs, and the process of decision making, in both economic and political endeavors.[34] Some of Gorbachev's indictments of the Soviet system have been more far-reaching and scathing than the criticisms of Western commentators. Whereas Leonid Brezhnev was apparently content to preside over the gradual demise of the USSR, Gorbachev has championed a broad reform program designed to revitalize Soviet society.[35] Although Gorbachev's proposed policies have apparently been resisted by conservative elements within the government, the general secretary appears mindful of the risks of continued Soviet stagnation. His admissions of Soviet fallibility do not represent a renunciation of superpower status, however. Quite the contrary, Gorbachev's initiatives reflect a desire to compete more vigorously with the United States in the international arena.[36]

U.S. Responses to Soviet Decline

It is not clear how much the United States can do to encourage a decline in Soviet power. Although U.S. policies have in some cases exacerbated Soviet difficulties, they have not created them. Furthermore, American proponents of applying pressure on the Soviets have often miscalculated the USSR's response to foreign challenges and overlooked the unintended consequences, particularly for U.S. security, of their policy prescriptions.

Specifically, conservatives seeking Soviet retrenchment have overestimated American influence by suggesting that the application of very modest challenges will bring about fundamental changes in the USSR. It is unreasonable to expect that any new development in the arms race will cause the Soviet system to buckle. The United States can force the Soviet Union to channel valuable resources away from the civilian to the military economy, but the USSR, since the earliest days of the atomic age, has shown a stubborn facility to keep up with (and in some fields surpass) the West in the strategic sphere. Vitaly Churkin, formerly the chief arms control expert at the Soviet embassy in Washington, bristled when asked about the Reagan administration's view that Moscow could not undertake an arms build-up: "I would like to point out that as you know, historically, if anything, we are very good at rising up to challenges. If we are challenged, we will certainly be able to respond in kind."[37] Indeed, the pattern of new strategic deployments—from MIRVs and high-accuracy terminal guidance systems to mobile missile technology—demonstrates the Soviet ability to keep pace with the United States in the nuclear competition. While new technologies of the arms race pose serious obstacles for the relatively inflexible Soviet system of military research and development, experience suggests the USSR will make necessary domestic sacrifices to meet military security requirements.

Likewise, it is difficult to imagine how the Reagan Doctrine will lead to the demise of the internal Soviet system. The USSR has in the past suffered many disappointments in the Third World: the overthrow of Allende of Chile; the expulsions of Soviet advisers from Sadat's Egypt;

and the total defeat of the Soviet-supplied Syrian air force in the skies over Lebanon. None of these humiliations led to a wholesale Soviet retreat from the Third World or triggered an internal crisis of confidence in the Soviet leadership. While the Reagan Doctrine can raise the costs of Soviet adventurism and "bleed" the Soviets on the peripheries, it is not likely to provoke the domestic cataclysm its conservative advocates promise.

Quite apart from policies that display a clear disproportion between stated ends and available means, the United States has in the past introduced certain anti-Soviet measures that stimulated the very developments they were designed to impede. For example, the U.S. decision in 1983 to boycott the USSR's natural gas pipeline to Western Europe goaded Soviet leaders into expending every effort to complete the project in record time, effectively disrupting the alliance the boycott was intended to preserve. Moreover, the implementation of some initiatives designed to press the Soviets into submission might threaten American security. For instance, conservatives have generally underestimated or ignored the potential Soviet response to a U.S. decision to deploy a strategic defense system or exceed the SALT II treaty limits in any meaningful way. A recent study by the Congressional Research Service found that, given the excess throw-weight of the Soviet Strategic Rocket Forces, the USSR could conceivably deploy up to 50 percent more warheads without adding any new means of delivery.[38] This sort of break-out would pose a severe threat to U.S. security.

The Soviet Response to Soviet Decline

The course of Soviet society will be fundamentally determined by internal economic and political forces and perhaps by contiguous developments in Eastern Europe. The United States can seek to aggravate these difficulties, or ease them, in some instances, but remains essentially a peripheral actor. The vast nuclear arsenal of the USSR serves as a useful deterrent to more ambitious American schemes to challenge the seriousness of the Brezhnev Doctrine in Eastern Europe or encourage ethnic discontent inside the USSR. It was no accident, as the Soviets have noted, that the countries chosen for the Reagan Doctrine did not include any important clients of the USSR in the Third World, let alone in Eastern Europe. Any U.S. initiatives to encourage a Soviet decline are likely to be less significant than the USSR's own responses to such a trend.

It is thus vital to take account of the potential Soviet responses to their own decline before we consider the likely U.S. initiatives to speed, further or maintain it. It is in this manner that the distinction between the *process* of Soviet decline and the *maintenance* of Soviet retrenchment will be made. Drawing on Gilpin's work on great powers in transition,[39] I would suggest there are six distinct strategies (Gilpin lists four) that the USSR might follow in reaction to its perceived slide: (1) improve domestic efficiency; (2) reduce foreign commitments; (3) seek rapprochement with "balancing" powers; (4) make concessions; (5) undertake further external expansion; and (6) wage hegemonic war. Several courses of action might be followed concurrently.

In the modern era of rapid economic growth and technological innovation, societal decline will almost necessarily be precipitous rather than gradual. In the premodern age the process of growth and decline often lasted many centuries; the Byzantine and Chinese empires both lasted a millennium and were in decline for several hundred years. In the contemporary world of heightened vulnerability, however, strategies to reverse the course of decline must show near-term results. A comprehensive set of strategies may increase the likelihood of bolstering a faltering position. Indeed, the USSR now appears to be testing elements of several strategies in hopes of reversing what are perceived to be negative trends. While the conditions of Soviet power are likely to change over the next generation, the choices available to Soviet leaders for coping with these changes will probably remain much the same over the long term.

Mikhail Gorbachev's determination to revitalize and retool the internal Soviet system appears to be based partly on a belief that the USSR must change to remain competitive with the capitalist West. (His immediate predecessors, in contrast, seemed willing to ignore signs of Soviet decline.) Gorbachev has virtually stated that the Soviet Union wishes to concentrate on domestic rather than foreign matters for the time being.[40] Here we are more concerned with the internal focus itself than with the specific reforms through which he hopes to make Soviet society more efficient. The Politburo has historically been willing to apply draconian methods, including starvation and internal military operations, to strengthen its domestic position and stifle unauthorized dissent, and it is not inconceivable that Gorbachev or a successor will again couple reforms with repression to strengthen the USSR.[41] Nevertheless, Gorbachev's initial response to Soviet decline has been to try to reverse the process internally so as to compete more vigorously with the West in the future.

If domestic initiatives alone cannot reduce its vulnerabilities, the USSR will probably cut back on its foreign commitments in the Third World. Unlike Great Britain, which depended on its empire as a source of raw materials and a market for finished products, the USSR gains only prestige from its global empire. The scattered Soviet allies in the Third World are as a whole miserably poor, besieged by domestic rivals and hostile powers, and virtually irrelevant to the Soviet economy. Many are so far from Soviet borders that they would have little military or strategic value to the USSR in a time of East–West crisis. Faced with diminishing resources and mounting domestic difficulties, the USSR might concede to scale back its support for fledgling members of the socialist community in the developing world.

Even now the USSR appears to be reassessing its Third World role. While Gorbachev has spoken extensively and often profoundly about nearly every aspect of Soviet life during his brief tenure as general secretary, he has said little about the future of Soviet policy in the Third World. A close reading of Soviet theoretical journals suggests that there are currently thinly veiled debates between elites about what the ultimate responsibility of the USSR in the Third World should be, with many arguing for a lower profile in the far corners of the globe.[42] The first step in such a retrenchment would be to avoid new involvements, followed perhaps by a stepping back from open-ended commitments to support floundering Marxist regimes. While Gorbachev has launched no new military initiatives in the Third World, the USSR has persevered and even stepped up its military support slightly in countries where he has inherited previous commitments. In the future, however, the Soviets may need to make hard choices concerning resource allocation and entangling foreign involvements in the Third World.

If faced by a powerful coalition of rival powers, the USSR might seek a rapprochement with "balancing" powers in the international system.[43] This need not imply a formal alliance in the strictest sense or even a fundamental transition from a bipolar to a multiple balance of power in the international system. Instead, the USSR might try to reach limited accords and undertake a range of confidence-building measures with the states bordering the Warsaw Pact, notably China, Japan, and Western Europe. By offering incentives carefully tailored for each of these states, the USSR would seek to block the formation of a threatening coalition of anti-Soviet nations.

Some of Gorbachev's regional initiatives appear designed to achieve this goal. In an important speech in Vladivostok during 1986, he held out the possibility of an Asian détente, offering a wide range of commercial, political, military, and territorial enticements. Specifically, Gorbachev publicly acceded to the long-standing Chinese position concerning the contested border; encouraged Japan to become more involved with the ambitious Soviet plans to develop Siberia; offered to participate in an all-Asian conference on the military situation; and pressed hard for an increase in trade between the USSR and the booming economies of the Asian Pacific. Gorbachev has also extended similar proposals to various Western European capitals. Nevertheless, China, Japan and Western Europe remain more interested in a reduction of the Soviet military threat than in an increase in state-to-state trade. (However, if the Soviet Union and its neighbors develop a mutual and enduring interest in trade and common security, this could lead to profound realignment in Eurasian politics and security.) Most of the initiatives, while unprecedented, are modest and should be seen as incentives rather than concessions.

While attempts at domestic reform, moves to rein in foreign commitments, and efforts to establish rapprochement with balancing powers might be viewed as simply adjustments in course, major Soviet concessions under duress would represent a fundamental departure. Such drastic measures might be taken if the Soviet leadership had exhausted the relatively painless remedies to Soviet decline and felt forced to consider bolder, more dangerous steps.

There are precedents in Soviet history for major territorial concessions to hostile powers. For instance, the Treaty of Brest-Litovsk in 1918 surrendered the Ukraine, Finland, the Baltic provinces, the Caucasus, White Russia, and Poland to the advancing German army.[44] While the Bolsheviks' depleted and dispirited army was then no match for the invading German troops, the contemporary Red Army would almost certainly fight before surrendering territory. Most Western commentators believe that the USSR would not retreat peacefully from occupied territory in Eastern Europe and would resist strenuously any attempts to dismember or divide the internal empire.[45]

There are other, perhaps more important, kinds of concessions to be considered in the modern nuclear age. Indeed, territorial reparations could be seen as an anachronism in the current era of arms control negotiations. It is conceivable that the USSR might enter into an unfavorable arms control regime with the United States if the alternatives seemed wholly unsatisfactory. In recent years American negotiators have exacted important concessions from Soviet representatives at least in principle (the USSR has acceded to the U.S. demand that it reduce the number of its land-based ICBMs in exchange for an American commitment to forgo the deployment of SDI), but these have not altered the strategic balance between the superpowers. Nevertheless, it is hard to imagine a Brest-Litovsk style scenario in arms control whereby the USSR allowed the United States a decisive nuclear superiority.

Significant concessions probably cannot be expected unless the international environment makes appeasement and accommodation palatable. Great Britain's graceful decline from world power before World War I was made possible by its "special relationship" with the United States, which allowed the rewards and responsibilities of power to shift gradually from Whitehall to Washington. Today, in contrast, the Soviet Union views itself as the only true manifestation of Marxist-Leninist power and the jumping-off point for the future worldwide communist revolution. There is no state to which it can hand off the responsibility of carrying the torch of the revolution (or in Lenin's words, the "spark" [Iskra] of the coming uprising). Thus national survival and the Marxist prophecies of nearly Biblical significance demand that the USSR maintain its power.

It has also been suggested that the USSR might seek to bolster its faltering international position by means of further expansion. Edward Luttwak, for example, has argued that "regime pessimism" about the course of Soviet decline might trigger an expansionist war into adjacent countries.[46] Such a desperate act, Luttwak acknowledges, would potentially have catastrophic consequences, both externally and internally. A Soviet strategy designed for the imperial military conquest of China or Europe might well trigger the nuclear war we seek to avoid.

On the subject of a hegemonic war, Gilpin has written, "The first and most attractive response to a society's decline is to eliminate the source of the problem. By launching a preventative war the declining power destroys or weakens the rising challenger while the military advantage is still with the declining power."[47] This is roughly the strategy for a surprise Soviet nuclear attack on the United States outlined in Richard Pipes's contentious article in Commentary. While we "consider nuclear war unfeasible and suicidal for both," Pipes wrote, "our chief adversary [the USSR] views it as feasible and winnable for himself."[48] While there is spirited debate among Western military specialists about whether Soviet strategic deployments and doctrine reflect a belief that nuclear war is winnable or not,[49] again, for the purposes of this study, a nuclear attack on the United States would be an unacceptable price to pay for Soviet decline.

The Soviet response to internal decline ultimately hinges on the internal psychology and calculus of Soviet decision making. Many Western commentators cite the historical propensity of Soviet leaders (and Russian leaders before them) to avoid risky foreign initiatives during periods of internal turmoil or uncertainty. Given an unsupportive domestic constituency or an unfavorable international environment, Soviet leaders tend to turn their attention inward, away from involvement in foreign adventures. This *peredyshka* (brief respite) is seen as a way to concentrate temporarily on domestic matters before re-emerging on the international scene more powerful than before. After the Great Patriotic War, for example, Stalin reportedly told Milovan Djilas, "We shall recover in fifteen or twenty years, and then we'll have another go at it."[50] Such caution has been predicated on the assumption that the USSR would ultimately triumph in the long run, despite short-term losses or setbacks. If, after failing at internal renovation and reform, the regime became convinced that Soviet power was irreversibly fading, it might well be tempted to use its military might to conquer abroad what it could not create at home. If an irreversible "regime pessimism" does set in among the Soviet leadership, the USSR could become a much more dangerous and risk-taking adversary.

Soviet Decline and the International System

If, through a combination of internal collapse and external restraint, the USSR declined peacefully and appreciably from superpower status, the task of the West would then be to maintain the Soviet downfall and prevent the recreation of Soviet power. In some respects, this would resemble the challenge faced by the West early in the Cold War, but with a goal of curtailing rather than containing Soviet power.[51] Two different kinds of international systems might result from a Soviet decline: (1) the United States stands alone as the predominant power in the world; or (2) the USSR faces a coalition of anti-Soviet states, with varying degrees of power and influence.

A world of unmatched American supremacy, with the United States enjoying a clear military advantage over the USSR, would be formidably difficult to maintain. Unless the Soviet nuclear arsenal were reduced drastically (or rendered irrelevant by a defensive system), even a sizable U.S. military edge would have little relevance. As Henry Kissinger poignantly observed, "In the nuclear age, it is no longer possible to assume that by patient accumulation of marginal advantage one can ultimately destroy one's opponent."[52] The Soviet ability to inflict unacceptable damage on American society with even a very small number of nuclear weapons makes political coercion exceedingly risky and dangerous.

Classical balance-of-power theory predicts that other powerful states in the system would side with the USSR to prevent unrivaled U.S. superiority and maintain the equilibrium of the international system. It has been argued that the rise of Soviet power in the 1960s curbed American indiscretions and deterred U.S. adventurism in the Third World.[53] Some European, Chinese, and Japanese observers might interpret Soviet decline as ushering in an era of unchecked American power. Many third parties wish to see both superpowers deterred and might well strike a bargain with the Soviets in order to ensure a balanced system. In addition, there would be significant domestic opposition to a U.S. effort to maintain a costly global military superiority, in the face of stiff economic competition from our allies.

In a world of Soviet decline and American hegemony, if indeed it is possible to arrive at such a destination, the risks of catastrophic nuclear war would probably be reduced. The USSR could fend off unwanted American intrusions into its domestic affairs, but Soviet leaders could pose no corresponding threat to the United States. The reduced Soviet deterrent could be used only in the most extreme instances, when the choice was between surrender and national suicide. However, this hypothetical world has some troublesome characteristics (mentioned above) that are not in U.S. interests.

A Soviet decline from superpower status would probably be coupled with an increase in the power of ascending states such as China, Japan, and West Germany. In this world, a coalition of rival powers, including the United States, would preside over Soviet retrenchment. However, unlike a world of American hegemony, a multiple alliance of states would be required to confront the USSR. Kenneth Waltz, among others, has argued that such a multipolar system would be much less stable than the present bipolar structure.[54] Furthermore, the proliferation of significant nuclear arsenals is perhaps more likely, with all the dangers that entails. While some studies have argued that the growth in the number of states that possess deliverable nuclear weapons would strengthen global deterrence in certain cases, most experts agree that proliferation increases the risks of accidental or inadvertent nuclear war.[55] Even if our allies' acquisition of nuclear weapons reduces the possibility of war between the United States and the Soviet Union, the effect on the other nations' foreign policy remains unclear. For instance, a Japanese nuclear capability might very well pose a threat to U.S. security. Indeed, it could be argued that the United States has managed its strategic competition with the Soviets better than its economic rivalry with Japan.[56] Furthermore, nuclear proliferation might serve as a catalyst for regional nuclear wars (as between India and Pakistan).

In a multipolar world as in one dominated by American power, states bordering the USSR would tend to seek a political accommodation with Moscow.[57] In either case it may well be easier for the USSR to undermine an anti-Soviet coalition than for the United States to maintain it. Furthermore, both alternative systems have the potential to decay into a world order marked by an anti-American coalition. Thus, while the maintenance of the new world order might involve less risk of conflict than the process of Soviet decline, U.S. security would not necessarily be enhanced over the long term.

Conclusion

The potential for Soviet decline will continue to play an important role in shaping American foreign policy. Indeed, the temptation to adopt more ambitious policies to challenge the Soviets will increase as the process of Soviet decline accelerates. A very real danger is that U.S. and Soviet expectations and world views might not be accurately attuned to the process of decline. Thus, the United States might demand a bigger international role sooner than would be merited by Soviet decline, while the USSR might require a large role long after its "objective" claim to such a position has faded (as some might argue Britain has done). These mismatched expectations could lead to confrontation and crisis, with the United States and the USSR seeking to extend or defend new international frontiers.

American policy makers should bear in mind the Soviet propensity to link all forms of internal dissent and opposition to "counter-revolutionary" and "imperialist" forces sponsored and directed by the United States. It is one thing to probe the Soviets on the peripheries and gingerly test the "global correlation of forces"; it is quite another to challenge Soviet national security directly. The existence of a large Soviet deterrent renders any fundamental change in the balance of power exceedingly dangerous. Although economic decline might reduce the USSR's ability to wage a protracted conventional war, this industrial downturn would not adversely affect the USSR's nuclear arsenal already in place. It is somewhat surprising, since nuclear weapons make an eclipse of Soviet power much more problematic, that conservative proponents of Soviet decline have so fiercely resisted arms control.[58]

A significant reduction in the Soviet arsenal is the most promising (and least threatening) way to manage a transition from a bipolar world to one with the Soviets in decline. The larger the gap between Soviet military power and domestic economic failure, the more American security will be jeopardized by the possibility of a Soviet-initiated conflict. The United States can exacerbate Soviet difficulties, but it has not created them. Similarly, the United States can help ease Soviet difficulties but cannot erase them. Soviet problems will be solved or exacerbated internally. In any case, given the perils of a declining superpower with a vast nuclear arsenal, the key question is whether the United States has an interest in maintaining a rough balance of power with the Soviet Union. At least one writer has said that Western realpolitik requires the survival of the Soviets as a superpower, because the alternatives are worse.[59]

It would be premature to suggest that the early signs of Soviet decline may not be irreversible. Indeed, the USSR has powerful reasons to expend every effort to recover from its recent stagnation. Soviet leaders probably consider themselves fortunate that the United States did not bring to bear its atomic monopoly in the early years of the Cold War. If the situations of the two nations had been reversed and Moscow alone possessed the secret of the bomb, Soviet leaders might not have exercised the same restraint. Having been allowed the opportunity to recover and take a position as a superpower, Soviet leaders do not plan to allow the United States a second chance at superiority.

CHAPTER 9

Internationalism: Contacts, Trade, and Institutions

David Welch

Imagine how much good we can accomplish, how the cause of peace would be served, if more individuals and families from our respective countries would come to know each other in a personal way. For example, if Soviet youth could attend American schools and universities, they could learn firsthand what spirit of freedom rules our land and that we do not wish the Soviet people any harm.

—Ronald Reagan [1]

Over time, trade and investment may lessen the autarkic tendencies of the Soviet system, invite gradual association of the Soviet economy with the world economy, and foster a degree of interdependence that adds an element of stability to the political equation.

—Henry Kissinger [2]

The only rational reply to the challenge which nationalism presents to the peace and order of the world is the voluntary cooperation of a number of nations with common interests for the purpose of creating supra-national institutions after the model of the specialized agencies of the United Nations and of the European Communities. These institutions would gradually take over the functions which the nation state has traditionally performed but is no longer able to perform today. If nation states acted in accord with the rational requirements of the age, they would strive, as it were, to make themselves superfluous.

—Hans Morganthau [3]

Some analysts would argue that the fundamental cause of international conflict is the existence and operation of the system of sovereign states

The author gratefully wishes to acknowledge the support of the Social Sciences and Humanities Research Council of Canada.

itself.[4] The more radical exponents of this view advocate abolishing that system altogether and replacing it with some form of supranational political authority, an approach that is examined in Chapter 10. Others, including many who deny that supranational authority is possible or desirable, advocate policies designed to constrain the action of states, limit their policy options, make conflict or uncooperative behavior unacceptably costly to them, and undercut the social and political bases of support for belligerence.

In this chapter, I examine three such schemes. The first, which I call the *contacts* approach, suggests that world politics can be pacified if parochial, nationalistic attitudes are eroded by exposure to other peoples and cultures; the second, or *web of trade*, approach, holds that increased global economic interaction would mollify interstate relations; and the third, or *institutions* approach, maintains that states would have less inclination, opportunity, or need to go to war with one another if their interactions were mediated by a complex and stable structure of international organizations and regimes.[5] All of these approaches may be called "internationalist" because their intent is to transform world politics so as to reduce the relevance of national boundaries—and hence the primacy of national governments—in world affairs.

In the international relations literature, these approaches are found most often in discussions of transnationalism and interdependence. Whereas sovereign states have been the primary actors in world politics since the seventeenth century, there have always been other influential actors extending and operating across national boundaries; historically, important "transnational actors" have included churches, multinational corporations, and modern international organizations.[6] Many believe that the rapid growth of transnational activities has fundamentally altered the nature of world politics by changing attitudes, increasing pluralism, constraining states' foreign policy options, affecting the ability of governments to influence each other, and altering the global agenda.[7] Groups such as Pugwash and International Physicians for the Prevention of Nuclear War, many believe, illustrate how transnational coalitions can be influential in all these respects, with beneficial effects on the climate and substance of international politics. Others argue that transnational actors cannot have any significant independent effect because they operate only at the pleasure of sovereign states.[8] While the trends and implications of transnationalism may be debated, it seems undeniable that new forces are now active in world politics, and it is important in the nuclear age to determine what risks and opportunities are associated with them.

The term *interdependence* has been used in a variety of ways by policy makers and scholars alike.[9] Not all uses of the term rely on the notion of transnationalism (though some writers use the terms almost interchangeably), nor does increasing transnational activity necessarily entail increasing interdependence. I shall simply use the term to indicate mutual reliance between states; thus a relationship is interdependent if its disruption would be significantly costly to the states concerned.[10] In the web of trade approach, which seeks explicitly to use greater interdependence as a force for peace, the interdependence is economic, and the agents spinning the webs are largely transnational actors. But not all forms of interdependence are economic. The aspect of Soviet–American relations most accurately described as interdependent today is the nuclear relationship: both states depend on the system of deterrence, and a violent breakdown of the deterrent relationship would be catastrophic for both. Those who object to relying on deterrence to preserve peace consider the risks associated with *this* form of interdependence unacceptable, and many would agree that "war prevention would rest on much safer ground . . . if gas lines and electric grids took the place of rockets."[11]

All three of the approaches examined here are aimed directly at reducing the likelihood of conflict between the superpowers, not its likely destructiveness.[12] None directly addresses the level or type of nuclear armament in the system, or the nature of nonnuclear technology—although, clearly, improved communication and transportation technologies can support a greater volume and variety of transnational contacts, economic transactions, and institutional arrangements.[13] Thus our focus will be on the structure, process, and domestic politics variables, for these are the ones internationalist approaches seek to manipulate to improve the prospects for peace, and these are the ones on which they stand or fall.

Contacts

President Reagan's remark quoted at the beginning of this chapter is a simple expression of the contacts thesis: that exposure to other peoples and cultures will increase mutual understanding, mutual sympathy, and hence the prospects for peace. Three different groups might be targeted as the beneficiaries of transnational contacts: citizens at large; the informed elite—journalists, businesspeople, professionals, and academics who have more direct influence on policy; and government officials themselves.

Can the contacts approach alter the nature of international politics so as to lessen the likelihood of conflict? The case for the affirmative was set out in greatest detail by Robert Angell in his pioneering 1969 work *Peace on the March*, which suggested that certain transnational experiences, other than purely communicative or transient contacts (such as tourism), have net positive effects on accommodative attitudes except when they take the form of overseas military service, missionary work, or residence abroad for business purposes.[14] Since it is impossible for whole societies to have the kinds of contacts found to be beneficial, Angell focused his attention on "the informed elite," which he believed had a disproportionate influence on policy makers.[15] Two important parts of Angell's thesis warrant attention: first, the claim that contacts have an accommodative effect on attitudes; second, the claim that the informed elite has the influence on policy making that he suggests.

Angell has been attacked on both counts. While some have agreed that transnational contact tends to erode nationalism and promote more cosmopolitan attitudes, others have argued that this occurs only under favorable conditions, which do not necessarily obtain.[16] Sociological work indicates that interpersonal interactions usually decrease antagonism, but not always; often the reverse is the case.[17] The effects of transnational contacts on attitudes seem to depend on several factors:

The prearrival characteristics of the participant
- Initial motives for contact
- Stage in life cycle
- Attitudes toward the home country
- Attitudes toward the host country
- Communication skills

The character of the transnational experience
- Cultural congruity
- Status discrepancy
- Duration of contacts
- Organizational context

Postreturn conditions related to the transnational experience

The effect of the transnational experience on policy depends on the participant's access to and influence on decision makers, and whether the experience was positive or negative. Under certain conditions, the contacts approach may be desirable and effective; under others, undesirable and counterproductive.[18]

Of particular concern is the case of U.S.–Soviet relations—the relationship of major tension in the international system. If the contacts approach will not help us realize a tangible gain here, it will be of limited value for reducing the risks of catastrophic war. Thus we must examine the plausibility and desirability of the contacts approach both in general terms and with respect to this "hard case."

What structural conditions would be conducive to the contacts approach? Clearly, the fewer negative prearrival characteristics participants have, the fewer obstacles they must overcome to realize a positive attitude shift. Likewise, the fewer points of conflict participants have during their transnational experiences, the more likely they are to come away with a more accommodative disposition. "Realist" theory suggests that, all other things being equal, the structure of the international system will affect these two variables: the two most powerful states in the system will always tend to be enemies and competitors, whereas states in a diffuse or multipolar system will tend to be more flexible in their alignments and more willing to explore cooperative policies with others, even former adversaries.[19] Even though the contacts approach might significantly improve accommodative attitudes between most peoples around the globe, realism suggests that it should not be expected to ameliorate U.S.–Soviet hostility substantially as long as the United States and the Soviet Union are the dominant powers in the system.

This is not to assume the accuracy of Realist theory in all its particulars; but historically the United States and the Soviet Union have indeed had difficulty cooperating on a broad range of issues and have never enjoyed a sustained period of cordial, constructive relations. The United States and the USSR have defined their material and ideological interests in largely incompatible ways, and the transnational experiences of Soviets and Americans have been handicapped as a result. Recent trends toward the erosion of the Cold War bipolar system suggest that opportunities for constructive transnational experiences between Soviets and Americans are increasing, but we should not expect a large-scale shift in attitudes unless the two countries begin to define their material and ideological interests more compatibly.[20] This redefinition of interests might conceivably occur without an erosion of bipolarity—realist tenets to the contrary—if there were a significant transformation in one of the superpowers' domestic politics.[21] A liberal democratic revolution in the Soviet Union, for example, would certainly ameliorate the ideological conflict and might increase the coincidence of material interests (allowing the development of mutually beneficial economic ties). If the Soviets seemed to be more "like us," transnational contacts could be expected to generate more accommodative attitudes because there would be fewer obstacles for them to overcome.[22]

American and Soviet domestic politics have not been particularly congenial to the contacts approach, though with *glasnost* and *perestroika* prospects would appear to be improving. Currently, however, Soviet and American political value systems differ so widely in certain crucial respects that transnational contacts are as likely to generate confusion, hostility, and defensiveness as understanding and mutual sympathy. Soviets consistently fail to understand American pluralistic politics and the virtues claimed for it; similarly they do not see why formal political rights and liberties are valued more highly in America than the universal provision of basic material needs. Similarly, Americans are inherently suspicious of centralized political systems and the denial of basic civil liberties.[23] The contacts thesis does not explain how such a clash in fundamental values can be overcome by transnational experiences. Moreover, despite their various cultural and ideological differences, Soviets and Americans consistently indicate that their hostilities are directed at each other's governments, rather than at each other's populations. Even if person-to-person contacts generated mutual sympathy and understanding, these attitude changes would be unlikely to have much effect on attitudes toward opposing policy makers, leaving the initial direction of influence on national foreign policy largely unchanged.

In the Soviet case at least, public attitudes have traditionally had virtually no bearing on policy choices, though they seem destined to become increasingly important. Public attitudes have a significantly greater bearing on American policy choices, since, among other things, citizens can express their approval or disapproval at the polls, and Congress can translate popular opinion into legislative fiat.[24] But we cannot expect the transnational contacts Angell found beneficial to have a major effect on mass opinion in the United States simply because of the difficulties of organizing contacts on that scale. The best we might hope for is a sustained attempt to improve the quantity and quality of vicarious contacts — through media coverage of life and politics in foreign lands, particularly the Soviet Union. In this way large segments of the population may have some opportunity to refine and reconsider their prior beliefs without residence abroad, and translate them into some degree of political influence. New communications technologies (such as direct-broadcast satellites) could facilitate such an effort, but it will also require the political willingness on both sides of the Iron Curtain to reduce existing constraints on broadcasts and receptions. Such a move is unlikely except in an improved climate of trust, simply because the broadcast media are vehicles of enormous power. Even if the airwaves were liberalized, it is not clear whether we should expect much in the way of positive attitude shifts. Much would depend on the content of the broadcasts, who controls them, their intended uses, their appeal, and their fairness.

Angell's emphasis on the importance of elite attitudes and direct transnational contacts neglects the potential importance of mass attitudes, at least in the United States. In any case it is not clear that the elite has the influence he attributes to it. The elite is a heterogeneous body in which competing interests and values struggle constantly to be heard. At any given time there may be a dominant tendency and a dominant direction of influence, but every impetus for change is resisted by the inertia of vested interests and by contrary pressures in other directions. In a climate of this sort, decision makers are more likely to be confirmed in their existing attitudes than moved to change them by the opinions of others. They are constrained in their flexibility by their own belief structures, their personal histories, their perceptions of their adversaries, and their understandings of their institutional roles. Thus they are selective in what they pay attention to, paying relatively greater heed to ideas that reinforce their own prior beliefs, and relatively less to dissonant notions.[25] Though these factors limit the influence of others on policy makers' behavior, they can be powerfully affected by their own transnational experiences, however. Among other things, these effects can include a reduction in knee-jerk hostility; a deeper understanding of an adversary's wants, needs, and insecurities; greater sensitivity to the cooperative and complementary dimensions of a relationship; and an improved understanding of the importance of concepts such as stability in a relationship.

The processes of international politics that would be most conducive to the contacts approach are simply those that would afford a greater number and variety of contacts under favorable conditions. Thus a world with multiple channels of communication and stable patterns of transnational activities would be better suited to the contacts approach than one in which states mediate and politicize most of the meaningful interactions between peoples. These channels by themselves will not necessarily improve attitudes—regular contacts frequently breed hatred and contempt, as has happened between the Russians and the Poles, the Greeks and the Turks, and the Arabs and the Israelis. But the contacts approach will have its most salutary effect if adversaries are already leaning in the direction of greater accommodation. This movement is unlikely to be the result of apolitical mass or elite contacts alone; but the evidence suggests that well-designed contacts at these levels will have some favorable effect on attitudes most of the time.[26] Over the long run, these contacts can help sustain improved political relationships by reinforcing predispositions toward cooperative relations. More fruitful—especially in the short run, perhaps—are direct contacts between government officials themselves, who often reap an immediate dividend from transnational encounters.

Contacts alone cannot solve tangible political problems and real conflicts of interest. Nevertheless the contacts approach may help cement positive attitudinal shifts so that, with generational change, traditional enmities—what Wolfers calls the "real evil" in international politics—may eventually be overcome.[27]

Trade

The web of trade is an idea familiar to students of détente. Henry Kissinger suggested that "by acquiring a stake in [an economic] network with the West, the Soviet Union may become more conscious of what it would lose by a return to confrontation. Indeed, it is our expectation that it will develop a self-interest in fostering the entire process of relaxation of tensions."[28] As State Department Counselor Richard Pederson put it, "expanded East–West trade can become a pivotal element in building a structure of peace."[29]

This notion dates back to the early liberal economic and political theorists, who supposed that international trade would transform conflict relations into peaceful ones.[30] Two versions of this view are associated with the Manchester School (so named because it flourished in the nineteenth-century British Midlands). The first version, a restatement of the contacts thesis, held that "the free flow of goods across national boundaries would . . . erase misunderstandings and differences of opinion among the world's peoples. Trade would break down national barriers because merchants carried in their packs fresh ideas and new visions."[31] The second version, on which I will focus here, held that international trade would eventually become so important and so beneficial to trading nations that war would price itself out of existence.[32] Thus Norman Angell argued in 1909 that European economic interdependence made war too costly and therefore impossible.[33]

He was tragically mistaken. World War I dealt a devastating blow to the Manchester School and inaugurated a long period in which the common wisdom held that trade had little or no positive effect on conflict; many even argued that nations that were interdependent in trade were more, not less, likely to engage in conflict.[34] As Kenneth Waltz puts it, close interdependence means closeness of contact and raises the prospect of at least occasional conflict. The fiercest civil wars and the bloodiest international ones have been fought within areas populated by highly similar people whose affairs had become quite closely knit together. It is hard to get a war going unless the potential participants are somehow closely linked. Interdependent states whose relations remain unregulated must experience conflict and will occasionally fall into violence. If regulation is hard to come by, as it is in the relations of states, then it would seem to follow that a lessening of interdependence is desirable.[35]

Geoffrey Blainey writes, "the Manchester creed cannot be a vital part of a theory of war and peace. One cannot even be sure whether those influences which it emphasizes actually have promoted peace more than war."[36]

The case for this pessimistic view seems superficially convincing. All ten of the bloodiest interstate wars have grown out of conflicts between countries that either bordered each other or actively traded with each other; people are generally far more dependent on domestic trade than international trade, and yet civil wars are more common than interstate wars; Germany was Russia's single largest trading partner in 1914, and also the Soviet Union's in 1941.[37] Accordingly, some critics have suggested that the web of trade approach mistakes effects for causes—that closer trade relationships may *follow* improved political relationships, but they cannot *lead* to them.[38] A disillusioned Henry Kissinger adopted this view after the failure of détente. The theory that trade will mellow Soviet behavior, he wrote ten years later, is contradicted by Soviet actions in Angola, Ethiopia, South Yemen, Afghanistan, and Poland during a period of expanding East–West trade.[39]

If the pessimistic view is accurate, then the web of trade approach would certainly be either useless or counterproductive. To examine the question properly, we must begin by distinguishing the various claims that are involved in the debate:

1. Trade guarantees peace.
2. Trade lessens the likelihood of war, all other things being equal.
3. Trade increases the likelihood of war, all other things being equal.
4. Trade has no relationship to the likelihood of war either way.

History clearly refutes the first claim, and it should not be seriously entertained. The web of trade approach would not be worth pursuing if the third proposition were true, unless the particular extenuating features of the East–West case made it attractive bilaterally; nor would it be worth pursuing *for security purposes* if the fourth claim were true.

The evidence and arguments mustered on behalf of the third claim are really quite weak. It is not at all surprising, for instance, that many of the bloodiest interstate wars are fought by neighbors. Bordering states have more to fight over—in particular, their borders—and it is certainly much easier for two neighbors to wage war than for two states with no common frontier. Being neighbors, being trading partners, and having disagreements on other issues are all highly correlated; in an explanation of the causes of war, the degree of trade may be a largely spurious factor.

Similarly, though people in domestic societies are generally more economically interdependent than states in the international system, comparatively few civil wars would occur in the absence of more pressing political, cultural, and religious disputes. The American civil war cannot be explained without primary reference to the slavery question; the Spanish civil war cannot be explained without primary reference to ideological divisions; and the current civil war in Lebanon cannot be explained without primary reference to religious factionalism. None of these civil wars can be explained well by appeal to the level of economic interdependence between warring parties.

Interdependence can increase the number of points of friction between societies, however, particularly where economic interests are less than fully harmonious.[40] But the key questions are whether (in general) the increased risks of conflict associated with the inherent stresses in a web of trade are offset by the incentives to seek cooperative solutions to economic disputes in interdependent relationships (especially in the nuclear age), and whether there are any *specific* conditions under which interdependence in trade will reduce the risks of conflict, despite even a *general* tendency in the opposite direction.

Occasionally, a dispute arising from an interdependent relationship may provide the grievance that ultimately leads to a conflict. Some states may even go to war in order to avoid having to rely on others for their economic well-being. Japanese aggression in World War II, for instance, may be interpreted as an attempt to secure the conditions for autarky.[41] But there are few examples of the Japanese kind, and most trading relationships have been peaceful ones. Comparatively few have resulted in saber-rattling, let alone war, even when there have been sharp disagreements over economic issues. The greatest trading partners of all time—the United States and Canada—perennially disagree on economic issues, and yet they form a model pluralistic security community. If interdependence were causally related to conflict, the world's longest undefended border would be virtually impossible to explain. Finally, though the costs of disrupting economic relationships have not always deterred outbreaks of war, as the world becomes increasingly interdependent, wars seem to break out less frequently and to have been largely displaced to the periphery.[42]

The second claim can account for these considerations. Where disruption of an interdependent relationship entails cost, those costs will weigh in the balance against armed conflict. It would certainly be difficult to argue that the prospect of disrupting such a relationship is an incentive to go to war.

Not all interdependent relationships will remain peaceful, however, since "all other things" are rarely equal. From time to time, the stresses of an interdependent relationships (particularly a grossly asymmetrical one) will lead to conflict where none would have occurred in the absence of interdependence. One of the many tasks still facing political science is that of identifying the conditions under which interdependence can reliably be expected to reduce risks of war. It may be, for instance (as Kant believed), that the risks will never be minimized until all states become constitutional republics.[43] But we can attempt to identify some of the conditions under which the web of trade approach would most likely yield the desired dividend. To do so, we will look again at structure, process, and domestic politics.

Some would argue that, in a system of sovereign states, webs of trade will always be fragile and difficult to spin, especially between the most powerful states in the system. Kenneth Waltz asserts, for example—somewhat incongruously given his argument above—that "interdependence is *always* a marginal affair in international relations," since it is a function of different units performing different functions and interacting on the basis of comparative advantages. In developed domestic economies, interdependence is always high; in international politics, however, the primary units (states) are structurally and functionally similar and tasks are duplicated rather than divided along lines of comparative advantage.[44]

Waltz's argument significantly underestimates the importance and implications of comparative advantages in world trade and politics. Not all states have the resources, the manpower, or the physical conditions needed to pursue autarkic economic policies, and what they cannot produce themselves must be traded for. If Waltz were correct, international trade would also be a "marginal affair"—and clearly it is not. But though Waltz seems to be wrong about global interdependence, his observations fit the East–West case fairly well. The United States and the Soviet Union are the two nations that best approximate the conditions for autarky, and East–West trade *is* largely a marginal affair, with the notable exception of the East bloc's dependence on Western Europe's goods and markets. (See Table 1.)

Table 1. East–West Interdependence in Trade

1a. Western Exports
Figures indicate the percentage of each source's total exports imported by the destination and the ratio of the value of those exports to the source's GNP.

		Destination			
		Socialist Countries of Eastern Europe (excluding USSR)		*USSR*	
Source	*Year*				
European developed market economies*	1960	2.5%	.0039	1.7%	.0027
	1970	2.6	.0048	1.6	.0029
	1975	3.4	.0073	2.5	.0054
	1979	2.4	.0057	1.9	.0044
United States	1960	0.8	.0003	0.2	<.0001
	1970	0.5	.0002	0.3	.0012
	1975	0.9	.0006	1.7	.0012
	1979	1.2	.0009	2.1	.0015

1b. Western Imports
Figures indicate the percentage of each destination's total imports exported by the source and the ratio of the value of those imports to the destination's GNP.

		Source			
		Socialist Countries of Eastern Europe (excluding USSR)		*USSR*	
Destination	*Year*				
European developed market economies*	1960	2.5%	.0043	1.8%	.0030
	1970	2.8	.0052	1.6	.0030
	1975	2.6	.0058	2.3	.0049
	1979	2.3	.0056	2.6	.0065
United States	1960	0.4	.0001	0.2	<.0001
	1970	0.4	.0002	0.2	.0001
	1975	0.5	.0003	0.2	.0001
	1979	0.6	.0005	0.3	.0002

1c. Soviet and Socialist East European Exports

Figures indicate the percentage of each source's total exports imported by the destination and the ratio of the value of those exports to the source's estimated GNP.

		Destination			
		European Developed Market Economies*		United States	
Source	Year				
Socialist Eastern Europe (exc. USSR)	1960	18.4%	.0117	0.7%	.0005
	1970	22.4	.0174	0.9	.0007
	1975	22.2	.0247	1.0	.0011
	1979	24.0	.0293	1.6	.0020
USSR**	1960	17.3	.0040	0.4	.0001
	1970	17.7	.0043	0.5	.0001
	1975	25.3	.0094	0.6	.0002
	1979	29.8	.0153	0.8	.0004

1d. Soviet and Socialist East European Imports

Figures indicate the percentage of each destination's total imports exported by the source and the ratio of the value of those imports to the destination's estimated GNP.

		Source			
		European Developed Market Economies*		United States	
Destination	Year				
Socialist Eastern Europe* (exc. USSR)	1960	16.7%	.0108	2.1%	.0013
	1970	21.0	.0159	1.4	.0010
	1975	26.4	.0315	2.0	.0024
	1979	23.3	.0298	2.8	.0036
USSR	1960	16.2	.0036	0.7	.0002
	1970	19.5	.0042	1.1	.0002
	1975	26.1	.0103	5.2	.0020
	1979	24.4	.0105	6.6	.0029

* Excluding trade conducted in accordance with the Supplementary Protocol to the Treaty on the Basis of Relations between the FRG and the GDR.

** The destinations of a marginal proportion of Soviet exports could not be reliably determined and are not included; actual Soviet exports are probably slightly higher than the figures shown.

Source: Calculated from United Nations Conference on Trade and Development (UNCTAD), Trends in World Production and Trade (New York: United Nations, 1983), pp. 24–27; World Bank, World Tables, 3d ed., vol. 1 (Baltimore: Johns Hopkins University Press, 1983); and National Foreign Assessment Center, Handbook of Economic Statistics 1981 (November 1981).

While East–West trade has been growing fairly rapidly in absolute terms, the United States and the Soviet Union are far from being bound in a web of interdependence. But there is a rough fit between the U.S. and Soviet economies. The Soviets have a pressing need for capital and technology to develop their resource potential; they consistently require significant imports of grain from foreign sources in quantities that depend on the size of the Soviet harvest; and they can make use of Western high technology to shore up inadequacies in their own civilian high-tech sector.[45] The United States could make use of Soviet raw and semi-processed materials, strategic metals (as a supplement to South African sources), and even oil (as a long-term alternative to OPEC sources).[46] Under favorable conditions, the potential would exist for a mutually beneficial U.S.–Soviet trading relationship.

Current conditions, however, are manifestly unfavorable. Since 1945 the two rival political systems have developed largely independent economic systems despite some obvious compatibilities.[47] To some extent this trend reflects an attempt to avoid economic interdependence that might be coercively exploited. The best of all possible worlds is to have an adversary dependent on you, but not vice versa; failing that, the tendency is to seek self-reliance, even at the cost of foregoing possible advantages from trade.[48]

This tendency can be reversed, but only if the partners to a trading relationship learn to trust each other not to play politics with trade. In the U.S.–Soviet case, this trust has been difficult to achieve, largely because of the temptation to use trade as a foreign policy weapon, to reward good behavior and to punish bad. But as the American experience with economic sanctions has shown, attempts to use trade in this way are often self-defeating; they may simply spur the target nation to change its practices so as to reduce its dependence and eliminate the possibility of further economic coercion. Thus after 1979, the Soviet Union diversified its grain sources so that it would no longer have to depend on unreliable American supplies.[49] The web of trade approach, recognizing that when trade is used as a weapon it can only inflame conflict, sees a different political role for interdependence—as a way to develop stable and lasting incentives to help pacify hostile relations, or to help preserve relatively peaceful relations if they may be attained through other means.[50]

A major obstacle to increased trade is the fact that the Soviet Union and the United States see themselves as adversaries and are suspicious of each other's motives for increasing economic interaction. Several developments might help alleviate this problem. If the Soviets were challenged by a burgeoning China or Japan, as seems likely over the next fifty years, they might be more willing to secure their western flank through political accommodation and they might be more interested in opening their economy to Western goods and capital in an attempt to maintain their Far Eastern position.[51] Independently—though even more so if concurrently—a stabilization of Western trade policies and a multilateral commitment not to use trade and investment as policy weapons might encourage the Soviets to sacrifice a degree of self-reliance for the sake of income and welfare gains.

Increased trade with the West would offer the USSR a renewed climate of détente and improved prospects for arms control; access to Western trade, technology, and credits to help replace the aging Soviet capital stock; and some increase in the regime's domestic popularity, brought about by the successes of a peace program and higher standards of living. Despite internal debate, recent statements suggest that the Soviet leadership is beginning to appreciate these advantages and is beginning to lean in the direction of greater ties:

> The party's course of accelerating the country's socioeconomic development makes serious demands on foreign economic activity. We proceed from the premise that in the modern world it is vitally necessary to actively develop economic, scientific, and technical ties and to participate in the international division of labor. We view this as an important means of maintaining and strengthening peaceful, good-neighborly relations among states and mutual assistance in resolving national economic problems. . . .
> The Soviet Union, true to the policy of peaceful coexistence, favors cooperation with developed capitalist states. We see quite considerable potential here. This applies to virtually all kinds of ties—trade, scientific, technical, financial, credit, and others.[52]

Mere expressions of interest, however, do not go very far in overcoming the many tangible barriers to increased trade that have to do with domestic politics and the differences between socialist and capitalist economic systems.[53]

Some of the more intractable barriers to trade are associated with the technicalities of East bloc central planning: currency inconvertibility;[54] commodity inconvertibility;[55] hard currency shortages;[56] and arbitrary, irrational pricing.[57] Others are a function of the typically inferior quality and dated design of East bloc manufactured goods, which are consequently seldom in demand in the West. The inferior quality of East bloc goods reflects aging plant and equipment, poor assimilation of research and development in the civilian sector, and (perhaps more than any-thing else) a productive system that rewards—or at least fails to punish—inefficiency, sloppy workmanship, and absenteeism. East bloc quality control has generally been so poor that very few Soviet and East European manufactures can compete with Western goods on the open market.

Dramatic improvements in trade will have to await relatively fun-damental and far-reaching economic reforms in the Eastern bloc, includ-ing limited currency convertibility, market pricing for certain types of goods, and a degree of decentralization of economic decision making. Such changes are not unlikely within the next half-century. Our expe-rience with Hungary and the People's Republic of China shows that changes of this kind *are* possible, and that a significant expansion in trade can follow very rapidly. It is difficult to gauge the likelihood of sweeping economic reforms of this kind in the Soviet Union; but to maintain its position against Far Eastern economic challenges, it may be forced to attempt successively longer steps toward liberalization, and this would bode well for the web of trade approach.

Further political barriers to trade arise on the American side. Some have to do with legitimate security concerns, such as attempts to stem the flow of sensitive technology to the Soviet bloc. The United States has been erratic in its application of export controls, however, and ham-handed in its attempts to secure allied cooperation. In combination with cross-issue linkages, this clumsiness has resulted in a reputation for un-reliability and paternalism, confirmed most forcefully when Secretary of Agriculture Earl Butz's 1972 promise that the USSR would be "abso-lutely safe" relying on U.S. grain to build up its livestock herds was vio-lated by a later administration.[58] The Jackson–Vanik amendment to the Trade Reform Bill of 1973, which linked the granting of most favored na-tion status and Eximbank loans to freer East European and Soviet emi-gration policies, was perceived in the Soviet Union as a tactless inter-ference in Soviet domestic affairs, and it ultimately proved damaging to economic and political relations with the Soviets.[59] Americans have al-ways played politics with Soviet trade, and the Soviets have learned from experience not to trust them.

Another important barrier is the fact that many Americans (typically conservatives) oppose increased trade with the Soviets, believing it tends to increase U.S. dependence on the Soviet Union and to subsidize re-pression and communist expansion.[60] In fact, confrontational politics are no more likely than constructive relations to reduce Soviet repression, and a properly managed trade policy can avoid gross asymmetries in dependence in the Soviets' favor. But as long as this constituency has the ear of policy makers in Washington, the United States is unlikely to take the first steps toward clearing away the obstacles to trade.

Western European states have already succeeded fairly well in cultivating trading relationships with the East, and the dependencies that do exist currently favor the West. The United States' lag in expanding trade with the East is itself a source of some concern; if Europe and Japan were the sole beneficiaries of expanded East–West trade, we might expect a further reduction in the United States' relative economic position and new cleavages in the Western alliance system. If improperly handled, these changes could prove destabilizing and might increase the risks of war. For these and other reasons, the web of trade approach will have its best chance of success if the United States, the world's largest economy, manages to get into the act. To do so, it will need to normalize and depoliticize its economic relations with the East; demonstrate a willingness to establish mutually beneficial ties on fair terms in the areas of trade, finance, and investment, and enter into serious negotiations on overcoming the technical and structural obstacles mentioned above.

Improved trade relationships may be more likely to *follow* improvements in political relations than to *lead* to them. Whether or not improved trade can lead to a fundamental pacification of international politics, it can certainly reinforce and stabilize political strategies designed to reduce tension between major players. If initiatives to overcome the barriers to East–West trade were undertaken as part of a broader political effort to establish and maintain a reliable, open global economic order, and if they accompanied serious confidence-building measures in an improved political climate, they would clearly be much more likely to succeed.[61]

If we could weave a web of trade between East and West, it would seem almost certainly desirable to do so. If properly managed, such interdependence could hardly increase the risks of war. A welcome irony of the current nuclear situation is that future East–West trade disputes would probably be dealt with particularly cautiously because of the existing premium on resolving conflicts without resort to arms. The web of trade can be nurtured in the shadow of nuclear deterrence, while reducing its importance. Thus there is little reason to expect that increased East–West economic interdependence would increase the likelihood of armed conflict if properly managed, and every reason to believe that it would make some contribution to reducing it. The sign of the effect is not in much doubt; the magnitude remains to be seen.

Institutions

Some of the more radical internationalist approaches suggest that the most direct and effective way to reduce the risks of war in a system of sovereign states is gradually to transfer a greater share of authority for international decision making to international institutions. The idea that international organizations (IOs) hold the key to world peace was first popularized in this century by Woodrow Wilson, and the League of Nations was the first attempt in that direction. The lessons of its failure led to the formulation of a more sophisticated version of the institutions approach, which David Mitrany called *functionalism*. I shall use it as my point of departure.[62]

Functionalism suggests that armed conflict could largely be eliminated from world affairs, and common welfare goals could more effectively be achieved, if a stable and complex structure of nonideological international institutions were created, with each institution given decision-making authority over a particular issue of international concern, and each structured (in membership and operation) in whatever way is most efficient for the successful discharge of its designated function. In each international institution, states would play a role corresponding to their relevance to the issue in question. Thus Norway (but not Switzerland) would play a major role in IOs governing shipping, while Switzerland (but not Norway) would play a major role in IOs governing international banking.[63] To be effective, it was supposed, these organizations would not require participating states to be politically or ideologically similar; a socialist USSR and a capitalist United States could participate together in a regime governing the emission of airborne pollutants, because their political structures are irrelevant to the choice of means necessary to deal effectively with that particular problem. Nor would functional institutions require any particular constitutional provision; they would be able to change in structure, membership, and operation as circumstances demanded—something rigid formal political organizations, such as the United Nations, cannot do.[64]

Functionalism had four main aims:

1. To reduce the incidence of conflict over issues on the international agenda by removing them from hands that politicize them.
2. To facilitate the resolution of conflicts by providing effective channels for management of disputes.

3. To improve the efficiency of decision making and resource allocation on issues of international concern (largely for purposes of social welfare).[65]
4. To provide the conditions under which nationalistic attitudes may be eroded in favor of cosmopolitan ones, paving the way, perhaps, for the eventual replacement of the system of sovereign nation states.[66]

It is difficult to evaluate functionalism's central propositions, simply because we do not have any experience of a true functionalist system. Though international institutions have proliferated at an impressive pace (Table 2), relatively few are designed on purely functionalist principles.[67] It seems clear, as Robert Keohane notes, that advocates of the institutions approach have generally been too optimistic about the prospects of completely reworking the international order; the harsh realities of power politics have proven less malleable than had been hoped.[68] The more grandiose visions of an institutionalized international system may never be realized; functionalism as it was originally conceived has few disciples, and even the word itself has been expropriated and put to other uses. Nevertheless, the notion of an international order effectively maintained by the operation of issue-specific institutions and regimes still captivates the policy and academic communities, and much effort has been exerted to understand how such institutions may be created, maintained, and put to constructive use improving security and welfare.[69]

Table 2. International Governmental Organizations

	1935–1939		1980	
Type	Number	Percent of Total	Number	Percent of Total
Limited membership, specific purpose	46	55%	506	81%
Universal membership, specific purpose	36	43	97	16
Limited membership, general purpose	1	1	17	3
Universal membership, general purpose	1	1	1	<1
Total	84	100%	621	100%

Source: Harold K. Jacobson, *Networks of Interdependence: International Organizations and the Global Political System*, 2d ed. (New York: Alfred A. Knopf, 1984), Table 3.3, p. 48.

Recent academic interest in institutions and regimes has resulted in some knowledge of their tendencies and effects, which can help frame a discussion of the conditions under which a true functionalist system—or the best possible approximation—might improve the long-term prospects for peace.

Does the evidence suggest that institutions and regimes reduce the incidence of conflict and facilitate its resolution? It is, of course, impossible to know what the incidence of international conflict would be if international affairs were less institutionalized than they are at present; but there are some interesting correlations. A relatively small proportion of states has engaged in international conflict since World War II; there have been few cases of forcible annexation; and the use of international governmental organizations (IGOs) for conflict settlement has increased dramatically.[70] Studies indicate that two out of three foreign policy actions are taken within the context of IGOs,[71] and that behavior is significantly more cooperative within IGOs than outside them.[72] While the limitations of the data used in these studies do not permit us to draw tight causal inferences, there is at least prima facie evidence to support the view that a world of IGOs and regimes is a more cooperative one. Keohane writes:

Regimes create a more favorable institutional environment for cooperation than would otherwise exist. . . . Such regimes are important not because they constitute centralized quasi-governments, but because they can facilitate agreements, and decentralized enforcement of agreements, among governments. They enhance the likelihood of cooperation by reducing the costs of making transactions that are consistent with the principles of the regime. They create the conditions for orderly multilateral negotiations, legitimate and delegitimate different types of state action, and facilitate linkages among issues within regimes and between regimes. They increase the symmetry and improve the quality of the information that governments receive. By clustering issues together in the same forums over a long period of time, they help to bring governments into continuing interaction with one another, reducing incentives to cheat and enhancing the value of reputation. By establishing legitimate standards of behavior for states to follow and by providing ways to monitor compliance, they create the basis for decentralized enforcement founded on the principle of reciprocity. . . .

The importance of regimes for cooperation supports the Institutionalist claim . . . that international institutions help to realize common interests in world politics.[73]

Some may worry that this increase in "cooperation" is more apparent than real, reflecting a shift in the arena of conflict, but not the profound changes in attitudes toward adversarial politics that would be needed to

establish durable norms. States may be trying to use transnational institutions and actors as instruments of their own self-interested policies
simply because military force has become less useful.[74] If this is so, a fundamentally adversarial relationship should not be expected to mellow
simply because the competition is now occurring on a different field. We
should guard against the complacent assumption that superficially cooperative behavior marks a fundamental change in attitudes; for a disruption of peaceful relations would be all the more dangerous if unexpected
or mishandled because of our misunderstanding of the true nature of a
relationship.

Sensible though this warning is, it has the potential to be self-fulfilling. Unwarranted suspicion can undo the beneficial effects of internationalism, and this factor as much as any other may explain why the
United States has been unable to break with its Cold War past. We need
to determine, at all times and under all conditions, what degree of suspicion is appropriate. *Some* cooperative behavior in IOs clearly indicates
the presence of common interests even between adversaries, and *some*
of the time the experience of cooperation itself has a favorable effect on
attitudes, as functionalism suggests. An analysis of speeches made by
members of Congress before and after their periods of service as dele-
gates to the United Nations General Assembly, for instance, shows that
the experience increases perceptions of the UN's salience and generates
more positive attitudes toward the organization.[75]

But there are limits both to the degree of common interests and to the
attitudinal changes we should expect as a result of participation in IGOs
and regimes, if only because many, and perhaps most, are still largely
political forums in which old political battles are still being fought.[76] Does
this observation challenge the functionalist assumption that institutions
can be nonpolitical, or does it confirm that improperly designed institutions will be unable to escape the political wrangling that stands as the
great barrier to a safer and more just world? If the latter interpretation is
correct, the institutional superstructure of world affairs may simply have
a long way to go before it approaches the functionalist ideal.[77] But attitudinal changes are not absolutely necessary for realizing a dividend
from the institutions approach. When states use international institutions and transnational actors as instruments of their own foreign policies—"the continuation of war by other means," as it were—their freedom of action *outside* the institutional context is eroded, and through
time the costs they incur through uncooperative behavior are increased.
Cooperation has a ratchet effect. Multiple channels of contact make it

more difficult to manipulate interdependence, to calculate expected costs and benefits of linkage strategies, and to foresee the effects of choices that disrupt the status quo, leading risk-averse states (the majority) to avoid rocking the proverbial boat.[78]

International cooperation can increase national influence over other actors, but it also increases dependence on the particular contributions of other states in the cooperative arena, and it increases the policy role of domestic bureaucracies charged with cooperative tasks.[79] The personal contacts and conflicts of interest between subunits of different governments can increase transgovernmental interactions and the incidence of cross-national coalition formation, resulting in "policy interdependence" between participating states.[80] All these effects can increase the importance of international organizations and regimes, because they can affect issue definition; serve as forums for contacts, coalition formation, and bargaining; provide points of policy intervention in transnational systems; and help set the international agenda itself.[81] International organizations may not yet be independent actors replacing states in world affairs, or powerful vehicles for attitude change; but even as largely political forums, they can still have beneficial effects.

Thus it appears that a superstructure of international institutions can constrain some of the tendencies of sovereign states that are associated with the risks of war—the tendencies to "go it alone," to pursue narrow short-term goals at the expense of long-term cooperative goals, to bluster rather than bargain, and to use the threat of disrupting relations to force concessions from others. The use of international institutions may have some beneficial effect on attitudes as well.

One of the most powerful objections to the institutions approach is that its most beneficial effects will come in precisely those areas that do not matter: the "low-politics" issues of economics, science, education, sports, and cultural affairs. If armed conflict is largely a function of competition over "high-politics" issues—territory, alliances, arms, and so on—then the institutions approach would largely be treating the wrong disease.[82] All we should expect of it is a marginal decrease in the likelihood of conflict, because armed conflicts over low-politics issues are rare and seldom catastrophic, and few international organizations are competent to deal with high-politics issues.

Some have responded that issues on the global agenda cannot be divided into such neat categories—that competition occurs on a wide variety of intricately linked chessboards, and it is no longer (if it ever was) accurate to dismiss low politics as subordinate to high politics.[83] For instance, the Soviet Union's awareness of falling behind economically seems to be influencing its arms and security policies—an indication that economics is more than merely "low politics" in the modern world. Others have suggested that cooperation through international institutions will spill over from low politics to high politics as participants seek to expand either the scope or level of their cooperative commitment in order to resolve lingering areas of dissatisfaction with the results of their more limited common endeavors.[84] Neither of these answers seems entirely satisfactory, however. The United States and the Soviet Union may well be able to settle their conflicts over fishing quotas in the Western Atlantic through the appropriate international organizations to which they belong; but it is altogether another matter whether they would be able to do so if the issue in question were West German nuclear weapons, widespread anti-Soviet revolution in Eastern Europe, or the deployment of a highly effective American strategic defense. Nor does the spill-over hypothesis offer a satisfying account of how or why they might do so *because of* their prior cooperation over fishing.

The real test of the institutions approach is whether it is adequate to the task in the high-politics areas of prestige and security. One study has indicated that high-politics IGOs are used more often than low-politics IGOs in world affairs, which suggests that states are at least willing to deal with their disputes over these issues in institutional forums.[85] But willingness is only half the battle; it remains to be shown that international institutions can be effective in resolving high-politics disputes in a timely and reliable way.

Our experience with the United Nations clearly demonstrates the weaknesses of formal political IOs as means of dealing with high-politics disputes. Only once, in Korea, did the UN succeed in a collective security action, and then only as a result of a Soviet diplomatic blunder that prevented it from exercising its veto—something we should not expect to be repeated. Only where the great powers are in substantial agreement on a course of action—as with the decision to deploy peace-keeping troops in the Middle East in 1967—can the UN play an active, independent role in conflict management. Only with the unanimous support of the great powers can it sustain a role of that kind, and even then it will be ineffective when the other parties concerned choose to ignore it, as in the Persian Gulf. None of this bodes well for the future of a highly politicized organization such as the UN as a forum for resolving crises that run risks of escalating to great-power war, except in the unlikely case of a crisis that has no basis in a material conflict of interest.

A brighter future may lie with "security regimes" such as the nonproliferation treaty or the Incidents at Sea Agreement. All nuclear powers have a common interest in settled, stable, predictable rules of the road that help avoid shocks to the system and conflicts of interest, and the Soviet and American experience with such regimes has generally been very positive.[86] None has yet been severely tested, and it is not clear how resilient they will be in the face of truly serious challenges. But there is already a good measure of circumstantial evidence for their usefulness in helping to avoid challenges of that kind.

In sum, our experience with a world of international organizations and regimes is encouraging, though less than conclusive. Under certain circumstances a deliberate attempt to pursue either the full functionalist vision or some less ambitious scheme might markedly improve the long-term prospects for peace. The structural circumstances most favorable to this attempt are precisely those appropriate to the web of trade approach: a world of eroding bipolarity in which the superpowers have incentives to seek cooperative solutions to common problems and to strike mutually satisfactory bargains on issues that divide them. The institutions could not have succeeded under classic Cold War conditions; but in a world in which both the United States and the Soviet Union are in relative decline, it looks rather more effective and appealing to both.

The process conditions most appropriate to the institutions approach are those we have already seen evolving in the Western industrial world, though to a much lesser extent between East and West. These are the processes associated with complex interdependence: an increased role for nongovernmental actors; increased reliance on regimes and institutions to mediate interstate relations; an increasing reluctance to use instruments of coercion to further policy goals; and regular, mutually beneficial economic transactions. How far these processes will supplant the traditional modes of state interaction in East–West relations in the next fifty years is still an open question; much will depend on the willingness of the two blocs to pursue some renewed form of détente.

Finally, the domestic political conditions most favorable to the institutions approach are also those most favorable to the other internationalist approaches. Reduced adversarial nationalism, the decline of domestic constituencies that favor traditional Cold War policies, increased willingness to seek cooperative solutions to age-old political conflicts, and increased openness to economic liberalization at home and in international trade would dramatically improve the chance that institutions could play a greater role in mediating and resolving conflicts. Whether or not institutions can be made adequate to the task of pacifying the traditional realm of high politics, these are the circumstances in which *low* politics dominate the international agenda, making it relatively easy to establish and maintain a stable superstructure of regimes and institutions.

Conclusions

While transnationalism and interdependence alone cannot be expected to prevent international conflict, they may be able to reduce its frequency and severity. Thus in the context of competitive and adversarial relationships that are also marked by certain basic shared interests (not least the avoidance of war), nuclear deterrence can be supplemented, and to some degree supplanted, by other forms of interdependence and through other modes of interaction. World politics can be reworked in more pacific ways, as internationalism suggests. It is difficult, however, to identify the most appropriate and effective ways to do this and to set the appropriate mechanisms in gear, largely because internationalist approaches tend to require as a precondition for success some degree of precisely what they seek to establish: a climate of international cooperation. This analysis suggests that none of the various internationalist approaches by itself is likely to make much progress toward that goal; but in concert, and as part of a wider attack on several fronts, they may have potent individual and collective effects.

Before the contacts approach will bear fruit, the barriers to effective direct and vicarious contacts must begin to erode; this will require the prior political will to open different cultures and societies to each other for the purpose of building affective bridges between peoples. The web of trade approach will require significant political and economic changes in the United States and the Soviet Union before the interdependencies can be built that will contribute to pacifying world politics. The institutions approach—clearly the most challenging, but the one that offers the greatest dividend over the long run—is fraught with unanswered questions concerning its ability to reduce the risks associated with conflicts on high-politics issues, but should prove useful in the context of improved East–West political relations, where high-politics would play a relatively less important role.

All these approaches are favored by the same environmental conditions, which are also those most amenable to U.S.–Soviet cooperation. These conditions all point in one direction: toward renewed détente. Though détente has its risks as well as its opportunities, and though our experience in the 1970s was both frustrating and disenchanting, it is a precondition for hurdling the fundamental obstacles to long-term cooperation and for transforming world politics in ways that can counteract the ugly tendencies of the system of sovereign states.[87] If we are to travel the road to détente once again, we must remember some lessons of the 1970s: that détente can collapse under the weight of unrealistic expectations; that it cannot survive the failure to work out symmetric norms of behavior; and that it cannot last unless atmospheric improvements in relations are backed up with substantive ones—political, economic, and institutional.[88]

Internationalism is neither a panacea nor a dead end. If the political will exists, on both sides of the Iron Curtain, to find ways of reducing the risks of catastrophic nuclear war, internationalism can play an important role in attaining and locking in the gains.

CHAPTER 10

World Government

Lee D. Neumann

> There are only two alternatives for mankind: world government
> or nuclear holocaust.
> *—Albert Einstein*

The General Assembly quieted as the new American president stepped
forward and began to speak.

Today, every inhabitant of this planet must contemplate the day when this planet
may no longer be habitable. Every man, woman and child lives under a nuclear
sword of Damocles, hanging by the slenderest of threads, capable of being cut
at any moment by accident or miscalculation or by madness. The weapons of
war must be abolished before they abolish us.
. . . it is in this spirit that we have presented with the agreement of the Soviet
Union [a program that] would achieve, under the eyes of an international disarmament organization, a steady reduction in force, both nuclear and conventional, until it has abolished all armies and all weapons except those needed for
internal order and a new United Nations Peace Force.[1]

Though these remarks could serve as a utopian vision of the beginning of a better world, they were made by President John F. Kennedy
in his first speech before the United Nations, on September 25, 1961,
four days after the signing of a landmark U.S.–Soviet proposal. In what
is now known as the McCloy–Zorin agreement, the two superpowers
worked out guidelines for negotiating the staged elimination of all military weapons and the establishment of an international force to uphold
the agreement and defend the peace.[2] In a follow-up document entitled
"A Blueprint for Peace," the United States called for arming the force "so
that no state could challenge it," thus providing the foundation for true
supranational authority.[3] As one analyst commented, "If militarily superior to any combination of national forces, an international force implies
(or is) some form of world government."[4]

World government, the common term for a global organization with the authority to make and enforce international law, has been a recurrent theme in contemporary thinking about solutions to the danger of nuclear war. Although many observers discount world government as an unreasonable alternative, the twentieth century has already witnessed two bold though unsuccessful attempts to limit war through international organization: the League of Nations and the United Nations. The urgency of the task in the atomic age motivated another ten years of effort by the Eisenhower and Kennedy administrations, which came closest to realizing their goal with the breakthrough in negotiations in 1961. Unresolved aspects of inspection procedures and several subsequent events—increased U.S.–Soviet tensions over Berlin and Cuba, the death of President Kennedy, and the intensification of the Vietnam conflict—buried the proposals under more immediate concerns.[5] Bills introduced in the last two congresses, however, reflect a renewed interest in the principles established by the McCloy–Zorin agreement.[6] As argued in Chapter 1, any dramatic bilateral or multilateral reductions in military strength will require some kind of international agency to enforce compliance and maintain stability.[7]

The basic argument for world government focuses on the inherently conflictual nature of a world crowded with separate states, each claiming absolute sovereignty and fighting over limited resources while threatening opponents with military arsenals of inconceivable destructive power. The history of civilization reveals the gradual merging of individual societies to spread the benefits of order and cooperation; given the danger of extermination by nuclear war, it seems absurd to let international society remain a last bastion of anarchy. In his best-selling *The Fate of the Earth*, Jonathan Schell asserts that "the peril of extinction is the price that the world pays . . . for its insistence on continuing to divide itself up into sovereign nations."[8] As discussed in Chapter 10, most national governments have already acknowledged the need for cooperative participation in international organizations to solve pressing problems; advocates of world government urge that such cooperation be extended to the arenas of war and conflict.

World government does not command a central position in the current nuclear debate, but many observers of international affairs believe it represents the only real chance of permanent peace.[9] A study published in 1971 revealed that only 29 percent of professional analysts directly involved in the formulation of American nuclear strategy disagreed with the statement that "some form of world government is the only long-term solution to the problem of the destructiveness of modern weapons and opposing nationalisms."[10] In 1982 an independent commission chaired by the late Olof Palme and including Cyrus Vance and Giorgi Arbatov argued for general and complete disarmament and the establishment of a supranational authority with enforcement capabilities.[11] Several political and professional organizations provide active support for world government, most notably the World Federalist Association, a Washington-based lobby whose former presidents include Senator Alan Cranston, two-term member of the Committee on Foreign Relations.[12] Although its near-term realization appears highly unlikely, world government's evident logic and perennial appeal as a permanent solution to war demand that it be considered.

Following a brief description of world government's form and operation, this chapter will analyze its potential to reduce the likelihood and destructiveness of war in the nuclear age. Consideration will be given to the risk of war between nations under world government, the world government itself as a threat to peace, and the problem of national and global civil war. A separate discussion examines the danger of conflict while establishing world government, as well as political challenges to its creation. The theme recurring in each section is the constant need, even under world government, for a commitment to peace and cooperation on the part of member nations. Without such a commitment, world government will possess no more strength, and provide no more security, than a house divided.

World Government: Its Form and Operation

World government has inspired innumerable impassioned declarations but few detailed plans.[13] Among contemporary works, the proposals developed by Grenville Clark and Louis Sohn in *World Peace through World Law* stand alone for their breadth and precision, in addition to their worldwide recognition.[14] A serious discussion of world government must therefore begin with an overview of the Clark–Sohn proposals, as well as those issues for which alternative proposals have received most attention.

Most advocates of world government, including Clark and Sohn, call for an international federation, proposing a supranational organization to maintain peace between nations while national governments retain full authority within them. Most plans also aspire to universal membership, but they differ in their recommendations for world government's initial composition. Emphasizing the need for broad international support at the outset, the Clark–Sohn proposals require voluntary participation by five-sixths of the world's nations (representing at least five-sixths of the world's population and including the four largest nations) before world government could begin. The American Blueprint for Peace focuses on the need for superpower support, requiring initial ratification by only the United States, the USSR, and "such other states as might be agreed" and then by other "militarily significant states" for the process to continue. Other proposals emphasize political cohesion, calling for a core world government based on regional federations or international associations free of significant political rivalry.[15]

After agreeing to world government, nations would begin an incremental program of general and complete disarmament. Clark and Sohn propose 10 percent reductions in military strength every six months for a period of five years, while the Blueprint for Peace proposes a three-stage process, with two three-year periods of 30 percent reductions and a final reduction over a period to be specified. Both plans result in complete disarmament, with national governments retaining only those forces necessary to ensure domestic order.[16] During the same period, an international police force would be formed from elements of the disbanding national forces. The Clark–Sohn proposals call for a permanent Peace Force of 200,000 to 500,000 members under a single unified command and a reserve force of about 500,000; the McCloy–Zorin agreement and the Blueprint for Peace do not specify the size of the force. According to Clark and Sohn, the international police would be armed with both a wide range of conventional equipment and a small number of nuclear weapons; the Blueprint for Peace, while asserting that the international corps should be able to "deter or suppress any threat or use of arms," does not define its nuclear capability. For reasons of political reliability, the Clark–Sohn proposals also limit the proportion of the force represented by any single nationality.[17] Finally, while the Blueprint for Peace would base national elements of the international police in their home country until called upon by the international assembly, the Clark–Sohn proposals locate the international force in various permanent bases around the world.[18]

Supreme authority in the Clark–Sohn world government would be vested in the assembly of national representatives.[19] Unlike the current United Nations procedure of one nation–one vote, national representation would take into account differences in national size and power. Clark and Sohn group nations in seven categories, assigning thirty representatives to each of the four most populous nations, twelve to each of the next ten, eight to the next fifteen, and so on down to the smallest nations, which have one representative each. Alternative proposals include bicameral assemblies or double voting procedures within a single assembly with different weightings assigned to each vote, but Clark and Sohn argue for simplicity and efficiency.[20] The international assembly would act as a parliamentary body with strictly defined constitutional powers. It would establish a seventeen-member executive council to oversee the international armed forces and manage an inspection agency ensuring compliance with the law against rearmament; in addition, it would operate a system of forums and tribunals to facilitate the peaceful settlement of international disputes. Clark and Sohn would also create a world development authority to promote development, primarily through financial assistance, and additional agencies to coordinate national policies on environmental protection and the exploitation of ocean resources. Only in matters directly related to the maintenance of peace, however, would the Clark–Sohn government have enforcement powers.

This description of world government touches on only the broadest outlines of the Clark–Sohn proposals and its alternatives, yet it reflects the type of thinking necessary to extend agreements of the McCloy–Zorin breed into real policy. In some respects, the proposals call for implementing certain objectives agreed to in the United Nations Charter but never carried out. World government's full significance, however, goes far beyond a strengthened UN—it would establish a new global polity based on a fundamental redistribution of political and military power. Nevertheless, Clark and Sohn make no explicit assumptions about international political relations, developments in military technology, or domestic politics as factors affecting a world government's chances for success. In fact, such considerations are likely to determine world government's effectiveness and ability to survive.

The Risk of War under World Government

War between Nations

Global disarmament would eliminate the weapons of war, but not its causes. To some extent, the good will and cooperation reflected in agreements on disarmament and negotiation might ease tensions, but the world government cannot expect to contain hostility solely through efforts at conciliation. Historical, political, and economic sources of international conflict will not vanish with the final land mine and grenade, nor will the danger of a resurgence in militant nationalism. As in domestic society, where effective law demands effective law enforcement, the burden of upholding the peace falls heavily on the shoulders of the international police, and their success, or failure, depends on both strategic and political variables.

The Military Dimension of Upholding the Peace. The ability of the international police to defeat handily any potential aggressor anywhere on the globe does not follow automatically from its monopoly on heavy weapons and strategic resources. The international force would face an enormous task. In 1985 alone, interstate conflicts embroiled nearly two dozen nations and over 3 million soldiers, and armed face-offs stretched for thousands of miles between military powers both great and small.[21] The international police might also find that their most powerful weapons conferred few battlefield advantages, since from moral and strategic points of view, the immense and indiscriminate destructiveness of nuclear and heavy conventional arms would limit their use. Keeping peace with humane methods in a world fraught with animosity would therefore require international forces of an imposing number, stationed around the world to facilitate rapid deployment, and trained not only in nuclear and conventional warfare but also in techniques for suppressing an opposing force with minimum violence and destruction.[22]

The international police would face a greater challenge if national forces armed themselves with more than the rifles and occasional machine gun or armored personnel carrier authorized to domestic police. As demonstrated by the American experience in Vietnam and the Soviet campaign in Afghanistan, technological advances in the accuracy and firepower of hand-carried weapons have increased the effectiveness of light, mobile units. While full-scale rearmament could not fail to attract the attention of the world government and hence trigger intervention by the international police, the clandestine production of arms might not be detected, and secretly hidden weapons or a black market in military hardware could provide alternative paths to rearmament. Ultimately, however, the international police, with their vastly superior military strength and the resources to support a prolonged engagement, could pursue a variety of strategies—enforcing an embargo, striking military facilities with air or ground attacks, invading the belligerent's territory—and eventually overcome even a substantially armed national contingent.

A particularly determined national force could nevertheless place tremendous pressure on world government forces. The sudden invasion of neighboring territory could provide large numbers of hostages to be used for bargaining, and the most sinister of governments could use portions of its own population. If armed with nuclear weapons obtained either through secret production or from a weapons cache, a belligerent could threaten even wider destruction. The international police might be able to foil a nuclear attack through its control of missile launch sites and international airspace, but ultimately, it would have to rely on its own nuclear arsenal to deter nuclear aggression. Whereas balanced bipolar or multipolar forces may have a stabilizing effect in today's world, any challenge to the world government's monopoly on nuclear arms would undermine its authority and demand a forceful response.

In sum, the nature and distribution of military power under a world government would greatly reduce both the destructiveness and likelihood of major interstate conflict. War, if fought, could occur only between neighboring nations, since the means for long-range transport of personnel and supplies would have largely disappeared. Even a considerably rearmed national force (assuming it could avoid detection by an unrestricted inspection service) could not realistically hope for victory against the extensive resources of a substantial international corps. Nevertheless, a potentially violent period of learning might be necessary to demonstrate the international force's capabilities, and the world government might have to accept the dangers of an atomic showdown, thus raising the potential human costs of world government beyond what many of its proponents may readily admit. Only one strategic threat could undermine the international police's ability to defend international law and punish the offender—the creation of a globally suicidal "doomsday machine" to be activated upon attack by world government forces. Such a machine would be no more likely under world government than it is today.

The Political Dimension of Upholding the Peace. The international police can be no more effective than the political machinery that controls it. Although world government rests largely on the principle of the illegality of war, an agreement to outlaw war does not guarantee prompt and impartial action by world government forces. If nations see that debate or dissent within the world government could delay or entirely prevent a forceful response, the risk of violations of international law will increase dramatically. Several potential obstacles to effective police action must therefore be recognized.

First, the ideological and economic divisions that create political blocs of East and West or North and South, or virulent disputes between major religious groupings, could permeate world government debate and pervert its decision-making process. After giving the nod to violent groups favored for their political outlook, a willful majority in the international assembly might defend an aggressor's actions and suspend police intervention. Basic differences over the meaning of international justice could also bog down efforts to keep the peace. Latin American anger over the United States' role in the Falklands war and European criticism of its 1984 bombing of Libya demonstrate that even communities sharing many of the same values may split over the proper response to international aggression.

Second, an injunction against war implies the inviolability of international borders — a nation's territory may not be entered without its permission — yet the precise locations of many borders are in dispute. As shown by the Falklands War in 1982, dormant territorial disputes can suddenly erupt into conflict and divide the international community as well. It is easy to imagine an international assembly in disagreement over even the wisest compromise, and its lack of consensus could translate into inaction by the international police even when faced with clear breaches of the peace.

A third obstacle to effective action involves political cohesion within the international police itself.[23] The force will comprise individuals with radically different values, backgrounds, and loyalties (in addition to different languages), yet they must form a well-integrated organization free from disruptive political frictions. Clark and Sohn recommend insulating the international police from the East–West conflict by limiting the participation of superpower nationals and by respecting cultural and political homogeneity in forming most units. Nevertheless, no matter how carefully international police units are composed, they will remain susceptible to the divisiveness of world government policy disputes.

Finally, there remains the complex question of how to treat a belligerent nation once its forces have been defeated. Although some authors, including Clark and Sohn, propose removing individual leaders to defuse the war-making machinery, popular domestic sentiment often supports violent foreign policies.[24] The indefinite stationing of international forces to restrain national leaders would smack of military occupation. Reforming national opinion or creating a peaceful government with domestic support—difficult tasks in themselves—might prove impossible in a context requiring the agreement of capitalists, socialists, and communists. One solution would be to divide the belligerent's territory into separate zones to be administered by different political elements of the world government, as was done with Germany following World War II. Such a course might seem repugnant to the defenders of national integrity (and thus perhaps deter national support for violent policies), but a world government failure to agree on a resolution would risk the collapse of peace.

Ideological divisions and political rivalries thus pose the greatest challenge to international peace under world government. Consider, for example, how a world government might deal with the current situation in the Middle East. Were the international assembly to remain politically neutral, world government mediators could try bringing belligerent leaders together while international forces held their armies apart. Negotiations would lose all meaning, however, if political conflicts overtook the assembly's agenda. An anti-Israeli coalition might challenge Israel's right to statehood and deny it the protection of the international police. Western economic security could be threatened by a coalition blocking measures to safeguard the flow of Middle East oil. An unholy alliance of such as Saudi Arabia, the United States, and the Soviet Union, accusing Islamic fundamentalism of spreading turmoil and unrest, might push for the dismantling of Iran's fundamentalist regime. Each of these projects would renew regional violence and deepen global tension. Their potential to replace peaceful negotiation with lethal pressures and force demonstrates the fragility of peace under a world government fractured with dispute.

The World Government as a Threat to National Security

Opposition to world government frequently focuses on the threat an omnipotent global authority would pose to national security. Critics warn that turning over all weapons to an international police creates a sure vehicle for world dictatorship. The design of a world government must therefore provide strong safeguards against the misuse of constitutional power and limit the dangers of an overthrow of legitimate authority.

World Government and the Freedom of Nations. Although established for a specific purpose—the enforcement of disarmament and the defense of peace—the world government might seek to use its power in ways unforeseen by its designers yet permitted under constitutionally granted authority. If approved by the vast majority of nations, the new uses of supranational power might vastly improve the well-being of mankind, but if designed to serve factional purposes while overruling the interests of a target minority, they would constitute a misuse of constitutional power, split the international community, and destabilize world order.

In an extreme case, a group of nations might band together to form a majority bloc in the international assembly and gain control of the international police. Because (according to the Clark–Sohn constitution) the world government could take forceful action against nations threatening the peace without waiting for an actual act of aggression, the controlling bloc could use the pretext of maintaining international security to assign the police any number of tasks. For example, charging that a particular economic or political system inevitably leads to international violence, or citing fictitious rumors of a plot for national rearmament, the world government could arrest a country's political leadership, impose temporary military rule, and bring the nation fully under world government command. A less ambitious coalition, seeking certain technical or industrial secrets, might assert that such capabilities could be turned to military use and order their seizure and transfer to international control. The Clark–Sohn proposals grant 20 percent of the votes in the international assembly to the world's wealthiest nations (which represent less than 20 percent of world population) and 10 percent to the Soviet bloc, offering wide latitude for the formation of a malevolent majority.

The legitimate pursuit of world government policy might also lead to interventions in national affairs. Clark and Sohn insist that domestic policy remain the exclusive province of national governments, but recognizing world government's inability to achieve certain goals without greater authority, they "leave to other generations any enlargement of the powers of the world organization that they may find desirable."[25] Intervention may not always seem inappropriate, but it will be difficult to limit its scope. In promoting human rights, the world government could demand the liberation of political prisoners and freedom for religious pursuits, but it might also insist on socialized medicine and the deprivatization of all educational institutions. In the name of international economic justice, a world government might rapidly improve technical and training opportunities in developing countries, but it could also impose ceilings on personal wealth. Some people may support all these goals, but they represent intrusions on national autonomy that would make world government permanently unacceptable to many.

The final and potentially gravest danger to national security legitimized under world government concerns the amendment of the world government constitution itself. Under the Clark–Sohn proposals, amendments would take effect after ratification by four-fifths of the member nations, including ten of the largest fourteen. Because the industrial democracies and their close allies represent ten of the largest fourteen nations and about one-quarter of all nations, they might feel themselves able to block unwanted amendments. On the other hand, if China, India, and the USSR reconstituted themselves into twelve separate nations (while presumably maintaining unofficial leadership structures within each), they would then make up twelve of the world's largest fourteen nations, and similar gerrymandering of other national boundaries could easily create the four-fifths majority necessary to remake the constitution.

The resolution of these threats to national freedom poses a difficult dilemma. Political power under a world government is founded on voting strength in the international assembly as well as the absolute number of nations supporting a particular cause. To prevent the tyranny of the majority, a larger proportion of positive votes could be required to carry a decision; but by facilitating a minority veto, such a rule also hamstrings the government. The hard fact is that no political structure will enable the founders of world government to define permanently the forms and limits of its power. As the history of the United States shows, large or determined majorities can, over time, effect drastic changes in the scope and functioning of governmental authority. While all nations may share an interest in limiting world government intervention, they may not agree on exactly where, or when, to draw the line.

Political Coups and Military Revolts. While the misuse of constitutional authority threatens the freedom of nations, the seizure of world government power by an individual or coalition followed by the nullification of the constitution raises the danger of major war. Even if the coup itself was relatively bloodless — a storming of the international assembly, the execution of resistant officials and the occupation of their offices, the announcement of the overthrow of the government and a demand for obedience — its aftermath would contain the seeds of large-scale violence, as in any revolution. The large number and broad dispersal of the international corps would challenge the leaders' ability to maintain discipline within the ranks, particularly after an upheaval of political and symbolic authority, and many of the police might remain loyal to the deposed government. The seizure of power could thus be quickly followed by extensive mutinies and rebellions within the international force, spreading the danger of anarchy and violence. As voices were raised against tyranny and a "government in exile" was established, military forces for and against the coup might tighten ranks and initiate a global battle of unpredictable proportions.

Two other scenarios illustrate the ominous consequences of a shift in police allegiance away from democratic world government. First, the military leadership itself might initiate a coup, shunting aside political figures and declaring military rule. Again, the possibility of widespread defections from the international corps to groups loyal to democratic world government raises the likelihood of war. Alternatively, a contingent of the international police in a particular region might revolt against world government authority and declare themselves independent rulers of their part of the globe. Unless it regained control of the maverick units, world government would collapse.

The risk of fragmentation within the international police makes control over its most powerful resource — nuclear weapons — of primary importance. While Clark and Sohn recommend placing nuclear materials in the hands of a civilian agency, it may prove more effective to disassemble nuclear weapons so that remaking them would require several months, giving opposing forces a chance to disrupt production. Such a scheme would not eliminate the possibility of an eventual nuclear monopoly, however, and it might set the scene for a two-contestant race to nuclear rearmament. Security devices, such as permissive action links (PALs) that require knowledge of special codes to launch a weapon, could make nuclear weapons less vulnerable to unauthorized use, but they also raise the likelihood of all-or-nothing control over nuclear forces with no guarantee on who will gain possession. Technical fixes thus have as many drawbacks as advantages.

In the final analysis, the best solution can only reduce the risk of revolt by the international forces, not eliminate it entirely. As Clark and Sohn themselves acknowledge, "Even with . . . elaborate safeguards, it is realized that the danger of possible misuse of the [international police] cannot be *wholly* eliminated. . . ."[26] Given the strength and dispersal of the international police, the clearest deterrent to would-be dictators is the virtual certainty of considerable resistance from within world government forces. The international community might contribute further to its security, however, and combat the lure of global power, by actively demonstrating its commitment to democratic world government as a framework for international order.

Civil Wars

The risk of civil war also represents a major threat to international peace. With the establishment of world government, civil war would include both conflicts between domestic groups competing for national power and the possibility of nations mobilizing their resources and populations for civil war on a global scale.

The Problem of National Civil War. In the last quarter-century, deaths in internal conflicts have outnumbered deaths in interstate conflict by more than ten to one.[27] In the early 1980s, more than twenty nations struggled with civil wars involving nearly 5 million combatants, and military governments held power over 700 million people in thirty-two nations.[28] For much of the world's population, the domestic environment thus rivals or surpasses the international as a threat to peace. While general and complete disarmament may enhance the long-run prospects for domestic as well as international stability, stripping national governments of their military strength would increase opportunities for antigovernment forces to vie for regional or national power and thus trigger a precipitous rise in internal conflict.

In the best of cases, a revolt would end with little violence. The relatively bloodless revolutions in the Philippines and Haiti demonstrate that nonviolent overthrow of a repressive regime is possible, but few governments topple peacefully. If domestic negotiations broke down and international councils failed to find an acceptable solution, sporadic gunfights might blaze into widespread conflict. Either side, or both, might call on the international police to halt the violence, or world leaders themselves might find it unacceptable to stand idly by. Furthermore, civil war within one country often acts as a destabilizing force for an entire region—if not for purely political reasons, then because of the flux of refugees seeking safety, rebel groups crossing borders for sanctuary, or traffic in black market weapons. The job of keeping peace within nations would place an extraordinary burden on world government, and long-term peace keeping by the international police could have the unfortunate effect of relieving disputing factions of the responsibility for settling their differences. There might be no alternative to such measures save walking out on a highly explosive situation.

The gravest danger posed by domestic conflict is that opposing factions will find support among different members of the world government, thereby raising domestic conflict to the international level. Were a world government responsible for peace in Nicaragua, for example, debate over contra versus Sandinista could be rapidly transformed into raw U.S.–Soviet confrontation. The complex Lebanese and South African situations could drive wedges between numerous international factions. By thus exacerbating differences within the international community, national civil wars could limit world government effectiveness and raise the danger of global civil war. Internal conflicts threaten the peace at local, regional, and international levels, yet domestic groups, not world government, have the power to resolve them.

The Danger of World Civil War. As in the American civil war, a knotty string of disputes tangled around a single major issue might unite one region of the world and provoke its withdrawal from the world federation. For example, frequent penalties against the industrial nations for pollution of the environment coupled with limitations on their access to raw materials, or constant pressure on totalitarian regimes to respect human rights and liberalize internal policies, might build demand for a return to national sovereignty. Or if world government forces failed to provide assurance of national security, countries might seek once again to rely on national resources for national defense. While it might seem the most straightforward solution to dissatisfaction with world government, the secession of a powerful and largely self-sufficient group of nations would initiate a dangerous era of political chaos. It would shatter the neat hierarchy of political and military authority, and as the global community divided like a massive cell, with each new unit vulnerable to further splits and divisions, international society would return to the disorder world government was meant to replace. Populations and industry would mobilize for defense, and uncertain leaders brace for war.

As in every challenge to world government authority, much would depend on the reaction of the international police. Unless supported by locally based international forces, secession would be extremely unlikely, since its foreseeable consequence would be rapid military occupation. Police support for the rebellion might therefore be sought by promising them greater wealth or power under a new regime, or perhaps by assuring them satisfaction on more substantive issues neglected by the world government—an end to mismanagement and poor leadership, for example, or the establishment of international policies more respectful of police values and beliefs. Even with wide police support, however, control over all or most nuclear weapons would be uncertain, and thus secession from world government would raise the danger of nuclear war.

The specter of escalation to a nuclear exchange might frighten all parties back from the brink and bring them to negotiation, but even with a peaceful resolution, successful armed coercion against the world government would alter fundamentally the notion of world government authority. Though preferable to nuclear war, it would set an ambiguous precedent. On the one hand, the world government might resolve never to permit international pressures to build to such intensity; on the other, a resort to arms might remain as a viable means of achieving political goals. Too great a reliance on military strength to maintain order and the neglect of serious political interchange would thus be a tragic mistake. As one commentator has pointed out, "the order-keeping function of government is not fulfilled by the winning of a civil war, but by its prevention... If the history of national government tells us anything about the problem of achieving international order, it seems to be this: There is no substitute for political adjustment as a means of managing relationships among the units which constitute complex human societies...."[29]

Challenges to the Creation of a World Government

Violence and War While Establishing a World Government

Both the Clark–Sohn proposals and the McCloy–Zorin agreement would establish world government in stages. As nations were called upon to join the international federation and begin disarmament, the risk of violence and war might rise significantly. During the first stage, as the issue of participation in world government gained momentum, intense domestic debate could spawn violent clashes between opposing groups; governments that relied on displays of military strength to achieve status might be particularly eager to quash support for general demilitarization. Domestic turmoil might well be generated by superpower intervention. To assure themselves of support in the international assembly, the superpowers might launch substantial initiatives, including military aid, to bring preferred factions to power.[30]

Once a consensus had formed in favor of world government and the disarmament process had begun, the refusal of some nations to participate would threaten the peace. The only solution, as noted by Clark and Sohn, is enforced compliance with international law, even at the risk of conflict.[31] Although the weight of world opinion, in addition to the threat of force, should prove highly influential, a forceful demonstration of international resolve might be necessary to convince stubborn hold-outs to yield.

The greatest threats to international peace would gradually make themselves felt after the disarmament process was under way. First, as the number of weapons declined, small advantages in strength would become increasingly significant; sudden rearmament or secret violations of disarmament could bring decisive superiority.[32] Moreover, mutual military reductions would increase opportunities to create local superiority by rapidly massing available forces on a particular location. Second, stability would become increasingly dependent on the nascent international police before they were ready for their responsibilities. National contingents would still be substantially armed, and the international police would lack training under new leadership and procedures. They might lack the strength to halt disarmament violations, or, if one country mounted a conventionally led attack, the international police might be unable to disengage aggressors and defenders without substantial losses to each. Finally neither the political mechanism for managing the international police nor political loyalty within the corps would have been firmly established. In short, the international police would face the greatest demands when their capabilities were least certain.

Political Challenges to the Creation of a World Government

The most formidable challenge to the creation of world government is the widespread resistance to relinquishing national power. Nations share a legitimate fear of world government intervention in domestic affairs, and foreign policies would also be vulnerable to significant constraints. The superpowers in particular would suffer a vast reduction in influence on world affairs by joining a sovereign international assembly that granted them together less than 10 percent of the vote. Moreover, while economic instruments or agreements on technological exchange might emerge as the main tools of international influence if the use of force were banned, they too could be curtailed in the name of distributive justice. Few nations, perhaps only the weakest, could anticipate direct benefits from these potential restrictions on national action.

A second challenge concerns ideological antagonisms. Despite numerous accords and cooperative exchanges between the United States and the Soviet Union, philosophical opposition might preclude their participation as equals in an international body endowed with true governmental authority. While the United Nations provides, at the minimum, a forum for international debates without obliging member nations to abide by their outcome, both superpowers might be unwilling to share responsibility for binding decisions with adherents of fundamentally opposed political and social values.

Finally, the attractiveness of world government hinges on its ability to provide member nations with what they need but cannot obtain (at a reasonable cost) even through the threat of war. Considering the vast arsenals of the nuclear superpowers and the relative economic self-sufficiency they enjoy with their allies, world government may have little to offer. The Soviet Union has shown no enthusiasm for unofficial American proposals for an international federation, contending that "there is nothing wrong with the United Nations as it is today. It just needs the political will of the nations to make it work."[33] A supranational organization responsible for world peace may appear more desirable, however, if the costs or pressures of nuclear deterrence reach unacceptable proportions. On the other hand, world government may have to await deterrence failure. The two most significant international organizations appeared only after the traumas of world war, and nuclear conflict may be the unfortunate prerequisite for further evolution in international authority. But major nuclear war, if it does not bring total destruction, might leave one power strong enough to impose a global order of its own design.[34]

Conclusion

Unless certain preconditions are met, world government is no panacea. At the international level, political relations between states must permit the settlement of disputes through judicial and diplomatic methods. While world government could rescue humanity from nuclear annihilation by limiting its capacity for self-destruction, consensual breakdown within the world government might turn the international forces against themselves, with possible augmentation from secret national arsenals, and ignite a short fuse to nuclear confrontation. At the domestic level, national groups must be able to share power harmoniously; otherwise local disputes could spark the violence world government is intended to contain.

World government offers neither a guarantee nor substitute for agreement—merely a framework. In the present environment of tension and distrust between major international blocs, this framework would provide only the illusion of security. If a particular voting coalition repeatedly imposed its will, if corruption or inefficiency spread through government agencies, or if rumors flashed of an impending coup, national leaders would no longer look to world government courts for security, but to control of the international police and their own ability to rearm. As some nations departed from regularized procedures, either through deliberate calculation or misunderstanding and fear, others would hasten to secure their own safety. Fear and uncertainty would thus unravel world government's legalistic design and propel nations toward conflict in uncharted strategic waters. Under these circumstances, the risk of nuclear war would go up, not down.

The first step in creating an effective world government is thus to lower the level of international hostility. Democratic government can operate effectively only if political conflicts threaten neither the existence of individual members nor the government itself; as stated by one political analyst, Lockian solutions cannot solve Hobbesian problems.[35] Several of the previous chapters offer ideas on how to defuse tensions in the strategic sphere, but developing the sense of trust and compatibility necessary for a stable world government requires a broader approach. Nations must treat each other with a respect based on rights, not power, and orient their policies toward global needs, not individual gain. National leaders and publics must learn to think in terms of cooperation and compromise, not conflict and conquest. Evidently, such shifts require a major reshaping of traditional attitudes and objectives, yet supporters of world government should not be daunted by this substantial task of education. They will be joining those already committed to reevaluating the norms and bases of foreign policy.[36] By thus furthering the cause of world government, they will advance the cause of peace.

Conclusion

Graham T. Allison, Albert Carnesale,
and Joseph S. Nye, Jr.

Two centuries ago, Immanuel Kant outlined the conditions of international and domestic politics that would, in his view, lead to the "ever widening pacification" of international life.[1] Kant's analysis is both subtle and complex, but simply stated his conditions for peace are three. The first and most important relates to the domestic political regime of states: peaceful nations must be "republics," by which Kant meant that citizens would have rights and governments depend on the consent of the governed. As he argued:

If the consent of the citizens is required to decide that war should be declared, nothing is more natural than that they would be cautious in commencing such a poor game, decreeing for themselves all of the calamities of war. Among the latter would be: having to fight, having to pay the costs of the war from their own resources, having painfully to repair the devastation war leaves behind, and to fill up the measure of evil, load themselves with a heavy national debt that would embitter peace itself.[2]

Kant's second condition focuses on economics: these republics should have market economies aimed at improving citizens' well-being. Then, given an international division of labor through free trade, economic interdependence will evolve. Benefiting from these arrangements, citizens will be more reluctant to break the ties of trade.

Third, because liberal states respect other liberal states, international law among such nations would have an ever-widening scope, ultimately leading to peace. War, Kant foresaw, was becoming increasingly destructive. Peace was therefore becoming more attractive and even necessary.

Kant did not think such a peace would come about quickly. Rather, he foresaw a lengthy process in which liberal republics would form an implicit "pacific union" among themselves. Peace would be the norm in relations between such states. As new liberal republics appeared, this pacific union would expand; by gradual extension, peace would become global and finally perpetual. And in fact, in the almost 200 years since Kant wrote, there has been virtually no war between liberal republics.[3] Although this phenomenon may have many causes, including the small number of liberal republics, Kant's analysis demonstrates the possibility of thinking hard and well about conditions that incline toward peace rather than war over the longer term. We share that goal.

The essays in this volume examine the major contending visions of peace that have been advocated since the dawn of the nuclear age, exploring their completeness, feasibility, and desirability. Not surprisingly, each vision has significant limits. In every case, some important assumptions are not spelled out, leaving ample room for debate over the practicality or utility of the vision. The challenge is to find ways to specify the visions more fully, and perhaps to combine promising portions of several visions to provide guidance and hope for the future.

We remain persuaded by the advice offered in our previous book, *Hawks, Doves, and Owls: An Agenda for Avoiding Nuclear War* (1985): "Don't assume that nuclear deterrence will last forever" and "Do intensify the search for alternatives to deterrence."[4] We did not then, nor do we now, believe deterrence soon will fail. In U.S.–Soviet relations, the current nuclear postures have substantially solved the problem of deterring deliberate nuclear attack. Under present conditions, no rational leader could conclude that his or her nation would be better off with a nuclear war than without one. But deliberate attack is not the only path to nuclear war. As we argued in *Hawks, Doves, and Owls*, the primary risks are "uncontrollable" accident, miscalculation, misperception, unintended consequences, and combinations of these factors that produce results no one would deliberately choose.

Current U.S. and Soviet strategic nuclear arsenals have virtually created the "doomsday machine" once satirized by the late Herman Kahn. As Kahn described it, a doomsday machine is "a device whose only function is to destroy all human life. The device is protected from enemy action and then connected to a computer which is in turn connected, by a reliable communications system to hundreds of sensory detectors all over the United States."[5] The computer is programmed so that the explosion of a certain number of nuclear bombs on the United States will trigger the device, and our planet will be destroyed. Under such conditions, any decision to attack would mean destroying all that one holds dear.

Kahn argued that the doomsday machine would provide ideal deterrence against an attack on the United States. It has all the desirable characteristics of a deterrent: it would be frightening, inexorable, pervasive, cheap, and relatively immune to accidents. Yet it is unacceptable on three grounds, he argued. The first is controllability. A doomsday machine could be designed to minimize the risk of simple accident or unauthorized launch—whereas today large numbers of nuclear weapons are spread among many alternative delivery systems, with many different hands on many different triggers. It could not, however, eliminate the possibility of an accident. By eliminating the chance of human intervention, control, and final decision, it risks too much without any chance for self-correction.

Second, the consequences of failure are too great for any rational or moral government to choose. Kahn's book was written almost three decades ago, before the superpower arsenals reached their current proportions and before discussions of phenomena such as nuclear winter. His judgment on what would be acceptable and unacceptable should give one pause. He writes:

Neither the 180 million Americans nor even the half billion people in the NATO alliance should or would be willing to design and procure a security system in which a malfunction or failure could cause the death of one or two billion people. If the choice were made explicit, the United States or NATO would seriously consider "lower quality" systems, i.e., systems which were less deterring, but whose consequences were less catastrophic if deterrence failed. They would even consider such possibilities as a dangerous degree of partial or complete unilateral disarmament if there were no other acceptable postures.[6]

The doomsday machine also fails in being unable to sustain public support. To quote Kahn again, "the closer a weapons system is to a Doomsday Machine the less satisfactory it becomes."[7] Indeed, neither NATO nor the United States, and possibly not even the Soviet Union, would be willing to spend billions of dollars to give a few individuals this particular kind of life and death power over the entire world."[8]

The aftermath of an all-out nuclear war between the United States and the Soviet Union would be no less horrifying than Kahn's vision. A vigorous search for alternatives to this modern doomsday machine is therefore imperative.

The search for feasible and more desirable alternatives should engage the strategic community as well as current visionaries. The visionaries too often resemble the judge of a singing contest who decided to award the prize to the second of two contestants after hearing only the first. Despite its flaws, the current system is not the least desirable arrangement that could be imagined. We must recognize that some, indeed many, alternatives that on the surface seem desirable would in fact be more likely to produce catastrophic war. On the other hand, our standards need not be too high. The appropriate test of an alternative is not that it be sane and reasonable—just *more* sane and *more* reasonable than the current system.

Although the visions explored in this volume are all deficient in some way, the national security community should not dismiss them out of hand. The current reliance on nuclear deterrence also rests on unspecified—and too often unexamined—assumptions about the long run. Macroanalysis of alternative worlds and the development of alternative security systems is extremely difficult. Methodologies for making sense of the bigger picture of the future are limited. Distinguishing between more sensible and less sensible visions calls for criteria and evidence of a sort most of us find unfamiliar. All in all, our analytic capacity for creating alternative visions is weak—a limitation rendered somewhat less dangerous by the fact that security systems are more evolved than planned. No one planned the current system of tens of thousands of nuclear warheads in the role of a doomsday machine. Many human choices, including national policy choices, contributed to this evolution. Technological opportunities helped shape it, and political competition fueled it. But no one specified the current system as his or her fateful vision for security in a dangerous world.

Formulating an alternative vision invariably involves difficult trade-offs. Fundamental paradoxes abound. For example, the superpowers seek to avoid nuclear war by maintaining arsenals large enough to make the consequences of such a war so catastrophic that no rational decision maker would intentionally start it. But if war did start through inadvertence, unforeseen escalation, sheer madness, or some other irrational means, it would probably be as horrible as we designed it in our attempt to avoid it. Small arsenals with reduced potential consequences may make nuclear war less unacceptable and therefore more likely; large arsenals with disastrous potential consequences may make it less likely. Which is less undesirable?

Consider another Catch-22: if the current nuclear powers move toward zero or near-zero nuclear arsenals, that would make it easier for other countries to achieve nuclear superpower status and thus encourage proliferation. If so, would the world be more or less safe? Suppose that

General Secretary Gorbachev's campaign to restructure the Soviet economy succeeds in closing the gap between the U.S. and Soviet economies. Would that mellow the Soviet Union's foreign policy or enhance its capabilities for foreign adventures? Simple answers to these questions are (and should be) suspect. What we don't know about the future is almost certain to be more important than what we do know.

Could we escape such dangerous complexities by withdrawing from the international arena? In a shrinking world, that option cannot promise peace. U.S. withdrawal from current commitments to Europe and Japan would arouse German and Japanese ambitions for military power sufficient to protect their national security—probably including nuclear weapons. Such developments, especially if they occurred precipitously, would greatly increase the risks of war.

No individual or government will be called on to choose an alternative fateful vision. Governments and individuals will, however, make important choices that can shape the future evolution of the system. The pressing need is for guidance that helps distinguish the better from the worse, and the more important from the less. Leaders responsible for shaping this evolution deserve far more help than they have received. Our hope is that this critique of alternative visions will enlist a wide community in debate about long-term futures. Engaged—or provoked—by this review of the competition, the reader is challenged to join in.

Summary and Critique

Each of the visions explored in this volume is incomplete. None specifies all of the parameters required to determine whether the hypothetical world would be workable or desirable. As noted in the Introduction, some theorists of international politics suggest that five major dimensions must be specified if such determinations are to be made. These dimensions form the columns in the table below: the structure or distribution of national power; the process and degree of moderation with which states interact; the nature of the domestic politics of the countries and their impact on foreign policies; the form and distribution of nuclear weaponry; and the nature and effects of other technological changes.

The table groups the visions discussed in the chapters in three major clusters: Chapters 1 through 5 focus on weapons, both offensive and defensive; Chapters 6 through 8 focus on U.S.-Soviet relations; and Chapters 9 and 10 focus on the larger international system in which U.S.-Soviet relations are embedded. Question marks indicate dimensions as to which a particular vision is silent or ambiguous. Thus there are entries

Publicly Debated Desirable Worlds

			Assumptions		
	Structure	Process	Domestic Politics	Nuclear Weapons	Other Technologies
Focus on Weapons and Defense					
1. Abolition and Near Zero	?	Some treaties	?	Zero or near-zero	?
2. Increased Accuracy	?	?	?	Accurate and limited	Accurate
3. Defense Dominance	?	?	?	Near-perfect defense	BMD
4. Lengthen the Fuse	?	?	?	Credible no first use (long fuse)	?
5. Nonprovocative Defense and Civilian Resistance	?	Unilateral action; some treaties	Broad support; reduced tension	Zero or near-zero	?
Focus on U.S.–Soviet Relations					
6. U.S.–Soviet Cooperation	?	Security regimes	?	?	?
7. Soviet Transformation	?	Moderation	Liberalization, reduced ideology	?	?
8. Soviet Decline	Hegemony or multipolarity?	?	Soviet internal problems	?	?
Focus on Transformation of the International System					
9. Internationalism	?	Institutions and regimes	Weakened nationalism	?	?
10. World Government	Single structure	Treaties and organizations	?	?	?

in the boxes related to the status of nuclear weaponry in the visions analyzed by the first five chapters; those boxes of the table have question marks for the last five chapters. Conversely, in the last five chapters, international political processes are more fully specified than in the first five chapters. The feasibility and desirability of a particular vision depends very much on how the various boxes are filled in.

Chapter 1 analyzed two related visions: abolition and near-abolition of nuclear weapons. Nuclear deterrence plays a role in both these worlds, since nuclear knowledge cannot be erased. Nuclear weapons could be quickly recreated, and that possibility will have a major effect on choices about war and peace. Rather than measuring military balances solely in terms of numbers and types of weapons, leaders and analysts would give great weight to mobilization timetables for reconstituting and expanding nuclear arsenals.

As James Miller pointed out, both visions reduce the catastrophic consequences of nuclear war if it should occur, but may increase the probability of nuclear war. There are three critical problem areas for both abolition and near-abolition: cheating and verification; proliferation; and conventional military balances, affecting prospects of conventional war. Neither abolition nor near-abolition would be stable unless nations had comparable abilities to hide nuclear weapons existing at the time of agreement and to build new ones. Given political distrust and uncertainty, verification would be a contentious issue. While the abolition of nuclear weapons would be a nondiscriminating nonproliferation regime, a drastic reduction of superpower arsenals could stimulate proliferation. The low threshold of entry into nuclear status might tempt more states or even private actors to cheat and become first-rank nuclear powers. Moreover, the abolition of nuclear weapons might make conventional war more probable. Conventional war, in turn, provides the conditions under which nuclear weapons are most likely to be reintroduced, thus breaking down the abolition agreement.

Other things being equal, one would expect both conventional war and its escalation to nuclear war to be somewhat more likely under abolition or near-abolition than they are now. But the potential destructiveness could be much less. A quantitatively oriented analyst would be interested in the expected consequences of a war: its potential destructiveness weighted by the probability that war would occur. Because such calculations depend on subjective judgments of the likelihood of war, they are very sensitive to political assumptions. For example, in a world where cooperative political processes facilitate and provide high confidence in verification, and where the conventional military balance is stable and robust, the expected destruction associated with abolition or near-abolition could be much lower than it is in today's world. Even under current circumstances, some people would prefer a higher probability of a series of smaller wars, such as World War II, to a lower probability of a single species-threatening nuclear conflict.

In a world of abolition or near-abolition, other things are *not* likely to be equal. In particular, nuclear disarmament could probably never be achieved without a marked change in the political relationships among states. Such fundamental political and social changes would have more impact on the fate of humanity than would the reduction or elimination of nuclear weapons.

Chapter 2 described a very different way to avoid catastrophe—increasing the accuracy of weapons. Greater accuracy should make it possible to substitute conventional weapons for nuclear weapons, and when nuclear weapons are used, to reduce their collateral damage. Proponents of this view argue that smaller, more usable weapons (rather than larger, less usable ones) would strengthen the credibility of deterrence and thereby reduce the risks of nuclear catastrophe. Others maintain that possession of small and usable accurate weapons might increase the probability of nuclear war. Not only would the weapons seem more usable to defense planners, but the distinction between conventional and nuclear systems might become blurred, making it easier to cross the nuclear threshold. Proponents counter that if deterrence did break down, the results would be less catastrophic because the military could hit what it wanted to hit and damage only what it wanted to damage. A critical question, of course, is whether such use would remain limited.

One technological approach to preventing catastrophic escalation is "lopping off the top"—that is, eliminating high-yield nuclear weapons so that only low-yield weapons remain. But that course is not often recommended by those who promote the vision of enhanced accuracy, and its technical and political feasibility is questionable. It would probably always be possible to combine a number of small accurate weapons for the purpose of destroying cities. In this vision, a safer nuclear world depends very much on rationality and restraint. It is too fragile in the face of the nonrational and inadvertent causes of war.

This vision is sensitive to assumptions about domestic politics. The rationality and restraint on which success would depend are less likely to prevail in a world of highly ideological and immoderate domestic politics, particularly in a time of war. Finally, this vision is very sensitive to changes in technologies other than those employed in nuclear forces.

For example, there may emerge new weapons of mass destruction based on other technologies (e.g., biological, chemical, climate modification, radiological) that would threaten the species.

The world of strategic defense examined in Chapter 3 has three major variants: perfect, near-perfect, and modest. Perfect defenses would be literally impenetrable; near-perfect defenses would suffer some leakage; and modest defenses would be effective only against attacks by small numbers of ballistic missiles. The prospects of catastrophic nuclear war are different in each case. Perfect defense, which is closest to President Reagan's SDI vision, would virtually eliminate the direct dangers of nuclear war. Moreover, as Charles Glaser argues in Chapter 3, the existence of perfect shields against nuclear deterrent forces would (other things being equal) increase the likelihood of conventional war. A perfect defense world would resemble an abolitionist world in the sense that small changes in the ability of the offense to penetrate the defense would be of substantial military significance. Thus, there would be strong incentives for a technological arms race. Since the outcome of such an arms race would be highly uncertain, each side could be tempted to pre-empt before the other gained an advantage.

Near-perfect defense would not make society invulnerable to a nuclear strike, but it might under certain conditions help to reduce the probability of war. For example, a near-perfect defense could improve the ability of retaliatory forces to survive attack and thereby discourage a first strike by an opponent. But as Glaser shows, the net effect of near-perfect defenses depends on several critical assumptions, among them the nature and extent of each side's defenses, the relative effectiveness of defenses against first strikes and retaliatory attacks, and the availability of delivery systems other than those for which the defense is intended.

In the third variant of the defense vision, a more modest defense acts as an insurance policy to protect against cheating or proliferation when political agreement has already led to the reduction or abolition of ballistic missiles. Transition to such a world would both reduce the probability and moderate the consequences of nuclear war. In contrast to the first two variants, which might (at least in theory) be achieved unilaterally, this modest defense world requires a high degree of political cooperation to achieve abolition. In such a world, the technology of defense somewhat mitigates the problems of cheating and proliferation.

Chapter 4 dealt with a set of visions summed up as "lengthening the fuse." This category includes concepts of no early use, no first use, and disengagement from political commitments. The common element is the idea of widening the firebreaks between political disputes and nuclear use. These visions would reduce the risk of nuclear catastrophe not by cutting the numbers of weapons, but by making their use less likely. If, despite these measures, the full nuclear arsenals were used, the consequences would be no less catastrophic than in today's world.

These visions aim at buying time. But since they leave weapons in place, they purchase less time than abolition would. Their potential flaws are analogous to those of the abolition vision, though perhaps to a lesser degree. Under some circumstances they may increase the probability of conventional war and hence the danger of escalation to nuclear war. Daniel Arbess and Andrew Moravcsik argue that the impact on the probability of nuclear war depends strongly on the nature of the U.S.–Soviet relationship as well as that between the United States and its allies. It is worth remembering that U.S. disengagement from Korea early in 1950 probably encouraged the Korean War. An American disengagement that allowed Soviet hegemony over Europe and Japan or provoked further proliferation by these countries would significantly increase risks to U.S. security rather than diminish them. A policy of no first use is far more modest than disengagement, but it could have serious effects on alliance cohesion. Acceptability of no first use may depend on achievement of symmetry in the conventional force balance. No early use is a still more modest proposal, with corresponding reductions in both potential benefits and potential costs.

The visions analyzed by Stephen Flanagan in Chapter 5 include nonprovocative defense and civilian-based defense. Both would reduce reliance on nuclear weapons, as well as on conventional offensive forces. Nonprovocative defense includes not only renunciation of first use of nuclear weapons, elimination of nuclear war-fighting systems, and abandonment of long-range military capabilities, but also conversion of armies to small forces equipped only with short-range weaponry for territorial defense. At some phase, many proponents of this vision would drop the nuclear capability entirely. Civilian-based defense goes a step further and eliminates all conventional military capabilities. It relies on nonviolent protest, noncooperation, and nonviolent intervention as means to raise the costs of aggression, in this way deterring attack and frustrating conquest. A trained and organized public rather than a trained and organized military, it is argued, makes a people unconquerable.

Those variants of nonprovocative defense that leave nuclear weapons as an insurance policy (at least in the early phases) resemble proposals for lengthening the fuse in their effects on prospects of nuclear catastrophe. But proposals to lengthen the fuse tend to stress strengthening conventional military capabilities, while proposals for nonprovocative defense call for reducing those capabilities to a level sufficient only for territorial defense. Civilian-based defense goes even further, denying the need for any military capabilities and relying on the organization of the body politic for defense.

Insofar as these proposals lead to renunciation of nuclear weapons, they are similar to abolition. They reduce the prospects of nuclear catastrophe at the cost of increasing the probability of conventional war. The magnitude of this cost depends on the credibility of the nonprovocative or civilian-based defense as a deterrent. The key assumption underlying these proposals is that elimination of offensive postures would significantly decrease the potential for war. But deeply rooted disputes could still lead to war, even if only guards were available to fight them.

One would expect nonprovocative defense to work best in circumstances of diffused power. If no one state predominates, it might be more difficult for any nation to use its border guards in an offensive manner. Agreements inhibiting intervention in other countries (including Third World countries) would help to remove many of the causes that could precipitate the misuse of allegedly defensive forces. Civilian-based defense would also work best in an international political structure with symmetry of power among the units. And, of course, popular support would be necessary to develop or maintain the organization necessary for civilian-based defense. Finally, the development of new technologies of mass destruction or the reintroduction of nuclear technology might pose a threat that could undermine the popular base of support on which civilian-based defense rests.

Chapters 6, 7, and 8 dealt with changes in the political dimensions of the U.S.-Soviet relationship rather than with armaments. These visions intend to reduce the prospect of nuclear catastrophe by making war between the major powers less likely. If war should occur nevertheless, its effects would still be catastrophic unless the improved U.S.-Soviet relationship somehow had led to radical reductions in weapons.

In Chapter 6, Sean Lynn-Jones and Stephen Rock discussed the prospects for deepening U.S.-Soviet cooperation and resolving the major issues dividing the two countries. Cooperation would take the form of either mutual disengagement from areas of potential conflict or a condominium for joint management of mutual problems. This deepening of cooperation could be stimulated in various ways. It could originate with a common enemy, as in 1941. Alternatively, it could stem from technological, economic, or domestic political changes or from a deliberate strategy of de-escalating conflicts driven by an increasing fear of nuclear war.

Lynn-Jones and Rock point out that cooperation is most likely to come about through mutually reinforcing changes in several of these dimensions, rather than just one. Paradoxically, they note, some conditions that appear to make U.S.-Soviet cooperation more likely might also make such cooperation less relevant to the problem of avoiding nuclear war. For example, the threat of a hostile major nuclear power on the world scene might lead the United States and the Soviet Union to cooperate as they did against Hitler. The prospects of nuclear war between the United States and the Soviet Union might then be diminished, but the overall chance of nuclear war could actually increase.

Chapter 7 examined the possibility of significant changes in Soviet foreign policy as a result of internal changes in the Soviet Union. In a sense, this vision has been a guiding light of U.S. foreign policy since 1947, when George Kennan formulated the concept of containment. Kennan hoped for a mellowing of Soviet aggressiveness as ideological zeal diminished and the Russian sense of isolation gave way to greater contacts with the outside world. In his words, "it would not take the ideological position that its own purposes cannot finally prosper unless all systems of government not under its control are subverted and eventually destroyed. It would dispense this paranoid suspiciousness we know so well."[9] Robert Beschel argues that Soviet foreign policy has its roots in Russian traditions of insecurity (which might be termed "paranoid"), ideological zeal and rigidity, and the normal expansive nature of a great power vis-à-vis its neighbors. While expansionist tendencies may persist, their intensity may be moderated by the same processes that have constrained other great powers. Thus if ideological zeal and paranoia are diminished by domestic reform and increased contact with the outside world, one would expect a gradual mellowing of Soviet foreign policy and a greater capacity to reach cooperative agreements.

In Chapter 8, Kurt Campbell analyzed a vision in which a decline in Soviet power renders nuclear catastrophe less likely. Proponents of this vision assume that the major sources of political conflict arise from Soviet expansionism combined with Soviet power. Whether the expansionist impulses wane or not, a decline in power would reduce the Soviet capability for military challenges. Awareness of weakness might cause the Soviet leadership to concentrate on domestic reform in order to regain its position. Continued decline might force the Soviet government to focus on maintenance of its innermost empire in Eastern Europe. It might even lead the Soviets to seek a rapprochement with their major adversary.

This vision poses risks as well as potential benefits. For example, if a sense of decline leads to less caution or a desperate attempt to regain an advantage through military adventure, then the prospects of nuclear catastrophe could be increased rather than diminished. The critical question is whether the decline in Soviet power would led to behavior like that of the multiethnic Austro-Hungarian Empire, which precipitated World War I, or the long and more graceful decline of the British Empire. And how would the perceived decline of Soviet power affect U.S. foreign policy? If it encouraged American policy makers to take increased risks, it could raise the risk of war. And if a decline in Soviet power led the Chinese or Japanese to press the Soviets in East Asia, this could lead to more risky Soviet policies.

Chapters 9 and 10 focused on transformations of the broader international system, going beyond the U.S.-Soviet relationship. According to David Welch, there are three variants of the internationalist argument: increased contacts will change those (mistaken) perceptions that exacerbate conflicts of interests; increased trade will create a new web of mutual interests to counter those conflicting interests that might lead to hostility; and development of international institutions and regimes will moderate conflicts and provide rules and procedures for dealing with any conflicts that do arise. While claims made for internationalism have often been exaggerated, its effects appear to be positive even if smaller than their proponents have asserted. For example, most observers would agree that the Soviet Union's sense of falling behind in technology provided an incentive for both domestic restructuring and increased international trade. Similarly, contacts may be more important than most Americans believe, primarily as they correct the misperceptions of individuals (especially decision makers) in relatively closed societies. Finally, international institutions and regimes can address security interests directly and indirectly. Examples include the regimes for slowing the proliferation of nuclear weapons and for dealing with incidents at sea, and the United Nations and regional institutional systems that help to cope with conflicts among member nations.

In Chapter 10, Lee Neumann examined the more ambitious scheme of world government. Here the risk of nuclear catastrophe would be reduced by creating an authority with a monopoly on nuclear technology, which would manage conflicts between its member nations. Indeed, if the world authority abolished nuclear weapons or dramatically reduced their numbers, it would reduce the effects as well as the probability of nuclear war. On the other hand, the mere establishment of such a world authority would not prevent the development of civil war, either within member countries or between coalitions formed within the world government. Moreover, given the enormous inequalities in today's world, it is hard to imagine how any authority's policy on wealth redistribution could be acceptable to all member nations.

Pointing to the Future

"Where there is no vision, the people perish." So concluded the Proverbs a millennium before Christ. So it remains in the fifth decade of the nuclear era.

At one level, uncertainty dominates any attempt to look into the future. A forecast made fifty years ago would have made no mention whatsoever of nuclear weapons. Clearly there can be no certainty in efforts to predict developments in the Soviet Union, the United States, China, or Japan, much less the interaction among them. Thus any proposed vision of the long-term future can easily be shown to be not only insufficiently specified but highly unlikely.

Nonetheless, political leaders' preferences and practices are informed and shaped by "visions"—combinations of assumptions, expectations, and hopes about where events are tending and in what direction they should be nudged. Leaders attempt not only to follow trends, but to bend them. While the visions that inform their actions are often incomplete and fuzzy, such hopes and fears allow them to act despite otherwise paralyzing complexity and uncertainty. Moreover, citizens demand some vision that offers both a sense of direction and hope. Leaders unable to offer a conception of the future will be displaced by others who propose more promising alternatives.

If the current security system were certain to fail catastrophically, prudence would demand that we choose an alternative. But the current system is not certain to fail catastrophically. There is some truth to Murphy's Law that if anything can wrong, it will. It does not always follow, however, that the worst that can happen, does. For example, history has proved that C.P. Snow was unduly pessimistic when he prophesied in 1960 that if events proceeded on their current course, nuclear war was "a certainty" within at most ten years.[10]

Many visionaries, and vision followers, are literally utopian: they seek a place that is nowhere in this world. Shaken by the awesome risks of the international system in the nuclear age, they demand some "final solution" to the problem of security. Most of the visions analyzed in this volume propose "endpoint utopias"—conditions that once achieved would resolve the problem. The sad truth is that this life offers no such resting place.

Are we left with no reasoned grounds for hope, no vision to provide guidance for policy makers and citizens intent on building peace? Fortunately not. We find considerable basis for optimism in what might be termed "process utopias": visions of a process for keeping the peace and reducing risks of war, even if no ultimate solution is possible. The chapters of this book offer a number of significant clues for the construction of process visions.

Neither technology nor political change alone offers a solution to the political dilemmas that stand in the way of a lasting peace. While most weapons- and defense-focused visions fail to specify the political context, and most visions of political change neglect the technological context, an adequate vision must address both. For the reasons given above, we find neither abolition nor near-abolition of nuclear weapons a realistic policy goal under current political conditions. Indeed, we believe that achievement of this goal without radical changes in other dimensions would make the use of nuclear weapons more likely, not less so. Perhaps the problems of cheating and verification, incentives to proliferation, and stable conventional deterrence could be overcome through changes in political conditions. If so, it would become very attractive to shrink nuclear arsenals to levels low enough to reduce significantly the risk of nuclear catastrophe. Thus the major policy direction derived from consideration of abolition or near-abolition is the desirability of having too few nuclear weapons to destroy civilization as we know it. But the essential prerequisite is major political change, both in U.S.–Soviet relations and in the behavior of other nations.

Technology is now marching in the direction of increased accuracy, which promises a reduction in the destructiveness of nuclear war. But despite the value of reducing collateral damage to civilians and to society as a whole, there is another, more worrisome, aspect of increasing accuracy. Blurring the distinction between nuclear and conventional weapons increases the chance that nuclear weapons would be treated as usable, normal weapons. The leap from this trend to a vision of a safer world thus requires heroic assumptions about governments' ability to limit nuclear war if it begins—assumptions on which we would not bet our planet. Moreover, as we have argued, while a strategy based on this vision might enhance deterrence of a rational, calculating adversary, the greater risks of nuclear war stem from nonrational factors. The vision of more accurate nuclear weapons thus offers modest policy guidance at best and could be highly misleading.

The nuclear age has been marked by the dominance of offense over defense. Even a few nuclear weapons penetrating a nation's defense would cause enormous destruction. The vision of a world in which citizens would be defended rather than avenged is attractive. Unfortunately, we see little prospect for perfect or near-perfect defense against a determined adversary. Nevertheless, we believe there may be a positive role for a modest defense against small attacks. Such a defense would provide some protection against inadvertent use of nuclear weapons by third parties. Moreover, if the world eventually moved toward abolition of nuclear weapons, this defense might help to deal with some problems of cheating and proliferation. It is crucial to remember, however, that such a limited defense would require a political understanding among the major powers and would not protect against all the means (e.g., airplanes, cruise missiles, or smuggled bombs) by which a proliferator could deliver weapons.

Nonprovocative military forces would reduce armies to the status of border guards, while civilian-based defenses would replace armies with organized civilians. Whether either approach would provide adequate deterrence depends very much on political conditions—conditions we cannot conceive being met in the foreseeable future. But there is a clue here in the reconfiguration of forces that most exacerbate insecurity. For example, reduction of forward-based armored divisions would be an important step in the right direction. Given the current geographical asymmetries, such reductions would initially require greater cuts by the Soviet Union than by the United States to avoid creating anxiety in Europe. Further in the future, more elaborate restructuring could take place, perhaps eventually leading to a marked reduction in military forces and greater dependence on civilian-based defense.

Broader internationalism, beyond improvements in the U.S.–Soviet relationship, becomes all the more relevant as the dominance of the superpowers diminishes and multipolarity emerges. It is not enough to lower the risks of war in the U.S.–Soviet competition if other risks grow even larger. The fostering of contacts, trade, and institutional arrangements could all reduce the nuclear risk if properly managed, though probably not as much as their strongest advocates expect. One risk is that the positive side of broader internationalism could be offset by the growth of ambitions and weakening of constraints that come with multipolarity. Nonetheless, greater internationalism has encouraging effects.

World government is perhaps the longest-standing vision of how to solve the problems of war, including the risk of nuclear catastrophe. Nevertheless, the concept remains underexamined. Both imagination and analysis are in short supply. Because it seems impossible that full world government could be created in the near future, more thought should be given to partial measures that create some degree of international authority. Ironically, such an exploration may lead us back toward a design suggested in 1945. There is considerable appeal in the idea of a United Nations Security Council acting as a condominium for a multi-polar world and having authority over only those issues that breached or threatened to breach the peace. In its first incarnation, unfortunately, this concept floundered on the realities of bipolarity and the ideological excesses of the Cold War. The time has come to devote fresh thinking to institutional authorities for maintaining common security.

In the editors' view, two paths together hold the greatest promise for policy makers today and scholarly exploration tomorrow. One begins with "lengthening the fuse" and extends to changing the military forces of the United States, our allies, and our adversaries enough to give the United States a credible conventional deterrent and only a minimal residual nuclear force. A successful program for achieving this objective would rely as much on political and organizational changes as on technological innovation. The second path, emerging from the chapters on U.S.–Soviet cooperation, Soviet mellowing, and Soviet decline, envisages a more fundamental, longer-term evolution of the U.S.–Soviet relationship.

The United States' nuclear strategy and the forces that have evolved to support it are remnants of a fundamentally different era. When U.S. nuclear forces and doctrine first began to take shape, there were no nuclear threats to American territory, forces, or allies, and no prospects for conventional aggression against the U.S. homeland. Our principal concern was the potential for Soviet conventional aggression in Europe. America's threat to meet such aggression with nuclear use was then a credible one, for we had both the means and the will to carry it out. With a nuclear monopoly, the United States felt safe from the societal destruction that nuclear weapons could inflict. As the Soviet Union obtained a countervailing nuclear arsenal, U.S. leaders could no longer count on nuclear war remaining one-sided, and the U.S. threat to meet Soviet conventional aggression in Europe (or elsewhere) with a nuclear response was slowly transformed into a threat of mutual suicide. It seemed more and more unlikely that a rational leader would take such action, and the threat to do so appeared less and less credible. Of course, the very existence of large numbers of nuclear weapons, their widespread integration with conventional forces in potential theaters of armed conflict, and the fragility of some of the systems for controlling their use create a danger of unintended nuclear escalation. But these factors not only contribute to deterrence; they also increase the danger of inadvertent and potentially catastrophic nuclear war. The West should and can modify its strategy and restructure its forces in ways that reduce these dangers while maintaining adequate deterrence.

The first step is to achieve a conventional military balance that will permit reduced reliance on nuclear weapons to deter conventional aggression. Negotiated reductions in conventional forces in Central Europe might be supplemented by qualitative improvements in the West's nonnuclear force, to compensate for Soviet quantitative advantages. In particular, technological innovations (such as smart weapons) permitting nonnuclear attacks against conventional forces previously vulnerable only to nuclear attack should be a high priority.

As the balance of conventional force becomes more even, shorter-range nuclear weapons could be withdrawn from potential areas of armed conflict. The military cost would be far less than imagined by those who fear stepping onto the "slippery slope" to denuclearization of Europe or other theaters. If, despite our effort to deter it, Soviet conventional aggression should occur, our longer-range missiles and aircraft could be employed against selected targets virtually anywhere in the world.

Nuclear and nonnuclear forces must be organizationally and geographically separate if a decision to use military force on a large scale is to be independent of a decision to use nuclear weapons. Yet, except for the strategic nuclear arsenal, most nuclear forces are integrated with general purpose forces. The army, navy, and air force maintain dual-use platforms and delivery vehicles, and separation of nuclear and nonnuclear systems would require all three services to abandon well-established command structures and deployment and training practices. These obstacles to change are formidable, but not insurmountable. It is worth noting that, unlike their army and air force counterparts, naval nuclear weapons are not now safeguarded by Permissive Action Links (PALs)—the electronic locks that help guard against unauthorized use. While an argument can be made for exempting submarine-based weapons (because of the difficulties of communicating with submarines), we see no compelling reason not to equip surface-ship-based nuclear weapons with PALs.

The nuclear fuse can be lengthened further by reducing each side's incentives for a pre-emptive attack against the other side's nuclear forces and/or associated command, control, and communication systems. Given the size and diversity of current nuclear arsenals, pre-emptive capabilities are inadequate to preclude a devastating retaliatory attack. Neither side faces a "use 'em or lose 'em" dilemma of meaningful proportion. This is a healthy state of affairs and should be maintained. Deep cuts in the nuclear arsenals of both superpowers (e.g., on the order of 50 percent or more) can be designed in ways that will reinforce the stability of the nuclear stalemate. The command, control, and communications networks associated with strategic and theater nuclear weapons, however, are less robust than the forces themselves. Strengthening these networks can add a substantial increment to the fuse, and efforts in that direction should continue to receive high priority.

The most important factor, however, is the process of change in U.S.–Soviet relations. Any comprehensive vision of a world beyond MAD must involve the political evolution of the U.S.–Soviet relationship to a point of significant superpower cooperation. Both Britain and France have nuclear arsenals that could destroy most American cities, yet few Americans lose sleep over this prospect. The Federal Republic of Germany and Japan have the economic and technical capacity to support a nuclear arsenal of superpower proportions, and both were bitterest enemies of the United States in World War II. Neither poses a military threat to the United States today.

Could U.S.–Soviet relations change over the next quarter-century as significantly as U.S.–Chinese relations have changed in the last fifteen years? Clues to the possibility of such change are to be found in the chapters on the decline of Soviet power, the mellowing of Soviet foreign policy ambitions, and the expansion of U.S.–Soviet cooperation. In some combination, these developments might constitute a path of political evolution to a world substantially different than today's.

It is becoming clear that the Soviet's centralized command-and-control economy is incompatible with successful advanced industrial economic development. Central management of a large industrial economy has proven inefficient in allocation and inept in incentives. In an era of rapid technological change in microelectronics and computers, a measure of decentralization and free thinking may be prerequisites for success. Nothing so constrains ambitions as the absence of capability. Soviet economic growth slowed nearly to stagnation in the early 1980s. Soviet GNP is now approximately equal to Japan's, and only half that of either Western Europe or the United States. This disadvantage has significant implications for the longer-term competition. As former Soviet Chief of the General Staff Orgakov recognized clearly, a nation that lags in its advanced technologies, such as computers and microelectronics, will inevitably fall behind.

The Cold War of the late 1940s and early 1950s was not merely a response to Soviet military power. Western Europeans and Americans also feared Soviet ideas and ideals, especially the possibility that Soviet communism could be an ideological firestorm sweeping countries in Europe and Japan much as Islam spread in the seventh century. Demoralized by a devastating war, exhausted economically, and threatened by communist parties within, several countries in Europe and Asia seemed especially vulnerable. Thus the first phase of containment focused on preventing a combination of ideological appeal and internal subversion from seizing power in countries such as Italy, France, and Greece. Today, communism's claim on the hearts and minds of anyone who has the chance to choose is minimal. While it remains a rationalization for some who hold power, few observers in either the West or the Soviet Union take seriously the prospect of communist ideology on the march. That change has consequences for Soviet foreign policy toward the Third World, as well as U.S. fears of Soviet or other communist advances.

The passage of time, interactions with the rest of the world, and the spread of communications are making Soviet policy makers more aware of the realities of the world outside. Contact with the outside world erodes the dogmatism of official truth, undermines misperceptions, and reduces paranoia. Awareness of the success of alternative political economies in producing high technology and consumer goods raises hard questions about previously accepted truths and encourages emulation.

General Secretary Gorbachev has put the point bluntly: unless the deterioration of the past decade is sharply reversed, the Soviet Union will not enter the twenty-first century as a great power. The current Soviet leadership is much clearer about the failures of performance than about prescriptions. But it seems plausible that for some time the Soviet Union will be preoccupied with internal affairs, as it concentrates first on righting its economy through common sense and pragmatism; experimenting with degrees of openness, liberalization, and democratization; and downgrading Soviet ambitions in the Third World.

Despite their risks, such circumstances, if wisely managed, could present the best opportunity of the postwar period to advance our interests and the cause of peace. Policy makers might begin by recognizing the real problems in the American economy that require urgent attention at home. Still more important should be the recognition that for the indefinite future the Soviet Union will remain capable of destroying what

Americans hold dear. Any sober assessment of the common threats the United States and Soviet Union face, and the parallel interests they share, should lead to a significant strengthening of processes of cooperation and parallel action.

No common interest is more fundamental than avoidance of the major nuclear war of which the superpowers would be the first victims. Other serious threats include the spread of nuclear weapons, the spread of advanced conventional weapons, terrorism, regional wars that could engage the superpowers, and worldwide environmental degradation. In each instance, the United States and the Soviet Union have common as well as competing interests. A sound American view, however, should emphasize the commonalities. Such cooperation could stop well short of condominium and still radically reduce the risks of nuclear war between the United States and the Soviet Union.

These twin visions of lengthening the fuse and political evolution are not only desirable but may actually be achievable. Indeed, though our crystal ball is quite hazy, it suggests that over the next half-century the Soviet Union will account for no more than half of the risk of mass destruction of Americans. If so, political evolution and cooperation beyond the superpowers will be a necessary condition for radically reducing nuclear risks, and an adequate process vision will have to include elements of internationalism and the strengthening of international institutions.

The acceptability of any process vision depends on avoiding C. P. Snow's error. The fact that nuclear war is possible does not mean that it is inevitable. If, through appropriate processes, the United States and Soviet Union can reduce the risks of nuclear war each year, then nuclear war need *not* even be likely.[11] Of course, no one can specify with confidence the risks of such a war today, or know exactly how much a given action would reduce the risks. The point is to expose the concept of pessimistic inevitability as misguided and mistaken.

Realization of the process visions sketched here will require significant changes in the behavior of both superpowers, and more from the Soviet Union than from the United States. This judgment reflects not only the authors' national identity, but also our conviction that the peaceful proclivities of liberal democracies offer the best hope for the long term.

Our process vision—though we believe it offers hope—is certainly not the only solution to the problem of avoiding nuclear catastrophe. This volume is an interim progress report, which we hope will stimulate further thinking. We offer not a conclusion, but a beginning.

Notes

Introduction

1. See symposium on "Nuclear Winter" in *Issues in Science and Technology* (Winter 1985): 112–33.
2. Richard Garwin, "Is There a Way Out?," *Harpers*, June 1985, pp. 35–47.
3. For an account of how a nuclear war might occur, see Graham Allison, Albert Carnesale, and Joseph S. Nye, Jr., eds., *Hawks, Doves, and Owls: An Agenda for Avoiding Nuclear War* (New York: Norton, 1985).
4. Arnold Toynbee, *Civilization on Trial* (New York: Oxford University Press, 1948).
5. "Defense Rejects Concept of a World Free of Atomic Arms," *New York Times*, February 1, 1987.
6. Jonathan Schell, *The Abolition* (New York: Knopf, 1984); see also his earlier book, *The Fate of the Earth* (New York: Knopf, 1982).
7. Robert S. McNamara, *Blundering into Disaster: Surviving the First Century of the Nuclear Age* (New York: Pantheon Books, 1986).
8. Albert Wohlstetter, "Bishops, Statesmen, and Other Strategists on the Bombing of Innocents," *Commentary* 75, no. 6 (June 1983): 15–35; Albert Wohlstetter, "Between an Unfree World and None: Increasing Our Choices," *Foreign Affairs* 63, no. 5 (Summer 1985): 962–94.
9. Morton H. Halprin, *Nuclear Fallacy* (Cambridge, MA: Ballinger, 1987).
10. Randall Forsberg, "Non-Provocative Defense: A New Approach to Arms Control," unpublished Institute for Defense and Disarmament Studies paper, October, 1986.
11. Gene Sharp, *Making Europe Unconquerable* (Cambridge, MA: Ballinger, 1986).
12. Aspen Institute for Humanistic Studies, International Group, *Managing East–West Conflict: A Framework for Sustained Engagement* (New York: Aspen Institute, 1984); also, W.W. Rostow, "On Ending the Cold War," *Foreign Affairs* 65, no. 4 (Spring 1987): 831–51; George Liska, "From Containment to Concert," *Foreign Policy* 62 (Spring 1986): 3–23; and Liska, "Concert through Decompression," *Foreign Policy* 63 (Summer 1986): 108–29; Marshall D. Shulman, "An Alternative Policy for Managing U.S.–Soviet Relations," in Arnold L. Horelick, ed., *U.S.–Soviet Relations: The Next Phase* (Ithaca, NY: Cornell University Press, 1986), pp. 259–75.

13. Reproduced in George F. Kennan, *American Diplomacy 1900–1950* (Chicago: University of Chicago Press, 1951).
14. See Robert Pear, "Push the Russians, Intellectuals Ask," *New York Times*, October 13, 1985; Richard Pipes, *Survival Is Not Enough: Soviet Realities and America's Future* (New York: Simon and Schuster, 1984).
15. David Mitrany, *A Working Peace System* (Chicago: Quadrangle Books, 1966).
16. Grenville Clark and Louis B. Sohn, *World Peace Through World Law* (Cambridge, MA: Harvard University Press, 1966).
17. For discussion of structure and process in international politics, see Kenneth Waltz, *Theory of International Politics* (Reading, MA: Addison-Wesley, 1979) and Robert O. Keohane and Joseph S. Nye, Jr., "'Power and Interdependence' Revisited," *International Organization* 41 (Fall 1987).

Chapter 1: Zero and Minimal Nuclear Weapons

1. U.S. Department of State, *Documents on Disarmament, 1945–59*, vol. 1, documents 4, 5 (Washington, DC: Government Printing Office, 1960). Reprinted in Trevor N. Dupuy and Gay M. Hammerman, *A Documentary History of Arms Control and Disarmament* (New York: R.R. Bowker Co., 1973), pp. 301–12.
2. "Gorbachev's Plan to Scrap All Nuclear Arms," *Current Digest of the Soviet Press* 38, no. 3 (1986): 6. Like the Soviet proposal to the United Nations forty years earlier, General Secretary Gorbachev's plan for abolition offered no specific steps for inspection and enforcement. Instead he proposed simply that "verification... would be carried out by both national technical means and through on-site inspection," declaring that "the Soviet Union is ready to negotiate on any additional verification measures."
3. See Michael Mandelbaum and Strobe Talbott, *Reagan and Gorbachev: The Chances for a Breakthrough in U.S.–Soviet Relations* (New York: Vintage Books, 1983), and James Schlesinger, "Reykjavik and Revelations: A Turn of the Tide?" *Foreign Affairs* 65, no. 3 (1987): 426–46.
4. Jonathan Schell, *The Fate of the Earth* (New York: Avon Books, 1982), p. 231.
5. Robert S. McNamara, *Blundering Into Disaster: Surviving the First Century of the Nuclear Age* (New York: Pantheon Books, 1986), p. 122.
6. Here I do not consider proposals that would leave nuclear arsenals with 1,000 or more nuclear warheads. Such proposals, although potentially interesting and quite different from today's world of more than 50,000 nuclear warheads, would not entail a radical reduction in the potential dangers of assured destruction. For example, George F. Kennan argues that "something well less than 20 percent of [present nuclear weapons] stocks would surely suffice for the most sanguine concepts of deterrence, whether as between the two nuclear superpowers or with relation to any of those other governments that have been so ill-advised as to enter upon the nuclear path" (George F. Kennan, *The Nuclear Delusion* (New York: Pantheon Books, 1983), p. 177).
7. See Leonard S. Spector, *Going Nuclear: The Spread of Nuclear Weapons 1986–1987* (Cambridge, MA: Ballinger, 1987).
8. "Gorbachev's Plan," p. 6 (note 2).
9. For a good brief overview of national technical means for verification, see David Hafemeister, Joseph J. Romm, and Kosta Tsipis, "The Verification of

Compliance with Arms-Control Agreements," *Scientific American* 252, no. 3 (March 1985): 39–45. For a more detailed discussion, see Kosta Tsipsis, David W. Hafemeister, and Penny Janeway, eds., *Arms Control Verification: The Technologies That Make It Possible* (Washington, DC: Pergamon-Brassey's, 1986).

10. "Reykjavik and American Security," report of the Defense Policy Panel of the Committee on Armed Services, United States House of Representatives (Washington, DC: Government Printing Office, 1987). For the view that extensive inspections would be consistent with the U.S. Constitution, see Louis Henkin, "Arms Inspections and the Constitution," *Bulletin of the Atomic Scientists* 15, no. 5 (May 1959): 192–97.

11. Even in the current unclassified literature on nonproliferation, there is much information about the status of nuclear programs for nations that appear to be edging closer to a nuclear capability. See, for example, Spector, *Going Nuclear* (note 7).

12. *Documents on Disarmament*, vol. 1, document 4, p. 11 (note 1).

13. See Bernhard G. Bechhoefer, *Postwar Negotiations for Arms Control* (Washington, DC: Brookings Institution, 1961), pp. 41–82.

14. *Documents on Disarmament*, vol. 1, document 4, p. 13 (note 1). World government is discussed in Chapter 10. For an extended argument that an international authority would be needed for abolition, but that the authority would *not* have to be a world government, see John H. Barton, "The Proscription of Nuclear Weapons: A Third Regime," in David C. Gompert, Michael Mandelbaum, Richard L. Garwin, and John H. Barton, *Nuclear Weapons and World Politics: Alternatives for the Future* (New York: McGraw-Hill Book Co., 1977). Barton's international authority may, however, be able to undertake a "disarming attack upon nuclear facilities" (p. 169) and to intervene in the "internal affairs" (p. 175) of a nation that violated the abolition agreement.

15. Schell, *The Fate of the Earth*, p. 188 (note 4). Schell argued that "the peril of extinction is the price the world pays not for 'safety' or 'survival' but for its insistence on continuing to divide itself up into sovereign states" (p. 210). Moreover, "nuclear disarmament cannot occur if conventional arms are left in place, since as long as nations defend themselves with arms of any kind they will be fully sovereign, and as long as they are fully sovereign they will be at liberty to build nuclear weapons if they so choose" (pp. 225–26).

16. Jonathan Schell, *The Abolition* (New York: Avon, 1984), pp. 152ff. Forty years earlier, J. Robert Oppenheimer, who served on the committee that produced the Baruch report, came to a similar conclusion. The International Atomic Development Authority should be used not to enforce compliance with the ban on atomic weapons, but to guarantee adequate warning time for other nations to respond if cheating occurred. Then "the violator would have raised the brightest red flag he can, and every other country will know that they are in for it" (*Bulletin of the Atomic Scientists* 1, no. 12 (June 1, 1946): 1–5).

17. Schell, *The Abolition*, p. 152 (note 16).

18. Schell, *The Abolition*, pp. 148–50 (note 16).

19. Thomas C. Schelling, *Arms and Influence* (New Haven: Yale University Press, 1966), p. 251.

20. *The Harris Survey*, March 14, 1985 (no. 21). The question was: "All in all, do you feel that the situation where the U.S. and the Soviet Union both know

that any use of nuclear weapons will result in instant retaliation has helped to keep the peace in the world, or not?" Of 1,256 adult respondents, 74 percent answered that it "has helped," 21 percent answered that it "has not helped," and 5 percent were not sure.

21. This point is recognized by Schell in *The Abolition*, p. 179 (note 16).
22. Charles Krauthammer argued, for example, that "the asymmetry regarding verification is crucial. One can be sure that if all strategic systems (or just ballistic missiles) were abolished, it would be extremely unlikely that they could be made clandestinely in the United States" (*New Republic*, November 17, 1986, p. 24). Similarly, Assistant Secretary of Defense Richard Perle asked rhetorically, "What Western leader would turn in his country's last remaining nuclear weapon on the strength of assurances—mere words—that the Soviets had done the same?" (*Boston Globe*, February 5, 1987, p. 15).
23. McNamara, *Blundering into Disaster*, pp. 122–23 (note 5). McNamara made the same argument in "The Military Role of Nuclear Weapons: Perceptions and Misperceptions," *Foreign Affairs* 62, no. 1 (Fall 1983): 59–80.
24. Jimmy Carter, *Keeping Faith* (New York: Bantam Books, 1982), p. 245.
25. A very good discussion of multipolar strategic deterrence appears in Richard Rosencrance, *Strategic Deterrence Reconsidered*, Adelphi Paper no. 116 (London: International Institute for Strategic Studies, 1975).
26. Attributed to Leonid Brezhnev by Freeman Dyson, in *Weapons and Hope* (New York: Harper and Row, 1984), p. 284.
27. This point is similar to the argument that "a major BMD [ballistic missile defense] initiative sparking widespread Soviet defense would in effect disarm our allies (to a degree depending on the nature of the Soviet deployment)" (Ashton B. Carter, *Directed Energy Missile Defense in Space*, background paper prepared for the Office of Technology Assessment, United States Congress (April 1984), p. 78). See also Lawrence Freedman, "The Small Nuclear Powers," in Ashton B. Carter and David N. Schwartz, eds., *Ballistic Missile Defense* (Washington, DC: Brookings Institution, 1984).
28. Thus, the United States would have exclusive control over 300 warheads. Either the United States or Great Britain could launch 100 warheads, and similarly for the United States and France. Obviously this "half-key" plan (as opposed to the present dual-key system for NATO) would require a high level of cohesion among the three partners. The potential problems with such a plan may be similar to those faced in the effort to establish a NATO multilateral nuclear force. See John Steinbrunner, *The Cybernetic Theory of Decision* (Princeton, NJ: Princeton University Press, 1974).
29. The notion of using international development of nuclear warheads to ease verification difficulties is similar to the proposal that the government recall all $100 bills and reissue red notes instead of green. Anyone turning in very large numbers of bills would have some explaining to do; drug dealers, who are believed to hold a disproportionate share of the stock of $100 bills, would have to choose between turning in their notes and attempting to explain, or losing vast sums of money.
30. McNamara, *Blundering into Disaster*, p. 122 (note 5).
31. Glenn S. Snyder, *Deterrence and Defense* (Princeton, NJ: Princeton University Press, 1961), p. 98.

32. Bernard Brodie, "On the Objectives of Arms Control," *International Security* 1, no. 1 (Summer 1976): 28.
33. Long-time strategist and arms control negotiator Paul Nitze has distinguished five nuclear strategies: minimum deterrence, requiring "a capacity to destroy a few key cities"; assured destruction, requiring the capability to "destroy many cities, many millions of people, and much productive capacity"; flexible response, which is present U.S. strategy; victory denial; and nuclear war winning ("Assuring Strategic Stability in an Era of Detente," *Foreign Affairs* 54, no. 2 (January 1976): 212–13). However, the difference between Nitze's "minimum deterrence" and "assured destruction" is largely one of degree — whether "a few key cities" or "many cities" must be threatened. Also, as Nitze notes, the bedrock of flexible response strategy is an assured destruction (or a "minimum deterrence") capability: flexible response is meant to "increase the credibility of deterrence" (p. 213).
34. Martin J. Bailey, "Deterrence, Assured Destruction, and Defense," *Orbis* 16, no. 3 (Fall 1972): 694.
35. Bailey, "Deterrence, Assured Destruction, and Defense," p. 683 (note 34). Donald Brennan referred to such a policy as a Russian Freeze, arguing (in 1967) that it would be consistent with prevailing Soviet views favoring damage limitation in a strategic war. See D.G. Brennan, "Post-Deployment Policy Issues in Ballistic Missile Defense," in D.G. Brennan and Johan J. Holst, *Ballistic Missile Defense: Two Views*, Adelphi Paper no. 43 (London: Institute for Strategic Studies, November 1967).
36. Paul C. Warnke, "Second Lecture," in James L. Buckley and Paul C. Warnke, *Strategic Sufficiency: Fact or Fiction?* (Washington, DC: American Enterprise Institute for Public Policy Research, 1972), p. 26.
37. Herman Kahn, "The Arms Race and Some of Its Hazards," in Donald G. Brennan, ed., *Arms Control, Disarmament, and National Security* (New York: G. Braziller, 1961), pp. 102–8.
38. Kennan, *Nuclear Delusion*, p. 177 (note 6).
39. McNamara, *Blundering into Disaster*, p. 123 (note 5).
40. Noel Gayler, "If Each Side Had Only 100 Nuclear Weapons," *Washington Post*, February 1, 1986, p. A17.
41. Paul H. Nitze, "Assuring Strategic Stability in an Era of Détente," *Foreign Affairs* 54, no. 2 (January 1976): 213.
42. Joseph S. Nye, Jr., *Nuclear Ethics* (New York: Free Press, 1986), p. 112.
43. Colin S. Gray, "Targeting Problems for Central War," in Desmond Ball and Jeffrey Richelson, eds., *Strategic Nuclear Targeting* (Ithaca, NY: Cornell University Press, 1986), p. 191.
44. For a critical discussion of ethnic targeting, see George H. Quester, "Ethnic Targeting: A Bad Idea Whose Time Has Come," chap. 10 in *The Future of Nuclear Deterrence* (Lexington, MA: Lexington Books, 1986).
45. Carl H. Builder, "Why Not First-Strike Counterforce Capabilities?" *Strategic Review* 7, no. 2 (Spring 1979): 33–34. See also Michael Howard, "Making the World Safe for Conventional War," *New York Times Book Review*, April 8, 1984, p. 7.
46. The crystal ball effect is discussed in The Harvard Nuclear Study Group's *Living with Nuclear Weapons* (New York: Bantam Books, 1983), pp. 43–44.

47. McNamara, *Blundering into Disaster,* pp. 119-21 (note 5); "Gorbachev's Plan," p. 6 (note 2).
48. Schell, *The Abolition,* pp. 176-77 (note 16).
49. See Randall Forsberg, "Parallel Cuts in Nuclear and Conventional Forces," *Bulletin of Atomic Scientists* 41, no. 7 (August 1985): 152-56. Stephen Flanagan evaluates defensive defenses in Chapter 5.
50. It is useful to distinguish five possible paths to nuclear war: a nuclear surprise attack ("bolt from the blue"), pre-emption in a crisis, the escalation of a conventional war, accidental or unauthorized use of nuclear weapons, and the catalytic use of nuclear weapons by a third party. See Graham T. Allison, Albert Carnesale, and Joseph S. Nye, Jr., *Hawks, Doves, and Owls: An Agenda for Avoiding Nuclear War* (New York: W.W. Norton & Company, 1985). In addressing the conditions for stable deterrence at low numbers, I investigated the first two of these paths.
51. This argument is made, for example, by Thomas Schelling in *Arms and Influence,* pp. 231-32 (note 19).
52. See Bruce G. Blair, *Strategic Command and Control: Defining the Nuclear Threat* (Washington, DC: Brookings Institution, 1985), pp. 289-94.
53. United States Arms Control and Disarmament Agency, "Treaty on the Non-Proliferation of Nuclear Weapons," *Arms Control and Disarmament Agreements* (Washington, DC: Government Printing Office, 1982), p. 93.
54. "Gorbachev's Plan," p. 6 (note 2).
55. See Robert Axelrod, *The Evolution of Cooperation* (New York: Basic Books, 1984).
56. See Michael T. Klare, "Securing the Firebreak," *World Policy Journal* 2, no. 2 (Spring 1985): 229-47.
57. For a convincing argument that conventional weapons may displace nuclear weapons in many military roles, but not in threatening cities, see Carl H. Builder, "The Prospects and Implications of Non-nuclear Means for Strategic Conflict," *Adelphi Paper* no. 200 (London: International Institute for Strategic Studies, 1985).
58. Donald L. Hafner, "Choosing Targets for Nuclear Weapons," *International Security* 11, no. 4 (Spring 1987): 138 (emphasis added).

Chapter 2: Smart Weapons and Ordinary People

1. In this chapter, as in virtually all of the literature dealing with strategic weapons policies, the words *accurate* and *precise* are used interchangeably to describe weapons that consistently arrive at or close to the targets at which they are fired. (In formal scientific usage, accuracy is a measure of how close the impact points are to the targets, while precision is a measure of how close the impact points from multiple firings at the same target are to each other.)
2. The Harvard Nuclear Study Group, *Living With Nuclear Weapons* (New York: Bantam Books, Inc., 1983), p. 34.
3. Albert Wohlstetter, "Between an Unfree World and None: Increasing Our Choices," *Foreign Affairs* 63, no. 5 (Summer 1985): 991.
4. Ibid., p. 990.

5. National Conference of Catholic Bishops, *The Challenge of Peace: God's Promise and Our Response*, A Pastoral Letter on War and Peace (Washington, DC: United States Catholic Conference, 1983), pp. 26–34.
6. Ibid., p. 31.
7. Ibid., pp. 31, 34.
8. Ibid., p. 34.
9. Albert Wohlstetter, "Bishops, Statesmen, and Other Strategists on the Bombing of Innocents," *Commentary* 75, no. 6 (June 1983): 19.
10. Ibid., p. 35.
11. *The Challenge of Peace*, p. v (note 5).
12. Ibid., p. 60.
13. Ibid., p. vi.
14. Carl H. Builder, "The Prospects and Implications of Non-nuclear Means for Strategic Conflict," Adelphi Paper no. 200 (London: International Institute for Strategic Studies, 1985), p. 31.
15. Ibid., p. 4.
16. Ibid., p. 21.
17. Ibid., p. 19.
18. Ibid., p. 19.
19. Wohlstetter, "Between an Unfree World," p. 992 (note 3).
20. Wohlstetter, "Bishops, Statesmen," p. 23 (note 9).
21. Builder, "Prospects and Implications," p. 27 (note 14).
22. Ibid., p. 23.

Chapter 3: Defense Dominance

1. An assured destruction capability is generally understood to be the capability, following a full-scale counterforce attack against one's forces, to inflict an extremely high level of damage on one's adversary. Most analysts are in rough accord with Robert McNamara, secretary of defense from 1960 to 1967, in specifying the levels of potential damage required for assured destruction. McNamara's criteria required that the United States be able to destroy, in a retaliatory attack, approximately 25 percent of the Soviet population and 50 percent of Soviet industry. See Alain C. Enthoven and K. Wayne Smith, *How Much is Enough? Shaping the Defense Program 1961–1969* (New York: Harper and Row, 1971), pp. 172–84, 207–10.
2. *New York Times*, March 24, 1983, p. 20.
3. On studies shortly following the president's speech, see Donald L. Hafner, "Assessing the President's Vision: The Fletcher, Miller and Hoffman Panels," *Daedalus* 114, no. 2 (Spring 1985): 91–107.
4. Lt. Gen. James Abrahamson, "Analysis: Star Wars," British Broadcasting Corporation radio documentary, October 10, 1984, quoted in Arms Control Association, *Star Wars Quotes* (Washington, DC: ACA, July 1986), p. 4.
5. Although *near-perfect* might be understood to describe less effective defenses, this more stringent definition is useful, identifying the range of defenses that, while imperfect, are sufficiently effective to move the superpowers out of MAD. I have borrowed the term from Ashton B. Carter, *Directed Energy Missile Defense in Space* (Washington, DC: Government Printing Office, 1984).

6. See, for example, Office of Technology Assessment, *Ballistic Missile Defense Technologies* (Washington, DC: Government Printing Office, 1985), and Carter, *Directed Energy Missile Defense in Space*, pp. 66-67 (note 5).

7. Exceptions include Thomas C. Schelling, "What Went Wrong With Arms Control," *Foreign Affairs* 64, no. 2 (Winter 1985/86): 231-33, and Robert J. Art, "Between Assured Destruction and Nuclear Victory: The Case for the 'MAD-Plus' Posture," *Ethics* 95, no. 3 (April 1985): 515-16.

8. A ballistic missile defense is a system capable of destroying ballistic missiles (or warheads) in flight. The terms *ballistic missile defense* (BMD) and *antiballistic missile* (ABM) are used interchangeably.

9. Union of Concerned Scientists, *The Fallacy of Star Wars* (New York: Vintage, 1984), p. 153. For a similar comment, see Office of Technology Assessment, *Ballistic Missile Defense Technologies*, p. 113 (note 6).

10. I use the term *defense* to refer only to area defense—that is, systems designed to protect cities and other "value targets" such as industry and other economic targets. BMD that would protect the United States by reducing the Soviet Union's ability to inflict damage is an area defense. By contrast, a point defense is designed principally to protect nuclear force capabilities. This distinction is important because these two types of defense have fundamentally different strategic implications. A country's area defense, if sufficiently effective, could reduce the size of the adversary's deterrent threat; a country's point defense, by protecting its offensive force against counterforce attack, could increase the size of its own deterrent threat.

11. Caspar W. Weinberger, *Annual Report to Congress, Fiscal Year 1988* (Washington, DC: Government Printing Office, January 1987), p. 52 (emphasis added).

   Many advocates of BMD favor asymmetric deployment—that is, U.S. strategic advantage provided in part by BMD. See, for example, Colin S. Gray, "Nuclear Strategy: The Case for a Theory of Victory," *International Security* 4, no. 1 (Summer 1979): 54-87, and Colin S. Gray and Keith Payne, "Victory Is Possible," *Foreign Policy* 39 (Summer 1980): 14-27.

12. For a review and analysis of the arguments surrounding these BMD systems, see Charles L. Glaser, "Do We Want the Missile Defenses We Can Build," *International Security* 10, no. 1 (Summer 1985): 25-57.

13. This terminology is somewhat unfortunate since in many ways MAD is a world of defense dominance. When countries maintain their security through deterrence by punishment, the ability to retaliate is defensive, while the ability to deny retaliatory capabilities—that is, to limit damage—is offensive. Retaliatory capabilities dominate damage-limitation capabilities in MAD, so MAD is defense dominant. Further, in MAD, strategic defenses—BMD and air defense—are offense, since these systems threaten the adversary's retaliatory capabilities. On these points see Robert Jervis, "Cooperation Under the Security Dilemma," *World Politics* 30, no. 2 (January 1978): 198, 206-10.

14. I have borrowed the term BAD from Robert J. Art, "The Role of Military Power in International Relations," in B. Thomas Trout and James E. Harf, eds., *National Security Affairs: Theoretical Perspectives and Contemporary Issues* (New Brunswick: Transaction Books, 1982), p. 23.

15. The following discussion assumes that both countries would know the effectiveness of their own and their adversary's defenses. In fact, there would always be uncertainties about the effectiveness of the defenses, and the implications of these uncertainties could be significant. But this simplifying assumption allows me to focus my examination of perfect defenses on the most basic issues. Some of the complications that would probably result from uncertainties about effectiveness are discussed later in this chapter.

    In certain cases uncertainty might create a safer world. For example, if defenses are in fact perfect, but decision makers do not know this, then they might act more cautiously—avoiding conventional confrontation—because they believed nuclear war was possible. However, if war occurred, nuclear attacks would not be damaging. In addition, uncertainty might reduce some dangers that stem from the sensitivity of BAD to small changes in either country's capabilities, but would exacerbate other dangers.

16. Many advocates of pursuing highly effective defense argue that even if the prospects for effective defense do not look extremely promising today, history suggests that major technological changes should be expected. For example, Keith B. Payne and Colin S. Gray observe that "all of recorded history has shown swings in the pendulum of technical advantage between offense and defense. For the strategic defense to achieve a very marked superiority would be an extraordinary trend in light of the last 30 years, but not of the last hundred or thousand years. Military history is replete with examples of defensive technology and tactics dominating the offense" ("Nuclear Policy and the Defense Transition," *Foreign Affairs* 62, no. 4 (Spring 1984), p. 826). This argument, however, would apply at least as well to the maintenance of the defense-dominant world they advocate and points to the major problems that would exist in BAD.

17. Some might question the utility of such an advantage, noting the limited value of the United States' nuclear monopoly following World War II. See, for example, Morton H. Halperin, *Nuclear Fallacy: Dispelling the Myth of Nuclear Strategy* (Cambridge, MA: Ballinger, 1987), pp. 23–47, and McGeorge Bundy, "The Unimpressive Record of Atomic Diplomacy," in Gwyn Prins, ed., *The Nuclear Crisis Reader* (New York: Vintage Books, 1984), pp. 42–54.

18. For an insightful discussion of why large nuclear arsenals reduce the probability of superpower conventional wars, even when neither superpower has an advantage in purely military terms, see Robert Jervis, "Why Nuclear Superiority Doesn't Matter," *Political Science Quarterly* 94, no. 4 (Winter 1979–80): 617–33, and *The Illogic of American Nuclear Strategy* (Ithaca: Cornell University Press, 1984). At the other end of the spectrum, Gray and Payne in "Victory Is Possible," p. 16 (note 11), find the U.S. strategic force inadequate to meet its extended deterrence commitments, but admit that U.S. strategic nuclear forces do contribute to deterrence of Soviet conventional attack in Europe. Strong proponents of a policy of no first nuclear use appear to believe that, independent of stated doctrine, the possibility of nuclear war would contribute somewhat to deterrence of conventional war; see, for example, McGeorge Bundy, "The Bishops and the Bomb," *New York Review of Books* (June 16, 1983), p. 6. For an opposing view on the effect of BAD on conventional war, which

is not inconsistent with his argument cited above, see Keith Payne, "Strategic Defense and Stability," *Orbis* 28, no. 2 (Summer 1984): 222–25.

19. This assertion depends on the assumption made above that both countries know that the defenses are perfect. If perfect defenses were not known to be so, then nuclear attack might be carried out (but would not result in damage) and nuclear threats might be used coercively.

20. In a counterforce attack the targets are military forces. The term usually refers even more narrowly to attacks against nuclear forces. In contrast, in a countervalue attack the targets are cities, industry, and other economic capabilities.

21. The probability of pre-emptive nuclear war also depends on the probability of crises. For example, a change in forces that increases crisis stability but also increases the probability or severity of crises could make pre-emptive nuclear war more likely. The following comparison of the probability of nuclear war in BAD and MAD does not consider the relative probability of crises. This simplification in the analysis probably favors BAD, since BAD is likely to increase tensions between the superpowers. Thus, this simplification tends to reinforce the best case which the analysis makes for BAD.

22. Some analysts argue that U.S. and Soviet leaders have different value structures and the United States therefore needs to threaten more than annihilation. Specifically, because the Soviet Union places great value on the political and military leadership, and on military forces, the United States must threaten these targets to deter Soviet aggression. Analysts who accept this view of Soviet values should see major problems with defenses, since using BMD to protect leadership and military targets (which can be protected from nuclear attack with concrete or by being located underground) is much easier than protecting cities and economic capabilities.

23. Freeman Dyson, *Weapons and Hope* (New York: Harper and Row, 1984), pp. 272–74. A similar argument is made by Donald Brennan in "The Case for Population Defense," in Johan J. Holst and William Schneider, Jr., eds., *Why ABM? Policy Issues in the Missile Defense Controversy* (New York: Pergamon Press, 1969), pp. 100–6. An earlier version of this argument appeared in Donald Bennan and Johan Holst, *Ballistic Missile Defense: Two Views*, Adelphi Paper No. 43 (London: International Institute for Strategic Studies, 1967), pp. 9–11.

Including uncertainty and imperfect information about the level of vulnerability to countervalue attack would weaken this argument. Redundant assured destruction capabilities are extremely large by any reasonable evaluation. There is little opportunity to misjudge this destructive potential, and assessments of damage are therefore not sensitive to relatively small differences in force size. In contrast, in BAD, with each country's ability to inflict damage greatly reduced, relative force capabilities would be harder to evaluate, and uncertainties, misevaluations, and misperceptions would be more likely to occur. On the one hand, if decision makers look cautiously at uncertainties, deterrence might be enhanced. On the other hand, a risk-taking decision maker might see strategic advantages that could result in a failure of deterrence. The probability of these deterrence failures might be reduced by the conservative nature of the equal countervalue requirement.

24. This does not mean that the Soviet Union would necessarily be unable to coerce the United States. As in MAD, if the Soviet Union could threaten convincingly to attack U.S. cities, then it might be able to coerce the United States. An equal countervalue capability, by making possible a highly credible retaliatory threat comparable to the Soviet threat, would make it difficult for the Soviet Union to make its coercive threat convincing. If the Soviet Union were able to coerce the United States, the key to its success would be a greater resolve and willingness to take risks, and not an advantage in nuclear forces.

25. See, for example, William C. Foster, "Strategic Weapons: Prospects for Arms Control," *Foreign Affairs* 47, no. 3 (April 1969): 414–15, and Robert L. Rothstein, "ABM, Proliferation and International Stability," *Foreign Affairs* 46, no. 3 (April 1969): 498–99.

26. Extensive discussions of crisis stability include Thomas C. Schelling, *Strategy of Conflict* (Cambridge, MA: Harvard University Press, 1960), pp. 207–54, and *Arms and Influence* (New Haven: Yale University Press, 1966), pp. 221–48; and Glenn H. Snyder, *Deterrence and Defense* (Princeton: Princeton University Press, 1961), pp. 97–114.

27. The assumption that decision makers would anticipate a countervalue strike is implicit in many discussions of crisis stability. It underlies the logic that says if a counterforce attack could reduce the adversary's countervalue potential, then there will be an incentive to strike first. A crisis, however, should provoke fears of a counterforce attack. If we assume the adversary's first strike would be counterforce, then the incentives to pre-empt are much smaller than if we assume the attack would be countervalue. For a good discussion of this argument see Snyder, *Deterrence and Defense*, pp. 104–9 (note 25). If we assume that both countries anticipate counterforce first strikes, then the effect of defenses on crisis stability is likely to be minimal. Given this assumption, the incentives to pre-empt would be small, or nonexistent, with or without defenses.

    The above arguments do not hold for decision makers who anticipate counterforce exchanges and believe that the ratio of surviving forces can confer political advantages during a nuclear war. In this case, even if significant damage limitation is infeasible, pre-emptive incentives could exist if the superpowers can shift the ratio of surviving forces.

28. If the defenses are vulnerable, then they could create pre-emptive incentives even when offenses can survive attack.

29. Valuable analysis of a variety of options for increasing ICBM survivability is found in Office of Technology Assessment, *MX Missile Basing* (Washington, DC: Government Printing Office, 1981).

30. *Arms race stability* is the standard measure of this characteristic of the nuclear situation. I use the term *robustness* to avoid the confusion that surrounds the other phrase. *Arms race stability* brings to mind at least two issues that are related to robustness but which are conceptually distinct. First, arms race stability is often considered an indicator of the likelihood and/or intensity of arms races that will occur in a specific nuclear situation. Arms races, however, can occur for a variety of reasons that are only peripherally related to the effect of building nuclear forces on the adversary's security. Consequently, arms races

can occur in highly robust nuclear situations, as has happened in our current world of highly redundant and diversified assured destruction capabilities.

Second, the use of the term *arms race stability* might seem to imply a belief that arms races increase the probability of war. There is substantial disagreement on this question. Nevertheless, one can assert that the probability of war depends on the robustness of the superpowers' nuclear capabilities without believing that, in general, arms races cause war. Robustness is a measure of how sensitive a country's security would be to the adversary's build-up of forces. It does not imply that the process of competitive armament itself leads to war. Rather, assuming the superpowers continue to build up forces, a war is more likely when the initial nuclear capabilities are less robust.

31. This is not to argue that the United States would necessarily be less secure when it is less vulnerable, for if war occurs, it would be less costly. I examine this tradeoff in more detail in the following section.

32. On this point see Carter, *Directed Energy Missile Defense in Space*, pp. 45–46 (note 5).

33. Moreover, when a country's defenses are not diversified, its low vulnerability is susceptible to catastrophic failure, because one offensive breakthrough by the adversary could render the country vulnerable to large attacks.

34. For a discussion of the factors that affect the probability that countries will be able to cooperate, see Jervis, "Cooperation Under the Security Dilemma," pp. 167–214 (note 13).

35. On these points see Glaser, "Do We Want the Missile Defenses We Can Build," pp. 37–40 (note 12); and Albert Carnesale, "Special Supplement: The Strategic Defense Initiative," in George E. Hudson and Joseph Kruzel, eds., *American Defense Annual: 1985–1986* (Lexington, MA: Lexington Books, 1985), p. 220.

36. On disarmament, see Chapter 1. Some argue that the effects of defenses are quite different when the superpowers have agreed to total nuclear disarmament than when they have agreed to very deep cuts, say of 500 weapons. According to this argument, in the former case defenses create fewer problems and complications; because the superpowers have disarmed, defenses do not reduce their ability to inflict damage. In the latter case, however, defenses create incentives to build offenses by reducing the ability to inflict damage. Whether this reaction would occur depends on how the superpowers manage the deployment of defenses. Because defenses might enhance robustness, the superpowers might prefer to achieve a given level of reduced vulnerability by deploying defenses instead of further reducing offenses. On the other hand, in the case of total disarmament defenses could increase uncertainties about the outcome of a rearmament race. Net assessments in each case require considering the risks stemming from a variety of static and dynamic uncertainties, and the related effect of defenses on superpower politics.

There does not appear to be a general answer as to whether the United States would be more secure in the cooperative or the competitive world. Although we tend to focus on the stability of military arrangements, it seems likely that U.S. security in the cooperative world would depend heavily on the continuation of the dramatically improved superpower relations that would probably be necessary for near-disarmament. Thus, this comparison requires knowledge of the superpower relationship that made extensive cooperation possible in the first place. Certain military comparisons are possible, however. For example, for defenses of a given effectiveness, cooperation could increase robustness, since decreasing the size of offenses would reduce the impact of a breakthrough in the ability of the offense to penetrate defenses. On the other hand, a general conclusion is not possible when comparing worlds that depend on defenses of unequal effectiveness.

37. By definition the costs of countervalue retaliation following pre-emptive attack would be lower in BAD than in MAD. In certain cases, however, the collateral damage from a pre-emptive attack would be higher in BAD than MAD. How the total costs in these wars compare depends on how the superpowers fight following the pre-emptive attack.

38. This analysis also leads to another controversial conclusion: the transition from MAD to low vulnerability might be less dangerous than the endpoint. For a more detailed discussion see Charles L. Glaser, "Managing the Transition," in Samuel F. Wells and Robert S. Litwak, eds., *Strategic Defenses and Soviet–American Relations* (Cambridge, MA: Ballinger, 1987). Glenn A. Kent and Randall J. DeValk have also analyzed the transition in *Strategic Defense and the Transition to Assured Survival*, R-3369-AF (Santa Monica, CA: Rand Corporation, October 1986).

39. For discussions of likely alliance reactions to extensive U.S. homeland defense, see Ivo H. Daalder and Lynn Page Whittaker, "SDI's Implications for Europe: Strategy, Politics, and Technology," in Stephen J. Flanagan and Fen Osler Hampson, eds., *Securing Europe's Future* (London: Croom Helm, 1986), and David S. Yost, "Ballistic Missile Defense and the Atlantic Alliance," *International Security* 7, no. 2 (Fall 1982): 154–58.

40. Dyson, *Weapons and Hope*, p. 284, makes a similar observation (note 22).

41. Kenneth N. Waltz, *Theory of International Politics* (Reading, MA: Addison-Wesley, 1979), p. 168. See also Waltz, "The Stability of a Bipolar World," *Daedalus* 93, no. 3 (Summer 1964): 881–909.

42. *New York Times*, March 30, 1983, p. 14.

Chapter 4: Lengthening the Fuse

1. In 1984, 81 percent of American citizens believed that it was U.S. policy to use nuclear weapons "if and only if" our adversaries used them against us first. Daniel Yankelovitch and John Doble, "The Public Mood," *Foreign Affairs* (Fall 1984): 45.

2. Morton H. Halperin, *Nuclear Fallacy: Dispelling the Myth of Nuclear Strategy* (Cambridge, MA: Ballinger, 1987), pp. 23–60; McGeorge Bundy, "The Unimpressive Record of Atomic Diplomacy," in Gwyn Pins, ed., *The Nuclear Crisis Reader* (New York: Vintage Books, 1984); Barry M. Blechman and Stephen S. Kaplan, *Force without War: U.S. Armed Forces as a Military Instrument* (Washington, DC: Brookings Institution, 1978).

3. William R. Kaufman, "Nuclear Deterrence in Central Europe," in John Steinbrunner and Leo Sigal, eds., *Alliance Security: NATO and the No-First-Use Question* (Washington, DC: Brookings Institution, 1978).

4. John Mearsheimer, "Nuclear Weapons and Deterrence in Europe," *International Security* (Winter 1984–85): 20.
5. Bernard W. Rogers, "The Atlantic Alliance: Prescriptions for a Difficult Decade," *Foreign Affairs* (Summer 1982): 1151–52.
6. McGeorge Bundy, George F. Kennan, Robert S. McNamara, and Gerard Smith, "Nuclear Weapons and the Atlantic Alliance," *Foreign Affairs* (Spring 1982): 757. Here, as elsewhere in this chapter, a discussion of Europe stands in for all possible situations in which nuclear weapons might be used first.
7. For a detailed history of changing U.S. conceptions toward first use, see Lawrence Freedman, *The Evolution of Nuclear Strategy* (New York: St. Martin's Press, 1979). In the 1950s, the view that aggression could be met by "massive retaliation" or by small mobile battlefield weapons succumbed to critics who pointed out that it was neither safe nor credible in a world in which the United States itself was vulnerable. In the 1960s, it was replaced, at least within NATO, by "flexible response," which assumed a longer conventional fuse.
8. See, for example, Robert McNamara, "The Military Role of Nuclear Weapons," *Foreign Affairs* (Winter 1983): 79.
9. Joseph S. Nye, Jr., "Nuclear Learning and U.S.–Soviet Security Regimes," *International Organization* (Summer 1987): 371–402.
10. John Lewis Gaddis, "The Long Peace: Elements of Stability in the Postwar International System," *International Security* (Spring 1986): 99–142; Blechman and Kaplan, eds., *Force without War* (note 2).
11. This was the conclusion of a classic debate in the history of nuclear strategy, held between 1957 and 1960 and involving, among others, Henry Kissinger, Robert Osgood, James E. King, Paul Nitze, Morton Halperin, Bernard Brodie, and William Kaufmann. The debate ended when Henry Kissinger acknowledged the "failure . . . to develop a coherent doctrine for tactical nuclear weapons." For a summary of the debate, see Freedman, *Evolution of Nuclear Strategy*, pp. 106–19 (note 7).
12. Bundy et al., "Nuclear Weapons," p. 765 (note 6). See also Halperin, *Nuclear Fallacy*, p. 102 (note 2).
13. Robert McNamara, "Military Role," p. 79 (note 8).
14. On the relative importance of these factors, see Graham Allison, Albert Carnesale, and Joseph S. Nye, Jr., *Hawks, Doves, and Owls: An Agenda for Avoiding Nuclear War* (New York: W.W. Norton, 1985); Richard Ned Lebow, *Nuclear Crisis Management: A Dangerous Illusion* (Ithaca: Cornell University Press, 1987); and Daniel Charles, *Nuclear Planning in NATO: Pitfalls of First Use* (Cambridge, MA: Ballinger, 1987).
15. McGeorge Bundy et al., "Back from the Brink," *Atlantic Monthly* (August 1986), p. 37.
16. Charles, *Nuclear Planning*, p. 36 (note 13).
17. Barry Posen, "Inadvertent Nuclear War? Escalation and NATO's Northern Flank," *International Security* (Fall 1982): 28–54.
18. Kurt Gottfried, Henry W. Kendall, and John M. Lee, "'No First Use' of Nuclear Weapons," *Scientific American*, March 1984, p. 34. The preceding two points were also stressed by the critics of the 1950s (note 11).
19. Earl C. Ravenal, "Europe without America: The Erosion of NATO," *Foreign*

Affairs (Summer 1985): 1024. See also Bundy et al., "Nuclear Weapons," pp. 761ff (note 6) and Halperin, *Nuclear Fallacy*, chap. 7 (note 2).

20. Earl C. Ravenal, "Counterforce and Alliance: The Ultimate Connection," *International Security* (Spring 1982): 26.
21. Sherle R. Schwenninger and Jerry Sanders, "The Democrats and a New Grand Strategy," *World Policy Journal* (Summer 1986): 387.
22. David Calleo, "Inflation and American Power," *Foreign Affairs* (Spring 1981): 781–812. See also David Calleo, *The Impervious Economy* (Cambridge, MA: Harvard University Press, 1982).
23. Melvyn Krauss, *How NATO Weakens the West* (New York: Simon and Schuster, 1986).
24. This distinction is found in Johan Holst, "Moving toward No First Use in Practice," In Steinbrunner and Sigal, *Alliance Security*, p. 188 (note 3).
25. Leon Sigal, "Political Prospects for No-First-Use," in Steinbrunner and Sigal, *Alliance Security*, p. 188 (note 3). Indeed, a declaration without corresponding changes in deployment and planning may degrade the deterrent without opening up any new defensive possibilities. See Earl Ravenal and Donald Haffner, "Letter," *Foreign Affairs* (Summer 1982): 1175–78.
26. They recommend that the matter should be studied, according to Bundy. McGeorge Bundy, "'No First Use' Needs Careful Study," *Bulletin of the Atomic Scientists* (June/July 1982): 6–8.
27. For example, Henry Kissinger, "Strategy and the Atlantic Alliance," *Survival*, September–October 1982, pp. 194–200.
28. Karl Kaiser, George Leber, Alois Mertes, and Franz-Josef Schulze, "Nuclear Weapons and the Preservation of Peace," *Foreign Affairs* (Summer 1982): 1171–80.
29. Rogers, "Atlantic Alliance" (note 5).
30. Samuel Huntington, "Conventional Deterrence and Conventional Retaliation," *International Security* (Winter 1983/84): 32–56.
31. Huntington's proposal does, however, go beyond the restoration of the status quo ante called for in the NATO official policy statement numbered MC 14/3. We acknowledge Dr. Stephen Flanagan for pointing this out.
32. Bundy et al., "Back from the Brink," p. 35 (note 15).
33. Bundy et al., "Back from the Brink," pp. 40–42 (note 15). For a selection of related proposals in what has become a very large literature, see Lawrence Freedman, "NATO Myths," *Foreign Policy* (Winter 1981–82): 62ff; Union of Concerned Scientists, *No First Use: Preventing Nuclear War* (Cambridge, MA: UCS, 1983); and William Kaufmann, "Nonnuclear Deterrence," in Steinbrunner and Sigal, *Alliance Security* (note 3).
34. Holst, "Moving toward No First Use," pp. 188–94 (note 24).
35. Halperin, *Nuclear Fallacy*, p. 123 (note 2). The summary below draws on pp. 76–123 passim.
36. Ravenal, "Europe without America," pp. 1020, 1035 (note 19).
37. Ravenal, "Europe without America," p. 1031 (note 19).
38. See the epigraphs to this chapter.
39. Josef Joffe, "The Political Role of Nuclear Weapons: No-First-Use and the Stability of the European Order," Institute for East–West Studies, Occasional Paper No. 3, n.d., p. 13.

40. An intriguing attempt to overcome these difficulties was made by Richard Betts in "Compound Deterrence Vs. No-First-Use: What's Wrong with What's Right," *Orbis* (Winter 1985): 695–718. Betts takes the probability of Soviet attack to be a function of (1) the Soviet desire to attack; (2) the probability that NATO conventional defense will fail; (3) the probability of deliberate escalation by the United States, France, or Britain; and (4) the probability of accidental escalation. Problems of scaling aside (e.g., *all* of the alternative postures he examines may pose unacceptable risks to the Soviets), the major weakness of Betts' analysis is that it ignores the crisis stability or controllability issues, except as inputs into the Soviet deterrent calculation.

41. We treat hypothetical scenarios with the methods recommended by Alexander George for examining real-world cases. See Alexander George, "Case Studies and Theory Development: The Method of Structured, Focused Comparison," in Paul Lauren, ed., *Diplomacy: New Approaches in History, Theory and Policy* (New York: Free Press, 1981). For the use of case studies in this context, see Allison et al., *Hawks, Doves, and Owls* (note 14).

42. Jonathan Dean, *Watershed in Europe* (Lexington, MA: Lexington Books, 1987), p. xiv.

43. Fen Osler Hampson, "Escalation in Europe," in Allison et al., *Hawks, Doves, and Owls*, pp. 80–114 (note 14).

44. Francis Fukuyama, "Escalation in the Middle East and the Persian Gulf," and Henry S. Rowen, "Catalytic Nuclear War," in Allison, et al., *Hawks, Doves, and Owls*, pp. 115–47, 148–63.

45. Michael MccGwire, *Military Objectives in Soviet Foreign Policy* (Washington, DC: Brookings Institution, 1987), p. 369.

46. The concept of a balanced deterrent, which lies at the heart of this analysis, deserves closer examination that it received in Allison et al., *Hawks, Doves, and Owls* (note 14). Marc Trachtenberg states the problem clearly: "We are talking here about a trade-off: we can drive down the probability that we might escalate...but in so doing we lose a bit of the deterrent effect. Is there anything that can be said about the terms of this trade-off?" Trachtenberg suggests that we employ the "general principle of diminishing marginal utility," by which he means that as the credibility of the deterrent decreases, the value of each increment increases. We diverge from Trachtenberg by arguing that the likelihood of a nonrational path to nuclear war, which he inexplicably ignores, is greater than that of a rational path, and that this ought to be viewed as a disadvantage of a first use defense. If we accept the metaphor of marginal utility, it follows that the safest place to be is at an equilibrium point between the two dangers, a point where any change would increase the overall probability of nuclear war. Since a longer fuse would reduce the probability of inadvertent first use while leaving the deterrent substantially intact, we conclude that lengthening the fuse would move us closer to equilibrium. Thus, whereas Trachtenberg finds more deterrence and less stability the safest policy, we propose the opposite. See Marc Trachtenberg, "The Question of No-First-Use," *Orbis* (Winter 1986): 753.

47. McGeorge Bundy, "Existential Deterrence and its Consequences," in Douglas MacLean, ed., *The Security Gamble* (Totowa, NJ: Rowman and Allanhead, 1984).

48. The following analysis draws heavily on Catherine Kelleher, "NATO Nuclear Operations," in Ashton B. Carter, John D. Steinbrunner, and Charles A. Zraket, eds., *Managing Nuclear Operations* (Washington, DC: Brookings Institution, 1987). See also J. Michael Legge, *Theater Nuclear Weapons and the NATO Strategy of Flexible Response* (Santa Monica, CA: Rand Corporation, 1983), p. 74.

49. Thus, as Representative Les Aspin points out, the removal of short- and medium-range weapons from Europe would "have us eliminate the weapons we should keep and keep the weapons we should eliminate." While less than ideal, it might still be argued that the zero-option and the momentum it creates toward further reductions are worth the risk. For a discussion, including the quotation above, see Graham Allison and Albert Carnesale, "Can the West Accept *Da* for an Answer?" *Daedalus* (Summer 1987): 69–94.

50. Kelleher, "NATO Nuclear Operations," (note 48).

51. See Huntington, "Conventional Deterrence" (note 30).

52. See Posen, "Inadvertent Nuclear War?" (note 17).

53. For the savings possible from even modest moves in the direction of a fully defensive posture, see Kaufmann, "Non-Nuclear Deterrence" (note 3).

54. To the extent that the avoidance of nuclear war has supplanted victory as the primary Soviet concern, there may be room for accommodation. See Mcc-Gwire, *Military Objectives*, pp. 88–89, 372–73 (note 45). The reasons for the fourteen-year stalemate at the conventional arms control talks in Vienna are complex, but recent breakthroughs at the negotiations on intermediate-range nuclear systems offer grounds for optimism.

55. There are good reasons to believe that situations in which the offense is perceived to have an advantage are extremely unstable. Robert Jervis, "Cooperation Under the Security Dilemma," *World Politics* 30, no. 2 (1978): 167–214. The paradigmatic case is World War I. See Steven Miller, ed., *Military Strategy and the Origins of World War I* (Princeton, NJ: Princeton University Press, 1984).

56. Thomas W. Graham, "Future Fission? Use of Nuclear Weapons, Extended Deterrence and American Public Opinion." Occasional Paper, Center for Science and International Affairs, Harvard University, forthcoming.

57. Halperin, *Nuclear Fallacy*, p. 147 (note 2).

58. Halperin, *Nuclear Fallacy*, p. 150 (note 2).

59. Stephen Flanagan, "NATO's Conventional Defense Choices in the 1960s," in Stephen Flanagan and Fen Osler Hampson, eds., *Securing Europe's Future* (London: Croom & Helm, 1986).

60. See Chapter 5, "Nonprovocative and Civilian-Based Defenses."

61. Henry Kissinger has voiced this fear with respect to no first use policies as well. The argument is more compelling in this context. See his "Strategy," p. 197 (note 27).

62. Dean, *Watershed in Europe*, p. 82 (note 42).

63. International relations theory contrasts these two responses to a shift in the balance of power. Finlandization and alliance disintegration constitute "bandwagoning," in which smaller nations ally with the stronger nation, while proliferation and stronger West European cooperation constitute "balancing," in which they strengthen themselves against it. The general evidence on alliance behavior suggests that states prefer to balance. This lends further support to our scepticism of Finlandization scenarios. See Stephen Walt,

"Alliance Formation and the Balance of World Power," *International Security* (Spring 1985): 3–43.

64. See "French Press Plan for Chemical Arms," *New York Times*, March 12, 1987, p. A15.

65. Joseph A. Yager, "Nuclear Supplies and the Policies of South Korea and Taiwan toward Nuclear Weapons," in Rodney Jones et al., eds., *The Nuclear Suppliers and Nonproliferation* (Lexington, MA: Lexington Books, 1985).

66. The most comprehensive literature review and the most sophisticated analysis can be found in Loretta De Luca, "Free-Riding in NATO: Reality or... Myth?" (Ph.D. Dissertation, Cornell University, August 1986).

67. Dean, *Watershed*, p. xiv (note 42).

68. For an overly sanguine view, see Randall Forsberg, "The Case for a Third-World Non-Intervention Regime," paper presented to the Third Sarnia Symposium, Guernsey, March 18–21, 1987.

Chapter 5: Nonprovocative and Civilian-Based Defenses

1. See Robert Jervis, *Perception and Misperception in International Politics* (Princeton, NJ: Princeton University Press, 1976), chap. 3, and "Cooperation Under the Security Dilemma," *World Politics* 30, no. 1 (January 1978): 167–214; and George Quester, *Offense and Defense in the International System* (New York: Wiley, 1977).

2. Social Democratic party of Germany, "Peace and Security," Motion for the Party Conference, Nuremberg, August 25–29, 1986, p. 5.

3. Randall Forsberg, "Nonprovocative Defense: A New Approach to Arms Control," unpublished paper, Institute for Defense and Disarmament Studies, October 1986. See also the revised version of this paper, "A Global Approach to Non-Provocative Defense," Alternative Defense Working Paper no. 6 (Brookline, MA: Institute for Defense and Disarmament Studies, June 1987).

4. Gene Sharp, *Making Europe Unconquerable* (Cambridge, MA: Ballinger, 1986). Other major works on these concepts include Anders Boserup, *War Without Weapons: Non-Violence in National Defense* (New York: Schocken, 1975), and Stephen King Hall, *Defense in the Nuclear Age* (London: Victor Gallancz, 1958). For an assessment of some of these concepts, see Adam Roberts, "Civilian Defense Twenty Years On," *Bulletin of Peace Proposals* 9, no. 4 (1978): 293–300.

5. Sharp, *Making Europe Unconquerable*, p. 15 (note 4).

6. For more recent scholarly analysis on the instability of offensive postures, see Jack Snyder, *The Ideology of the Offensive* (Ithaca, NY: Cornell University Press, 1984), and Stephen Van Evera, "The Cult of the Offensive and the Origins of the First World War," *International Security* 9, no. 1 (Summer 1984): 58–107.

7. Lutz Unterseher, "Emphasizing Defense: An Ongoing Non-Debate in the Federal Republic," in Frank Barnaby and Marlies ter Borg, eds., *Emerging Technologies and Military Doctrine* (New York: St. Martin's, 1986), pp. 116–18.

8. Quoted in Adam Roberts, *Nations in Arms*, 2d ed. (New York: St. Martin's, 1986), p. 258.

9. "Report of the Fourth Workshop of the Pugwash Study Group on Conventional Forces," *Pugwash Newsletter* 23, no. 4 (April 1986): 113.

10. "Peace and Security," p. 7 (note 2).

11. *Arms Control Reporter*, Section 402 (Brookline, MA: Institute for Defense and Disarmament Studies, 1986, 1987).
12. Karsten Voigt, "Interim Report of the Sub-Committee on Conventional Defence: New Strategies and Concepts," North Atlantic Assembly, November 1986, pp. 20–27.
13. Egbert Boecker and Lutz Unterseher, "Emphasizing Defense," in Barnaby and ter Borg, p. 89 (note 7).
14. Carl von Clausewitz, *On War*, Book 6, trans. Michael Howard and Peter Paret (Princeton, NJ: Princeton University Press, 1976), p. 358.
15. Dr. Albrecht A.C. von Müller of the Max Planck Institute, Starnberg, West Germany, has provided a lucid exposition of this argument in his unpublished paper, "Integrated Forward Defense: Outlines of a Modified Conventional Defense for Central Europe," 1985, p. 8, and *Pugwash Newsletter*, p. 114 (note 9).
16. Von Müller, "Integrated Forward Defense" (note 15).
17. Boeker and Unterseher, "Emphasizing Defense," p. 91 (note 14).
18. Hew Strachan, "Conventional Defence in Europe," *International Affairs* (London) 61, no. 1 (Winter 1984/85): 31. See also Horst Afheldt, *Verteidigung und Frieden* (Munich: Deutsche Taschenbuch Verlag, 1979).
19. Jochen Loser, "The Security Policy Options for Non-Communist Europe," *Armada International* 2 (March/April 1982): 66–75.
20. Von Müller, "Integrated Forward Defense," pp. 19–25 (note 15), and Norbet Hannig, "Can Western Europe Be Defended By Conventional Means?" *International Defense Review* 1 (1979): 27–34.
21. Boeker and Unterseher, "Emphasizing Defense," pp. 102–3 (note 14).
22. Frank Barnaby and Stan Windass, *What Is Just Defense?* (Oxford: Just Defence, 1983).
23. Report of the Alternative Defence Commission, *Defence Without the Bomb* (New York: Taylor & Francis, 1983), pp. 8–11, 249–79.
24. Richard Smoke, "For a NATO Defensive Deterrent," unpublished manuscript, Brown University.
25. Forsberg, "Non-Provocative Defense" (note 3).
26. Ibid., pp. 32–33.
27. Ibid., pp. 33–34.
28. Sharp, *Making Europe Unconquerable*, p. 11 (note 4).
29. King-Hall, *Defense in the Nuclear Age*, pp. 145–59 (note 4).
30. Gene Sharp, *The Politics of Non-Violent Action* (Boston: Porter Sargent, 1973), pt. 2.
31. Sharp, *Making Europe Unconquerable*, chap. 3 (note 4).
32. Government of the Netherlands, Ministry of Defense, Memorandum by the Minister of Defence, Jacob de Ruiter, "Reinforcement of the Conventional Defense and 'Emerging Technologies,'" June 26, 1985, paragraph 26.
33. H.W. Hofmann, R.K. Huber, and K. Steiger, "On Reactive Defense Options," in R.K. Huber, ed., *Modeling and Analysis of Conventional Defense in Europe* (New York: Plenum Press, 1986), pp. 92–140.
34. Wilhelm Nolte, "Cofunction of Civilian Resistance and Military Defence?" Paper presented at Consultation on Non-Nuclear Alternatives in Europe, University of Bradford, England, July 1986.

Chapter 6: From Confrontation to Cooperation

1. The results of the competition and portions of many of the essays can be found in Earl W. Foell and Richard A. Nenneman, eds., *How Peace Came to the World* (Cambridge: MIT Press, 1986).
2. See George F. Kennan, *The Nuclear Delusion* (New York: Pantheon, 1982); Robert S. McNamara, *Blundering into Disaster: Surviving the First Century of the Nuclear Age* (New York: Pantheon, 1986); Jonathan Schell, *The Abolition* (New York: Knopf, 1984); and Richard H. Ullman, "Nuclear Arms: How Big a Cut?" *New York Times Magazine*, November 16, 1986, pp. 70–78.
3. See Chapters 1 and 2 for discussions of proposals to change the size or character of U.S. and Soviet nuclear arsenals. Chapter 3 assesses the prospects for a world in which near-perfect defenses against nuclear missiles are deployed. Other prominent visions of the future suggest that the risk of nuclear war will not decline until there is a fundamental change in the character or relative power of the Soviet Union. Such arguments, which have exerted a powerful hold on many members of the Reagan administration, are discussed in depth in Chapters 7 and 8.
4. Britain and France now have a greater capability to inflict destruction on the United States than the Soviet Union did at the time of the Cuban missile crisis in 1962.
5. Lawrence Freedman, *The Evolution of Nuclear Strategy* (New York: St. Martin's, 1980), p. 400.
6. Michael MccGwire, "Deterrence: The Problem—Not the Solution," *International Affairs* 62, no. 1 (Winter 1985–86): 70, 67. See also E.P. Thompson, *Beyond the Cold War* (New York: Pantheon, 1982), pp. 154–55, and Seweryn Bialer, "Soviet–American Conflict: From the Past to the Future," in Seweryn Bialer, Lee Hamilton, Jerry Hough, and John Steinbrunner, *U.S.–Soviet Relations: Perspectives for the Future, Alternatives for the 1980's*, no. 14 (Washington, DC: Center for National Policy, 1984), pp. 11–12.
7. Michael MccGwire, "Dilemmas and Delusions of Deterrence," *World Policy* 1, no. 4 (Summer 1984): 766.
8. William G. Hyland, "Paging Mr. X," *New Republic*, June 18, 1984, p. 37.
9. See W.W. Rostow, "On Ending the Cold War," *Foreign Affairs* 65, no. 4 (Spring 1987): 831–51; George Liska, "From Containment to Concert," *Foreign Policy* 62 (Spring 1986), pp. 3–23; and Liska, "Concert Through Decompression," *Foreign Policy* 63 (Summer 1986), pp. 108–29.
10. For discussions of defining détente and the need to distinguish détente from further-reaching forms of accommodation, see Gordon A. Craig and Alexander L. George, *Force and Statecraft: Diplomatic Problems of Our Time* (New York: Oxford University Press, 1983), pp. 238–42; Richard W. Stevenson, *The Rise and Fall of Détente: Relaxations of Tension in U.S.–Soviet Relations, 1953–84* (Urbana: University of Illinois Press, 1985), pp. 1–11; and Raymond L. Garthoff, *Détente and Confrontation: Soviet–American Relations from Nixon to Reagan* (Washington, DC: Brookings Institution, 1985), p. 25.
11. See Karl W. Deutsch et al., *Political Community and the North Atlantic Area: International Organization in the Light of Historical Experience* (Princeton: Princeton University Press, 1957), p. 5.

12. See Rostow, "On Ending the Cold War," pp. 847–49 (note 9); Randall Forsberg, "The Obstacles to a Stable Disarmed Peace and How to Set Our Priorities to Overcome Them," *Bulletin of Peace Proposals* 15, no. 4 (1984): 333–39; and the remarks of Robert R. Bowie at a 1986 conference on U.S.–Soviet relations, published in Robert K. German, ed., *The Future of U.S.–Soviet Relations: Lessons from Forty Years without World War* (Austin, TX: Lyndon B. Johnson School of Public Affairs, 1986), pp. 158–59.
13. See Thomas Powers, "What Is It About?" *Atlantic*, January 1984, pp. 35–55.
14. Rostow, "On Ending the Cold War," pp. 847–48 (note 9).
15. See Chapter 3 for a discussion of the need for U.S.–Soviet cooperation to stabilize a world in which strategic defenses are deployed.
16. See Joseph S. Nye, Jr., "ReStarting Arms Control," *Foreign Policy* 47 (Summer 1982): 108–10.
17. Rostow, "On Ending the Cold War," p. 848 (note 9).
18. Ibid.
19. Liska, "Concert Through Decompression," p. 116 (note 9).
20. For examples, see Thompson, *Beyond the Cold War*, pp. 153–88 (note 6); Klaus Bloemer, "Freedom for Europe, East and West," *Foreign Policy* 50 (Spring 1983): 23–38; Mary Kaldor, "Beyond the Blocs: Defending Europe the Political Way," *World Policy* 1, no. 1 (Fall 1983): 1–22; and George Konrád, "A Path Toward Peace," *Atlantic*, March 1984, pp. 71–76.
21. For an opposing argument that a continued American presence in Europe is needed to prevent conflicts from emerging among West European countries, see Josef Joffee, "Europe's American Pacifier," *Foreign Policy* 54 (Spring 1984): 64–82.
22. See Alexander L. George, *Managing U.S.–Soviet Rivalry: Problems of Crisis Prevention* (Boulder, CO: Westview, 1982), and Garthoff, *Détente and Confrontation* (note 10).
23. Early proposals for a superpower condominium were made in the 1960s. See, for example, John Strachey, *On the Prevention of War* (London: Macmillan, 1962). For a discussion of the history and meaning of the concept of *condominium*, see Carsten Holbraad, "Condominium and Concert," in Carsten Holbraad, ed., *Super Powers and World Order* (Canberra: Australian National University Press, 1971), pp. 1–24.
24. Alton Frye, "Inching Beyond Containment: Détente, Entente, Condominium — and Orchestraint," in Terry L. Deibel and John Lewis Gaddis, eds., *Containment: Concept and Policy*, vol. 2 (Washington, DC: National Defense University Press, 1986), p. 650.
25. Liska, "From Containment to Concert," pp. 4, 20 (note 9).
26. Randall Forsberg, "Confining the Military to Defense as a Route to Disarmament," *World Policy* 1, no. 2 (Winter 1984): 313. See also Michael May, "The U.S.–Soviet Approach to Nuclear Weapons," *International Security* 9, no. 4 (Spring 1985): 150–53, and Jerry W. Sanders, "Security and Choice," *World Policy* 1, no. 4 (Summer 1984): 709–10.
27. Forsberg's proposals in particular also assume that peace can be guaranteed by confining the militaries of all countries to purely defensive postures. See Chapter 5 for a discussion of this concept.
28. Liska, "Concert Through Decompression," p. 114 (note 9).

29. Quoted by John Lewis Gaddis in German, ed., *The Future of U.S.-Soviet Relations*, p. 163 (note 12).

30. Robert W. Tucker, "Toward a New Détente," *New York Times Magazine*, December 9, 1984, p. 95.

31. Robert S. McNamara and Hans A. Bethe, "Reducing the Risk of Nuclear War," *Atlantic*, July 1985, p. 47. See also Kennan, *The Nuclear Delusion*, p. 66 (note 2); Stanley Hoffman, "Détente," in Joseph S. Nye, Jr., ed., *The Making of America's Soviet Policy* (New Haven: Yale University Press, 1984), p. 260; Marshall D. Shulman, "What Kind of Relationship Do We Want with the Soviet Union?" *Arms Control Today* 15, no. 9 (November–December 1985): 7; and Garthoff, *Détente and Confrontation*, p. 1092 (note 10).

32. For a prominent example of this view, see Kenneth N. Waltz, *Theory of International Politics* (Reading, MA: Addison-Wesley, 1979).

33. Marshall D. Shulman, "The Future of the Soviet–American Competition," in *Soviet–American Relations and World Order: The Two and the Many*, Adelphi Papers, no. 66 (London: International Institute for Strategic Studies, 1970), p. 1.

34. Liska, "Concert Through Decompression," p. 113 (note 9).

35. For this reason, many advocates of U.S.-Soviet cooperation consider a belief in the irreversibility of the current strategic balance to be a necessary condition for improved relations. See Roy Bennett, "Design for a New Détente," *Social Policy* 16, no. 2 (Fall 1985): 6–14, and Chapter 8.

36. See Chapter 7 for a more comprehensive discussion of these arguments.

37. "Excerpts from President's Speech in California on U.S.-Soviet Relations," *New York Times*, August 23, 1987, p. A8.

38. Quoted in "Moving into a Warmer East–West Climate," *Christian Science Monitor*, August 28, 1987, p. 7.

39. See Robert W. Tucker, "Would a Socialist America Behave Differently?" in Thomas G. Paterson, ed., *The Origins of the Cold War*, 2d ed. (Lexington, MA: D.C. Heath, 1974). See also Stephen M. Walt, "Alliance Formation and the Balance of World Power," *International Security* 9, no. 4 (Spring 1985): 18–26, and Kenneth N. Waltz, *Man, the State, and War* (New York: Columbia University Press, 1959), pp. 80–158.

40. Michael Doyle, "Kant, Liberal Legacies, and Foreign Affairs," *Philosophy and Public Affairs* 17, nos. 3 and 4 (Summer and Fall 1983): 205–35, 323–53.

41. George F. Kennan, "America's Unstable Soviet Policy," *Atlantic*, November 1982, p. 80. For a comprehensive discussion of the domestic problems of managing U.S. policy toward the Soviet Union, see Nye, *The Making of America's Soviet Policy* (note 31).

42. Rostow, "On Ending the Cold War," p. 840 (note 9).

43. Ibid., pp. 840–47.

44. Sherle R. Schwenninger and Jerry W. Sanders, "The Democrats and a New Grand Strategy," *World Policy* 3, no. 3 (Summer 1986): 384.

45. See Chapter 9.

46. Norman Angell, *The Great Illusion* (New York: G.P. Putnam's Sons, 1910).

47. Herman Kahn, *Thinking About the Unthinkable* (New York: Avon Books, 1962), pp. 155–56. For a discussion of the Clark–Sohn plan, see Chapter 10.

48. The term *malignant social process* was coined by Morton Deutsch. See his "The Prevention of World War III: A Psychological Perspective," *Political Psychol-*

ogy 4, no. 1 (March 1983): 3–31, and *The Resolution of Conflict: Constructive and Destructive Processes* (New Haven: Yale University Press, 1973).

49. On hostility spirals, see Robert Jervis, *Perception and Misperception in International Politics* (Princeton: Princeton University Press, 1976), pp. 62–84.

50. Charles E. Osgood, *An Alternative to War or Surrender* (Urbana: University of Illinois Press, 1962). See also his earlier articles, "Suggestions for Winning the Real War with Communism," *Journal of Conflict Resolution* 3, no. 4 (December 1959): 295–325, and "A Case for Graduated Unilateral Disengagement," *Bulletin of the Atomic Scientists* (April 1960): 127–31. The strategy was termed "the policy of mutual example" by a Soviet writer. See B. Dimitriev, "The Policy of Mutual Example," *Izvestia* (December 15, 1964), in *Current Digest of the Soviet Press* (January 16, 1965), p. 16.

51. For recent discussions of GRIT, see Mark Sommer, *Beyond the Bomb: Living Without Nuclear Weapons* (Massachusetts: Expro Press, 1985), pp. 58–63; Charles Osgood, "The Way GRIT Works," in Don Carlson and Craig Comstock, eds., *Securing Our Planet* (Los Angeles: Tarcher/St. Martin's, 1986), pp. 24–30; and Dennis Paulson, ed., *Voices of Survival* (Santa Barbara: Capra Press, 1986), pp. 236–42. A good partial survey of the literature on GRIT and the related strategy of gradualism is C.R. Mitchell, "GRIT and Gradualism— 25 Years On," *International Interactions* 13, no. 1 (August 1986): 59–90.

52. Amitai Etzioni, *The Hard Way to Peace: A New Strategy* (New York: Collier Books, 1962).

53. Robert Axelrod, *The Evolution of Cooperation* (New York: Basic Books, 1984).

54. See the special issue of *International Organization* published as Stephen D. Krasner, ed., *International Regimes* (Ithaca: Cornell University Press, 1983).

55. See Joseph S. Nye, Jr., "The Superpowers and the Non-Proliferation Treaty," in Albert Carnesale and Richard N. Haass, eds., *Superpower Arms Control: Setting the Record Straight* (Cambridge, MA: Ballinger, 1987), pp. 165–90.

56. See Condoleezza Rice, "SALT and the Search for a Security Regime," in Alexander L. George, Philip J. Farley, and Alexander Dallin, eds., *U.S.–Soviet Security Cooperation* (New York: Oxford University Press, forthcoming).

57. Joseph S. Nye, Jr., "Nuclear Learning and U.S.–Soviet Security Regimes," *International Organization* 41, no. 3 (Summer 1987): 371–402.

58. For an analysis of some of these areas, see George, Farley, and Dallin, eds., *U.S.–Soviet Security Cooperation* (note 54), and Nish Jamgotch, Jr., ed., *Sectors of Mutual Benefit in U.S.–Soviet Relations* (Durham, NC: Duke University Press, 1985).

59. Donald M. Kendall, "U.S.–Soviet Trade, Peace and Prosperity," in Fred Warner Neal, ed., *Détente or Debacle: Common Sense in U.S.–Soviet Relations* (New York: Norton, 1979), p. 40. See Chapter 9 of this volume for a more detailed discussion of such proposals.

60. Edward Teller, in Dennis Paulson, ed., *Voices of Survival in the Nuclear Age* (Santa Barbara: Capra Press, 1986), p. 157.

61. Daniel Deudney, "Forging Missiles into Spaceships," *World Policy* 2, no. 2 (Spring 1985): 273.

62. Aspen Institute for Humanistic Studies, International Group, *Managing East–West Conflict: A Framework for Sustained Engagement* (New York: Aspen Institute, 1984).

63. Nye, "Nuclear Learning and U.S.–Soviet Security Regimes," pp. 398–401 (note 55).
64. Deutsch, *Resolution of Conflict*, p. 363 (note 46).
65. Ralph K. White, *Fearful Warriors: A Psychological Profile of U.S.–Soviet Relations* (New York: Free Press, 1984), pp. 160–67.
66. Arthur A. Stein, "Coordination and Collaboration: Regimes in an Anarchic World," in Krasner, ed., *International Regimes*, p. 139 (note 52). See also Deutsch, *Resolution of Conflict*, p. 365 (note 46).
67. Deutsch, *Resolution of Conflict*, p. 364 (note 46).
68. For a general discussion of the evidence, see Martin Patchen, "Strategies for Eliciting Cooperation from an Adversary: Laboratory and Internation Findings," *Journal of Conflict Resolution* 31, no. 1 (March 1987): 164–85.
69. Mitchell, "GRIT and Gradualism" (note 49). Other authors have cited a number of instances in which the strategy was employed, but Mitchell argues that these lacked one or more of GRIT's defining characteristics.
70. The term *Kennedy Experiment* was coined by Etzioni. See his "The Kennedy Experiment," *Western Political Quarterly* 20, no. 2 (Spring 1967): 361–80. Both Etzioni and Charles Osgood place the end of the process at Kennedy's assassination in November 1963, but Mitchell argues that it continued until mid-1965. See "GRIT and Gradualism," pp. 78–79 (note 49).
71. Steven L. Spiegel, "America's Détente Dilemma," Research Note No. 18, Center for International and Strategic Affairs, University of California, Los Angeles, September 1986.
72. See Deborah Welch Larson, "The Austrian State Treaty," *International Organization* 41, no. 1 (Winter 1987): 27–60.
73. For a comparison of de-escalation strategies in Egyptian–Israeli and U.S.–Soviet relations, see Louis Kriesberg, "Carrots, Sticks, De-escalation: U.S.–Soviet and Arab–Israeli Relations," *Armed Forces and Society* 13, no. 3 (Spring 1987): 403–23.
74. See the pointed critique of "nuclear depth psychology" by James G. Blight, "How Might Psychology Contribute to Reducing the Risk of Nuclear War," *Political Psychology* 7, no. 4 (December 1986), especially pp. 631–32, and Blight, "Toward a Policy-Relevant Psychology of Avoiding Nuclear War: Lessons for Psychologists from the Cuban Missile Crisis," *American Psychologist* 42, no. 1 (January 1987), especially pp. 22–24.
75. Herbert C. Kelman, "An Interactional Approach to Conflict Resolution," in Ralph K. White, ed., *Psychology and the Prevention of Nuclear War: A Book of Readings* (New York: New York University Press, 1986), pp. 172–73.
76. See Stephen R. Rock, "Why Peace Breaks Out: Power, Economics, and Socio-Culture in Great Power Rapprochement" (Ph.D. diss., Cornell University, August 1985).
77. Liska admits that this problem exists, but claims it is not insurmountable. First, a condominial form of cooperation could well involve some devolution of authority to large regional powers, "decreasing the scope for anything like a two-headed dictatorship." Second, superpower collusion that might otherwise be unacceptable would be supported because it would help insure international stability and avert a nuclear disaster. See Liska, "Concert Through Decompression," pp. 112–13, 122 (note 9).

78. Hedley Bull suggests that the emergence of China as a great power has ended the possibility of a U.S.–Soviet condominium. See his *The Anarchical Society: A Study of Order in World Politics* (London: Macmillan, 1977), p. 227. However, as Liska and Rostow observe, the combined power of the United States and the Soviet Union would remain formidable if the two countries cooperated in any regional conflict. See Rostow, "On Ending the Cold War," p. 849 (note 9), and Liska, "Concert Through Decompression," p. 115 (note 9).

79. For a rejection of the idea that the Soviets are motivated by fear, see Richard Pipes, "How to Cope with the Soviet Threat: A Long-Term Strategy for the West," *Commentary*, August 1984, p. 13.

80. See Strobe Talbott, "Social Issues," in Nye, ed., *The Making of America's Soviet Policy*, pp. 204–5 (note 31).

81. Liska, "Concert Through Decompression," p. 111 (note 9). See also Michael H. Shuman and Gale Warner, "Effectiveness of the New Diplomats," in Don Carlson and Craig Comstock, eds., *Citizen Summitry: Keeping the Peace When It Matters Too Much to be Left to Politicians* (Los Angeles: Jeremy P. Tarcher/Ark Communications Institute, 1986), p. 145.

82. Rostow, "On Ending the Cold War," p. 847 (note 9).

83. See, for example, Eugene V. Rostow, "The Case Against SALT II," *Commentary*, February 1979, pp. 23–34.

84. Stevenson, *The Rise and Fall of Détente*, p. 165 (note 10). See also Coral Bell, "The October Middle East War: A Case Study in Crisis Management during Détente," *International Affairs* (London) 50, no. 4 (October 1974): 531–43, and William Quandt, "Soviet Policy in the October Middle East War," *International Affairs* (London) 53, no. 3 (July 1977): 377–89, and no. 4 (October 1977): 587–603.

85. Stevenson, *The Rise and Fall of Détente*, pp. 196–202 (note 10).

Chapter 7: The Long-Term Modernization of Soviet Foreign Policy

1. For example, see Walter Clemens, "A Foreign Policy Innovator," *Christian Science Monitor*, December 18, 1986, p. 16.

2. On this point, see Benson L. Grayson, ed., *The American Image of Russia* (New York: Frederick Ungar, 1977), and Robert Dallek, "How We See the Soviets," in Mark Garrison and Abbott Gleason, eds., *Shared Destiny: Fifty Years of Soviet–American Relations* (Boston: Beacon Press, 1985).

3. In two potential scenarios a moderation in Soviet foreign policy might be dangerous for the United States. If a militant third party arose that required a vigorous Soviet response to counteract it, and if a more pacific bent in Soviet policy withheld that response, then the risks and dangers of a nuclear war might increase. Americans could argue that a more belligerent stance on the part of Britain and France in the 1930s would have been helpful in preventing World War II.

   A moderation in Soviet foreign policy could also be dangerous if it caused the United States to seriously underestimate the dangers of Soviet intervention in response to certain American actions. A recent study of the outbreak of World War I argued that the improvement in Anglo-German relations in the years immediately preceding 1914 misled the Germans into believing that the British would not intervene against them. This prompted the Germans to be somewhat bolder in pursuing their continental strategy than they would have been otherwise, which in turn ultimately brought about British intervention. See Sean Lynn-Jones, "Détente and Deterrence in Anglo-German relations, 1911–1914," *International Security* 11, no. 2 (Fall 1986): 121–50.

4. Walter Lippman, quoted by William Zimmerman in "The Soviet Union and the West," in Stephen Cohen, Alexander Rabinowitch, and Robert Sharlet, eds., *The Soviet Union Since Stalin* (Bloomington: Indiana University Press, 1980), p. 308.

5. Kennan's thoughts were originally laid down in a lengthy telegram from the American embassy in Moscow in 1946. He published this essay with minimal revisions under the pseudonym "X" in the July 1947 edition of *Foreign Affairs*. It can currently be found in Kennan's book *American Diplomacy: 1900–1950* (Chicago: University of Chicago Press, 1951), pp. 107–28.

   Kennan would later identify himself with many of Lippman's criticisms. This chapter will address their arguments as they were originally outlined in the 1940s and will not attempt to trace the evolution of their thought. For an example of Kennan's more recent thinking on U.S.–Soviet relations and the problem of nuclear war, see George Kennan, *The Nuclear Delusion* (New York: Pantheon Books, 1983), and "Containment Then and Now," *Foreign Affairs* 65, no. 4 (Spring 1987): 885–90.

6. Kennan, *American Diplomacy*, p. 107 (note 5).

7. Kennan, *American Diplomacy*, p. 115 (note 5).

8. This list was developed by John Lewis Gaddis. See his *Strategies of Containment* (New York: Oxford University Press, 1982), pp. 25–53.

9. Kennan, *American Diplomacy*, p. 120 (note 5). Kennan has maintained that he originally viewed containment as being political, not military, in nature. See his *Memoirs: 1925–1950* (New York: Pantheon Books, 1967), pp. 358–59, and "Containment Then and Now," pp. 885–86 (note 5). However, this point has been contested on the basis of archival research. See Eduard Mark, "The Question of Containment: A Reply to John Lewis Gaddis," *Foreign Affairs* 56, no. 2 (January 1978): 430–40. See also John Lewis Gaddis's response in the same issue, pp. 440–41.

10. Kennan, *American Diplomacy*, pp. 125–28 (note 5).

11. George F. Kennan, "America and the Russian Future," *Foreign Affairs* 29, no. 3 (April 1951): 351–70. Reprinted in *American Diplomacy* (note 5); the citation is from p. 137. Kennan also believed that such a Russia would also need to stop short of totalitarianism in its domestic exercise of power (see pp. 136–43). He originally envisioned that the character of Soviet policy would mellow in ten to fifteen years. In his memoirs in 1967, he argued that this shift had already taken place, rendering the doctrine of containment irrelevant.

12. The articles were later collected in Walter Lippman, *The Cold War: A Study in U.S. Foreign Policy*, ed. Ronald Steel (New York: Harper Torchbooks, 1972).

13. Lippman, *Cold War*, p. 16 (note 12).

14. Ibid., p. 26.

15. Ibid., pp. 5–7.

16. Ibid., pp. 32–42, 50–52.

17. Richard Pipes, *Survival Is Not Enough* (New York: Simon and Schuster, 1984),

pp. 214–20. However, Pipes also believes that containment's success depended on two factors that no longer apply today—American nuclear superiority and clearly defined aggression on the part of the Soviet Union or its clients.

18. Ibid., pp. 17–48, 102.
19. Pipes maintains that contemporary Soviet ailments—a slumping economy, declining birthrate, increasing alcoholism, and so on—combine to create what Lenin would have called a "revolutionary situation" within the Soviet Union. Ibid., p. 200. For Kennan's view on this topic, see his *American Diplomacy*, p. 125 (note 5), and Gaddis, *Strategies of Containment*, pp. 46–47 (note 8).
20. On the relationship of external expansion to domestic legitimacy, see Pipes, *Survival*, pp. 40–42 (note 17).
21. He writes that "such changes for the better that one can expect in the nature of the Soviet government and in its conduct of foreign relations *will come about only from failures, instabilities, and fears of collapse and not from a growing confidence and sense of security*" (ibid., p. 204). Emphasis in the original.
22. Ibid., p. 207.
23. Contrary to the popular wisdom, which views the Soviet Union as self-sufficient and practically impervious to Western economic sanctions, Pipes argues that Western technical and financial assistance has always been of crucial importance in allowing the Soviet economy to function. Ibid., pp. 259–73.
24. These criticisms are taken from Marshall Shulman, "A Rational Response to the Soviet Challenge," *International Affairs* 61, no. 3 (Summer 1985): 375–84. Although Shulman does not mention Pipes by name, the context makes it clear that his remarks are directed against Pipes's argument.
25. Shulman argues that it is "wrong to base our policy on the assertion that Soviet behavior can only change if there is a change in the Soviet system. It obscures the main point, which is that there can be and there has been modification in Soviet behavior even in spite of the continuing nature of the Soviet system" (ibid., p. 381).
26. Ibid., p. 380.
27. Marshall Shulman, "What Does Security Mean Today," *Foreign Affairs* 49, no. 4 (July 1971): 613. Shulman acknowledges that a "residual ideological commitment" leads the Soviet Union to deny the legitimacy of the current status quo. But he maintains that this "is of diminishing relevance in a world in which . . . Soviet Marxism has little to offer as a guide to the future." In 1970, he wrote that "the Soviet–American relationship has been mainly a nation-state rivalry for military power and for political influence, complicated by differences in political culture and ideology" (Shulman, "The Future of the Soviet–American Competition," in *Soviet–American Relations and World Order: The Two and the Many*, Adelphi Paper no. 66 (March 1970), p. 1).
28. Shulman, "A Rational Response," pp. 380–81 (note 24).
29. See Marshall D. Shulman, *Beyond the Cold War* (New Haven: Yale University Press, 1966), p. 100.
30. See Marshall D. Shulman, "The Future of the Soviet–American Competition," pp. 1–10 (note 27), and *Beyond the Cold War*, pp. 18–32 (note 29).
31. Shulman, "A Rational Response," p. 382 (note 24).
32. Shulman, *Beyond the Cold War*, pp. 2–3 (note 29).

33. See ibid., pp. 93–95; "The Future of the Soviet–American Competition," pp. 7, 10 (note 27); "A Rational Response to the Soviet Challenge," pp. 382–83 (note 24); "What Does Security Mean Today," pp. 616–18 (note 27); and "Toward a Western Philosophy of Coexistence," *Foreign Affairs* 52, no. 1 (October 1973): 55–56.

34. Shulman, "A Rational Response," pp. 382–83 (note 24).

35. Throughout the 1950s, the Socialist Democratic Party in Germany advocated German neutrality and reunification in opposition to Konrad Adenauer's policy of integrating the Federal Republic into Western economic and security blocs. In 1952, the Soviet Union attempted to block German rearmament by proposing the creation of an independent, unified, and rearmed Germany—a proposal that Winston Churchill suggested be considered "at the highest level." In a series of essays and public broadcasts in 1957, George Kennan advocated the neutralization of Germany along terms that were almost identical to Lippmann's earlier recommendations. And today, there are numerous proposals—from the Green Party's advocacy of a unilateral German withdrawal from NATO to less radical calls for a purely European defense—reflecting a belief that at least Europe (and perhaps the world) would be safer if the superpowers did not confront each other directly on the European continent. If one believes that geographical proximity is the key factor determining hostility in superpower relations, then superpower disengagement from Europe would play a role in reducing Soviet and American enmity.

36. In addition, the Mutual Balanced Force Reduction talks have demonstrated that important political and military asymmetries complicate the process of superpower military disengagement from Europe. Heavy armored divisions in the western USSR could be reintroduced into Europe more quickly than similar divisions stationed in the continental United States. American and Soviet troops in Europe serve different functions, and the Soviets have frequently found it necessary to rely on their forces to ensure the compliance of client regimes.

37. For an excellent critical analysis of alternative strategies for European defense, see Fen Osler Hampson, "Is There an Alternative to NATO?" in Stephen J. Flanagan and Fen Osler Hampson, eds., *Securing Europe's Future* (Dover, MA: Auburn House, 1986), pp. 191–217.

38. See Fen Osler Hampson, "Escalation in Europe," in Graham T. Allison, Albert Carnesale, and Joseph S. Nye, Jr., eds., *Hawks, Doves, and Owls: An Agenda for Avoiding Nuclear War* (New York: W.W. Norton, 1985), pp. 80–114. See also A.W. DePorte, *Europe Between the Superpowers* (New Haven: Yale University Press, 1979), pp. 243–44. It is possible that contemporary European stability will disintegrate over time; the German question may heat up again, and the Soviet Union may find its position in Eastern Europe increasingly tenuous.

39. Shulman, "The Future of Soviet–American Competition," p. 10 (note 27). He writes that North–South issues "generate tensions which will cut across the Soviet–American competition, exacerbating it in some cases but producing common or parallel interests in others" (p. 2).

40. This position was more widely held in the 1970s than it is today (although it is still fashionable in some circles). For a typical example, see Seyom Brown,

"The Changing Essence of Power," *Foreign Affairs* 51, no. 2 (January 1973). See also Richard Nixon's Second Annual Report to the Congress on United States Foreign Policy, in *Public Papers of the Presidents, 1971* (Washington, DC: Government Printing Office), pp. 219–28.

41. Those who argue that bipolarity is optimal emphasize the stability of the system in the face of third-party realignment. The great disparity in power between the superpowers and the other states ensures that the security of the United States or the USSR will not be decisively threatened by the defection of smaller powers. It also enables an aggressor to estimate more accurately the strength of the coalition that it will oppose. Those who see multipolarity as preferable argue that a multipolar system creates increased flexibility in alignment, which erodes the rigidity of the various blocs. This increases the uncertainty that a power faces in determining who will align against it. It also generates additional issues that downgrade the importance of the central superpower relationship. For contrasting arguments, see Kenneth N. Waltz, *Theory of International Politics* (Reading, MA: Addison-Wesley, 1979), pp. 161–93; Morton Kaplan, *System and Process in International Politics* (New York: Wiley, 1964); and Hans Morgenthau, *The Purpose of American Politics* (New York: Alfred Knopf, 1961).

42. See Waltz, pp. 176–83 (note 41).

43. For a discussion of the complex theoretical issues involved in assessing power, see David A. Baldwin, "Power Analysis and World Politics: New Trends versus Old Tendencies," *World Politics* 31, no. 2 (January 1979): 161–93.

44. Unfortunately, "balance of power" is a rather slippery term. It is used to describe an inherent tendency within international politics for states to resist the domination of a particular hegemon by producing a coalition that offsets the threatening distribution of power.

45. Shulman does not advocate a policy of unilateral conciliation. He writes, "Paradoxically, either extreme—toughness or weakness—may have the effect of encouraging greater Soviet militancy, and the combination of firmness (which is different than toughness), clarity, and fairness is most likely to evoke corresponding qualities in Soviet negotiating behavior." See Marshall Shulman, "Tell Me, Daddy, Who's the Baddy," in Erik P. Hoffman, ed., *The Soviet Union in the 1980s* (Montpelier, VT: Capital City Press, 1984), p. 181.

46. See Pipes, *Survival*, pp. 216–18 (note 17).

47. See Henry Kissinger, *The White House Years* (Boston: Little, Brown and Co., 1979), pp. 118–19.

48. The quotation is from President Carter's speech on Soviet–American relations at the U.S. Naval Academy in June, 1978, which Shulman helped draft (*New York Times*, June 8, 1978, p. A22). Similar statements can be found in Carter's address at the University of Notre Dame on May 22, 1977. See *Public Papers of the Presidents*, vol. 1 (Washington, DC: Government Printing Office, 1977), pp. 954–62.

49. At the 27th Party Congress, Gorbachev stated that "What is required is firmness in defending principles and positions coupled with tactical flexibility. . . ." Quoted in Dimitri Simes, "Gorbachev: A New Foreign Policy?" *Foreign Affairs* 65, no. 3: 491.

50. Pipes recently stated in an interview in *Time Magazine* (July 27, 1987) that "Aggressiveness is embedded in a system where there is a dictatorial party that can justify its power only by pretending there is a continual warlike situation." See also note 20.

51. See, for example, Michael Voslensky, *Nomenklatura* (Garden City: Doubleday & Co., 1984), pp. 319–55; Irving Kristol, "Coping With an 'Evil Empire,'" *Wall Street Journal*, December 17, 1985; and Adam Ulam, "The World Outside," in Robert F. Byrnes, ed., *After Brezhnev: Sources of Soviet Conduct in the 1980s* (Bloomington: Indiana University Press, 1983), pp. 347–48. A less extreme version of this view holds that the traditional patterns of investment and resource allocation, which greatly favor industrial-military power over popular consumption, are legitimized primarily in terms of international imperatives.

52. See Seweryn Bialer, *Stalin's Successors: Leadership, Stability and Change in the Soviet Union* (New York: Cambridge University Press, 1980), pp. 194–95.

53. See Walter D. Connor, "Mass Expectations and Regime Performance," in Seweryn Bialer, ed., *The Domestic Context of Soviet Foreign Policy* (Boulder, CO: Westview Press, 1981), p. 58. This conclusion is consistent with several Western studies of the roots of political legitimacy, which emphasize the importance of economic development as a precondition for a stable political system in a nontraditional society. Seymour Martin Lipset's *Political Man* (Garden City, NY: Doubleday, 1960) is probably the foremost work in this genre.

54. On this point see Jerry Hough, *The Struggle for the Third World: Soviet Debates and American Options* (Washington, DC: Brookings Institution, 1986), pp. 18–22.

55. Khrushchev refuted one of Lenin's cardinal tenets—that war between communism and capitalism was inevitable—by arguing that the atomic bomb "does not adhere to the class principle" and has therefore made Lenin's formulation obsolete.

56. See Loren Graham, "Science and Computers in Soviet Society," in Erik P. Hoffmann, ed., *The Soviet Union in the 1980s* (Montpelier: Capital City Press, 1984), p. 131. For a discussion of the structural shortcomings of the Soviet economy, see Seweryn Bialer, *The Soviet Paradox* (New York: Alfred Knopf, 1986), pp. 57–80, and Marshall Goldman, *USSR in Crisis: The Failure of an Economic system* (New York: W.W. Norton, 1983).

57. For example, computers—like photocopiers—can be housed in institutions and controlled by institution officials; microcomputers could also be linked to a central network that would record manuscript files, and so on. For a discussion of these and other measures, see Graham, "Science and Computers," p. 120 (note 56).

58. See Charles Gati, "The Stalinist Legacy in Foreign Policy," in Stephen F. Cohen, Alexander Rabinowitch, and Robert Sharlet, eds., *The Soviet Union Since Stalin* (Bloomington: Indiana University Press, 1980), pp. 279–301.

59. See Simes, "Gorbachev: A New Foreign Policy?" p. 479 (note 49).

60. See "Soviet Perceptions of the U.S.: Results of a Surrogate Interview Project," Research Memorandum (Washington, DC: United States International Communication Agency, 1980), and David Shipler, *Russia: Broken Idols, Solemn Dreams* (New York: Times Books, 1983), especially chap. 7. See also William

Zimmerman and Deborah Yarsike, *Inter-Generational Change and Soviet Foreign Policy*, Working Paper #24, Soviet Interview Project, University of Illinois at Urbana-Champaign, July 1986.

61. For an interesting contemporary reformulation of this view, see Michael Doyle, "Kant, Liberal Legacies and Foreign Affairs," *Philosophy and Public Affairs* 12, nos. 3 and 4 (Summer and Fall 1983).

62. Pipes made this statement at a seminar sponsored by Harvard's Avoiding Nuclear War Project in April 1987.

63. These factors include Stalin's break with Tito in the late 1940s; his death in 1953, which marked the end of an era in which one man had the stature and power to be the ultimate interpreter of Marxist dogma for the entire communist movement; later events, such as the Sino-Soviet split and the invasion of Czechoslovakia in 1968, which greatly weakened Moscow's authority and reputation among the left; the Soviet pursuit of détente with West European governments at the expense of their local Communist parties; and the growth of Eurocommunism.

64. See *Pravda*, March 4, 1987, p. 2.

65. Quoted by Gaddis in *Strategies of Containment*, p. 47 (note 8).

66. On this point, see Joan Barth Urban, "The Soviets and the West European Communist Parties," in Herbert J. Ellison, ed., *Soviet Policy Toward Western Europe* (Seattle: University of Washington Press, 1983), pp. 91–129.

67. See Francis Fukuyama, "Gorbachev and the Third World," *Foreign Affairs* 64, no. 4 (Spring 1986): 715–31.

68. See Morton Schwartz, *Soviet Perceptions of the United States* (Berkeley: University of California Press, 1980), and Franklyn Griffiths, "The Sources of American Conduct: Soviet Perspectives and Their Policy Implications," *International Security* 9, no. 2 (Fall 1984). However, Griffiths also observes that the evolution of these perceptions is not irreversible, and that a movement toward greater orthodoxy occurred in the late Brezhnev years.

69. Quoted by F. Stephen Larrabee and Allen Lynch, in "Gorbachev: The Road to Reykjavik," *Foreign Policy* 65 (Winter 1986–87): 7.

70. See Schwartz, *Soviet Perceptions*, pp. 155–57 (note 68).

71. See Hough, *Struggle for the Third World*, p. 260 (note 54). See also George Breslauer, "Ideology and Learning in Soviet Third World Policy," *World Politics* 39, no. 3 (April 1987): 429–48.

72. See Roman Kolkowicz, "The Military," in H. Gordon Skilling and Franklyn Griffiths, eds., *Interest Groups in Soviet Politics* (Princeton: Princeton University Press, 1971), pp. 103–4.

73. On these points, see Raymond L. Garthoff, *Détente and Confrontation* (Washington, DC: Brookings Institution, 1985), p. 557; Andrew Cockburn, *The Threat: Inside the Soviet Military Machine* (New York: Random House, 1983), pp. 104–6; Arkady N. Schevchenko, *Breaking with Moscow* (New York: Alfred Knopf, 1985), p. 202; and Strobe Talbott, *Endgame: The Inside Story of Salt II* (New York: Harper and Row, 1979), p. 73.

74. H. Gordon Skilling, "Group Conflict in Soviet Politics," in Skilling and Griffiths, eds., *Interest Groups*, pp. 395–96 (note 72).

75. Frederick Barghoorn, "The Security Police," in Skilling and Griffiths, eds., *Interest Groups*, p. 109 (note 72).

76. Western estimates of the amount of production allocated to defense range from about 11 to 18 percent of Soviet GNP. This includes nine ministries (Aviation, Defense, Shipbuilding, Electronics, Radio, Means of Communication, Medium Machine Building, General Machine Building, and Machine Building), 134 major final assembly plants, and another 3,500 individual installations that provide support for these plants. See David Holloway, *The Soviet Union and the Arms Race* (New Haven: Yale University Press, 1984), pp. 118–20.

77. Military officers up to the rank of general are stationed in plants specializing in defense production. The former minister of defense, Dimitri Ustinov, made his career in the defense industry.

78. On this point, see Shevchenko, *Breaking with Moscow*, pp. 206–7 (note 73).

79. For example, see Kolkowicz, "The Military," p. 167 (note 72); Jerry Hough and Merle Fainsod, *How the Soviet Union is Governed* (Cambridge: Harvard University Press, 1979), p. 395; and Holloway, *The Soviet Union and the Arms Race*, p. 159 (note 76).

80. When Politburo members who are not yet secure in their positions have attempted to go against the military, they have usually been ousted by more conservative opponents. Thus Malenkov's attempts at liberalization left him vulnerable to Khrushchev's reassertion of traditional Stalinist priorities in 1954, and Podgorny and Kosygin were vulnerable to Brezhnev on this point ten years later. However, once a general secretary has secured his position, he is much less vulnerable. Both Khrushchev and Brezhnev were able to go against the interests of the military, although Khrushchev's challenge was much more fundamental and may have contributed to his downfall in 1964.

81. When Ukrainian party boss Petr Shelest strenuously objected to Brezhnev's decision to proceed with the 1972 summit in spite of the American mining of Haiphong harbor, he was quickly denounced as a "dogmatic negativist." He was expelled from the Politburo in 1973.

82. For a discussion of these beliefs, see Stephen Cohen, *Sovieticus* (New York: W.W. Norton, 1985), pp. 97–101, 136–40, and Hedrick Smith, *The Russians*, rev. ed. (New York: Ballantine Books, 1984), pp. 557–86.

83. Seweryn Bialer, *The Soviet Paradox* (New York: Alfred Knopf, 1986), pp. 267–68.

84. For a discussion of the pivotal importance of Eastern Europe to the Soviet Union, see Sarah Meiklejohn Terry, "The Soviet Union and Eastern Europe: Implications for U.S. Policy," in Dan Caldwell, ed., *Soviet International Behavior and U.S. Policy Options* (Lexington, MA: Lexington Books, 1985), pp. 11–59, and testimony by Melvin Croan, Zygmunt Friedemann, Charles Gati, George Hoffman, Andrzej Korbonski, and Gerhard Wettig before the United States Senate Committee on Foreign Relations, in *Perceptions: Relations Between the United States and the Soviet Union* (Washington, DC: Government Printing Office, 1978).

85. China is probably the nation with the most potential to alter the structure of world politics and bring about this type of change in U.S.–Soviet relations. However, because of its low level of industrial development and the need to distribute its economic output among a vast population, China will not be capable of posing a serious threat to Soviet security for at least a generation.

86. Gorbachev made this declaration at the 27th Party Congress. See *Pravda*, February 26, 1986, p. 3.
87. Kennan, *American Diplomacy*, p. 128 (note 5).

Chapter 8: Prospects and Consequences of Soviet Decline

1. For a review of the Council on Foreign Relations delegation to Moscow, see Henry A. Kissinger, "How to Deal with Gorbachev," *Newsweek*, March 2, 1987.
2. Leon Trotsky's famous phrase, cited in Adam Ulam, *Expansion and Coexistence* (London: Secker and Warburg, 1968), p. 61.
3. These remarks were all made at a symposium sponsored by the Committee for the Free World. See Robert Pear, "Push the Russians, Intellectuals Ask," *New York Times*, October 13, 1985.
4. Henry S. Rowen, "Living with a Sick Bear," *National Interest* (Winter 1986): 25.
5. This is the sort of outcome offered by Zbigniew Brzezinski, in *Game Plan: A Geostrategic Framework for the U.S.–Soviet Contest* (Boston: Atlantic Monthly Press, 1986), and encouraged by Raymond L. Garthoff, in *Détente and Confrontation* (Washington, DC: Brookings Institution, 1985).
6. Many commentators have supported such a development in Soviet society. See, for instance, Frederick C. Barghoorn, *Détente and the Democratic Movement in the USSR* (New York: Free Press, 1976).
7. This is a problematic viewpoint to cite in the literature, for obvious reasons. Perhaps the closest approximation is the hidden agenda of Richard Perle described by Strobe Talbott, *Deadly Gambits* (New York: Alfred A. Knopf, 1984); Marshall Goodman has also spoken about Western experts who are concerned about the prospects and payoffs of Soviet reform.
8. The CIA report is classified, but its findings are summarized in Rowen, "Living with a Sick Bear," pp. 14–26 (note 4).
9. Kenneth L. Adelman, "Why We Need to Scrap SALT II," *New York Times*, September 16, 1986.
10. Kristol's remarks are cited in Pear, "Push the Russians" (note 3).
11. Pipes is quoted in Pear, "Push the Russians" (note 3). See also Richard Pipes, *Survival Is Not Enough: Soviet Realities and America's Future* (New York: Simon and Schuster, 1984).
12. Conservatives have also spoken out against grain sales to the USSR. For a good review of American attempts to use trade sanctions against the USSR, see Bruce Parrott, ed., *Trade, Technology and Soviet–American Relations* (Bloomington: Indiana University Press, 1985). On the issue of Soviet military uses of Western technology, see *Soviet Acquisition of Military Significant Western Technology*, U.S. Department of Defense (September 1985).
13. This is a major point of contention between "decliners" and "reformers."
14. See, for instance, V.I. Lenin, "Soviet Economic Development and World Evolution," in Robert C. Tucker, ed., *The Lenin Anthology* (New York: Norton, 1975), pp. 635–36; Morton Schwartz, *Soviet Perceptions of the United States* (Berkeley: University of California Press, 1978); and the interesting anecdotes in Arkady N. Shevchenko, *Breaking with Moscow* (New York: Ballantine, 1985).

15. The full text of Gorbachev's address appeared in *Pravda*, February 20, 1986.
16. Leslie H. Gelb, "Policy Struggles by U.S. and Soviets on Verge of Shift," *New York Times*, April 5, 1986.
17. President Reagan's UN address of October 24, 1985, is discussed in Lou Cannon and David Hoffman, "Arms Control, Regional Peace," *Washington Post*, October 25, 1985.
18. See Henry Kissinger, *White House Years* (Boston: Little, Brown and Co., 1979), and the section on "eroding hegemony" in Robert O. Keohane and Joseph S. Nye, Jr., *Power and Interdependence* (Boston: Little, Brown and Co., 1977), pp. 42–46.
19. Richard K. Betts, "A Nuclear Golden Age? The Balance Before Parity," *International Security* 2, no. 3 (Winter 1986/1987): 3–32.
20. See, for instance, C. Robert Zelnick, "The Foundering Soviets," *Foreign Policy* (Winter 1984): 92–107, and George W. Breslauer, *Five Images of the Soviet Future* (Berkeley: Institute of International Studies, 1978).
21. Joint Economic Committee, U.S. Congress, *Soviet Economy in the 1980's: Problems and Prospects* (Washington, DC: Government Printing Office, 1983), and Boris Rumer, "Realities of Gorbachev's Economic Program," *Problems of Communism* 35 (May–June 1986): 20–31.
22. Bruce Parrott, *Politics and Technology in the Soviet Union* (Cambridge: MIT Press, 1983), and Marshall I. Goldman, *The USSR in Crisis: The Failure of an Economic System* (New York: Norton, 1983).
23. For an informative look into the world of Soviet computers, see Alex Beam, "The USSR: Atari Bolsheviks," *Atlantic* 257, no. 3 (March 1986): 28–32.
24. The most authoritative work on dissent among nationality movements to date is Ludmilla Alexeyeva, *Soviet Dissent: Contemporary Movements for National, Religious, and Human Rights* (Middletown, CT: Wesleyan University Press, 1985).
25. See Helene Carrere d'Encausse, *Decline of an Empire* (New York: Newsweek Books, 1979).
26. See, for instance, Jerry F. Hough, *Soviet Leadership in Transition* (Washington, DC: Brookings Institution, 1980), and Seweryn Bialer, *Stalin's Successors: Leadership, Stability and Change in the Soviet Union* (Cambridge: Cambridge University Press, 1980).
27. Michael Tatu, *Power in the Kremlin* (New York: Viking Press, 1969), and Zbigniew Brzezinski, ed., *Dilemmas of Change in Soviet Politics* (New York: Columbia University Press, 1969).
28. This point is underlined in Rowen, "Living with a Sick Bear" (note 4).
29. See Daniel S. Papp, "Soviet Non-fuel Mineral Resources: Surplus or Scarcity," *Resources Policy* 8, no. 3 (September 1982); Rae Weston, *Gold: A World Survey* (London: Croom Helm, 1983); Michael Kaser, "Soviet Gold Production," *Soviet Economy in a Time of Change*, vol. 2, Joint Economic Committee, Congress of the United States (Washington, DC: Government Printing Office, 1979); and Marshall I. Goldman, *The Enigma of Soviet Petroleum: Half Full or Half Empty* (New York: Norton, 1980).
30. Andrei Amalrik, *Will the Soviet Union Survive Until 1984?* (New York: Harper and Row, 1970).

31. See the collected essays in Sarah M. Terry, *Soviet Policy in Eastern Europe* (New Haven: Yale University Press, 1984).

32. See Richard H. Shultz, Jr., "Countering Third World Marxist-Leninist Regimes: Policy Options for the United States," in Institute for Foreign Policy Analysis, *Third World Marxist-Leninist Regimes: Strengths, Vulnerabilities and U.S. Policy* (Cambridge: IFPA, 1985), pp. 111–25.

33. Robert W. Tucker, "The New Reagan Doctrine Rests on Misplaced Optimism," *New York Times*, April 9, 1986.

34. Thane Gustafson and Dawn Mann, "Gorbachev's First Year: Building Power and Authority," *Problems of Communism* 35 (May–June 1985): 285–305.

35. On Brezhnev, see Timothy J. Colton, *The Dilemma of Reform in the Soviet Union* (New York: Council on Foreign Relations Books, 1986), pp. 6–31.

36. For a recent discussion of this long-term objective, see "Would a Rich Russia be a Cuddly Russia?" *Economist* (February 20, 1987), pp. 13–14.

37. Churkin is quoted in Walter Pincus, "After SALT II, Can Moscow Afford a Big Arms Buildup?" *Washington Post Week in Review*, September 16, 1986.

38. Jonathan Medalia and Al Tinajero, *Strategic Nuclear Forces Potential US/Soviet Trends with or Without SALT 1985–2000*, Congressional Research Service, Report No. 86-135F, July 15, 1986.

39. Robert Gilpin, *War and Change in World Politics* (New York: Cambridge University Press, 1981), pp. 186–211.

40. Philip Taubman, "Gorbachev Avows a Need for Peace to Pursue Domestic Reform," *New York Times*, February 17, 1987.

41. For a historical account of the often brutal Soviet measures of modernization, see the essays in Robert C. Tucker, ed., *Stalinism* (New York: Norton, 1977).

42. See Francis Fukuyama, *Moscow's Post-Brezhnev Reassessment of the Third World*, Rand R-3337-USP (February 1986), and, for an interesting review of Soviet writings on the Third World, Jerry F. Hough, *The Struggle for the Third World: Soviet Debates and American Options* (Washington, DC: Brookings Institution, 1986).

43. See the discussion on the balance of power in Martin Wight, *Power Politics* (Middlesex, England: Penguin, 1979).

44. Ulam, *Expansion and Coexistence*, pp. 51–76 (note 2).

45. This point is made in a wide range of the literature on Soviet foreign and military policies. See Seweryn Bialer, *The Soviet Paradox: External Expansion, Internal Decline* (New York: Alfred A. Knopf, 1986); Raymond Garthoff, *Soviet Military Policy* (New York: Praeger, 1966); and Malcolm MacKintosh, *Juggernaut: A History of the Soviet Armed Forces* (New York, Macmillan, 1967).

46. Edward Luttwak, *The Grand Strategy of the Soviet Union* (New York: St. Martin's Press, 1983). His analysis builds on his earlier study of Rome's decline, *The Grand Strategy of the Roman Empire—From the First Century A.D. to the Third* (Baltimore: Johns Hopkins University Press, 1976).

47. Robert Gilpin, *War and Change*, pp. 191 (note 39).

48. Richard Pipes, "Why the Soviet Union Thinks It Could Fight and Win a Nuclear War," *Commentary* 64 (July 1977): 21–34.

49. For contrasting views, see William Scott, *Soviet Sources of Military Doctrine and Strategy* (New York: Crane, Russak, 1975); Paul Nitze, "Deterring our Deter-

rent," *Foreign Policy* 25 (Winter 1976): 195–210; and C.G. Jacobsen, *Soviet Strategic Initiatives* (New York: Praeger, 1979).

50. Cited in Bialer, *The Soviet Paradox*, p. 270 (note 45).

51. For an excellent discussion of the early theory and practice of containment, see John Lewis Gaddis, *Strategies of Containment* (New York: Oxford University Press, 1982).

52. Cited in *Newsweek*, June 12, 1972.

53. This point was made by Hedley Bull, Cyril Foster Memorial Lecture, Oxford University, England, November 1982, and by N.S. Khrushchev, "Report of the Central Committee to the Twentieth Party Congress," *Current Digest of the Soviet Press* 8, no. 4 (March 7, 1956): 6–12.

54. Kenneth N. Waltz, *Theory of International Politics* (Reading, MA: Addison-Wesley, 1979).

55. See Michael D. Intriligator, "Nuclear Proliferation and the Probability of Nuclear War," in Brodie, Intriligator, and Kolkowicz, eds., *National Security and International Stability* (Cambridge, MA: Oelgeschlager, Gunn, & Hain, 1983), pp. 257–72.

56. See Joseph S. Nye, Jr., "Nuclear Learning Between the Superpowers," draft article, Center for Science and International Affairs, Kennedy School of Government, Harvard, 1986.

57. Hedley Bull, *The Anarchical Society: A Study of Order in World Politics* (London: Macmillan, 1977), pp. 101–26.

58. Richard Pipes, "Why Hurry Into an Arms Accord?" *International Herald Tribune*, October 11, 1986.

59. Martin Walker, *The Waking Giant: Gorbachev's Russia* (London: Pantheon, 1986).

Chapter 9: Internationalism

1. From his speech to the nation on November 14, 1985; quoted in *Surviving Together*, Institute for Soviet–American Relations, no. 8 (February 1986), p. 3.

2. Statement delivered to the Senate Foreign Relations Committee, September 19, 1974. Reprinted in Henry A. Kissinger, *American Foreign Policy*, 3d ed. (New York: W.W. Norton & Co., 1977), pp. 158–59.

3. In the introduction to David Mitrany, *A Working Peace System* (Chicago: Quadrangle Books, 1966), pp. 10–11.

4. See, for example, Louis Rene Beres and Harry R. Targ, *Constructing Alternative World Futures* (Cambridge, MA: Schenkman, 1977), p. 148.

5. A regime is commonly defined as a set of "implicit or explicit principles, norms, rules and decision-making procedures around which actors' expectations converge in a given area of international relations." Stephen D. Krasner, "Structural Causes and Regime Consequences: Regimes as Intervening Variables," in Krasner, ed., *International Regimes* (Ithaca, NY: Cornell University Press, 1983).

6. *Transnational relations* refers to both nonstate relations across national boundaries and transgovernmental relations, or the relations between subunits of different national governments. International organizations (IOs) are ordinarily categorized either as international governmental organizations (IGOs),

such as the United Nations, or as international nongovernmental organizations (INGOs), such as Foster Parents Plan.

7. Cf. Robert O. Keohane and Joseph S. Nye, Jr., eds., *Transnational Relations and World Politics* (Cambridge: Harvard University Press, 1970), p. xvii. See also Seyom Brown, *New Forces in World Politics* (Washington, DC: Brookings Institution, 1974).

8. See, for example, Robert Gilpin, "The Politics of Transnational Economic Relations," in Keohane and Nye, *Transnational Relations and World Politics*, pp. 53–54 (note 7).

9. On interdependence as an analytic concept, see Robert O. Keohane and Joseph S. Nye, Jr., *Power and Interdependence: World Politics in Transition* (Boston: Little, Brown and Co., 1977), pp. 8–11. For a detailed survey of the many dimensions of interdependence and their importance in the international system, see Harold K. Jacobson, *Networks of Interdependence: International Organizations and the Global Political System*, 2d ed. (New York: Alfred A. Knopf, 1984).

10. My use of the term *interdependent* is purely descriptive of particular relations. It is consistent with Keohane and Nye's "Complex Interdependence," a paradigm of international relations competing with Realism, but the two uses of the word should not be confused. An ideal "complex interdependent" relationship would be marked by (1) multiple channels of communication; (2) absence of hierarchy among issues; and (3) a minor role for military force. It describes a mature form of a pacific relationship, and can be thought of as partly describing an internationalist's utopian vision of world politics. See *Power and Interdependence*, pp. 24–37 (note 9).

    My use of the term is intended to capture two dimensions of interdependence identified by Keohane and Nye as *sensitivity* and *vulnerability* (pp. 12ff). The first refers to the degree of responsiveness in a relationship—that is, how quickly (and to what extent) changes in one country result in costly changes in another. The second refers to a state's long-term liability to suffer costs imposed by external events.

11. Walter C. Clemens, Jr., *The Superpowers and Arms Control: From Cold War to Interdependence* (Lexington, MA: D.C. Heath, 1973), p. xxiv.

12. The institutions approach is intended epiphenomenally to reduce the likely destructiveness of conflict by improving the chance that a major war could be terminated quickly and at a low level of violence, by increasing the number and quality of channels of communication between belligerents.

13. On this point see Brown, *New Forces in World Politics*, p. 146 (note 7). Nonnuclear technology is relevant to the effectiveness of all three approaches, but may be presumed to advance unilinearly without much relevant variation. For this reason I shall not be treating it as a variable with potentially diverse effects on the desirability of these approaches.

14. Robert Angell, *Peace on the March*, New Perspectives in Political Science no. 19 (New York: Van Nostrand Reinhold Co., 1969), pp. 188–89. In general, according to Angell, "international trade does not qualify as transnational participation" because of the intermediation of a market and the normal distance between parties to a transaction (p. 24). Effective forms of transnational participation include involvement in international organizations and residences

abroad for study, teaching, research, technical assistance, and Peace Corps duty.

15. Ibid., p. 21.
16. For an expression of agreement, see James A. Field, Jr., "Transnationalism and the New Tribe," in Keohane and Nye, *Transnational Relations and World Politics*, pp. 3–22 (note 7). For a detailed critique of Angell, see Donald P. Warwick, "Transnational Participation and International Peace," in Keohane and Nye, ibid., pp. 305–24. Robert Gilpin claims that, despite the increase in transnational contacts, "the political fragmentation of the world has increased in recent decades" (*War and Change in World Politics* (Cambridge: Cambridge University Press, 1981), p. 225).
17. See, for example, Louis Kreisberg, "Applied Sociology and International Relations," *Sociological Practice* 1, no. 2 (1976), especially pp. 123–24. One way in which transnational contacts can increase antagonism is by raising the expectations of less fortunate groups exposed to more fortunate groups, generating resentment and political upheaval in the less fortunate state (p. 124).
18. For detailed argument on these points, see Warwick, "Transnational Participation" (note 16).
19. See Chapter 7.
20. The work of Karl Deutsch suggests that it is difficult to realize positive attitude changes even under conditions more closely resembling complex interdependence. But there is a point at which some states realize that they have nothing to fear from one another and everything to gain from cooperation. Then a sense of commonality may develop that results in a "pluralistic security community"—one in which "there is real assurance that the members of that community will not fight each other physically, but will settle their disputes in some other way" (Karl W. Deutsch et al., *Political Community and the North Atlantic Area* (New York: Greenwood Press, 1957), pp. 5–6, 36). The idea that the United States and the USSR might form a pluralistic security community seems fantastic at present; but major shifts in the structure of the international system may over the long run significantly reduce the role of the implicit threat of force in U.S.–Soviet relations.
21. British–American relations in the twentieth century, for example, failed to follow the course predicted by Realist theory; thus Realism should at best be treated as a means of generating a first approximation of the distribution of power and enmity in the system. Usually, domestic political, cultural, and other factors will be needed to explain patterns of relations that from the Realist perspective would be counterintuitive.
22. We might be able to expect more *accommodative* attitudes, but empirical work suggests that we should not necessarily expect a *convergence* of attitudes and values. High degrees of contact and relevance do not seem to have any effect on convergence; largely for that reason, an amalgamated world community in the strong sense is simply not in the cards. See Roger W. Cobb and Charles Elder, *International Community: A Regional and Global Study* (New York: Holt, Rinehart and Winston, 1970).
23. For a fuller discussion of U.S. and Soviet attitudes toward each other, see Chapter 7.

24. For a thorough discussion of domestic political limitations on major policy shifts, see Alexander L. George, "Domestic Constraints on Regime Change in U.S. Foreign Policy: The Need for Policy Legitimacy," in Ole R. Holsti, Randolph M. Siverson, and Alexander L. George, eds., *Change in the International System* (Boulder, CO: Westview Press, 1980), pp. 233–62.

25. See generally Robert Jervis, *Perception and Misperception in International Politics* (Princeton, NJ: Princeton University Press, 1976), and Donald R. Kinder and Janet A. Weiss, "In Lieu of Rationality: Psychological Perspectives on Foreign Policy Decision Making," *Journal of Conflict Resolution* 22, no. 4 (1978): 707–35.

26. See Herbert C. Kelman and Raphael S. Ezekiel, *Cross-National Encounters* (San Francisco: Jossey-Bass, 1970), pp. 300–30.

27. Arnold Wolfers, *Discord and Collaboration* (Baltimore: Johns Hopkins University Press, 1962), p. 56.

28. Quoted in Raymond L. Garthoff, *Détente and Confrontation* (Washington, DC: Brookings Institution, 1985), p. 30.

29. Quoted in David A. Jodice and Charles Lewis Taylor, "Détente and its Effects: A Measurement of East–West Trade," in Daniel Frei, ed., *Definitions and Measurements of Détente* (Cambridge, MA: Oelgeschlager, Gunn & Hain, 1981), p. 153.

30. For instance, Kant wrote that "the *spirit of commerce* sooner or later takes hold of every people, and it cannot exist side by side with war." Immanuel Kant, *Perpetual Peace: A Philosophical Sketch*, in Hans Reiss, ed., *Kant's Political Writings*, trans. H.B. Nisbet (Cambridge: Cambridge University Press, 1970), p. 114 (emphasis in the original). For a discussion of the historical arguments for capitalism's promise to pacify international relations, see Albert O. Hirschman, *The Passions and the Interests: Political Arguments for Capitalism Before Its Triumph* (Princeton, NJ: Princeton University Press, 1977).

31. George W. Ball, *Diplomacy for a Crowded World* (Boston: Little, Brown and Co., 1976), pp. 102–3.

32. For more detailed discussion of the Manchester School, see Geoffrey Blainey, *The Causes of War* (New York: Free Press, 1973), pp. 18–32, and Keith L. Nelson and Spencer C. Olin, Jr., *Why War? Ideology, Theory and History* (Berkeley: University of California Press, 1979), pp. 35–43.

33. Norman Angell, *Europe's Optical Illusion* (London: Simpkin Marshall, 1909).

34. See Bruce M. Russett, *International Regimes and the International System* (Chicago: Rand McNally and Co., 1967), p. 198.

35. Kenneth N. Waltz, "The Myth of National Interdependence," in Charles P. Kindleberger, ed., *The International Corporation: A Symposium* (Cambridge: MIT Press, 1970), p. 205.

36. Blainey, *Causes of War*, p. 31 (note 32).

37. See Melvin Small and J. David Singer, *Resort to Arms: International and Civil Wars, 1816–1980* (Beverly Hills, CA: Sage Publications, 1982), pp. 92–99, 102, 229–32. Small and Singer note that between 1945 and 1980 there were forty-four civil wars and thirty interstate wars.

38. See Blainey, *Causes of War*, p. 30 (note 32). Richard Rosecrance directly contradicts this, arguing that "it is possible for relationships among states to be

entirely transformed by the low politics of trade" (*The Rise of the Trading State* (New York: Basic Books, 1986), p. xi).

39. Henry Kissinger, "Trading with the Russians: A Political Strategy for Economic Relations," in Gary K. Bertsch and John R. McIntyre, eds., *National Security and Technology Transfer: The Strategic Dimensions of East–West Trade* (Boulder, CO: Westview Press, 1983), p. 219. It should be noted that though East–West trade was expanding it remained negligible throughout the period in question.

40. Robert O. Keohane, *After Hegemony* (Princeton, NJ: Princeton University Press, 1984), pp. 5, 243.

41. I am indebted to Stephen Van Evera for suggesting this point. If this is so, Japan relies today on international trade to secure what it fought for in World War II—economic welfare. See Rosecrance, *The Rise of the Trading State*, p. 16 (note 38).

42. In an important sense, Norman Angell was right. A costs-and-gains calculation based on hindsight shows that, from the perpetrators' perspectives, neither world war *was* worth the costs of disrupting the status quo. States sometimes go to war for apparently irrational reasons, or because of misperceptions and misunderstandings. Sometimes they simply miscalculate likely costs and benefits. And, on occasion, the likely gains of war *do* outweigh the costs of disrupting an interdependent relationship.

43. *Perceptual Peace*, p. 100 (note 30).

44. Waltz, "Myth," p. 206 (note 35) (emphasis in quotation added). Rosecrance and Stein note that Waltz's point about interdependence in general is clearly mistaken—interdependent military relationships such as NATO's, for instance, do not require divisions of labor along lines of comparative advantage. See Richard Rosecrance and Arthur Stein, "Interdependence: Myth or Reality," *World Politics* 26, no. 1 (1973): 3.

45. In a bad harvest year, Soviet imports of grain amount to as much as 35 percent of the nation's own harvest. Grain imports cost the USSR $5–6 billion in 1981, or one quarter of its hard-currency import bill. See Marshall I. Goldman, *U.S.S.R. in Crisis: The Failure of an Economic System* (New York: W.W. Norton & Co., 1983), p. 130. Of course, Soviet grain imports are in the form of livestock feed and are intended only to boost meat production; even in a bad harvest year the Soviets grow enough grain to meet their carbohydrate needs.

46. Cf. Cord D. Hansen-Strum, "The Comparative Benefits of Trade," in United States Senate Committee on Foreign Relations, *Perceptions: Relations Between the United States and the Soviet Union* (Washington, DC: Government Printing Office, 1979), p. 374.

47. See Robert Gilpin, "The Politics of Transnational Economic Relations," in Keohane and Nye, *Transnational Relations and World Politics*, p. 53 (note 7).

48. Robert Gilpin writes that, historically, autarky and security values have been more highly prized than income and welfare gains from the free operation of world markets. See "Economic Interdependence and National Security in Historical Perspective," in Klaus Knorr and Frank W. Trager, eds., *Economic Issues and National Security* (Lawrence, KS: Regents Press of Kansas, 1977), p. 22.

49. The experience of 1979 seems to suggest that a largely autarkic nation with access to alternative sources cannot be successfully coerced by a unilateral embargo, and that attempts to do so destroy whatever leverage might have existed in the first place. Cf. Robert Paarlberg, "Lessons of the Grain Embargo," *Foreign Affairs* 59, no. 1 (1980): 144–62.

50. Some have argued that trade links could paralyze the West in the face of others' misbehavior. Henry Kissinger writes, "There is little doubt that the negotiating balance in East–West trade has been reversed over the past decade. In every crisis, the West invents new excuses for declining to interrupt economic relations. Indeed, economic relations have done much more to induce Western restraint in the face of Soviet misconduct than to encourage Soviet restraint in international relations" ("Trading with the Russians," p. 218 (note 39)). This observation seems wholly incompatible with the rather marginal but still one-sided economic dependence that currently exists.

51. Such a structural change would also result in a relative decline in the American share of the world economy. Robert Gilpin suggests that under these circumstances, a liberal international economic order will be increasingly difficult to maintain, in part because the United States will be retrenching. Thus the structural conditions that improve the prospects for East–West trade may be unfavorable to a liberal global economic order as a whole. (See Gilpin, "Economic Interdependence," pp. 57–58 (note 48)). Keohane's work, on the other hand, convincingly demonstrates that under certain conditions, even cooperative arrangements established hegemonically may be retained after the hegemon's decline because of their demonstrated utility. See *After Hegemony*, p. 244 (note 40).

52. Ryzhkov Report on Basic Guidelines at 3 March Session (Party Congress), *FBIS* Soviet Union Supplement 3, no. 43 (March 5, 1986): O-23–O-24. Ryzhkov went on to criticize the United States for its history of using economics as a foreign policy tool, and he called for a world congress on problems of economic security, "at which it would be possible to discuss everything that is encumbering world economic ties" (p. O-24).

53. For good detailed discussions of the intricacies of and constraints on U.S.–Soviet trade, see Marshall I. Goldman, *Détente and Dollars* (New York: Basic Books, 1975); John W. DePauw, *Soviet–American Trade Negotiations* (New York: Praeger Publishers, 1979); and Joan Edelman Spero, *The Politics of International Economic Relations*, 2d ed. (New York: St. Martin's Press, 1981), chap. 10, pp. 289–328.

54. A planned economy cannot be managed successfully if production, distribution, and consumption patterns are subject to the erratic and unpredictable forces of supply and demand, as they would be under conditions of open trade with decentralized economies. Currency inconvertibility is thus necessary to protect the precarious planning system; without it, international transactions and currency exchanges would make it impossible to forecast needs and to set production quotas and prices in any ordered and manipulable way.

55. The absence of slack in planned economies often means that inventories are consistently spoken for ahead of time and that Eastern goods are not available for purchase unless they have been so allocated well in advance—often too far ahead for importers who must match sources to demands in a timely

and flexible way. Commodity inconvertibility restricts the degree to which East bloc nations can generate the foreign exchange they need to buy Western goods and services, perpetuating the vicious cycle that frustrates the generation of greater levels of trade. See Spero, *Politics*, p. 307 (note 53).

56. Low levels of trade caused by currency and commodity inconvertibility make it difficult for East bloc nations to generate hard currency through exports; thus many Western goods and services have to be bartered or bought on credit, limiting transactions.

57. Because prices in East bloc states are determined by bureaucrats, rather than by market force, they generally fail to reflect the true value of goods. Eastern goods sold at artificially high prices will not move on Western markets, while goods sold at artificially low prices will unfairly undercut comparable Western products in violation of international trading norms. Western entrepreneurs seeking to sell goods or establish production facilities in Eastern countries cannot be guaranteed a reasonable profit margin or return on their investment because they must deal with irrational pricing. These among other risks discourage investors from seeking access to Soviet and East European markets. Other risks include uncertainties caused by the instability of the political relations between East and West, restrictions on the trade of sensitive goods, and so forth.

58. Paarlberg, "Lessons," p. 161 (note 49).

59. See Spero, *Politics*, pp. 317–18 (note 53).

60. See, for example, Lawrence J. Brady, "East–West Trade Policy: Maintaining the Present Course," in W. Bruce Weinrod, ed., *Confronting Moscow: An Agenda for the Post Détente Era* (Washington, DC: Heritage Foundation, 1985).

61. For an argument that East–West prospects for trade interdependence follow political cycles rather than comparative advantages, and that Western inroads are likely only to follow détente and stabilization of economic relations, see John P. Hardt and Donna L. Gold, "Soviet Commercial Behavior with Western Industrial Nations," in Dan Caldwell, ed., *Soviet International Behavior and U.S. Policy Options* (Lexington, MA: D.C. Heath, 1985).

62. Mitrany's ideas were first formulated in *The Progress of International Government*, chap. 3, "The Communal Organization of World Affairs" (London: Allen & Unwin, 1933), but most thoroughly developed in *A Working Peace System: An Argument for the Functional Development of International Organisation* (London: Royal Institute for International Affairs, 1943), reprinted in 1966 with an introduction by Hans J. Morgenthau.

63. This division of authority by issue, Mitrany claims, reconciles the tension between the principle of the formal equality of all states, and the manifest substantive inequalities between states, both in general terms of raw power and in particular terms of the specific items on the international agenda of interest and concern to each state. It does so by giving each state exactly the degree of authority appropriate to its international role and by giving each state the same opportunity to participate on the same terms as every other state in the workings of the functionalist system as a whole. See ibid., pp. 63–66. Mitrany's view accords with Stanley Hoffmann's observation that "there is no longer one hierarchy based on military or geo-military power. There are

separate functional hierarchies, and in each one the meaning of being 'top dog' is far from simple." *Primacy or World Order* (New York: McGraw-Hill, 1978), pp. 117–18.

64. Mitrany, *A Working Peace System*, pp. 70–71 (note 62).
65. Functionalism is founded on the implicit assumption that all states have a common interest in economic expansion, all other things being equal. Mitrany also seems to believe that the failure to satisfy common demands for improvements in standards of living is itself a source of conflict. Cf. Harold K. Jacobson, William M. Reisinger, and Todd Mathers, "National Entanglements in International Governmental Organizations," *American Political Science Review* 80, no. 1 (1986): 142.
66. Mitrany, *A Working Peace System* (1966 ed.), p. 29 (note 62). Cf. Paul Taylor's introduction to David Mitrany, *The Functional Theory of Politics* (London: Martin Robertson & Company Ltd., 1985), p. x.

    There is a central ambiguity in functionalism: are the *institutions* or the *sense of community* responsible for peace? Which of these is the precondition for the other? See Andrew Wilson Green, "Review Article: Mitrany Reread with the Help of Haas and Sewell," *Journal of Common Market Studies* 8, no. 1 (1969). A careful reading of Mitrany's work indicates that he believes both institutions and a nascent sense of community will serve the cause of peace, and that they will interact in a mutually reinforcing manner. The question of which is the precondition for which is not well formed; once the initial step is made of recognizing the cooperative possibilities of mutual interests, the two will grow in concert.
67. Of 880 IGOs for which the date of founding is available, 94.1 percent were established after 1939, and 70.3 percent were established between 1960 and 1981. See Jacobson et al., "National Entanglements," p. 144 (note 65).
68. *After Hegemony*, pp. 7–10 (note 40).
69. See, for example, Keohane, *After Hegemony* (note 40); the essays in Krasner, ed., *International Regimes* (note 5); and Oran R. Young, "International Regimes: Problems of Concept Formation," *World Politics* 32, no. 3 (1980): 331–56.
70. Jacobson, *Networks of Interdependence*, p. 198 (note 9).
71. Using the CREON data set, James M. McCormick and Young W. Kihl put the figure at 66.1 percent for the period 1959–68. See "Inter-Governmental Organizations and Foreign Policy Behavior: Some Empirical Findings," *American Political Science Review* 73, no. 2 (1979): 497.
72. James M. McCormick, "Intergovernmental Organizations and Cooperation Among Nations," *International Studies Quarterly* 24, no. 1 (1980): 85. Jacobson, Reisinger, and Mathers have found that an increase in the number of IGOs in the system appears to lessen states' mean proneness to war; but while this accurately describes the system as a whole, the relation does not hold for the behavior of any state in particular (pp. 141–59) (note 65).
73. Keohane, *After Hegemony*, pp. 244–45 (note 40).
74. "IGOs are used by nations primarily as selective instruments for gaining foreign policy objectives," write McCormick and Kihl, pp. 502–3 (note 71). Cf. Wolfers, p. 23 (note 27); Keohane and Nye, *Power and Interdependence*, p. 225

(note 9); Edward L. Morse, "The Transformation of Foreign Policies: Modernization, Interdependence, and Externalization," *World Politics* 22, no. 3 (1970): 379–83.

75. The speeches also show that previously extreme attitudes, both positive and negative, were moderated as a result of the experience. Robert E. Riggs, "One Small Step for Functionalism: U.N. Participation and Congressional Attitude Change," *International Organization* 31, no. 3 (1977): 515–39.

76. See Victor-Yves Ghebali, "The Politicisation of U.N. Specialized Agencies: A Preliminary Analysis," *Millennium* 14, no. 3 (1985), especially pp. 330–31. Ghebali looks at politicization within the ILO, UNESCO, and UNCTAD, arguing that it is a manifestation of dysfunction that threatens the very idea of cooperation through IOs. Politicization is a "purely negative" phenomenon, since international cooperation is not a zero-sum game; it systematically hurts Western interests without benefit to the Third World or Eastern Europe.

77. The politicization of IGOs, among other things, leads Robert Keohane to proclaim that functionalism's "predictions" have been falsified and that it is an idea whose time has passed (Robert O. Keohane, review essay on David Mitrany's *The Functional Theory of Politics, American Political Science Review* 72, no. 2 (1978)). But Mitrany made prescriptions, not predictions, and his "ought" cannot be defeated by treating it as an "is." At most , we can say that Mitrany was overly optimistic about the likelihood of a true functionalist order.

78. Cf. Keohane and Nye, *Power and Interdependence*, p. 34 (note 9).

79. See, for example, Stephen M. Shaffer and Lisa Robock Shaffer, "The Politics of International Cooperation: A Comparison of U.S. Experience in Space and in Security," *Monograph Series in World Affairs*, vol. 17, book 4 (Denver, CO: Graduate School of International Studies, 1980).

80. Robert O. Keohane and Joseph S. Nye, "Transgovernmental Relations and International Organization," *World Politics* 27, no. 1 (1974): 39–62, and Robert O. Keohane and Joseph S. Nye, Jr., "International Interdependence and Integration," in Fred I. Greenstein and Nelson W. Polsby, eds., *Handbook of Political Science*, vol. 8 (Reading, MA: Addison-Wesley Publishing Co., 1975), pp. 371–74.

81. See Keohane and Nye, *Power and Interdependence*, pp. 35–37 (note 9); "Transgovernmental Relations and International Organizations," pp. 39–62 (note 80); and *Transnational Relations and World Politics*, pp. xix–xx (note 7).

82. Keohane and Nye concede that the role of transnational actors in areas of national security appears to be less important because governments insist on tighter controls (*Transnational Relations and World Politics*, p. 170 (note 7)).

83. Keohane and Nye, *Transnational Relations and World Politics*, pp. 378–79 (note 7).

84. Philippe C. Schmitter, "Three Neo-Functional Hypotheses about International Integration," *International Organization* 23, no. 1 (1969): 162. On the spillover hypothesis, see Kjell Skjelsbaek, "The Growth of International Nongovernmental Organization," in Keohane and Nye, *Transnational Relations and World Politics*, especially pp. 88–92 (note 7); Stanley Hoffman, "European Process at Atlantic Cross-Purposes," *Journal of Common Market Studies* 3, no. 2 (February 1965): 85–101; and Karl Kaiser, "The U.S. and the EEC in the Atlan-

tic System: The Problem of Theory," *Journal of Common Market Studies* 5, no. 4 (June 1967): 388–425.

85. McCormick and Kihl, "Inter-Governmental Organizations," pp. 497–98 (note 72). For the period studied, high-politics IGOs were used 62 percent and low-politics IGOs 38 percent of the time.

86. See Joseph S. Nye, Jr., "Nuclear Learning and U.S.–Soviet Security Regimes," *International Organization* 41, no. 3 (Summer 1987): 371–402.

87. See Sean M. Lynn-Jones, "Détente and Deterrence: Anglo–German Relations, 1911–1914," *International Security* 11, no. 2 (Fall 1986): 121–50.

88. See Raymond L. Garthoff, "American–Soviet Relations in Perspective," *Political Science Quarterly* 11, no. 4 (Winter 1985–86): 541–59, especially pp. 548–51.

Chapter 10: World Government

1. *Public Papers of the Presidents, 1961* (Washington, DC: Government Printing Office, 1962), p. 387.

2. "Joint Statement of Agreed Principles for Disarmament Negotiation," Arms Control and Disarmament Agency, Disarmament document series 26 (1961).

3. "A Blueprint for Peace: Outline of Basic Provisions of a Treaty on General and Complete Disarmament in a Peaceful World," Arms Control and Disarmament Agency, Publ. 4, General Series 3 (May 1962), p. 33.

4. Thomas Schelling, "The Role of Deterrence in Total Disarmament," *Foreign Affairs* 40, no. 3 (April 1962): 392–406.

5. See the exchange of letters between Zorin and McCloy, Arms Control and Disarmament Agency, Disarmament document series 28 (1961).

6. The bills were introduced as H. Con. Res. 123 and S. Con. Res. 125 in the 98th Congress, and H. Con. Res. 392 in the 97th Congress. S. Con. Res. 125 was introduced by Senator Claiborne Pell, ranking Democrat on the Senate Foreign Relations Committee, but none of the bills ever mustered the 100 sponsors required for a hearing.

7. In the words of Hans Morgenthau, "total disarmament and world government go hand in hand" ("The Political Conditions for an International Police Force," *International Organization* 17, no. 2 (Spring 1963): 393–403.

8. Jonathan Schell, *The Fate of the Earth* (New York: Knopf, 1982), p. 210.

9. For a review of historic comments concerning supranational government, see A. Fonseca Pimentel, *Democratic World Government and the United Nations* (Brasilia: Escopo Editora, 1980).

10. Roy E. Licklikder, *The Private Nuclear Strategists* (Columbus: Ohio State University Press, 1971).

11. Independent Commission on Disarmament and Security Issues, *Common Security: A Blueprint for Survival* (New York: Simon and Schuster, 1982).

12. For other organizations supporting world government or enforceable international law, see Melinda Fine and Peter M. Steven, eds., *American Peace Directory* (Cambridge, MA: Ballinger, 1984); C. Maxwell Stanley, *Managing Global Problems* (Muscatine, IA: Stanley Foundation, 1979); and Duane Sweeney, ed., *The Peace Catalog* (Seattle: Press for Peace, 1984).

13. For example, see Charles R. Beitz and Theodore Herman, eds., *Peace and War* (San Francisco: W.H. Freeman and Co., 1973), pp. 145–211; Louis R. Beres, *Constructing Alternative World Futures: Reordering the Planet* (Cambridge, MA: Schenkman, 1977); Leonard W. Doob, *The Pursuit of Peace* (Westport, CT: Greenwood Press, 1981), pp. 229–76; Ronald J. Glossop, *Confronting War* (Jefferson, NC: McFarland, 1983); Robert Pickus and Robert Woito, "Five Approaches to World Order: The Idea and the Discussion in the U.S.," reprinted in Grenville Clark and Louis Sohn, *Introduction to World Peace through World Law* (Chicago: World Without War Publications, 1973), pp. 65–69; and C. Maxwell Stanley, *Managing Global Problems* (Muscatine, IA: Stanley Foundation, 1979).

14. Grenville Clark and Louis B. Sohn, *World Peace through World Law* (Cambridge: Harvard University Press, 1958; rev. 1966). For a summary and updated version of their proposals, see Clark and Sohn, *Introduction to World Peace through World Law* (note 13). Their work has been translated into over a dozen languages.

15. In *Union Now* (New York: Harper, 1939; 2d ed., 1949) and *Freedom's Frontier* (New York: Harper, 1961), Clarence K. Streit proposes an extendable "Union of the Free" initially made up of democratic states in North America and Europe. T. Caplow proposes a coalition of European and Third World countries to avoid superpower rivalry in a new world government; see T. Caplow, *A Feasibility Study of World Government* (Muscatine, IA: Stanley Foundation, 1977), p. 27.

16. In determining the size of the domestic police, Clark and Sohn propose a maximum of seven police for each 100,000 of population, not to exceed a total of 100,000 police.

17. No nationality would exceed 3 percent of the force's total strength, and no more than 5 percent of the force would be nationals from the fourteen largest nations. See Clark and Sohn, *Introduction to World Peace through World Law*, p. 29 (note 13).

18. Clark and Sohn also advise against basing international forces in the world's largest countries, where they may be vulnerable to an attack. Thomas Schelling offers an alternative strategy, asserting that large nations represent the greatest threat to peace and recommending that the international forces be based in populous countries, where they will be closest to the anticipated sources of aggression. See Thomas C. Schelling, "Strategic Problems of an International Armed Force," *International Organization* 17, no. 2 (Spring 1963): 465–85.

19. T. Caplow calls for the direct participation of national heads of state; see *Feasibility Study*, p. 21 (note 15). A.F. Pimentel proposes the creation of a strong executive based on the American presidential model; see *Democratic World Government*, p. 82 (note 9).

20. For a discussion of different proposals on voting procedures, see C. Maxwell Stanley, *Managing Global Problems*, pp. 196–97 (note 12).

21. Statistics compiled from G.D. Kayge, D.A. Grant, and E.J. Edmond, *Major Armed Conflict: A Compendium of Interstate and Intrastate Conflict, 1720 to 1985* (Ottawa: Operational Research and Analysis Establishment, 1985).

22. For ideas on the training of the international police, see Richard Falk, *A Study of Future Worlds* (New York: Free Press, 1985), p. 243.

23. Several authors deal with the problem of political reliability within the international police: Henry V. Dicks, "National Loyalty, Identity, and the International Soldier," *International Organization* 17, no. 2 (Spring 1963): 425–64; Hans J. Morgenthau, "The Political Conditions for an International Police Force," *International Organization* 17, no. 2 (Spring 1963): 393–403; Schelling, "Strategic Problems" (note 18); and Stanley Hoffman, "Erewhon or Lilliput?" *International Organization* 17, no. 2 (Spring 1963): 404–24.

24. For comments on this issue, see Schelling, "The Role of Deterrence," p. 402 (note 4); Falk, *A Study of Future Worlds*, pp. 245–46 (note 22); R.J. Glossop, *Confronting War*, p. 241 (note 13); and Inis L. Claude, Jr., *Power and International Relations* (New York: Random House, 1962), p. 267.

25. Clark and Sohn, *Introduction to World Peace through World Law*, p. 14 (note 13).

26. Ibid., p. 32.

27. Kayge et al., *Major Armed Conflict* (note 21). For comments on the problem of national civil wars, see Caplow, *A Feasibility Study* (note 15); Glossop, *Confronting War* (note 13); and Lincoln P. Bloomfield, "International Force in a Disarming—but Revolutionary—World," *International Organization* 17, no. 2 (Spring 1963): 444–64.

28. Ibid.; Michael Kidron and Dan Smith, *The War Atlas* (New York: Simon and Schuster, 1983), Map #35.

29. Claude, *Power and International Relations*, pp. 267–70 (note 24).

30. This problem is considered in Bloomfield, "International Force" (note 27).

31. See also Falk, *A Study of Future Worlds*, p. 243 (note 22).

32. See Chapter 2 on instabilities in nuclear disarmament.

33. *World Federalist—Newsmagazine of the World Federalist Association* 12, no. 1 (Winter 1987): 1.

34. See Herman Kahn, *On Thermonuclear War* (Princeton, NJ: Princeton University Press, 1961), p. 6.

35. Inis L. Claude, Jr., *Swords into Ploughshares* (New York: Random House, 1956), p. 249.

36. See, for example, Stanley Hoffman, *Duties Beyond Borders* (Syracuse, NY: Syracuse University Press, 1981), and the new publication *Ethics in International Affairs* 1 (1987).

Conclusion

1. Michael Doyle, "Kant, Liberal Legacies, and Foreign Affairs, Part I," *Philosophy and Public Affairs* 12, no. 3 (Summer 1983): 225.

2. Immanuel Kant, "Perpetual Peace," cited in Peter Gay, ed., *The Enlightenment* (New York: Simon and Schuster, 1974), pp. 790–92; see Doyle, "Kant," p. 229.

3. See Doyle, "Kant," especially pp. 213–24.

4. Graham T. Allison, Albert Carnesale, and Joseph S. Nye, Jr., eds. *Hawks, Doves, and Owls: An Agenda for Avoiding Nuclear War* (New York: W.W. Norton and Co., 1985), pp. 224–26.

5. Herman Kahn, *On Thermonuclear War*, 2d ed. (Princeton: Princeton University Press, 1961), p. 145.
6. Ibid., pp. 149–50.
7. Ibid., p. 148.
8. Ibid., p. 147.
9. George F. Kennan, "America and the Russian Future," *Foreign Affairs* 29, no. 3 (April 1951): 351–70; reprinted in Kennan's *American Diplomacy, 1900–1950* (Chicago: University of Chicago Press, 1951), pp. 137ff.
10. C.P. Snow, "Risk of Disaster or a Certainty," speech of 1960 reprinted in *New York Times*, August 17, 1981, as cited in *Living with Nuclear Weapons*, Carnesale et al., eds. (Cambridge, Mass. and London: Harvard University Press, 1983), p. 234.
11. For example, if the probability of catastrophic nuclear war this year were 1 percent (which is higher than most experts would estimate), and if the superpowers could reduce that likelihood of war by 20 percent this year and every subsequent year (i.e., from 1 percent this year to 0.8 percent next year, to 0.64 percent the following year, and so on), the chance of having a catastrophic nuclear war during the next thousand years would be less than 5 percent. See Richard Garwin, quoted in "Is There a Way Out?" *Harper's*, June 1985, p. 39.

Index

About the Editors

Joseph S. Nye, Jr., is the director of the Center for Science and International Affairs and Ford Foundation Professor of International Security, Kennedy School of Government, Harvard University. He received his bachelor's degree summa cum laude from Princeton University in 1958; did post-graduate work at Oxford University on a Rhodes Scholarship, earning a degree in philosophy, politics, and economics in 1960; and received a Ph.D. degree in political science from Harvard University in 1964. He is a fellow of the American Academy of Arts and Sciences, a senior fellow of the Aspen Institute, and director of the Aspen Strategy Group. From January 1977 to January 1979, he served as deputy to the under secretary of state for security assistance, science and technology, and chaired the National Security Council Group on Non-Proliferation of Nuclear Weapons. A member of the editorial boards of *Foreign Policy* and *International Security*, Dr. Nye is the author of many articles in professional journals. His most recent books are *Living with Nuclear Weapons* (co-authored), *The Making of America's Soviet Policy*, *Hawks, Doves, and Owls: An Agenda for Avoiding Nuclear War* (with Albert Carnesale and Graham T. Allison), and *Nuclear Ethics*.

Graham T. Allison is the dean of Harvard's John F. Kennedy School of Government and the Don K. Price Professor of Politics, having served as a professor at Harvard since 1972. A North Carolinian educated at Harvard and Oxford, he is also a director of the Council on Foreign Relations and several private corporations. Professor Allison's teaching and research focuses on political analysis, American foreign policy, and ethics and public policy. He is the author or co-author of numerous books and articles, including *Essence of Decision* and *Hawks, Doves, and Owls: An Agenda for Avoiding Nuclear War*. An expert on foreign policy decision-making, the U.S.–Soviet competition, and alliance relations, Dean Allison has been a consultant to various government agencies since the 1960s. He served as special advisor to former Secretary of Defense Caspar Weinberger.

Albert Carnesale is a professor of public policy and the academic dean at Harvard University's John F. Kennedy School of Government. His teaching and research interests are in international security and U.S.–Soviet relations, with emphasis on policies and issues associated with nuclear weapons. He consults for several agencies of the U.S. government, served on the U.S. delegation to the Strategic Arms Limitation Talks (1970–72), and is a co-author of *Hawks, Doves, and Owls: An Agenda for Avoiding Nuclear War* and *Living with Nuclear Weapons*.

About the Contributors

Daniel J. Arbess is an attorney practicing in New York City. He received his LL.B from Osgoode Hall Law School in Toronto and his LL.M from the Harvard Law School. He is a member of the Committee on International Arms Control and Security Affairs of the Association of the Bar of the City of New York, a fellow at the World Policy Institute, and the former executive director of the Lawyers' Committee on Nuclear Policy. Arbess is co-author of a forthcoming book on alternative defense concepts and has published articles on legal aspects of nuclear weapons policies, arms control, and international security.

Robert P. Beschel, Jr., is currently enrolled in a Ph.D. program in International Relations at the Government Department of Harvard University. He received his B.A. from the University of Washington and his master's in public administration from Harvard's Kennedy School of Government. He has worked as a policy analyst and consultant for the Department of Defense and served as coordinator for the Harvard Project on Avoiding Nuclear War. He has published works on Soviet–American relations and crisis management.

Kurt M. Campbell is the assistant director of the Center for Science and International Affairs and a lecturer in public policy at Harvard's Kennedy School of Government. He received a D.Phil. in international relations from Oxford University and served as a research associate at the International Institute for Strategic Studies in London. Campbell was selected as a Council on Foreign Relations International Affairs fellow for 1987. He is the author of *Soviet Policy Towards South Africa*.

Stephen J. Flanagan is a senior fellow in the Strategic Concepts Development Center of the National Defense University, Washington, D.C.

From 1984 to 1987 he was executive director of the Center for Science and International Affairs at Harvard University's John F. Kennedy School of Government, where he also taught international relations. He was also a professional staff member of the U.S. Senate Select Committee on Intelligence for five years, a fellow of the Council on Foreign Relations, and a research associate of the International Institute for Strategic Studies (IISS). He has published widely on European security, arms control, and intelligence issues and is the author of the forthcoming *NATO's Conventional Defences: Options for the Central Region* and editor of *Securing Europe's Future*. Dr. Flanagan serves on the editorial boards of *International Security* and *The Fletcher Forum* and is a member of the Council on Foreign Relations and the International Institute for Strategic Studies.

Charles L. Glaser is an assistant professor of political science at the University of Michigan and a research associate at the university's Institute of Public Policy Studies. His research interests are in international security, focusing on the theoretical underpinnings of nuclear weapons policy. His recent publications include "Do We Want the Missile Defenses We Can Build" and "Managing the Transition."

Sean M. Lynn-Jones is managing editor of *International Security* and a research fellow at the Center for Science and International Affairs, Harvard University.

James N. Miller, Jr., is a fellow at the Center for Science and International Affairs. He received a master's degree in public policy from Harvard's John F. Kennedy School of Government in 1985, after completing undergraduate training in economics at Stanford University.

Andrew M. Moravcsik is a doctoral candidate in the Department of Government, Harvard University, and a Harvard MacArthur Fellow at the Center for Science and International Affairs. He received an M.A. in international relations from The Johns Hopkins University and a B.A. in history from Stanford University. He has served as a trade negotiator for the U.S. Department of Commerce, as an editor and economic analyst in the Office of the Deputy Prime Minister of South Korea, and as the editor of the *SAIS Review*.

Lee D. Neumann wrote his chapter while working as research assistant at the Center for Science and International Affairs. He holds a bachelor's degree in engineering from Princeton University and a master's degree in international relations from the London School of Economics. He has also studied at the Institut d'Etudes Politiques in Paris and participated in a project on international services trade at the Atlantic Institute for International Affairs in Paris. He is currently studying law at Columbia University.

Stephen R. Rock is currently an assistant professor of political science at Vassar College. He received his A.B. from Miami University and his M.A. and Ph.D. from Cornell. Prior to becoming research fellow of the Avoiding Nuclear War Project, Dr. Rock taught at Centenary College of Louisiana.

David Welch is a research fellow at the Center for Science and International Affairs at Harvard University, as well as coordinator for the Center's Project on Avoiding Nuclear War. He holds a B.A. in both international relations and philosophy from the University of Toronto, and a master's degree in political science from Harvard. Welch is currently a doctoral candidate in Harvard's Department of Government, completing a dissertation on international justice and conflict reduction.